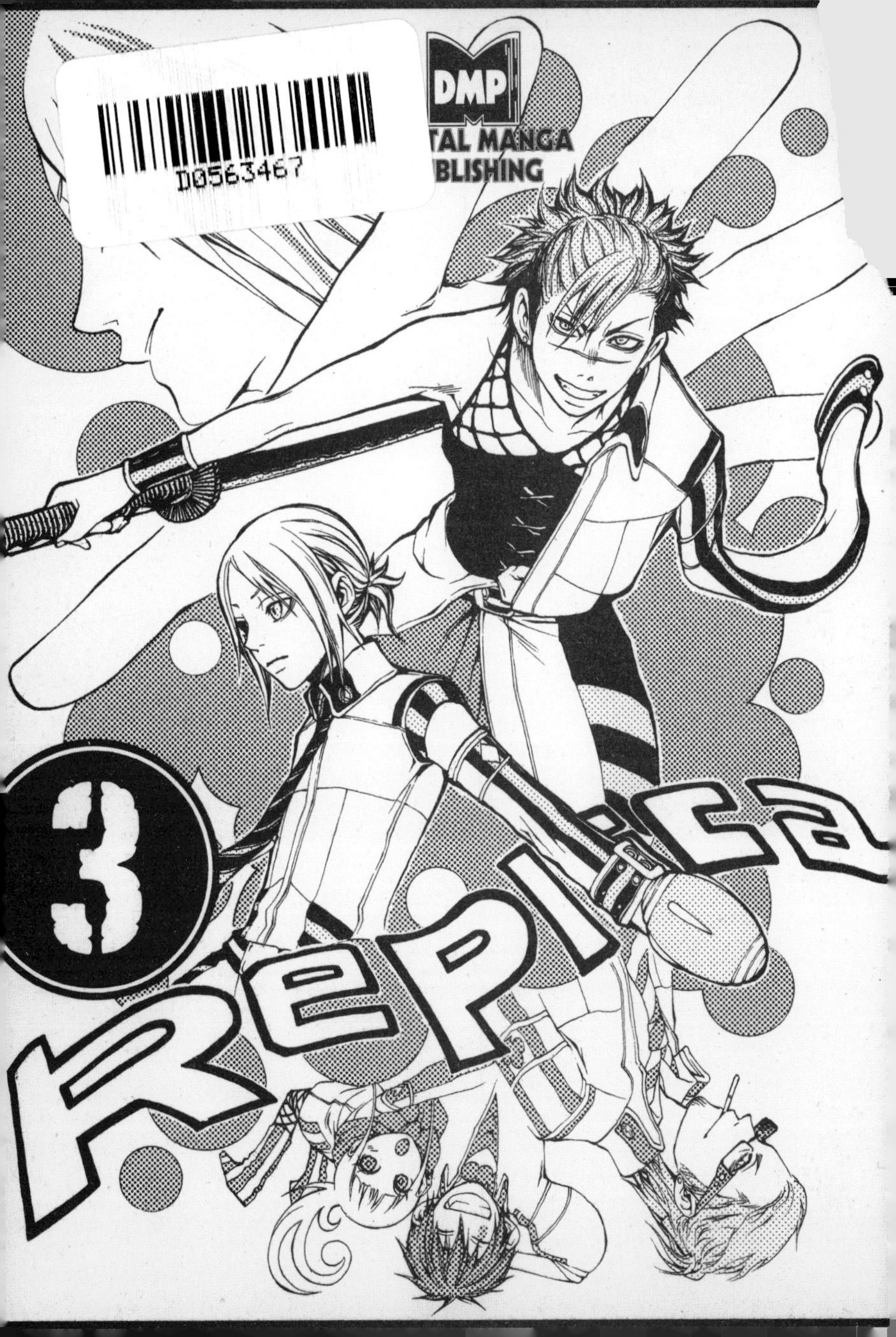
DMP
TAL MANGA
BLISHING
3
Replica

Replica

3

Translation	Duane Johnson
Lettering	Erika Terriquez
Sales & Distribution	Yoko Tanigaki
Graphic Design	Matt Akuginow / Amy Lee Koga
Editing	Stephanie Donnelly
Editor in Chief	Fred Lui
Publisher	Hikaru Sasahara

English Edition Published by
DIGITAL MANGA PUBLISHING
A division of DIGITAL MANGA, Inc.
1487 W 178th Street, Suite 300
Gardena, CA 90248

www.dmpbooks.com

First Edition: July 2012
ISBN-10: 1-56970-262-4
ISBN-13: 978-1-56970-262-8
1 3 5 7 9 10 8 6 4 2

Printed in Canada

Read digital titles at
www.emanga.com

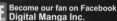
More print titles at
www.akadot.com

Become our fan on Facebook
Digital Manga Inc.

Follow us on Twitter
@DigitalManga

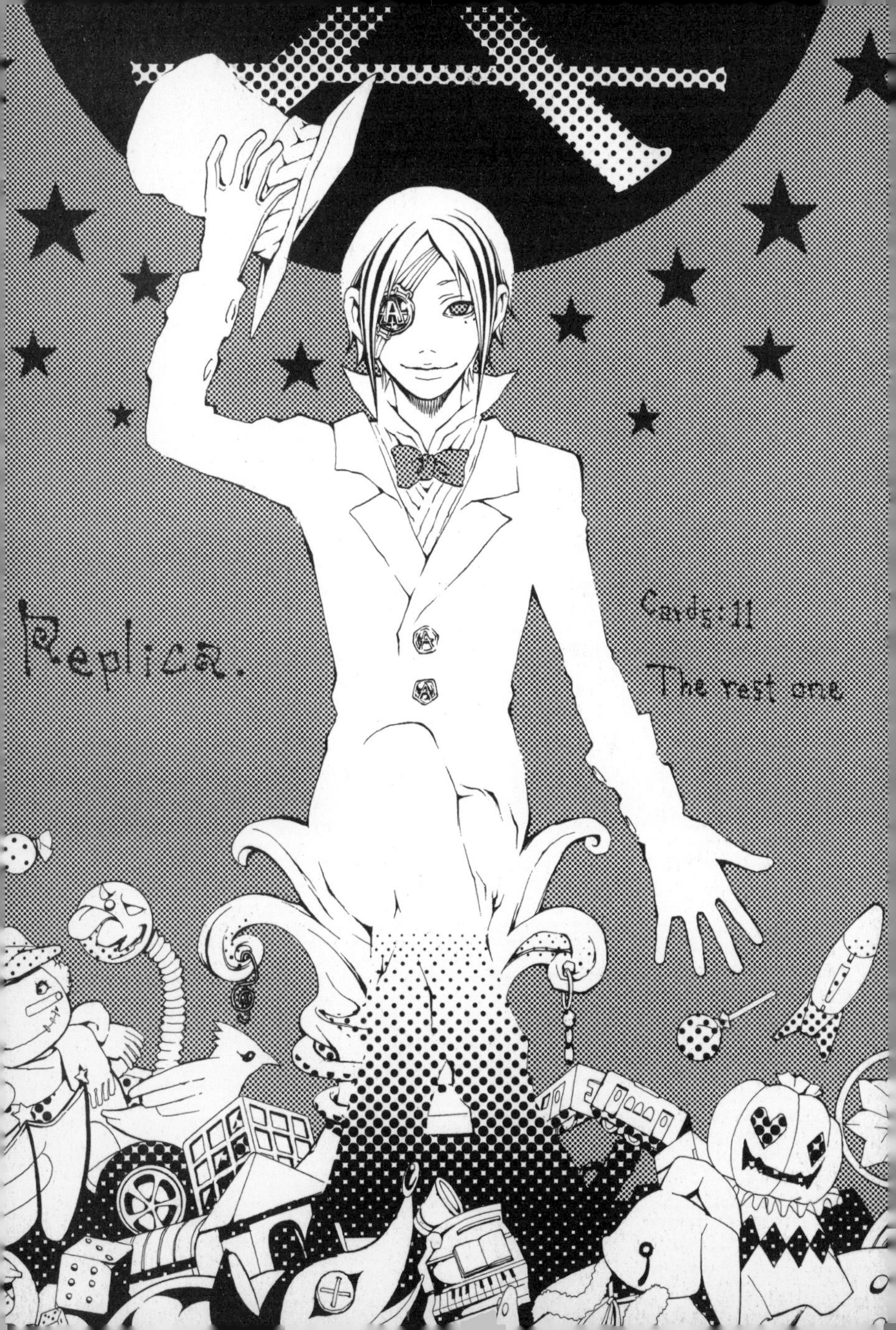
Replica.
Cards:11
The rest one

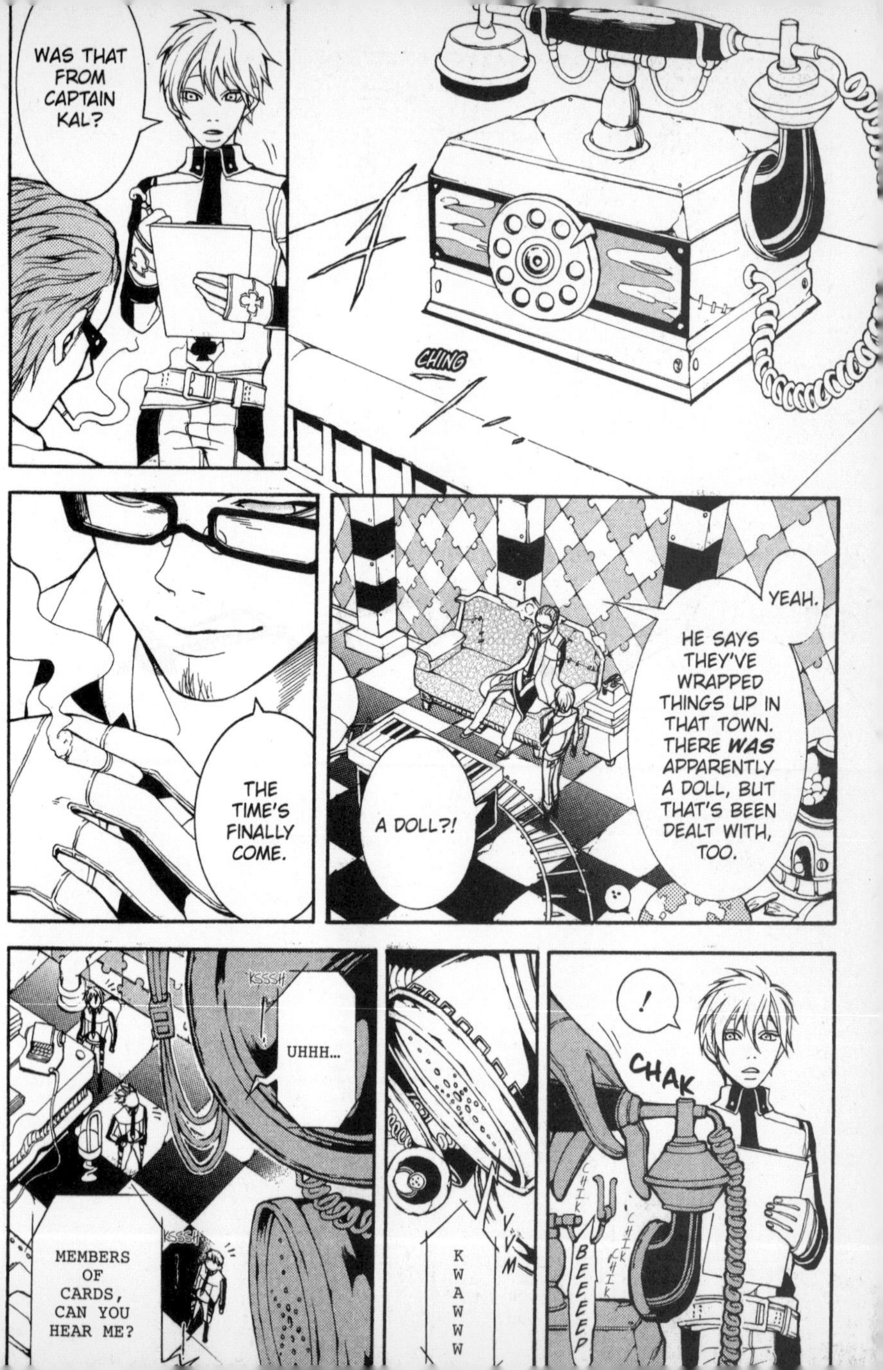
CHING
WAS THAT FROM CAPTAIN KAL?
YEAH.
HE SAYS THEY'VE WRAPPED THINGS UP IN THAT TOWN. THERE ***WAS*** APPARENTLY A DOLL, BUT THAT'S BEEN DEALT WITH, TOO.
A DOLL?!
THE TIME'S FINALLY COME.
!
CHAK
CHIK
CHIK
CHIK
BEEEEP
KWAWWW
KSSSH
UHHH...
KSSSH
MEMBERS OF CARDS, CAN YOU HEAR ME?

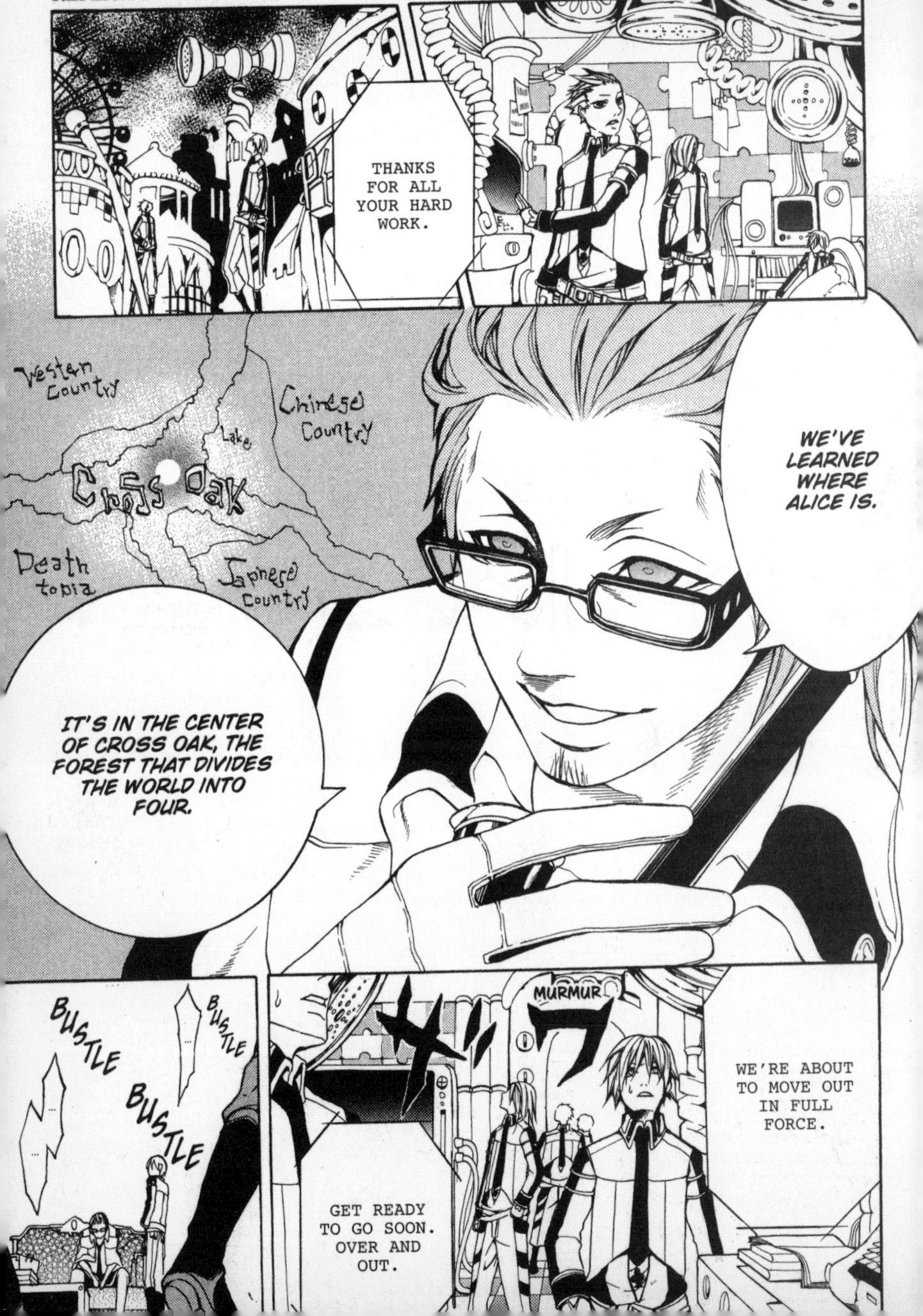
THANKS FOR ALL YOUR HARD WORK.
WE'VE LEARNED WHERE ALICE IS.
Westen Country
Chinese Country
Lake
Cross Oak
Death topia
Japanese Country
IT'S IN THE CENTER OF CROSS OAK, THE FOREST THAT DIVIDES THE WORLD INTO FOUR.
MURMUR
WE'RE ABOUT TO MOVE OUT IN FULL FORCE.
GET READY TO GO SOON. OVER AND OUT.
BUSTLE
BUSTLE
BUSTLE
...
...
...

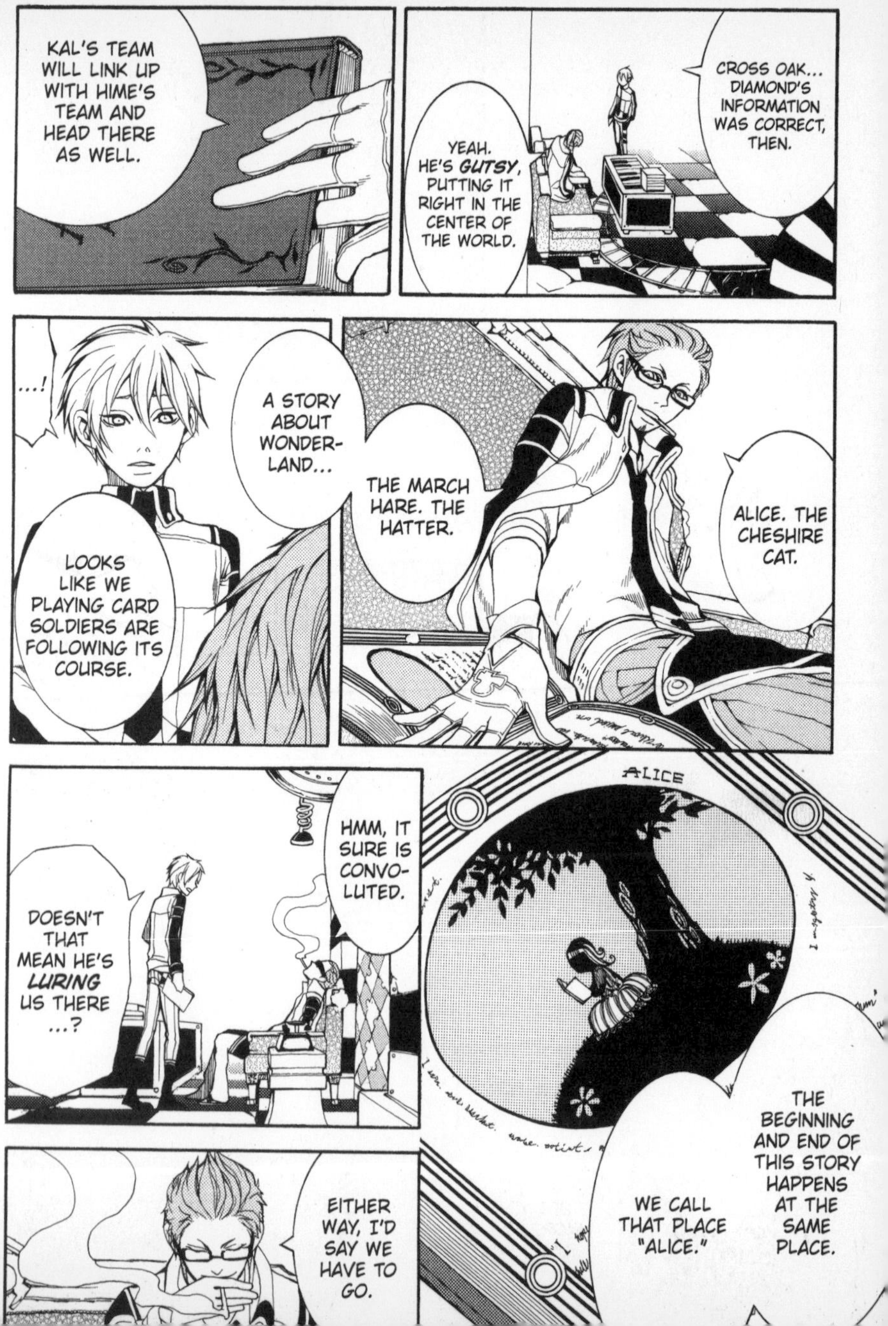
CROSS OAK... DIAMOND'S INFORMATION WAS CORRECT, THEN.
YEAH. HE'S *GUTSY*, PUTTING IT RIGHT IN THE CENTER OF THE WORLD.
KAL'S TEAM WILL LINK UP WITH HIME'S TEAM AND HEAD THERE AS WELL.
ALICE. THE CHESHIRE CAT.
THE MARCH HARE. THE HATTER.
A STORY ABOUT WONDER-LAND...
...!
LOOKS LIKE WE PLAYING CARD SOLDIERS ARE FOLLOWING ITS COURSE.
ALICE
THE BEGINNING AND END OF THIS STORY HAPPENS AT THE SAME PLACE.
WE CALL THAT PLACE "ALICE."
HMM, IT SURE IS CONVO-LUTED.
DOESN'T THAT MEAN HE'S *LURING* US THERE ...?
EITHER WAY, I'D SAY WE HAVE TO GO.

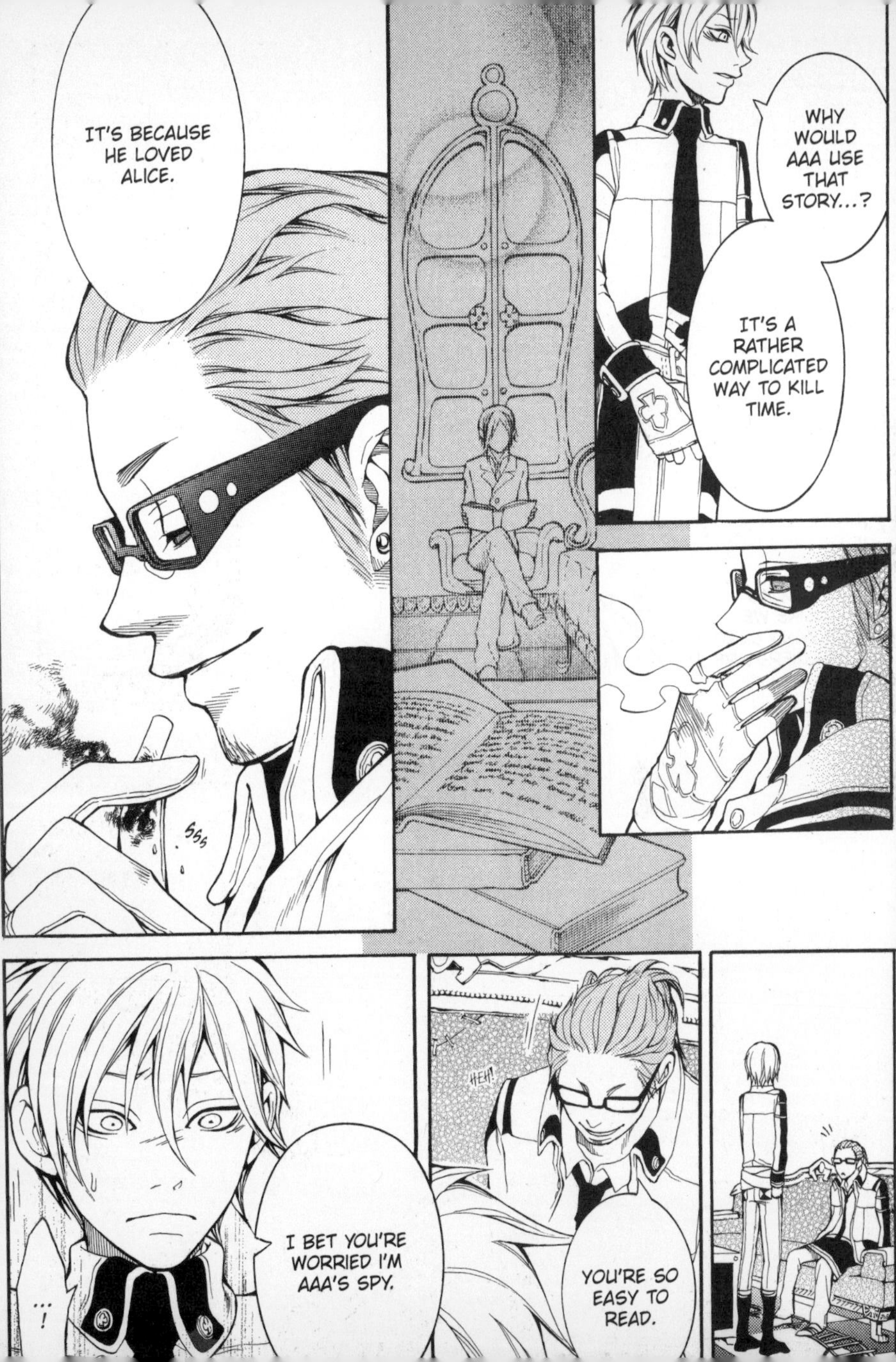
WHY WOULD AAA USE THAT STORY...?
IT'S A RATHER COMPLICATED WAY TO KILL TIME.
IT'S BECAUSE HE LOVED ALICE.
SSS
HEH!
YOU'RE SO EASY TO READ.
I BET YOU'RE WORRIED I'M AAA'S SPY.
...!

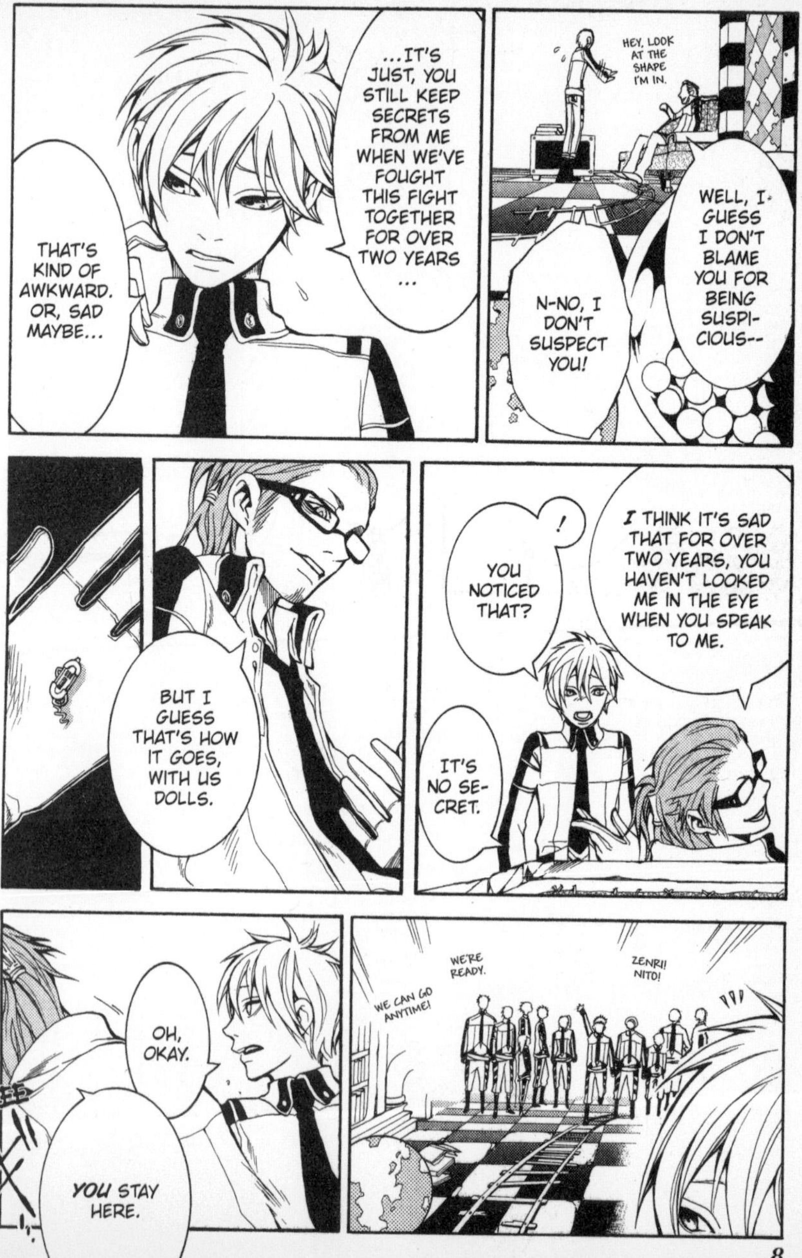
HEY, LOOK AT THE SHAPE I'M IN.
WELL, I GUESS I DON'T BLAME YOU FOR BEING SUSPICIOUS--
N-NO, I DON'T SUSPECT YOU!
...IT'S JUST, YOU STILL KEEP SECRETS FROM ME WHEN WE'VE FOUGHT THIS FIGHT TOGETHER FOR OVER TWO YEARS ...
THAT'S KIND OF AWKWARD. OR, SAD MAYBE...
I THINK IT'S SAD THAT FOR OVER TWO YEARS, YOU HAVEN'T LOOKED ME IN THE EYE WHEN YOU SPEAK TO ME.
!
YOU NOTICED THAT?
IT'S NO SECRET.
BUT I GUESS THAT'S HOW IT GOES, WITH US DOLLS.
ZENRI! NITO!
WE'RE READY.
WE CAN GO ANYTIME!
OH, OKAY.
YOU STAY HERE.
GREE

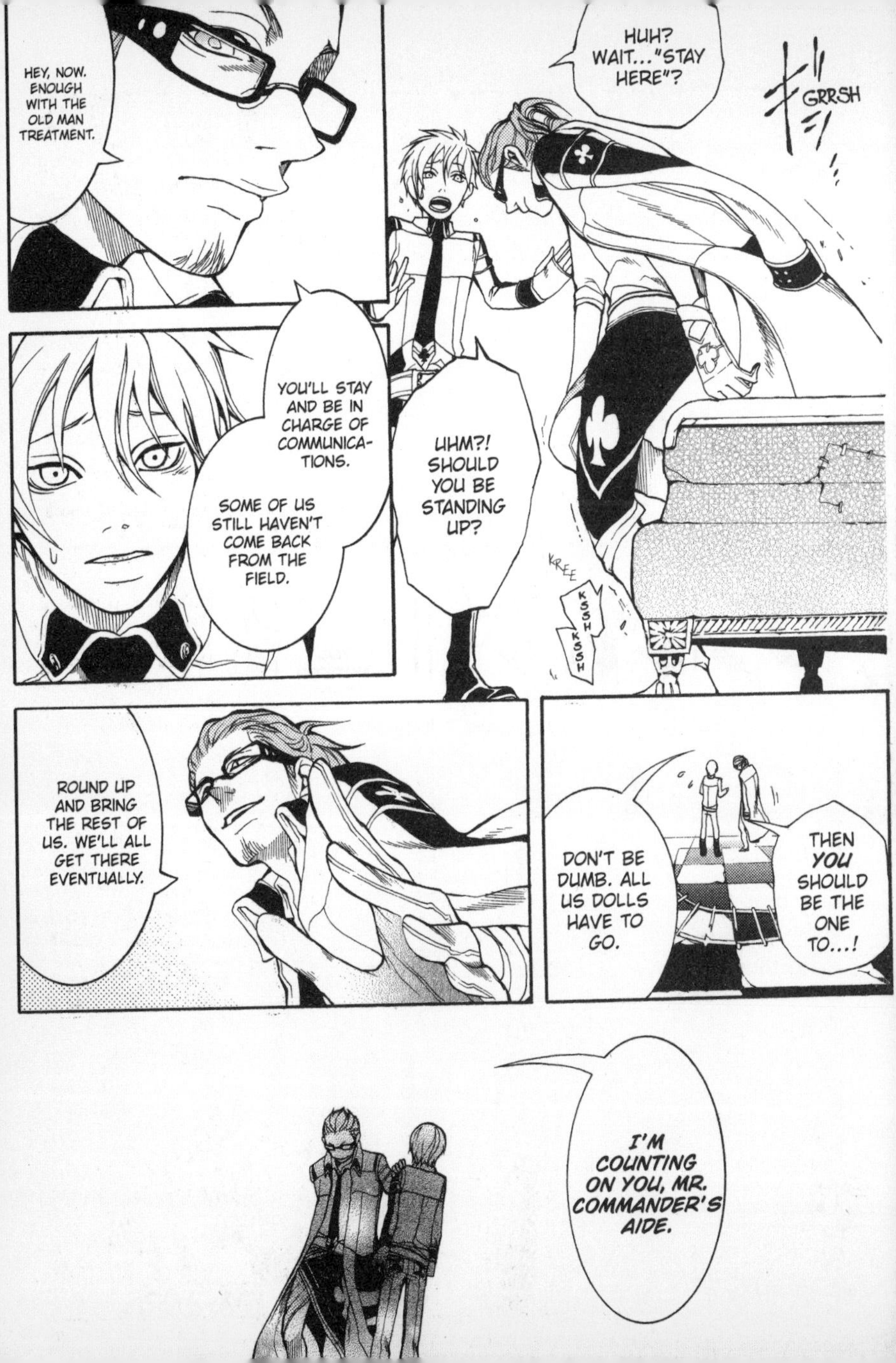
HUH? WAIT..."STAY HERE"?
GRRSH
UHM?! SHOULD YOU BE STANDING UP?
KREE
KSSH KSSH
HEY, NOW. ENOUGH WITH THE OLD MAN TREATMENT.
YOU'LL STAY AND BE IN CHARGE OF COMMUNICATIONS.
SOME OF US STILL HAVEN'T COME BACK FROM THE FIELD.
THEN *YOU* SHOULD BE THE ONE TO...!
DON'T BE DUMB. ALL US DOLLS HAVE TO GO.
ROUND UP AND BRING THE REST OF US. WE'LL ALL GET THERE EVENTUALLY.
I'M COUNTING ON YOU, MR. COMMANDER'S AIDE.

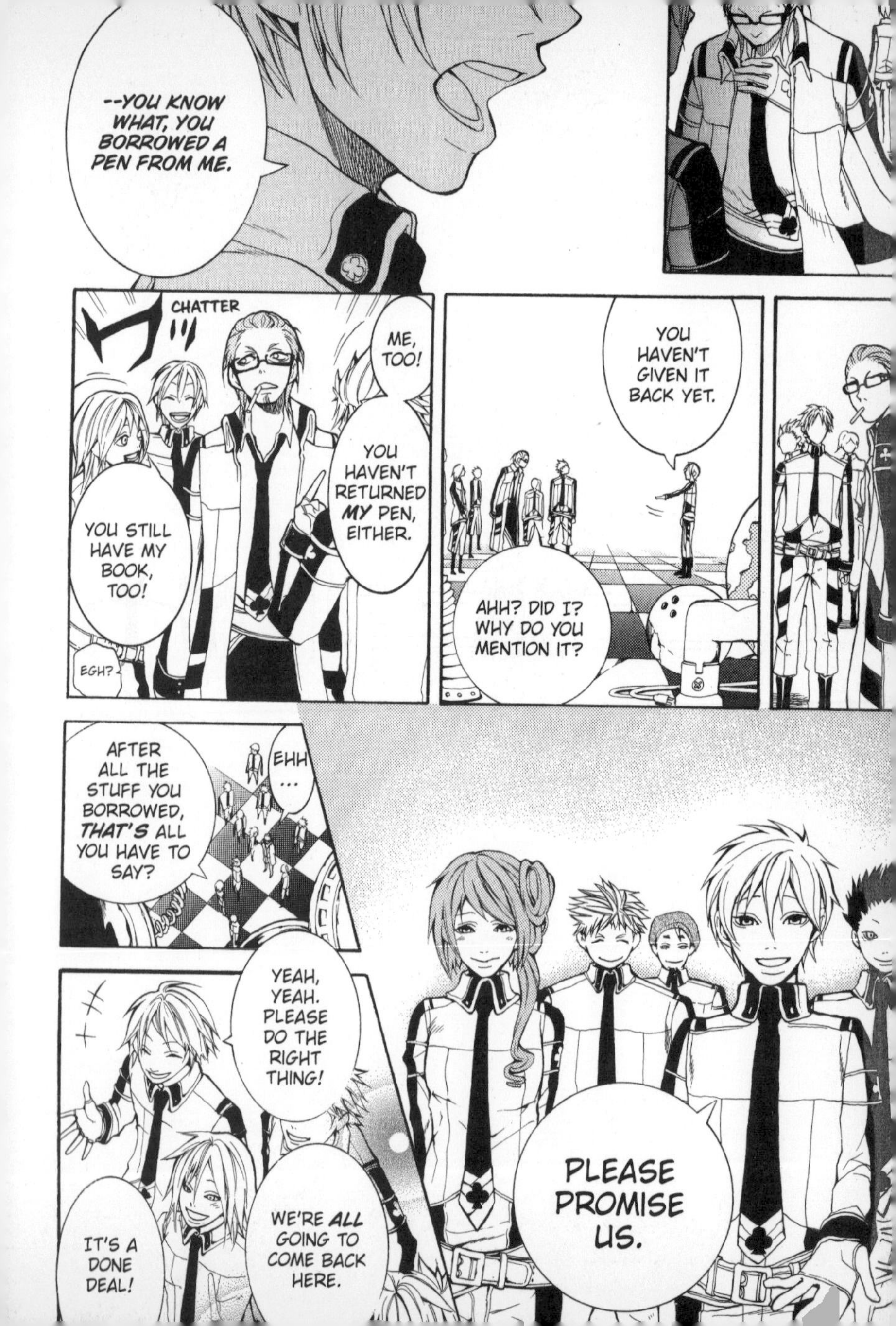
--YOU KNOW WHAT, YOU BORROWED A PEN FROM ME.
YOU HAVEN'T GIVEN IT BACK YET.
AHH? DID I? WHY DO YOU MENTION IT?
CHATTER
ME, TOO!
YOU HAVEN'T RETURNED *MY* PEN, EITHER.
YOU STILL HAVE MY BOOK, TOO!
EGH?
PLEASE PROMISE US.
EHH...
AFTER ALL THE STUFF YOU BORROWED, *THAT'S* ALL YOU HAVE TO SAY?
YEAH, YEAH. PLEASE DO THE RIGHT THING!
WE'RE *ALL* GOING TO COME BACK HERE.
IT'S A DONE DEAL!

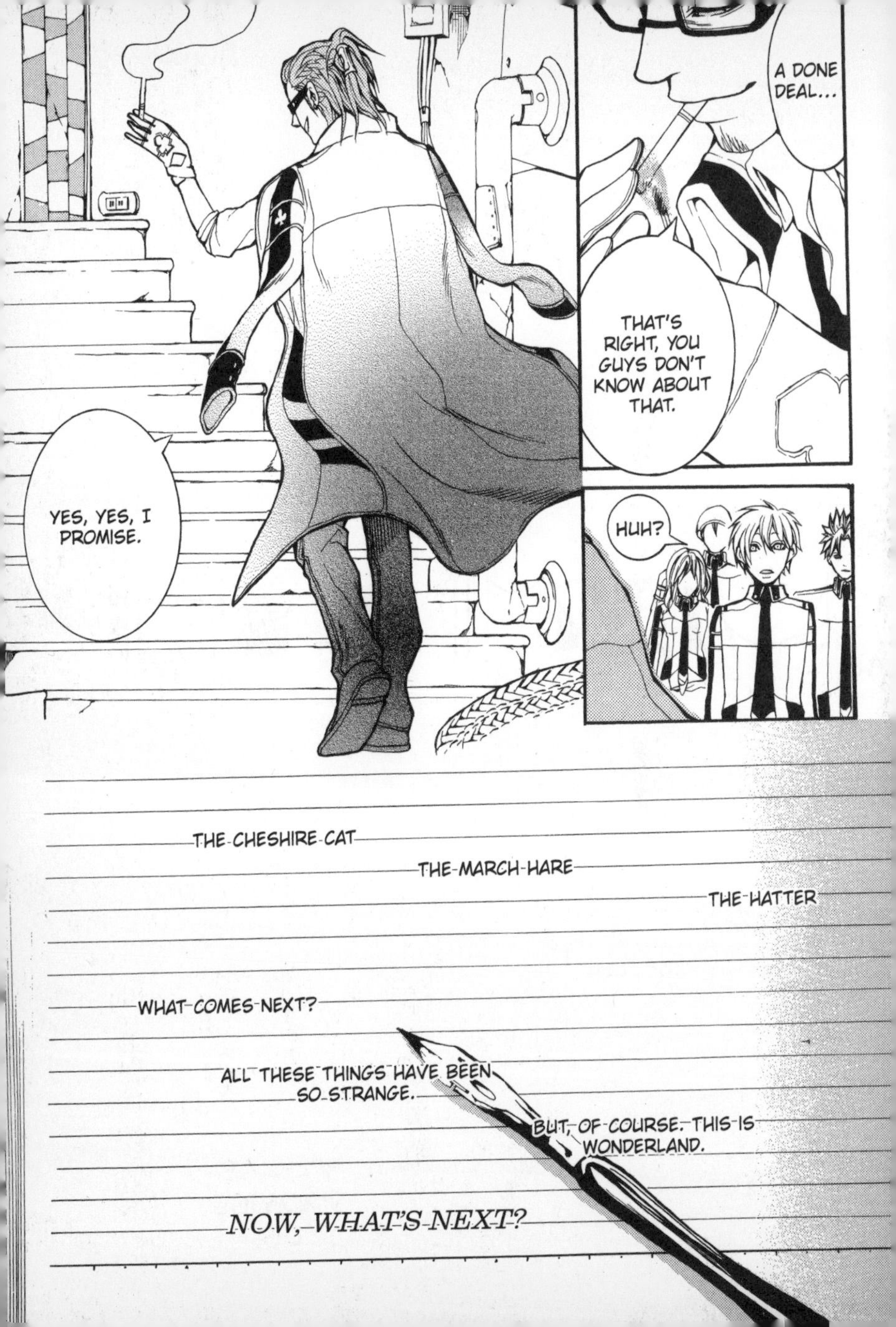
A DONE DEAL...
THAT'S RIGHT, YOU GUYS DON'T KNOW ABOUT THAT.
HUH?
YES, YES, I PROMISE.
THE CHESHIRE CAT
THE MARCH HARE
THE HATTER
WHAT COMES NEXT?
ALL THESE THINGS HAVE BEEN SO STRANGE.
BUT, OF COURSE. THIS IS WONDERLAND.
NOW, WHAT'S NEXT?

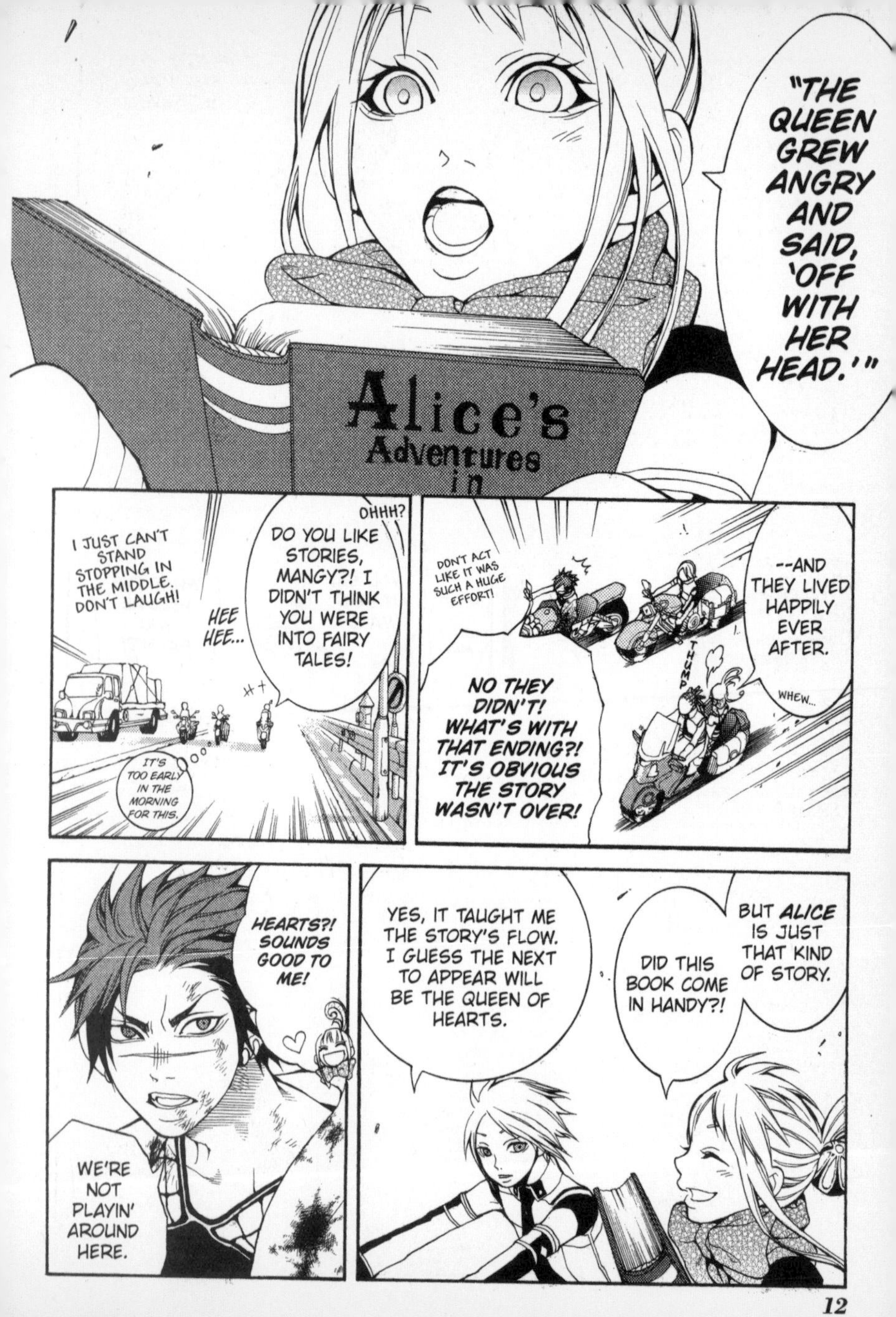
"THE QUEEN GREW ANGRY AND SAID, 'OFF WITH HER HEAD.'"
Alice's Adventures in
--AND THEY LIVED HAPPILY EVER AFTER.
WHEW...
THUMP
DON'T ACT LIKE IT WAS SUCH A HUGE EFFORT!
NO THEY DIDN'T! WHAT'S WITH THAT ENDING?! IT'S OBVIOUS THE STORY WASN'T OVER!
OHHH?
DO YOU LIKE STORIES, MANGY?! I DIDN'T THINK YOU WERE INTO FAIRY TALES!
HEE HEE...
I JUST CAN'T STAND STOPPING IN THE MIDDLE. DON'T LAUGH!
IT'S TOO EARLY IN THE MORNING FOR THIS.
BUT ALICE IS JUST THAT KIND OF STORY.
DID THIS BOOK COME IN HANDY?!
YES, IT TAUGHT ME THE STORY'S FLOW. I GUESS THE NEXT TO APPEAR WILL BE THE QUEEN OF HEARTS.
HEARTS?! SOUNDS GOOD TO ME!
WE'RE NOT PLAYIN' AROUND HERE.

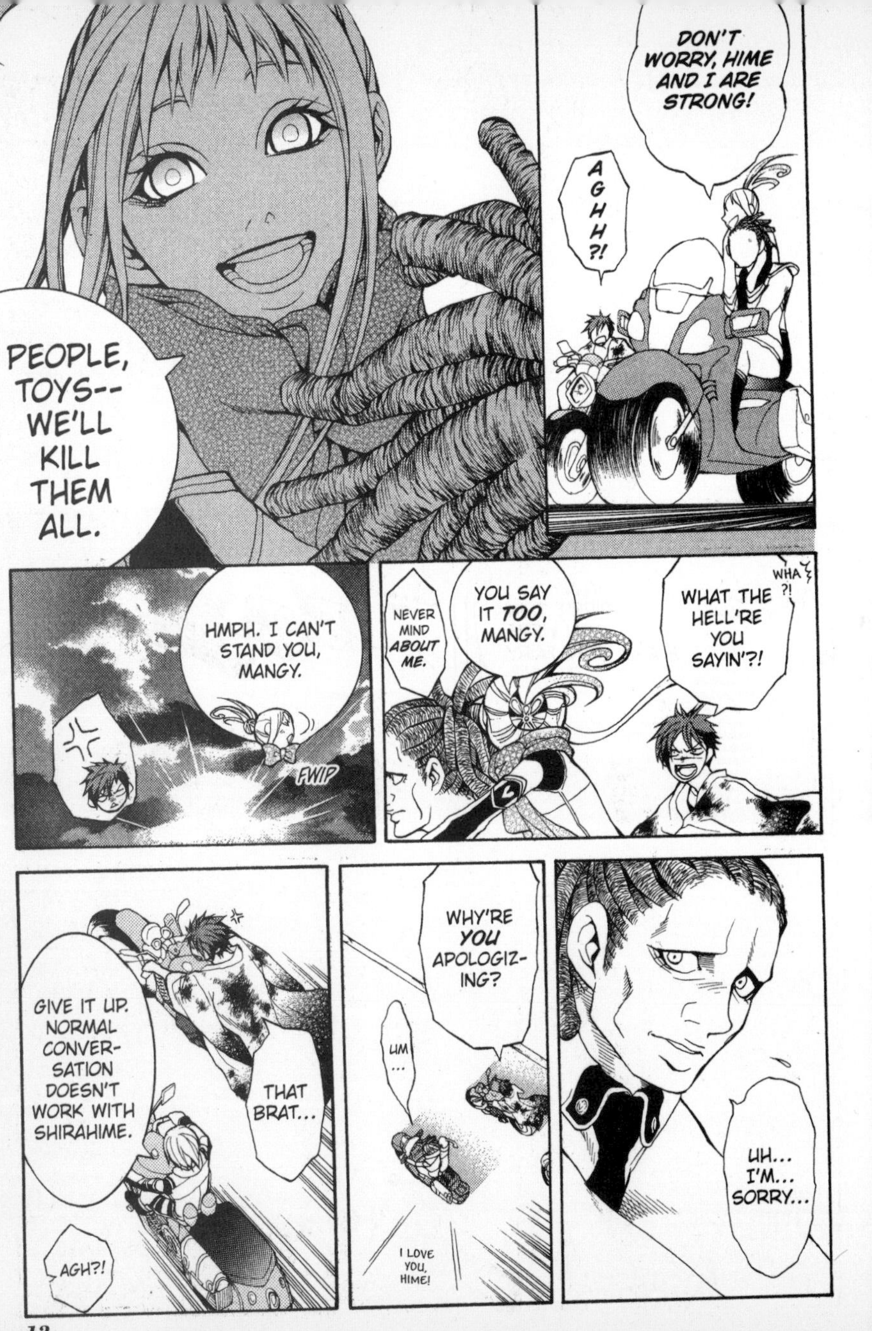
DON'T WORRY, HIME AND I ARE STRONG!
AGHH?!
PEOPLE, TOYS-- WE'LL KILL THEM ALL.
WHA ?!
WHAT THE HELL'RE YOU SAYIN'?!
YOU SAY IT *TOO*, MANGY.
NEVER MIND *ABOUT ME.*
HMPH. I CAN'T STAND YOU, MANGY.
FWIP
UH... I'M... SORRY...
WHY'RE *YOU* APOLOGIZ-ING?
UM ...
I LOVE YOU, HIME!
THAT BRAT...
GIVE IT UP. NORMAL CONVER-SATION DOESN'T WORK WITH SHIRAHIME.
AGH?!

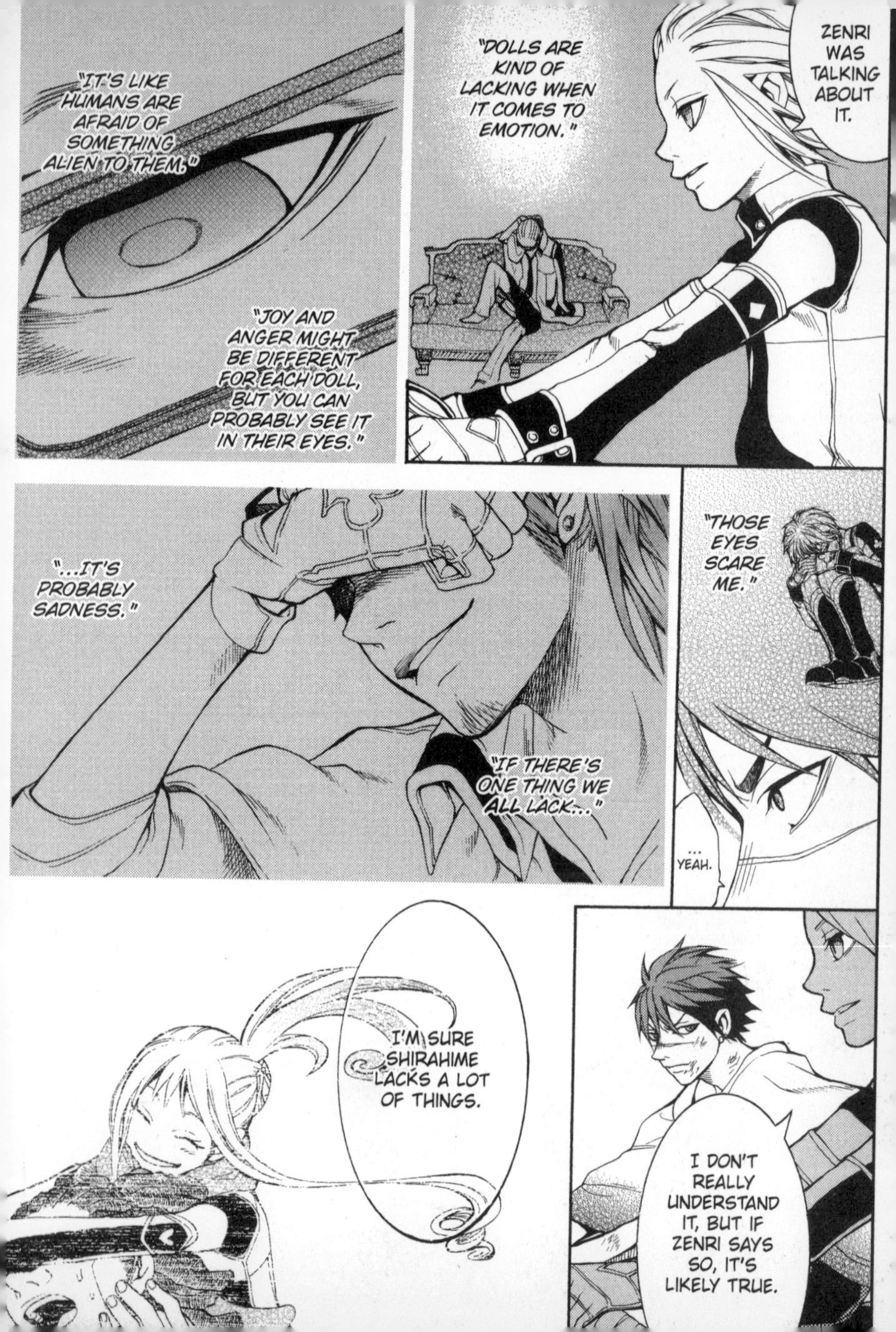
ZENRI WAS TALKING ABOUT IT.
"DOLLS ARE KIND OF LACKING WHEN IT COMES TO EMOTION."
"IT'S LIKE HUMANS ARE AFRAID OF SOMETHING ALIEN TO THEM."
"JOY AND ANGER MIGHT BE DIFFERENT FOR EACH DOLL, BUT YOU CAN PROBABLY SEE IT IN THEIR EYES."
"THOSE EYES SCARE ME."
...YEAH.
"IF THERE'S ONE THING WE ALL LACK..."
"...IT'S PROBABLY SADNESS."
I DON'T REALLY UNDERSTAND IT, BUT IF ZENRI SAYS SO, IT'S LIKELY TRUE.
I'M SURE SHIRAHIME LACKS A LOT OF THINGS.

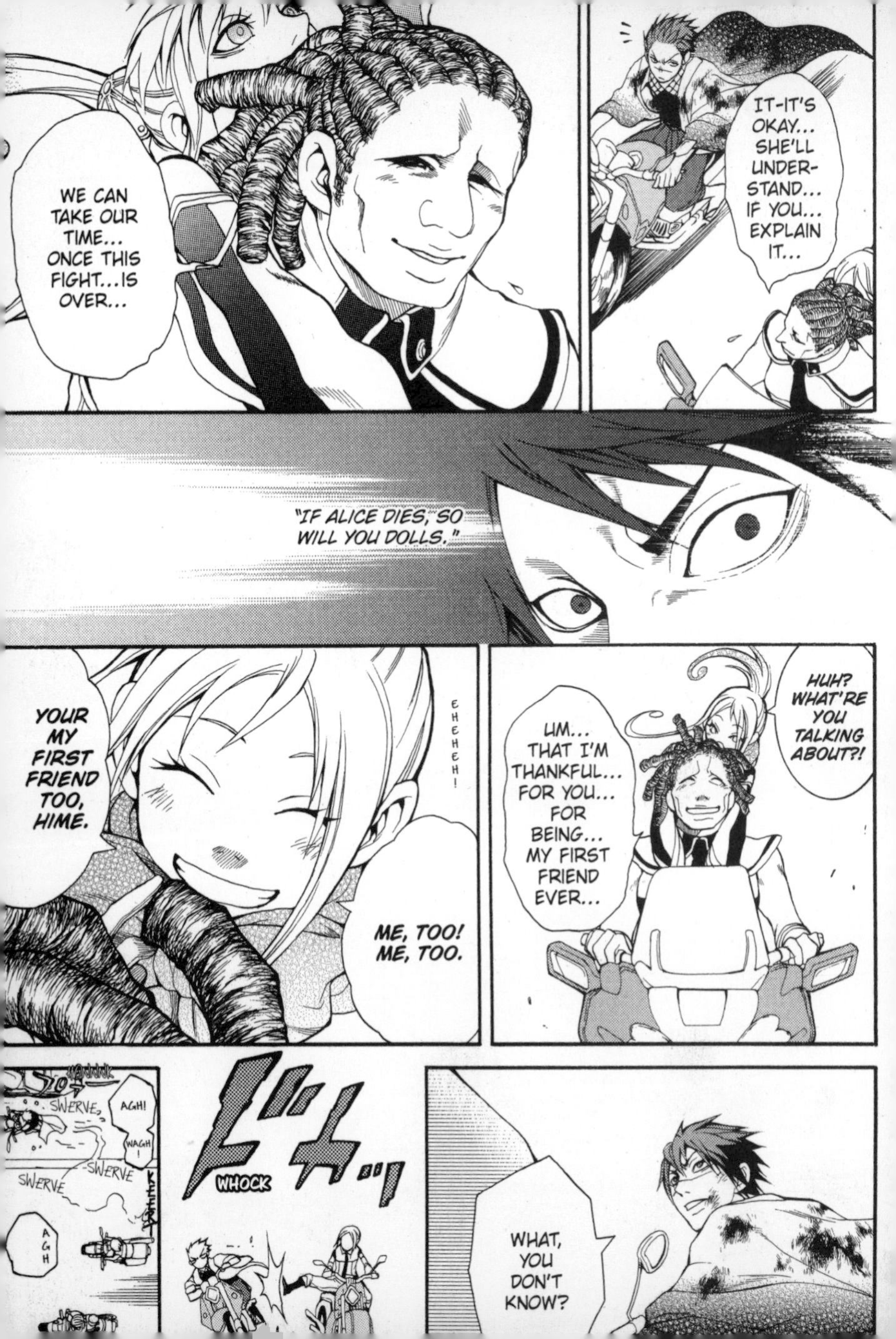

IT-IT'S OKAY... SHE'LL UNDER-STAND... IF YOU... EXPLAIN IT...
WE CAN TAKE OUR TIME... ONCE THIS FIGHT...IS OVER...
"IF ALICE DIES, SO WILL YOU DOLLS."
HUH? WHAT'RE YOU TALKING ABOUT?!
UM... THAT I'M THANKFUL... FOR YOU... FOR BEING... MY FIRST FRIEND EVER...
EHEHEH!
YOUR MY FIRST FRIEND TOO, HIME.
ME, TOO! ME, TOO.
WHAT, YOU DON'T KNOW?
WHOCK
SWERVE
AGH!
WAGH!
SWERVE
SWERVE
AGH

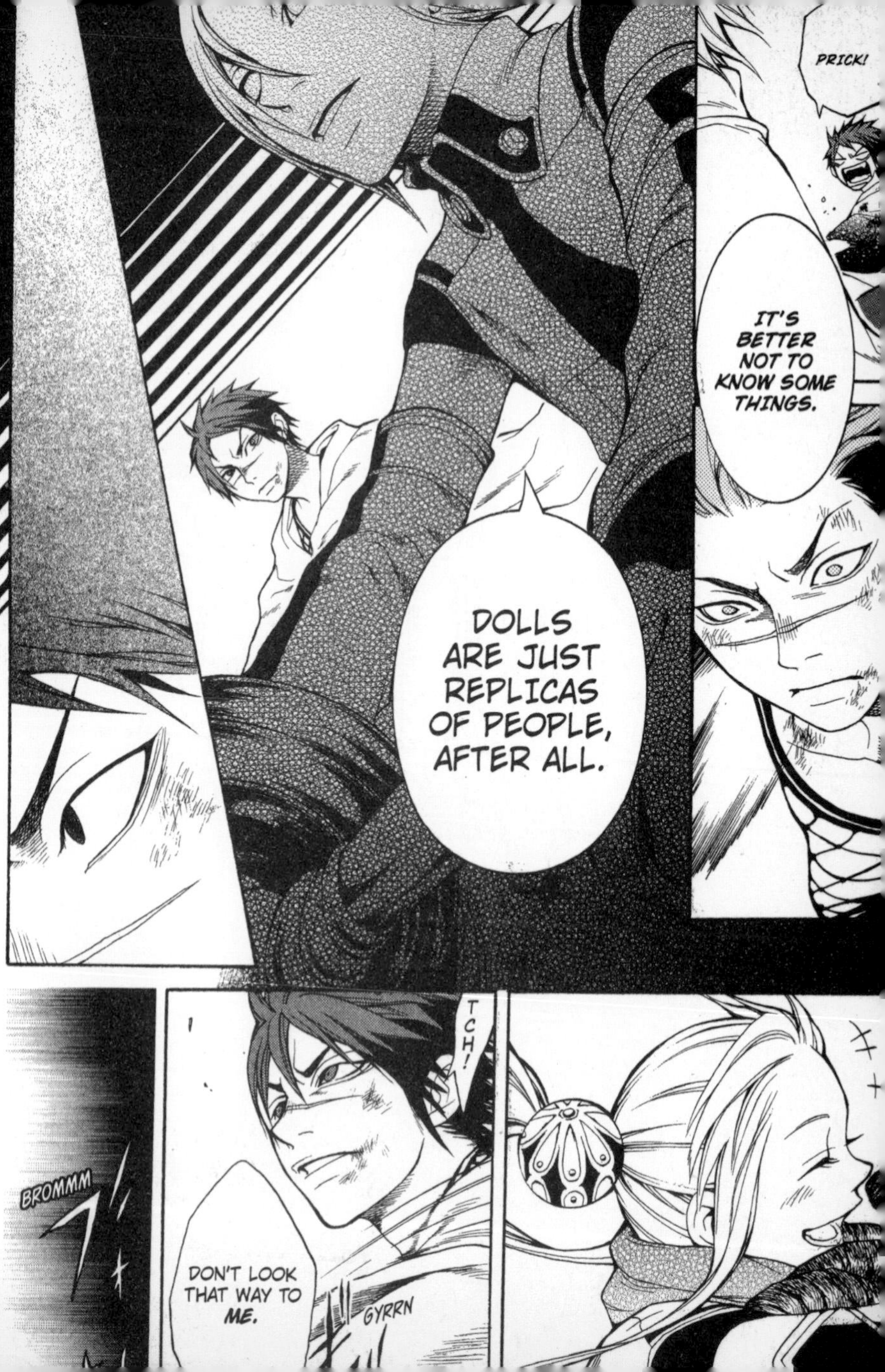
PRICK!
IT'S BETTER NOT TO KNOW SOME THINGS.
DOLLS ARE JUST REPLICAS OF PEOPLE, AFTER ALL.
TCH!
DON'T LOOK THAT WAY TO ME.
GYRRN
BROMMM

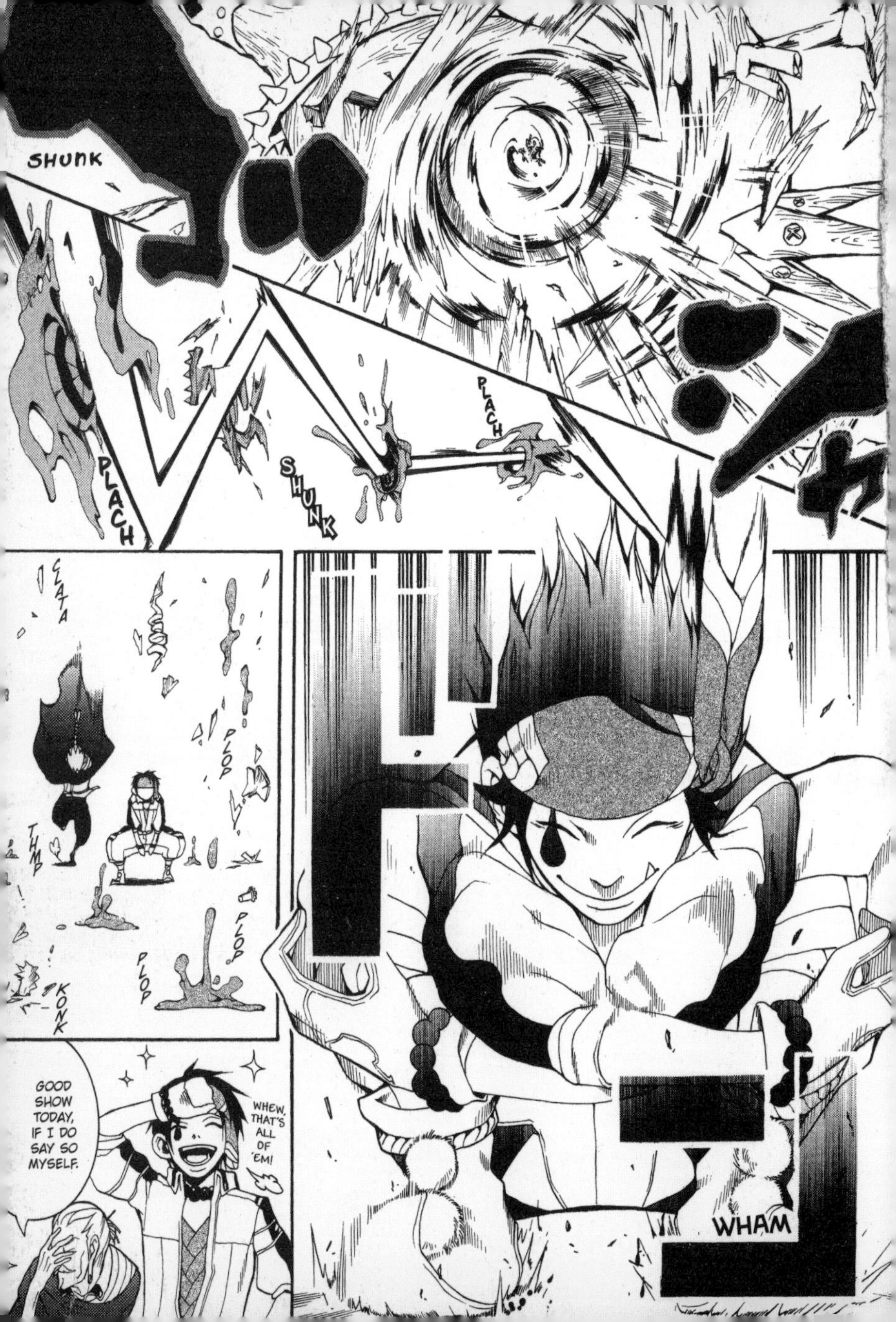
PLACH
SHUNK
SHUNK
PLACH
WHAM
CLATA
PLOP
THMP
PLOP
PLOP
PLOP
KONK
WHEW, THAT'S ALL OF 'EM!
GOOD SHOW TODAY, IF I DO SAY SO MYSELF.

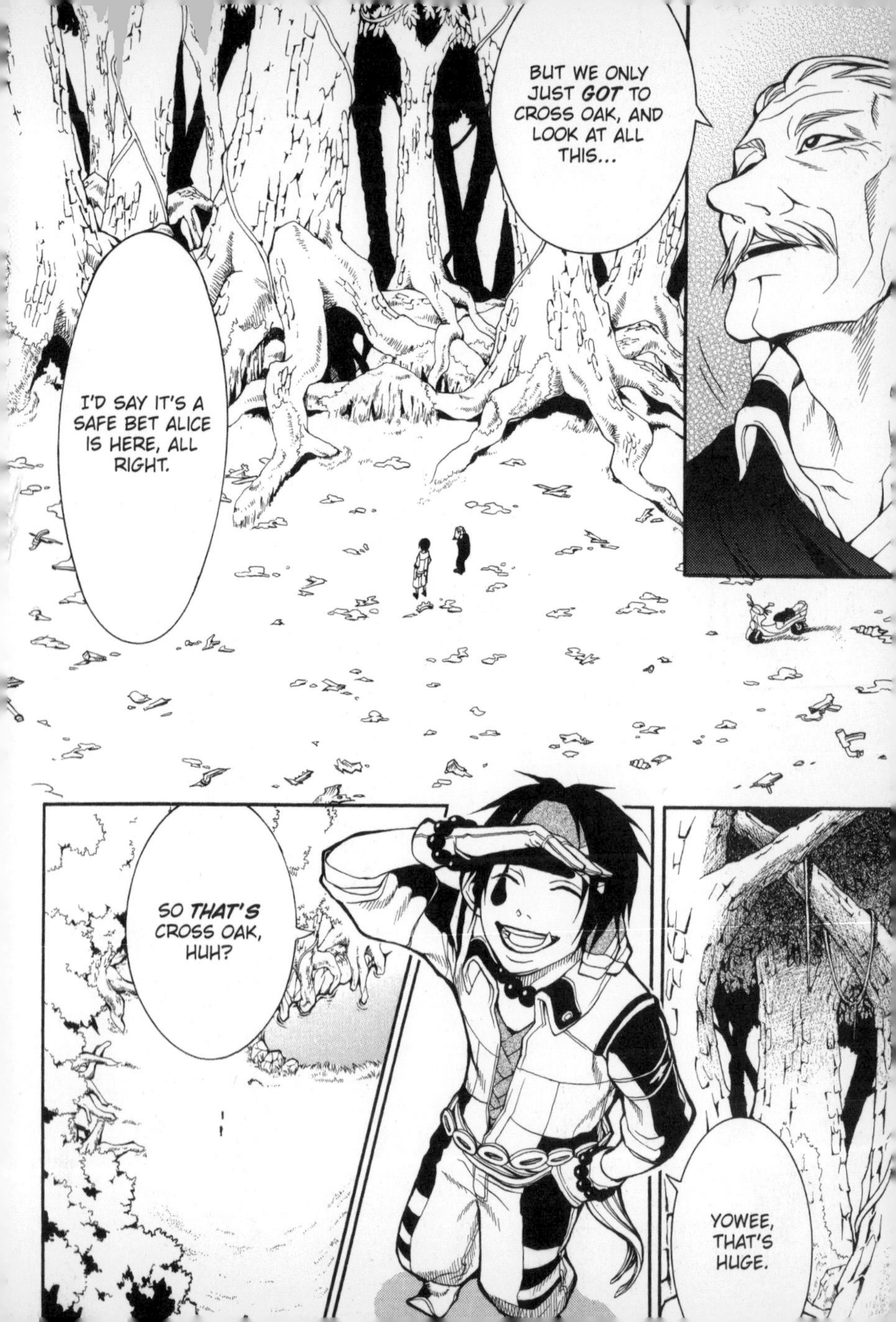
BUT WE ONLY JUST *GOT* TO CROSS OAK, AND LOOK AT ALL THIS...
I'D SAY IT'S A SAFE BET ALICE IS HERE, ALL RIGHT.
YOWEE, THAT'S HUGE.
SO *THAT'S* CROSS OAK, HUH?

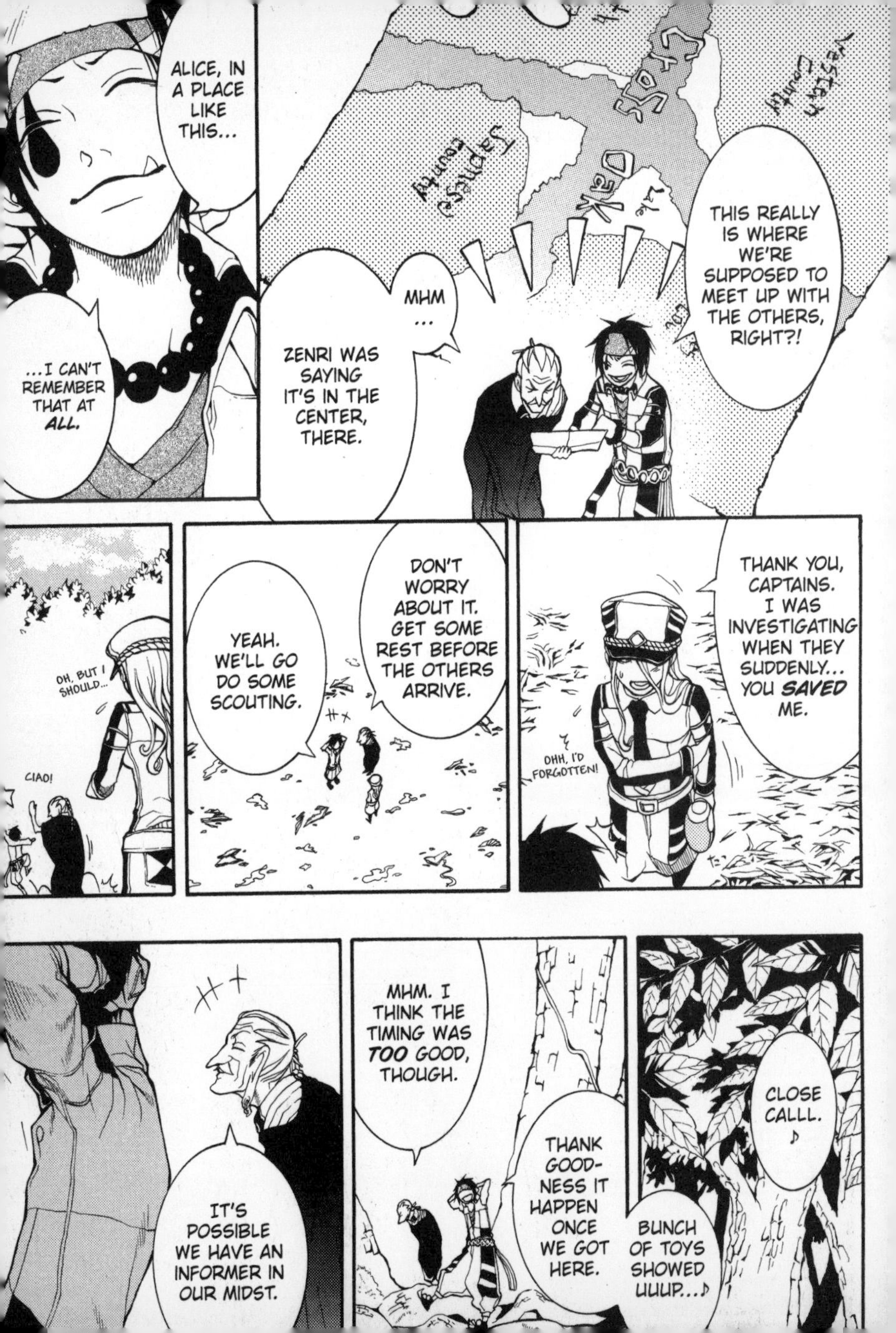
THIS REALLY IS WHERE WE'RE SUPPOSED TO MEET UP WITH THE OTHERS, RIGHT?!
MHM ...
ZENRI WAS SAYING IT'S IN THE CENTER, THERE.
ALICE, IN A PLACE LIKE THIS...
...I CAN'T REMEMBER THAT AT **ALL.**
THANK YOU, CAPTAINS. I WAS INVESTIGATING WHEN THEY SUDDENLY... YOU **SAVED** ME.
OHH, I'D FORGOTTEN!
DON'T WORRY ABOUT IT. GET SOME REST BEFORE THE OTHERS ARRIVE.
YEAH. WE'LL GO DO SOME SCOUTING.
OH, BUT I SHOULD...
CIAO!
CLOSE CALL. ♪
BUNCH OF TOYS SHOWED UUUP...♪
THANK GOODNESS IT HAPPEN ONCE WE GOT HERE.
MHM. I THINK THE TIMING WAS **TOO** GOOD, THOUGH.
IT'S POSSIBLE WE HAVE AN INFORMER IN OUR MIDST.

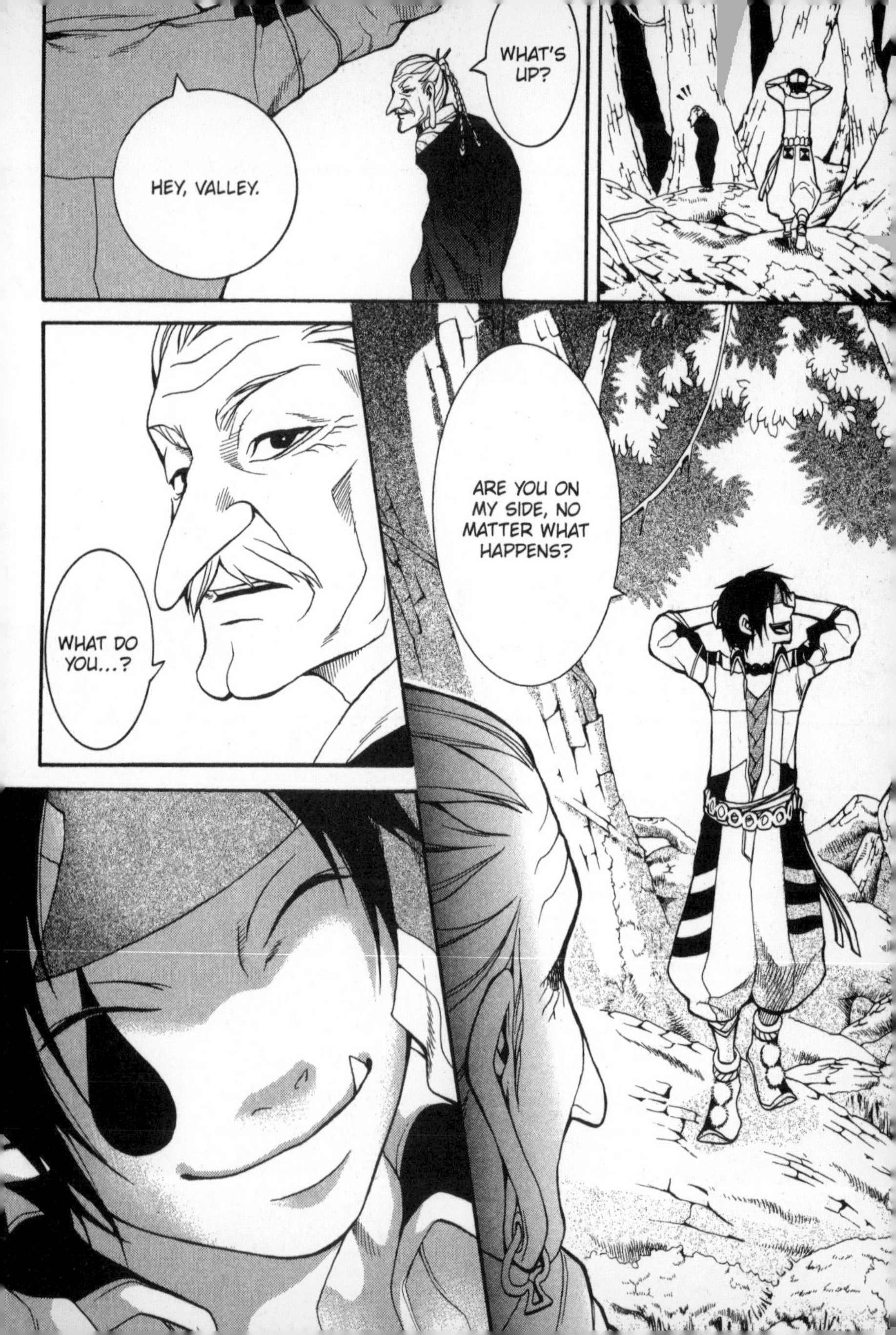
HEY, VALLEY.
WHAT'S UP?
ARE YOU ON MY SIDE, NO MATTER WHAT HAPPENS?
WHAT DO YOU...?

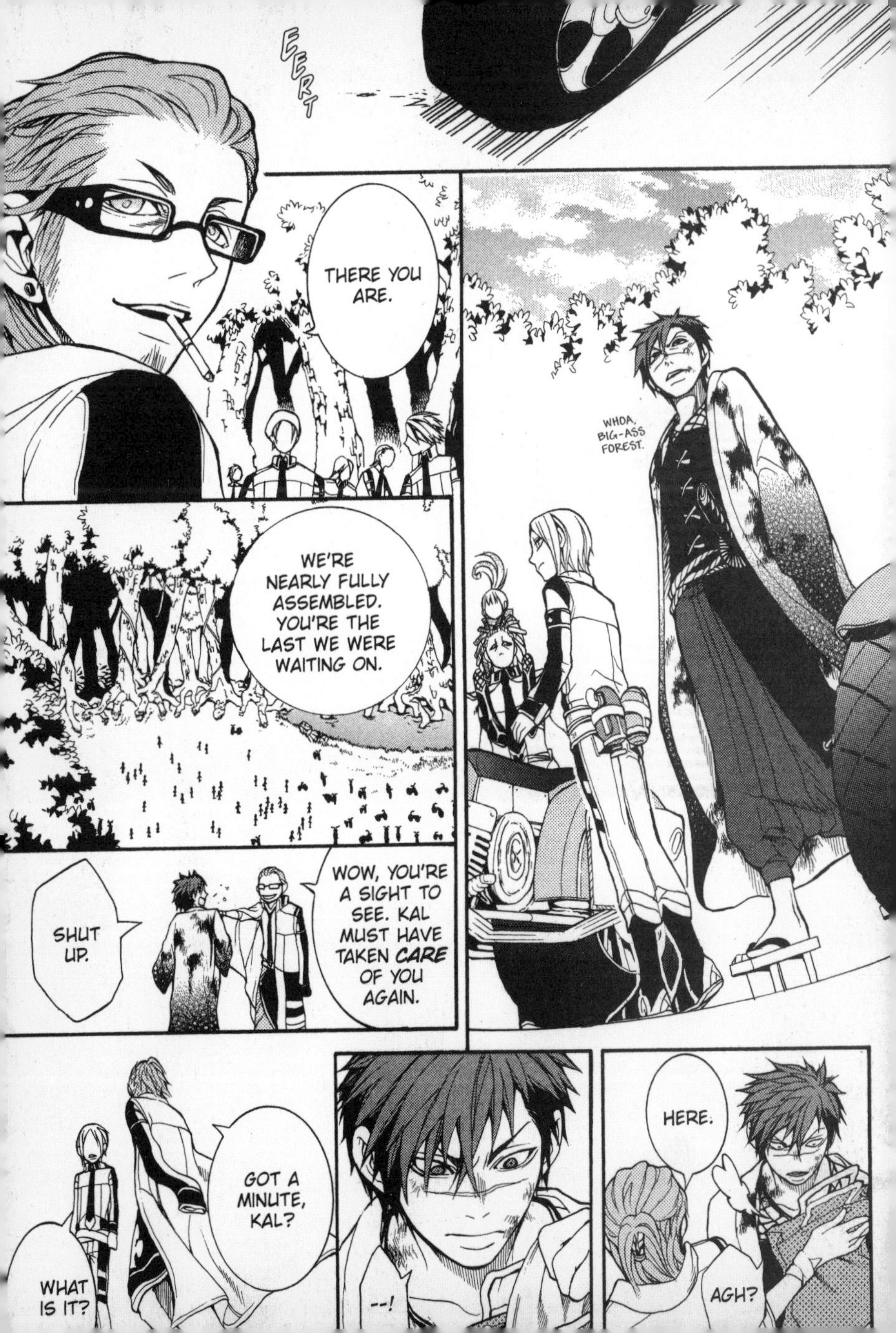
EERT
WHOA, BIG-ASS FOREST.
THERE YOU ARE.
WE'RE NEARLY FULLY ASSEMBLED. YOU'RE THE LAST WE WERE WAITING ON.
WOW, YOU'RE A SIGHT TO SEE. KAL MUST HAVE TAKEN *CARE* OF YOU AGAIN.
SHUT UP.
HERE.
AGH?
--!
GOT A MINUTE, KAL?
WHAT IS IT?

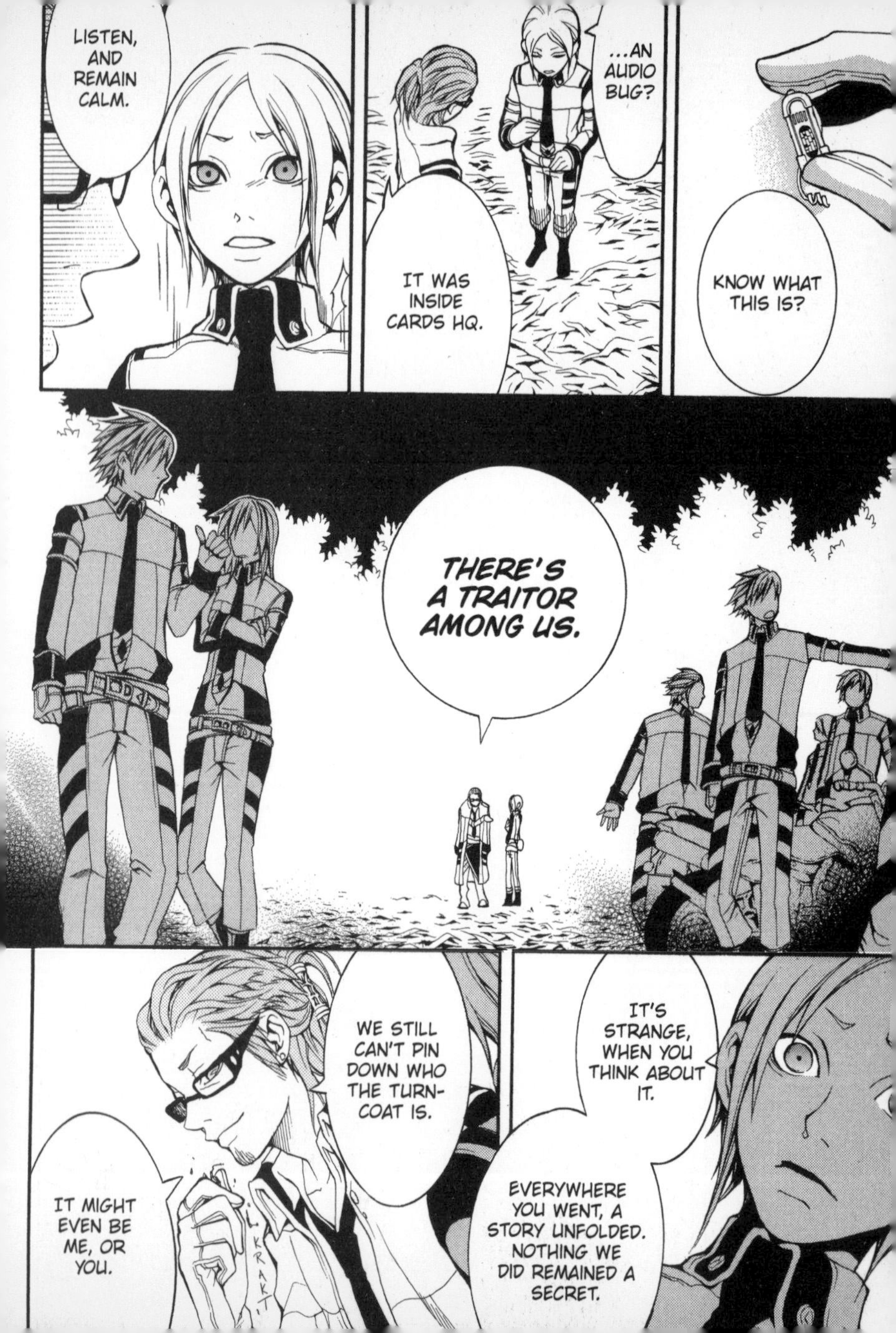
KNOW WHAT THIS IS?
...AN AUDIO BUG?
IT WAS INSIDE CARDS HQ.
LISTEN, AND REMAIN CALM.
THERE'S A TRAITOR AMONG US.
IT'S STRANGE, WHEN YOU THINK ABOUT IT.
EVERYWHERE YOU WENT, A STORY UNFOLDED. NOTHING WE DID REMAINED A SECRET.
WE STILL CAN'T PIN DOWN WHO THE TURN-COAT IS.
IT MIGHT EVEN BE ME, OR YOU.
KRAKT

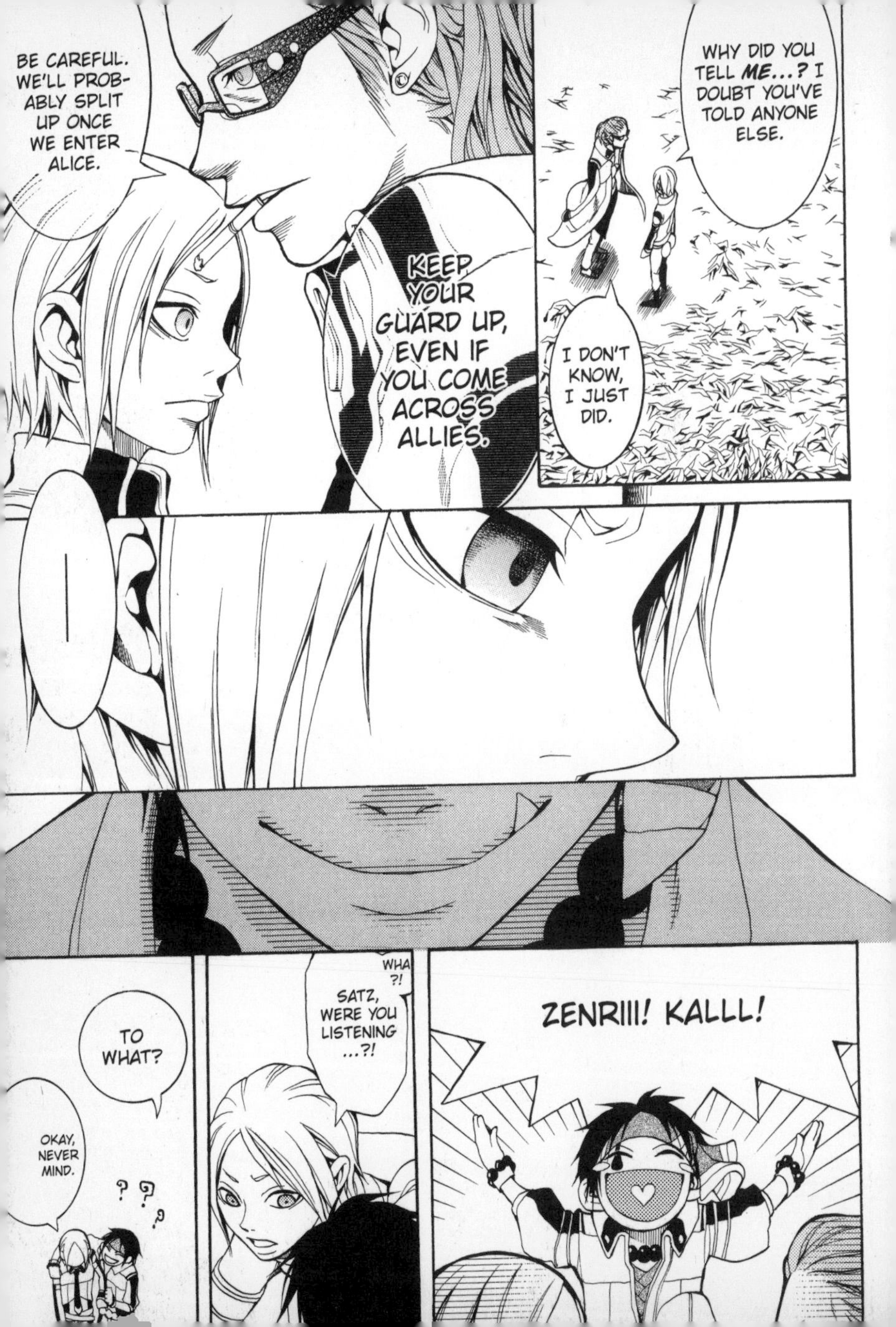
WHY DID YOU TELL ME...? I DOUBT YOU'VE TOLD ANYONE ELSE.
I DON'T KNOW, I JUST DID.
BE CAREFUL. WE'LL PROB-ABLY SPLIT UP ONCE WE ENTER ALICE.
KEEP YOUR GUARD UP, EVEN IF YOU COME ACROSS ALLIES.
ZENRIII! KALLL!
WHA ?!
SATZ, WERE YOU LISTENING ...?!
TO WHAT?
OKAY, NEVER MIND.
? ? ?

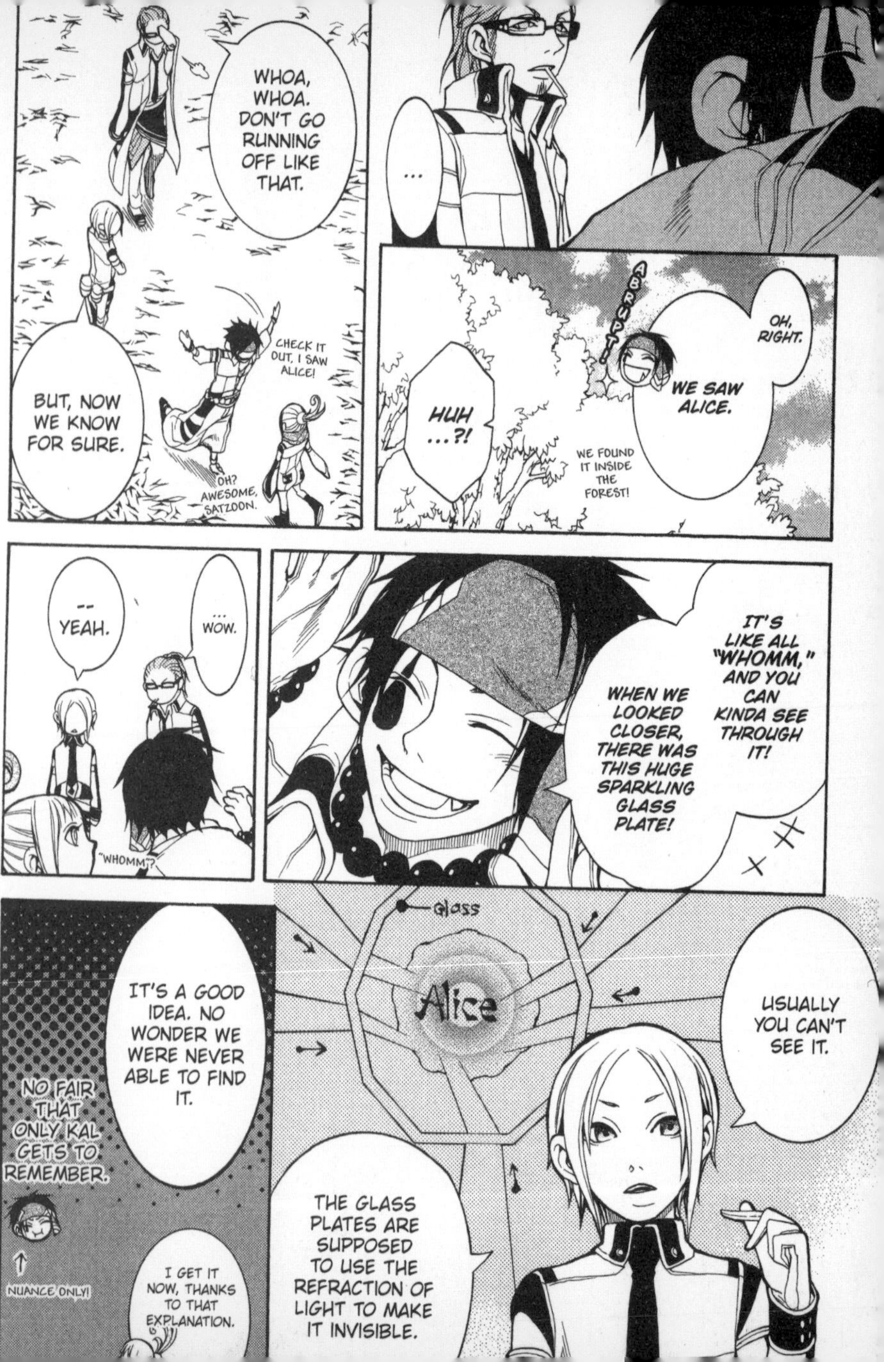
...
ABRUPT!
OH, RIGHT.
WE SAW ALICE.
WE FOUND IT INSIDE THE FOREST!
HUH ...?!
WHOA, WHOA. DON'T GO RUNNING OFF LIKE THAT.
CHECK IT OUT, I SAW ALICE!
BUT, NOW WE KNOW FOR SURE.
OH? AWESOME, SATZOON.
IT'S LIKE ALL "WHOMM," AND YOU CAN KINDA SEE THROUGH IT!
WHEN WE LOOKED CLOSER, THERE WAS THIS HUGE SPARKLING GLASS PLATE!
... WOW.
-- YEAH.
"WHOMM"?
USUALLY YOU CAN'T SEE IT.
Glass
Alice
THE GLASS PLATES ARE SUPPOSED TO USE THE REFRACTION OF LIGHT TO MAKE IT INVISIBLE.
IT'S A GOOD IDEA. NO WONDER WE WERE NEVER ABLE TO FIND IT.
NO FAIR THAT ONLY KAL GETS TO REMEMBER.
I GET IT NOW, THANKS TO THAT EXPLANATION.
NUANCE ONLY!

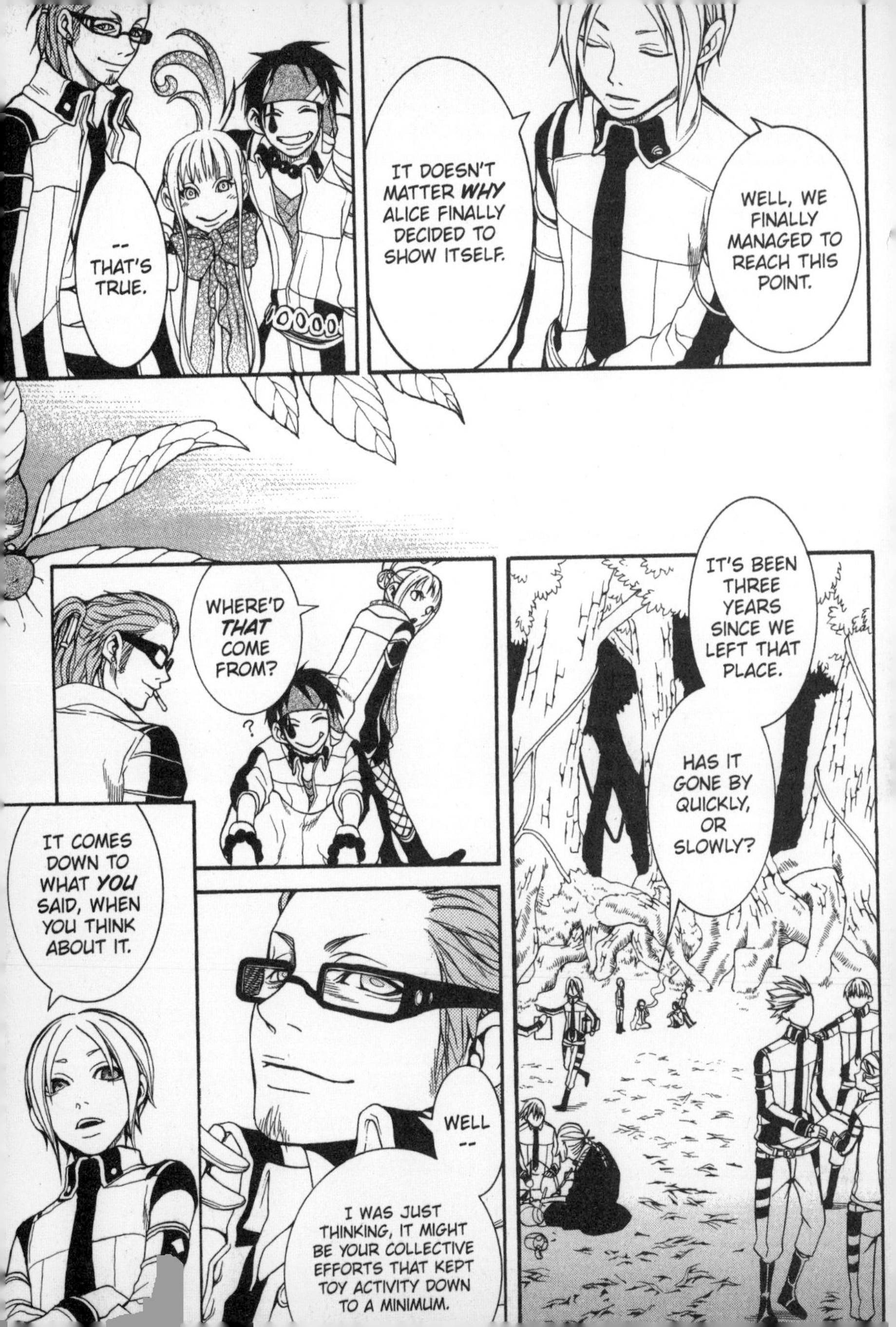
WELL, WE FINALLY MANAGED TO REACH THIS POINT.
IT DOESN'T MATTER ***WHY*** ALICE FINALLY DECIDED TO SHOW ITSELF.
-- THAT'S TRUE.
IT'S BEEN THREE YEARS SINCE WE LEFT THAT PLACE.
HAS IT GONE BY QUICKLY, OR SLOWLY?
WHERE'D ***THAT*** COME FROM?
?
WELL --
I WAS JUST THINKING, IT MIGHT BE YOUR COLLECTIVE EFFORTS THAT KEPT TOY ACTIVITY DOWN TO A MINIMUM.
IT COMES DOWN TO WHAT ***YOU*** SAID, WHEN YOU THINK ABOUT IT.

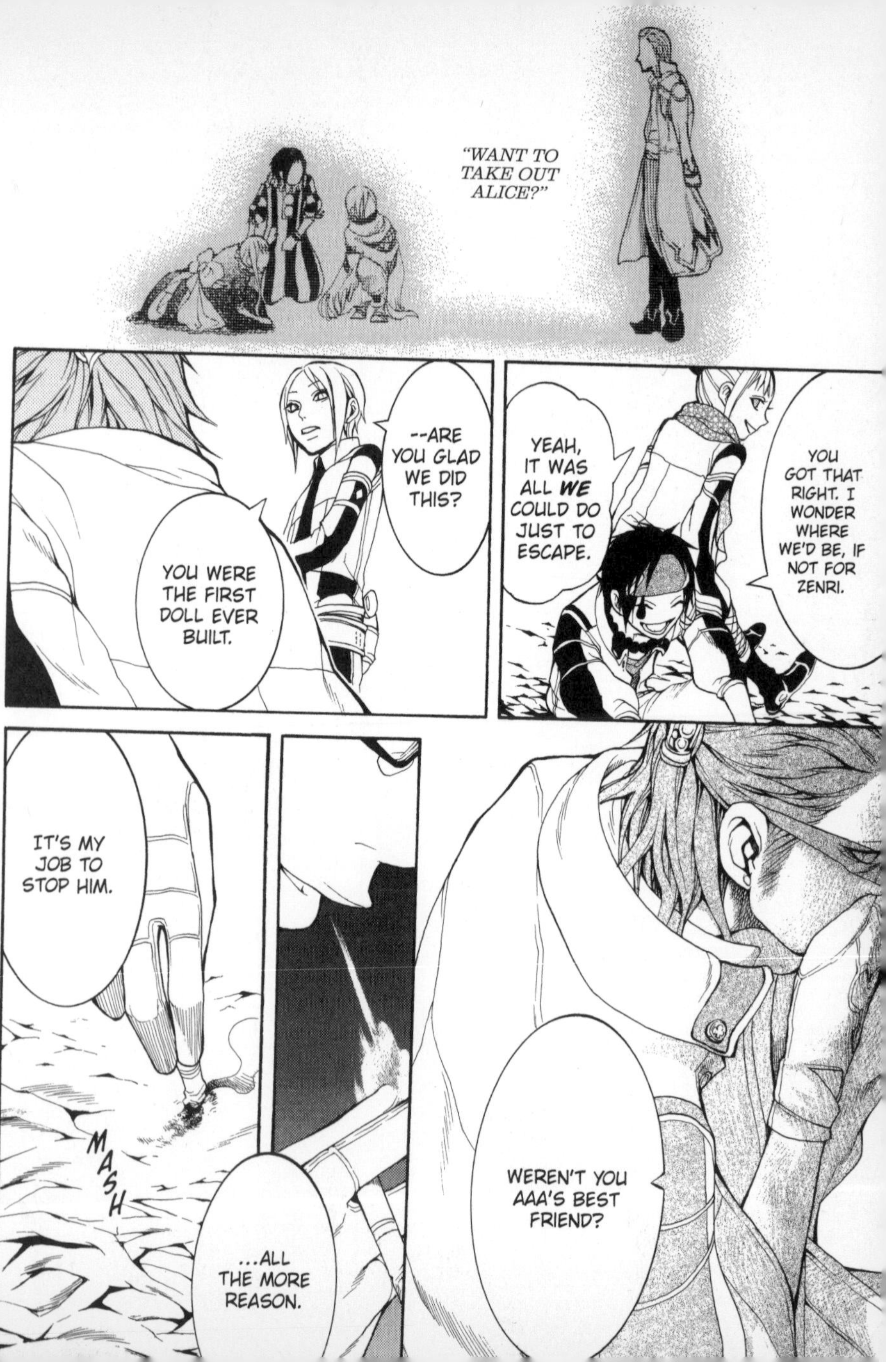
"WANT TO TAKE OUT ALICE?"
YOU GOT THAT RIGHT. I WONDER WHERE WE'D BE, IF NOT FOR ZENRI.
YEAH, IT WAS ALL WE COULD DO JUST TO ESCAPE.
--ARE YOU GLAD WE DID THIS?
YOU WERE THE FIRST DOLL EVER BUILT.
WEREN'T YOU AAA'S BEST FRIEND?
...ALL THE MORE REASON.
IT'S MY JOB TO STOP HIM.
MASH

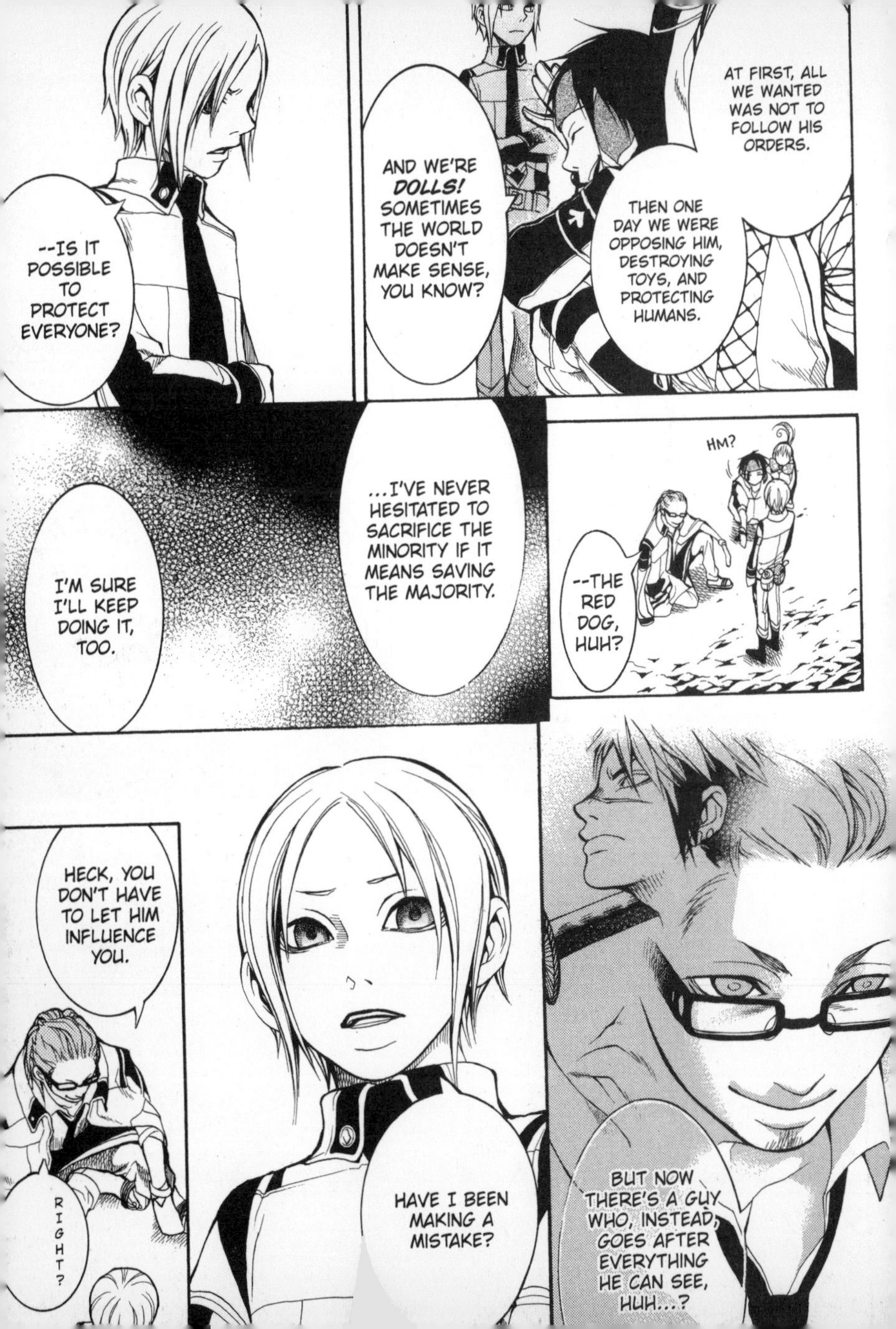

AT FIRST, ALL WE WANTED WAS NOT TO FOLLOW HIS ORDERS.
THEN ONE DAY WE WERE OPPOSING HIM, DESTROYING TOYS, AND PROTECTING HUMANS.
AND WE'RE ***DOLLS!*** SOMETIMES THE WORLD DOESN'T MAKE SENSE, YOU KNOW?
--IS IT POSSIBLE TO PROTECT EVERYONE?
HM?
--THE RED DOG, HUH?
...I'VE NEVER HESITATED TO SACRIFICE THE MINORITY IF IT MEANS SAVING THE MAJORITY.
I'M SURE I'LL KEEP DOING IT, TOO.
BUT NOW THERE'S A GUY WHO, INSTEAD, GOES AFTER EVERYTHING HE CAN SEE, HUH...?
HAVE I BEEN MAKING A MISTAKE?
HECK, YOU DON'T HAVE TO LET HIM INFLUENCE YOU.
RIGHT?

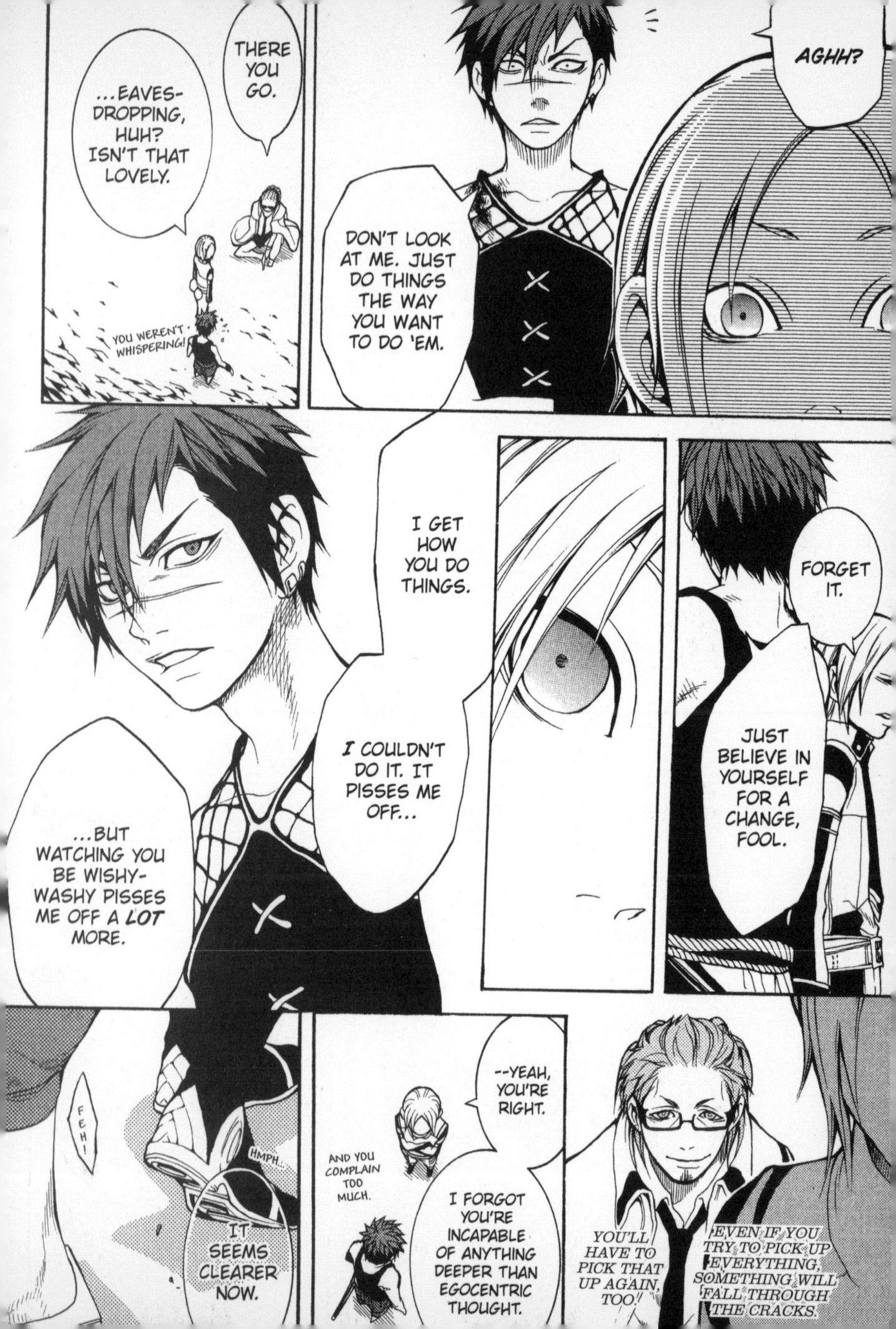
AGHH?
DON'T LOOK AT ME. JUST DO THINGS THE WAY YOU WANT TO DO 'EM.
THERE YOU GO.
...EAVES-DROPPING, HUH? ISN'T THAT LOVELY.
YOU WEREN'T WHISPERING!
FORGET IT.
JUST BELIEVE IN YOURSELF FOR A CHANGE, FOOL.
I GET HOW YOU DO THINGS.
I COULDN'T DO IT. IT PISSES ME OFF...
...BUT WATCHING YOU BE WISHY-WASHY PISSES ME OFF A LOT MORE.
EVEN IF YOU TRY TO PICK UP EVERYTHING, SOMETHING WILL FALL THROUGH THE CRACKS.
YOU'LL HAVE TO PICK THAT UP AGAIN, TOO!
--YEAH, YOU'RE RIGHT.
I FORGOT YOU'RE INCAPABLE OF ANYTHING DEEPER THAN EGOCENTRIC THOUGHT.
AND YOU COMPLAIN TOO MUCH.
FEH!
HMPH...
IT SEEMS CLEARER NOW.

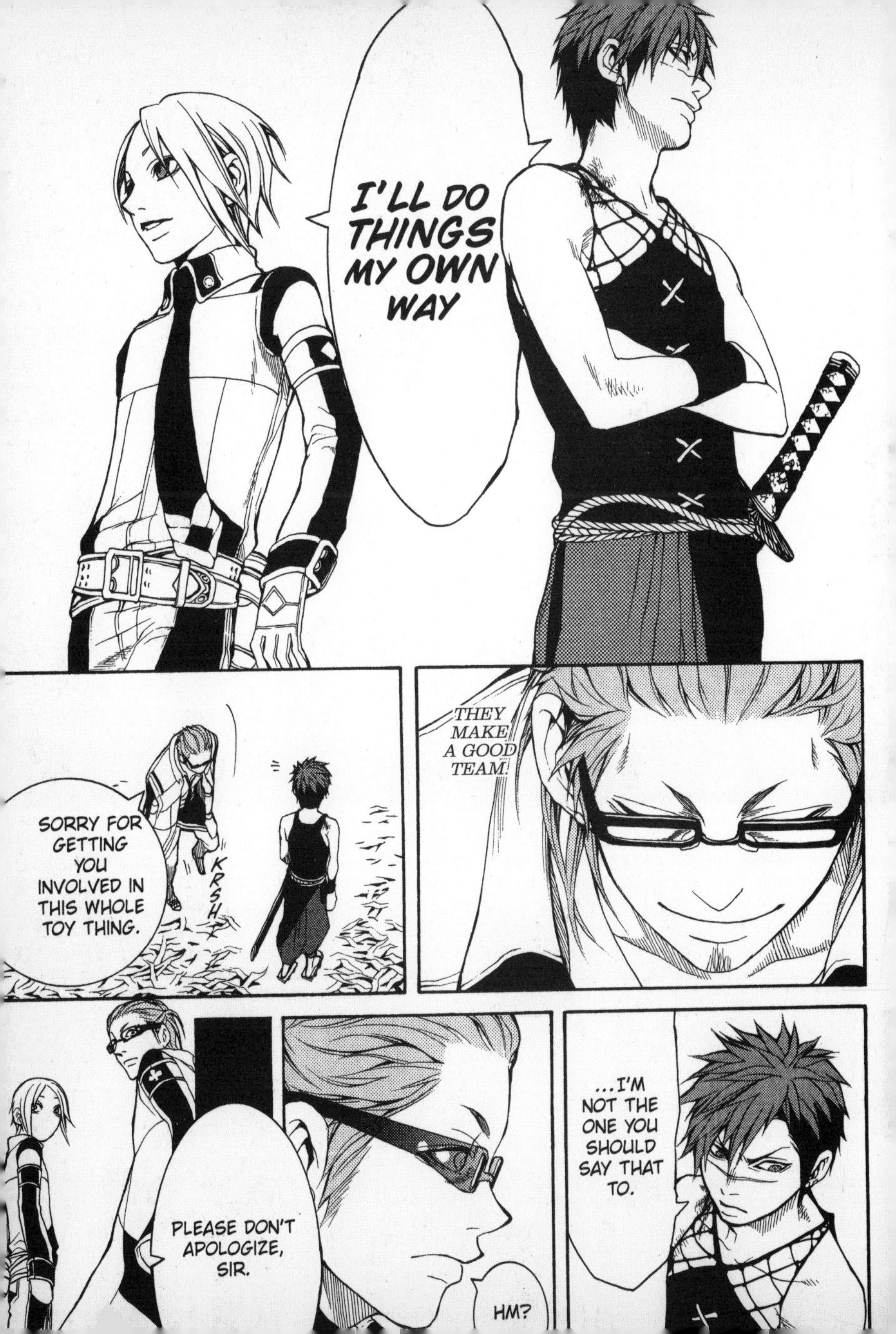
I'LL DO THINGS MY OWN WAY
THEY MAKE A GOOD TEAM.
SORRY FOR GETTING YOU INVOLVED IN THIS WHOLE TOY THING.
KRSH
...I'M NOT THE ONE YOU SHOULD SAY THAT TO.
HM?
PLEASE DON'T APOLOGIZE, SIR.

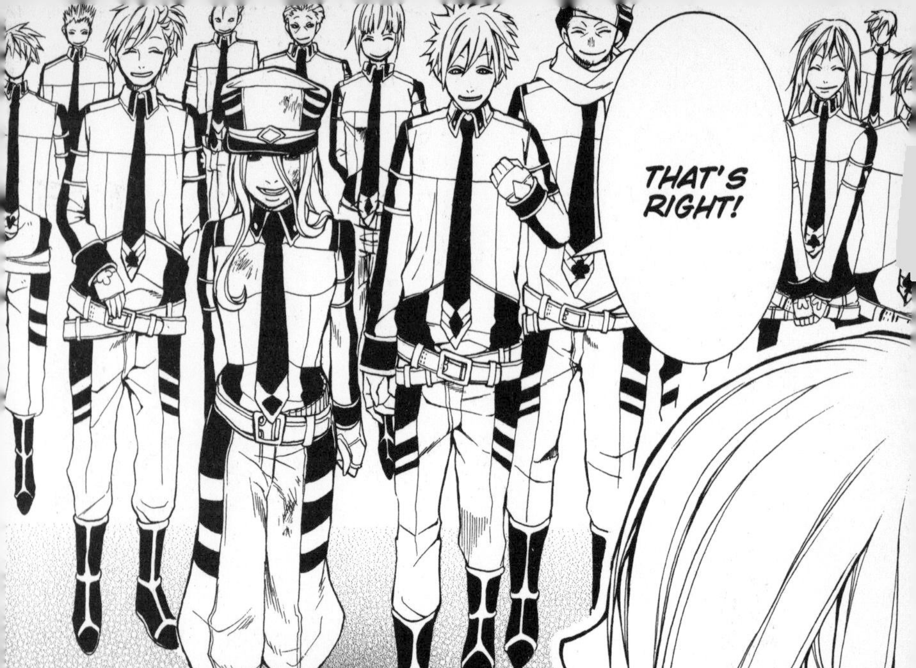
THAT'S RIGHT!

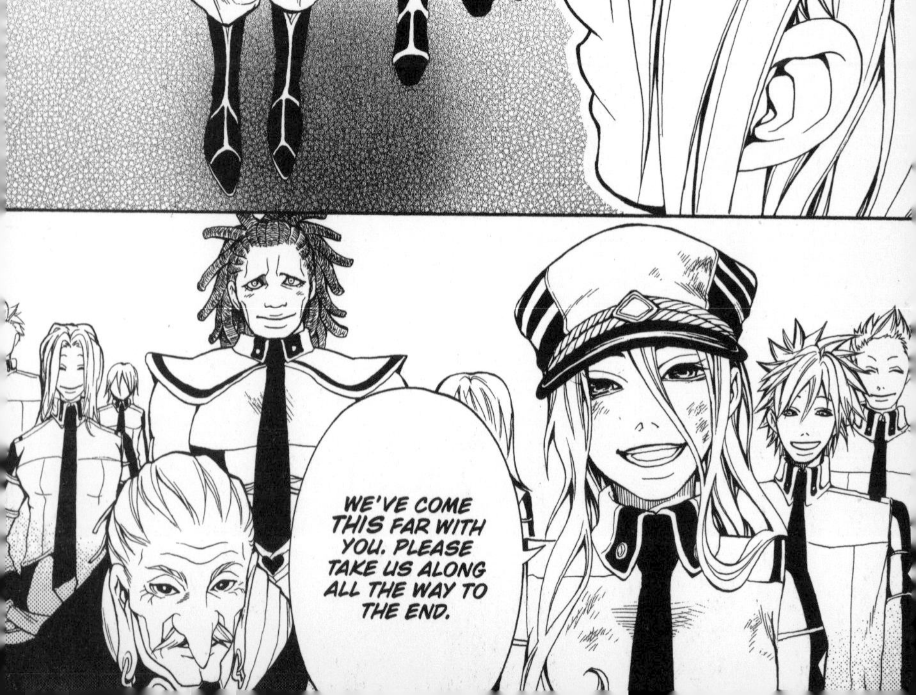
WE'VE COME THIS FAR WITH YOU. PLEASE TAKE US ALONG ALL THE WAY TO THE END.

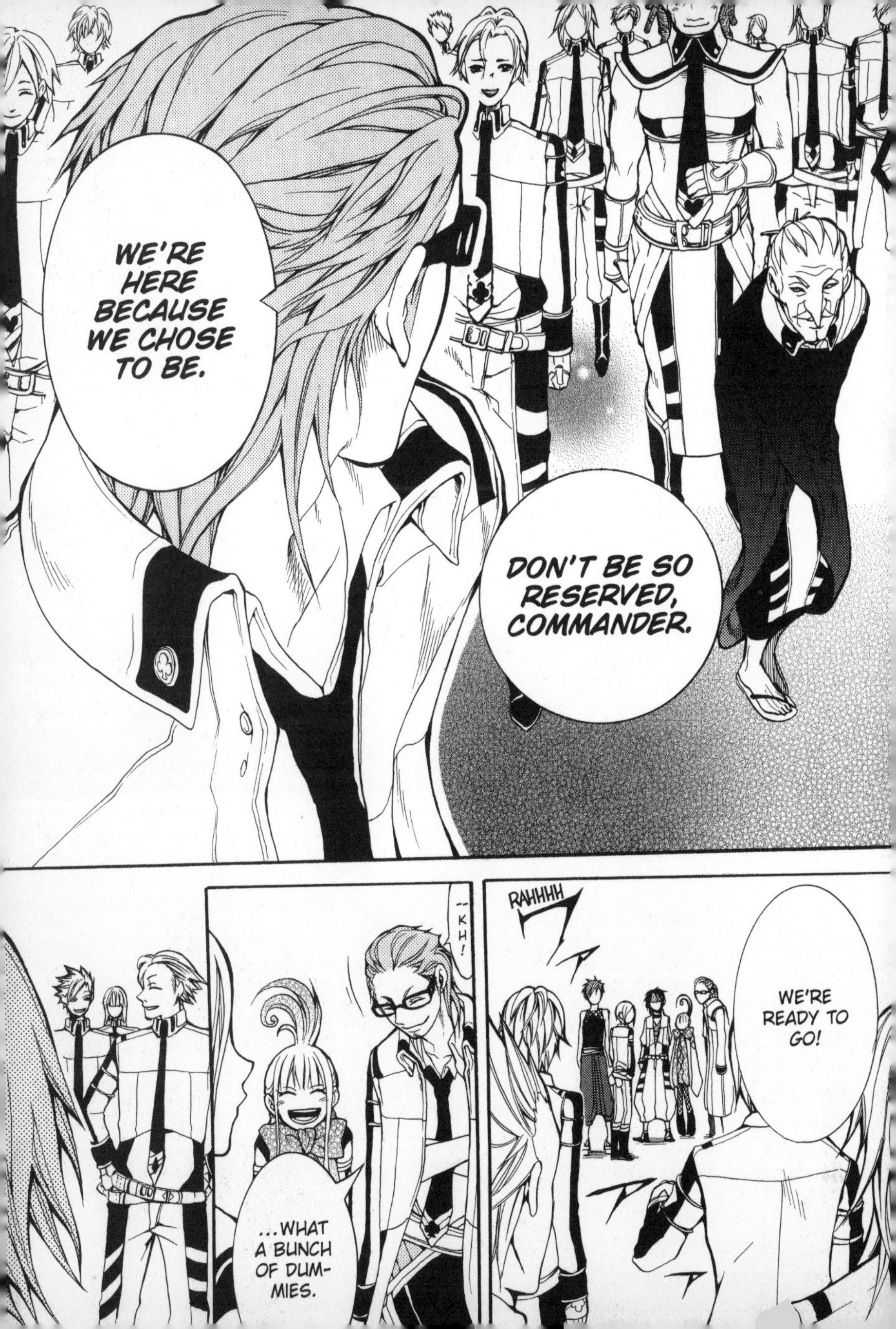
DON'T BE SO RESERVED, COMMANDER.
WE'RE HERE BECAUSE WE CHOSE TO BE.
RAHHHH
WE'RE READY TO GO!
--KH!
...WHAT A BUNCH OF DUM-MIES.

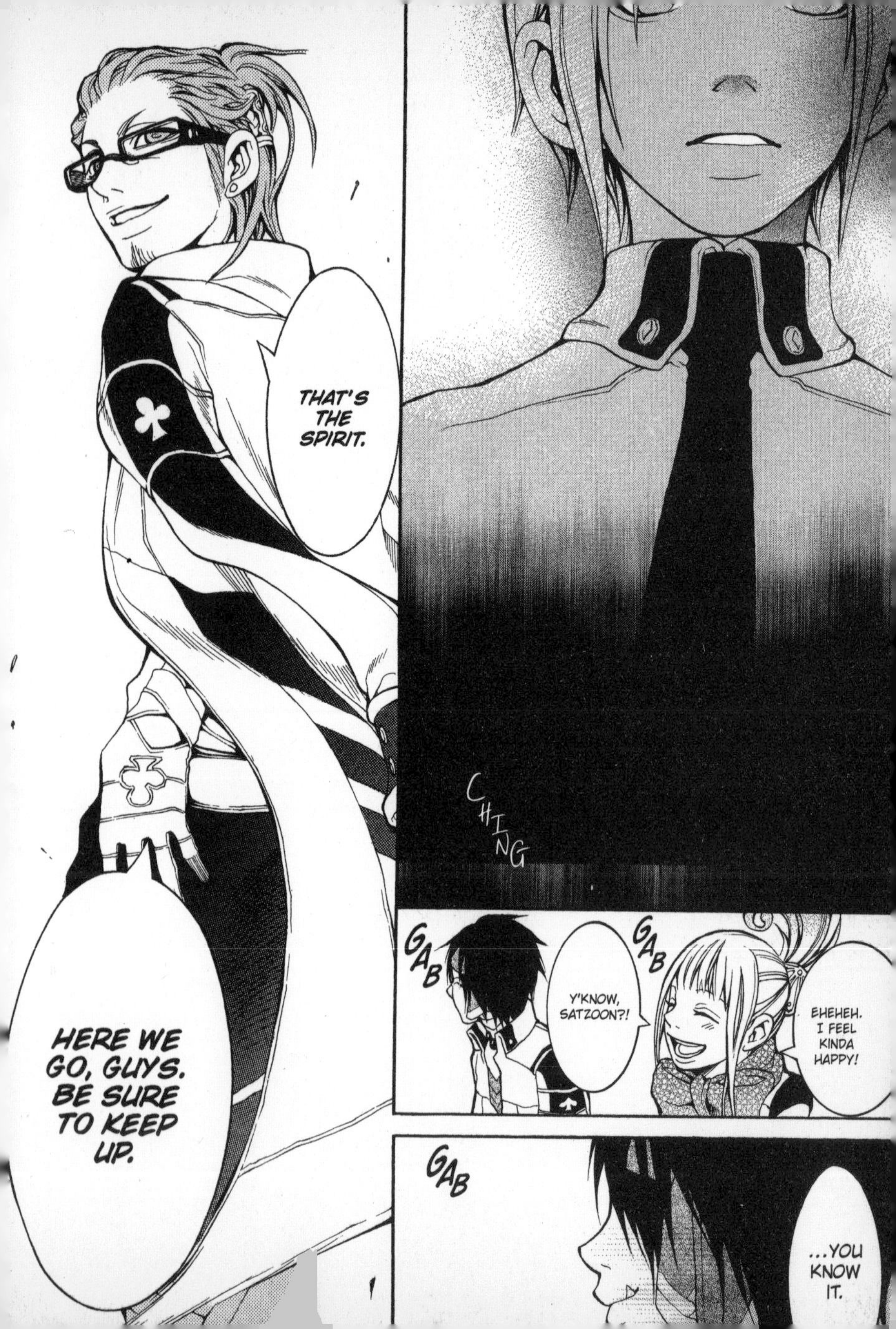
CHING
EHEHEH. I FEEL KINDA HAPPY!
GAB
Y'KNOW, SATZOON?!
GAB
...YOU KNOW IT.
GAB
THAT'S THE SPIRIT.
HERE WE GO, GUYS. BE SURE TO KEEP UP.

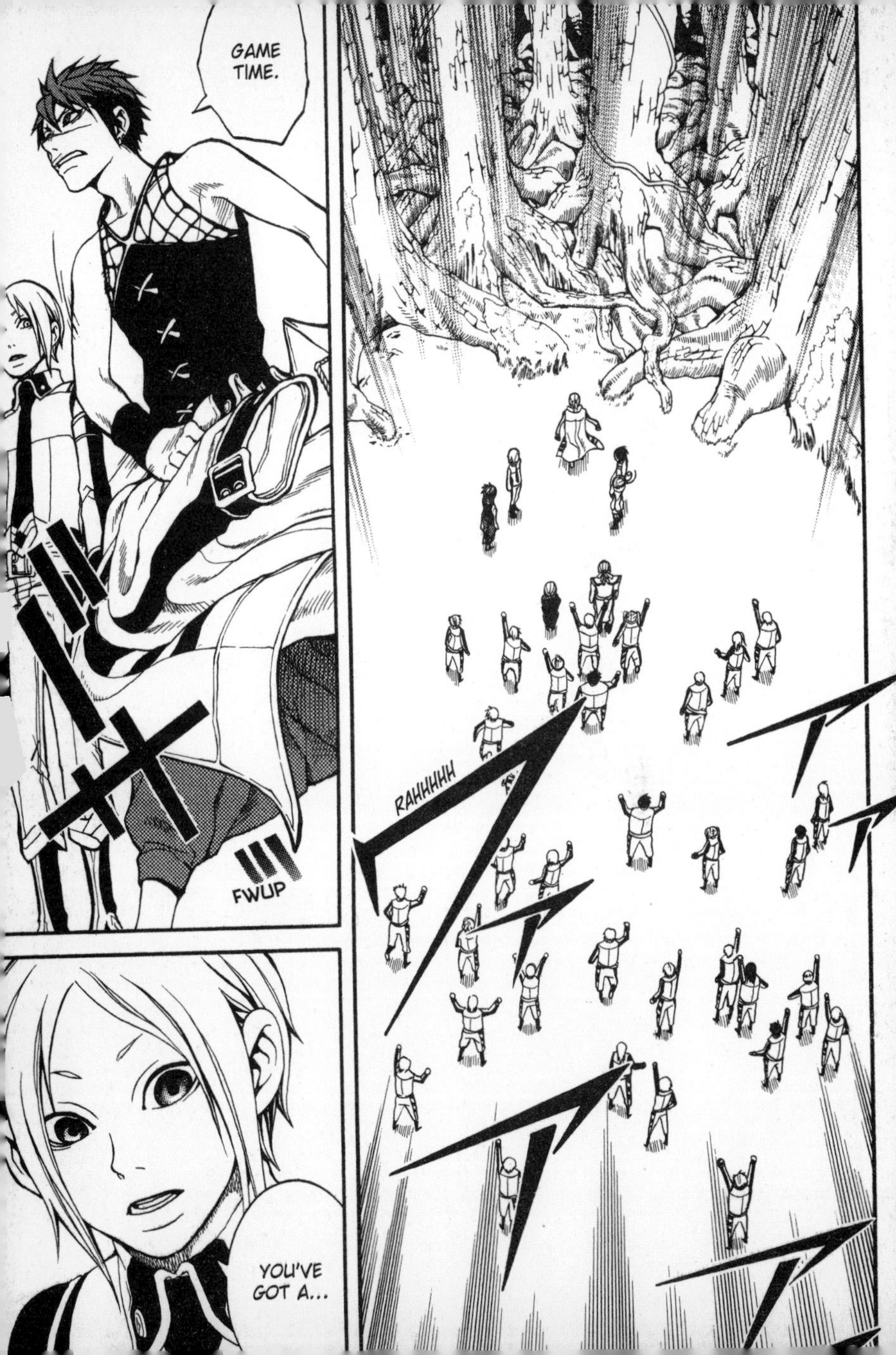
RAHHHHH
GAME TIME.
FWUP
YOU'VE GOT A...

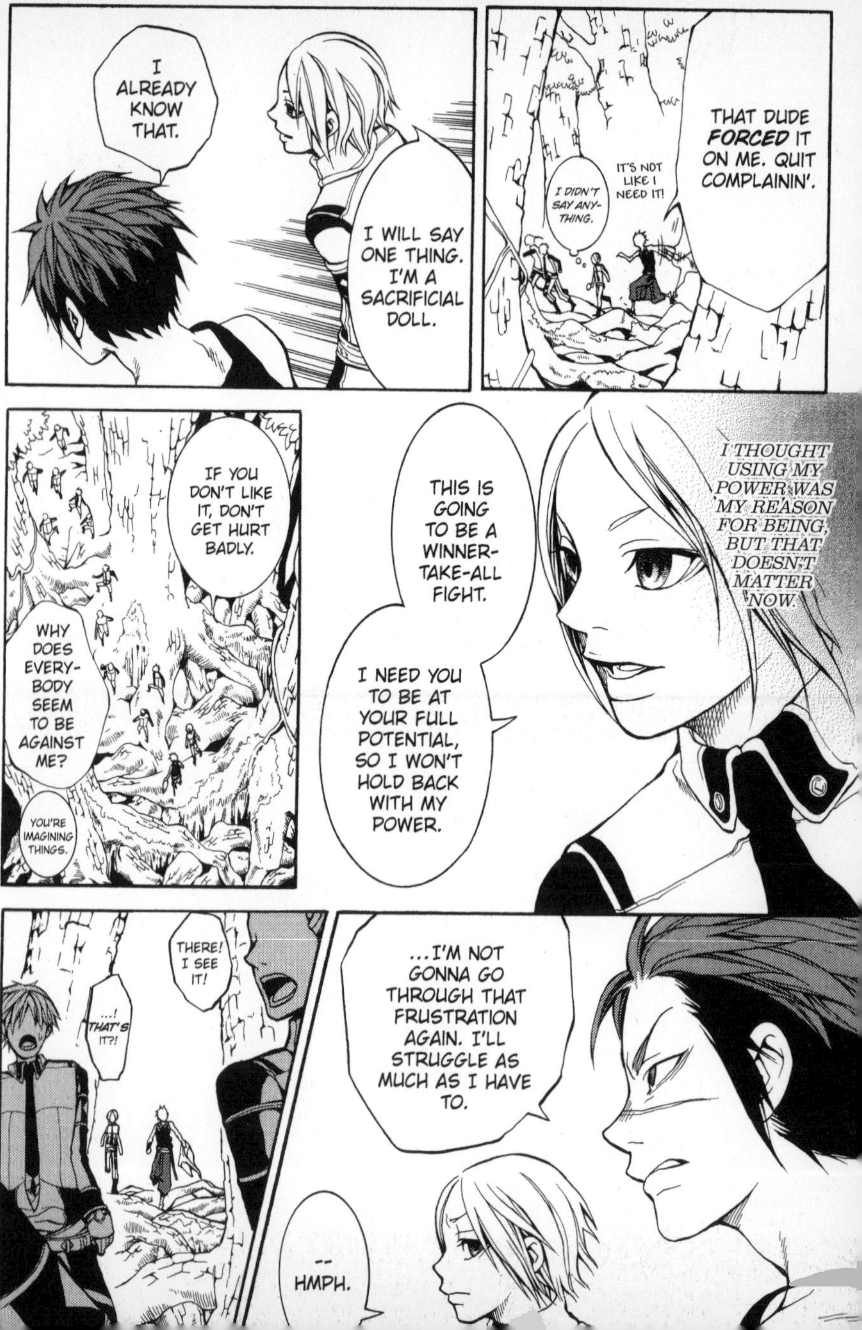
THAT DUDE FORCED IT ON ME. QUIT COMPLAININ'.
IT'S NOT LIKE I NEED IT!
I DIDN'T SAY ANYTHING.
I WILL SAY ONE THING. I'M A SACRIFICIAL DOLL.
I ALREADY KNOW THAT.
I THOUGHT USING MY POWER WAS MY REASON FOR BEING, BUT THAT DOESN'T MATTER NOW.
THIS IS GOING TO BE A WINNER-TAKE-ALL FIGHT.
I NEED YOU TO BE AT YOUR FULL POTENTIAL, SO I WON'T HOLD BACK WITH MY POWER.
IF YOU DON'T LIKE IT, DON'T GET HURT BADLY.
WHY DOES EVERYBODY SEEM TO BE AGAINST ME?
YOU'RE IMAGINING THINGS.
...I'M NOT GONNA GO THROUGH THAT FRUSTRATION AGAIN. I'LL STRUGGLE AS MUCH AS I HAVE TO.
--HMPH.
THERE! I SEE IT!
...! THAT'S IT?!

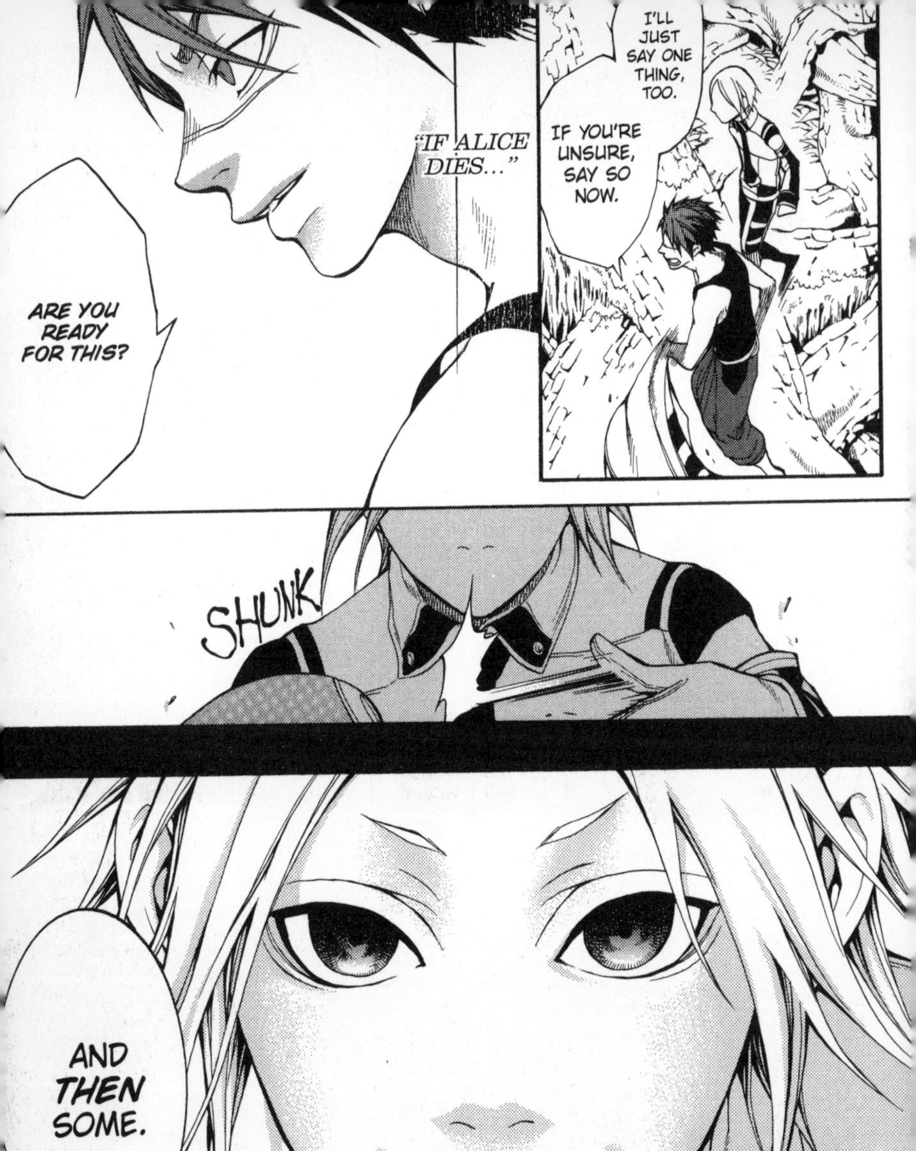
I'LL JUST SAY ONE THING, TOO.
IF YOU'RE UNSURE, SAY SO NOW.
"IF ALICE DIES..."
ARE YOU READY FOR THIS?
SHUNK
AND THEN SOME.

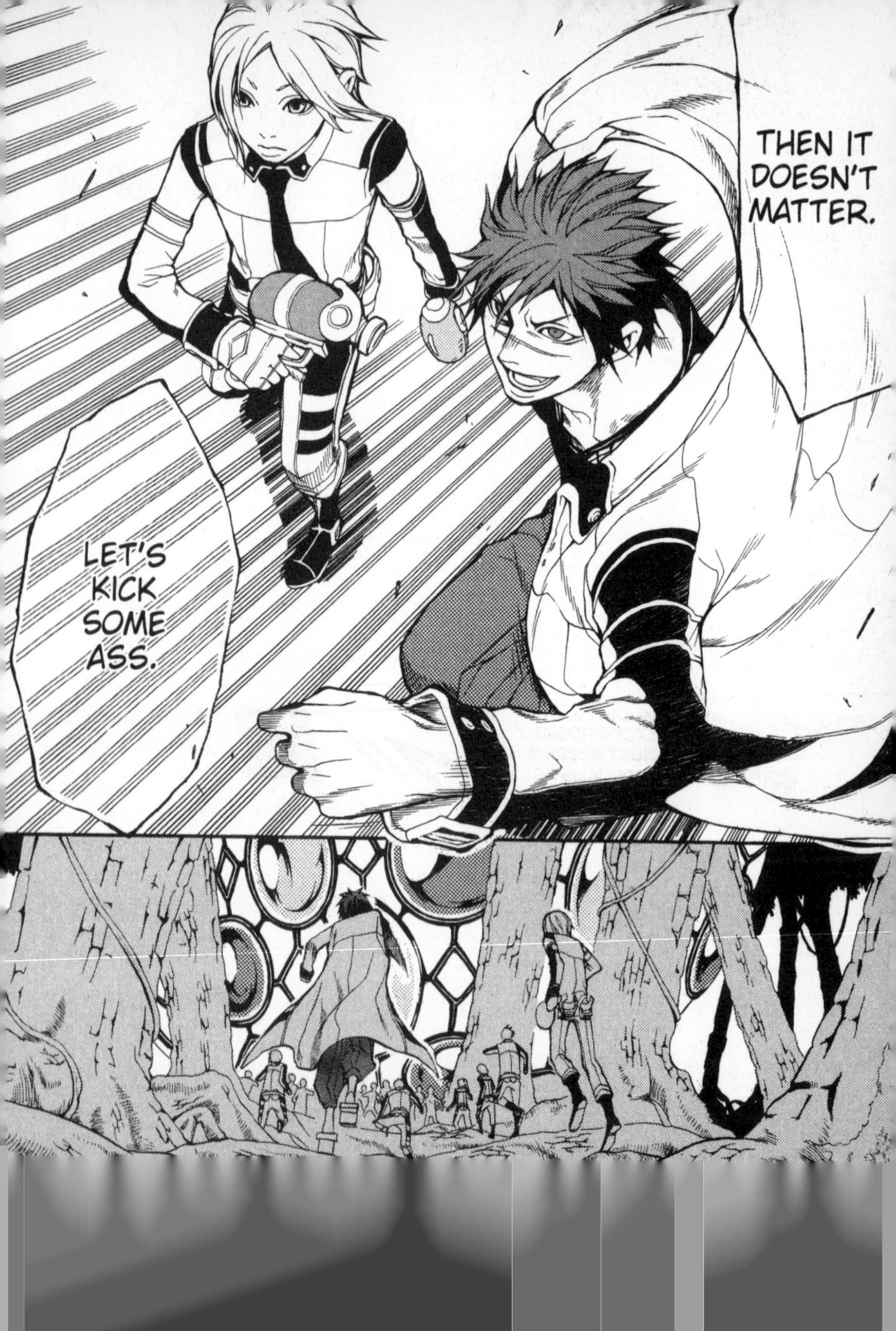
THEN IT DOESN'T MATTER.
LET'S KICK SOME ASS.

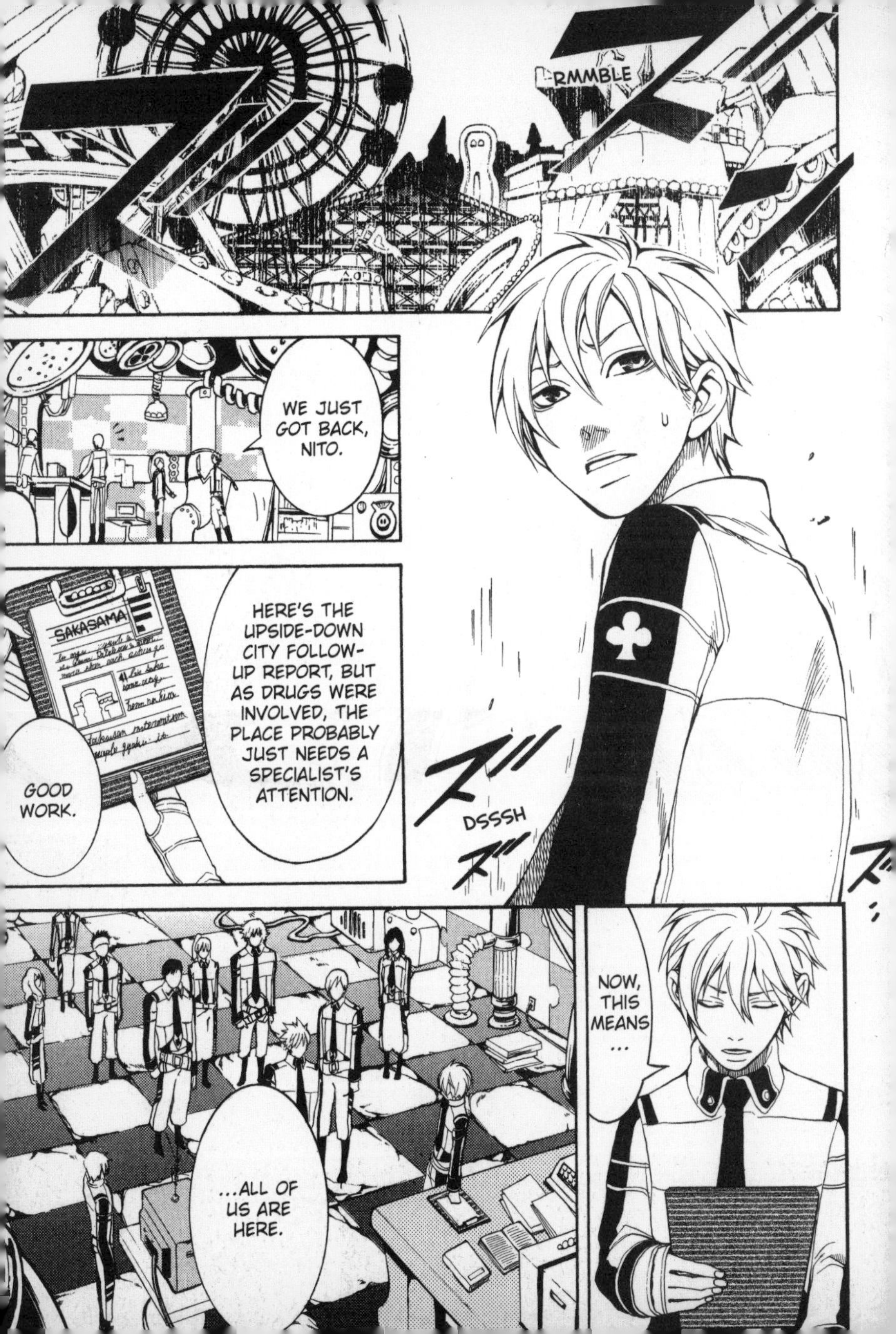
RMMBLE
DSSSH
WE JUST GOT BACK, NITO.
HERE'S THE UPSIDE-DOWN CITY FOLLOW-UP REPORT, BUT AS DRUGS WERE INVOLVED, THE PLACE PROBABLY JUST NEEDS A SPECIALIST'S ATTENTION.
SAKASAMA
GOOD WORK.
NOW, THIS MEANS ...
...ALL OF US ARE HERE.

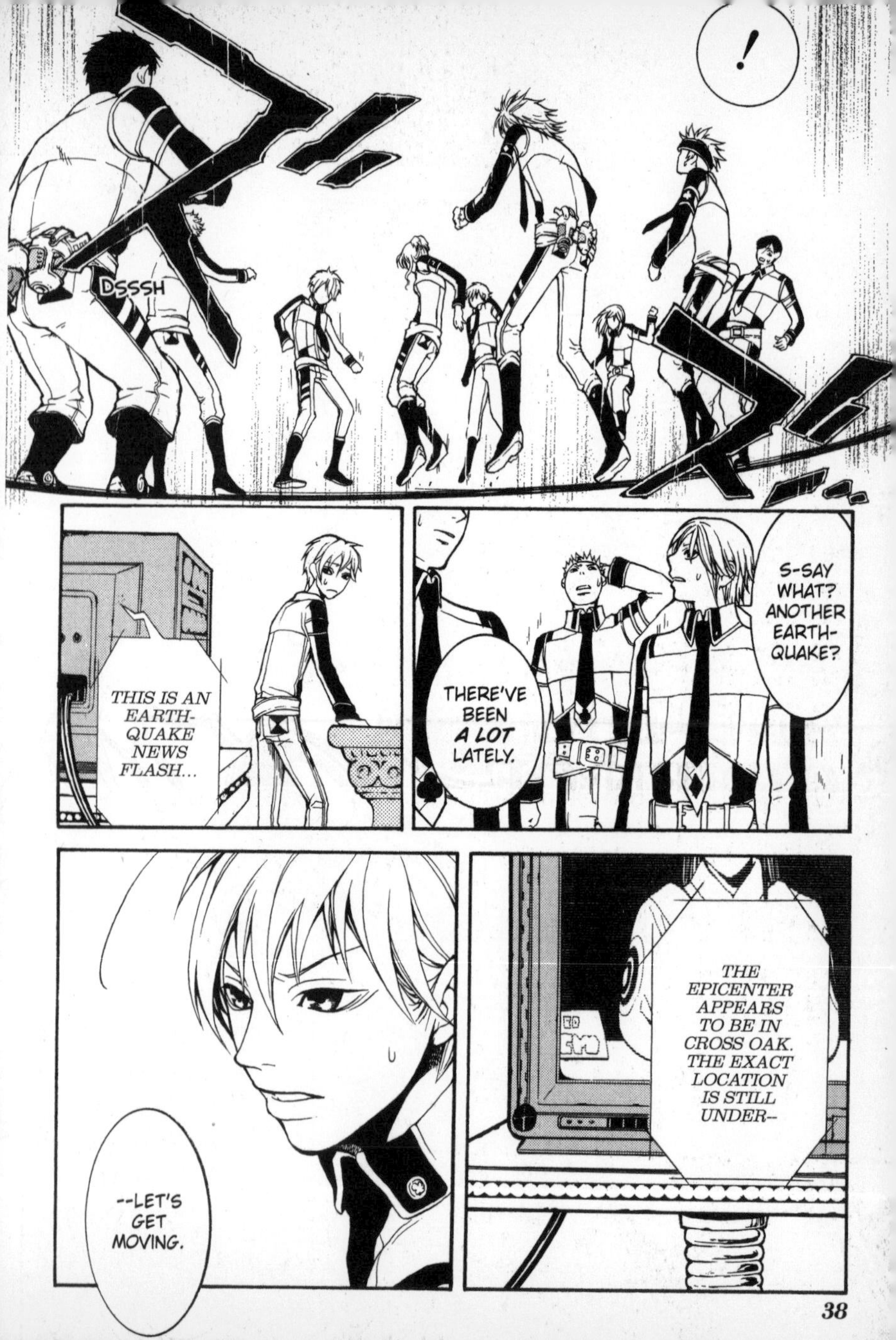
!
DSSSH
S-SAY WHAT? ANOTHER EARTH-QUAKE?
THERE'VE BEEN A LOT LATELY.
THIS IS AN EARTH-QUAKE NEWS FLASH...
THE EPICENTER APPEARS TO BE IN CROSS OAK. THE EXACT LOCATION IS STILL UNDER--
--LET'S GET MOVING.

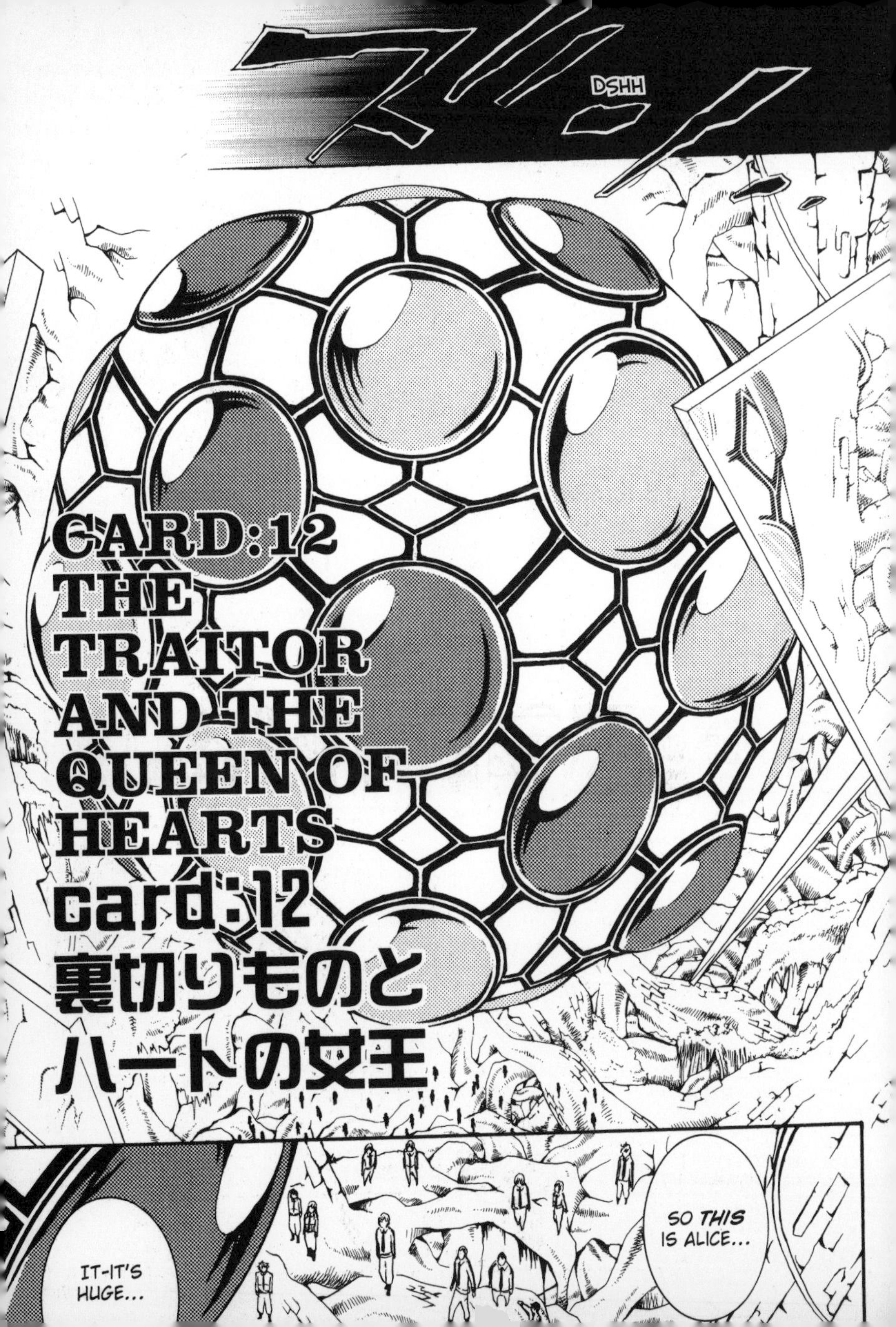
DSHH
CARD:12
THE TRAITOR AND THE QUEEN OF HEARTS
card:12
裏切りものとハートの女王
SO THIS IS ALICE...
IT-IT'S HUGE...

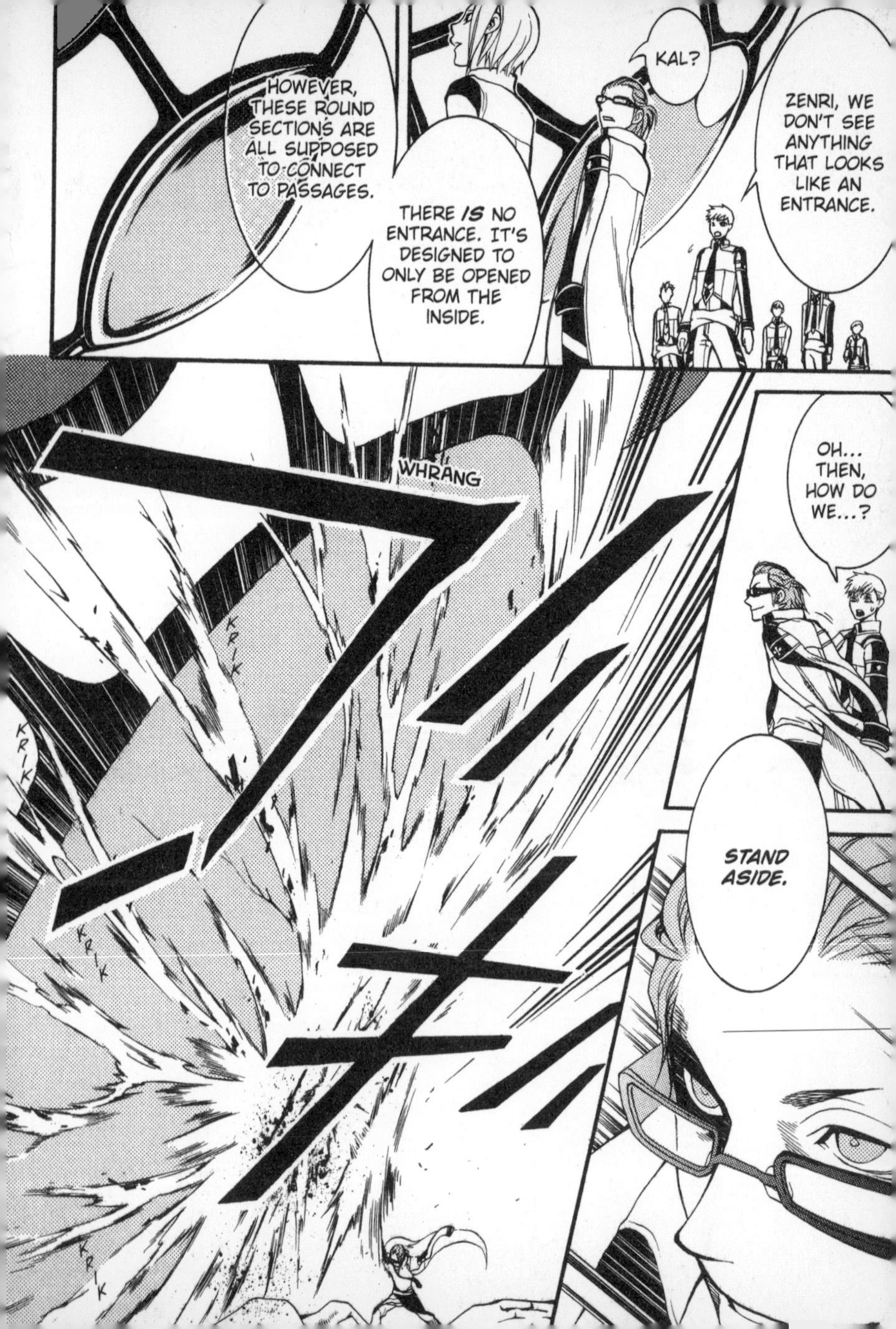
KAL?
ZENRI, WE DON'T SEE ANYTHING THAT LOOKS LIKE AN ENTRANCE.
THERE IS NO ENTRANCE. IT'S DESIGNED TO ONLY BE OPENED FROM THE INSIDE.
HOWEVER, THESE ROUND SECTIONS ARE ALL SUPPOSED TO CONNECT TO PASSAGES.
OH... THEN, HOW DO WE...?
STAND ASIDE.
WHRANG
KRIK
KRIK
KRIK
KRIK

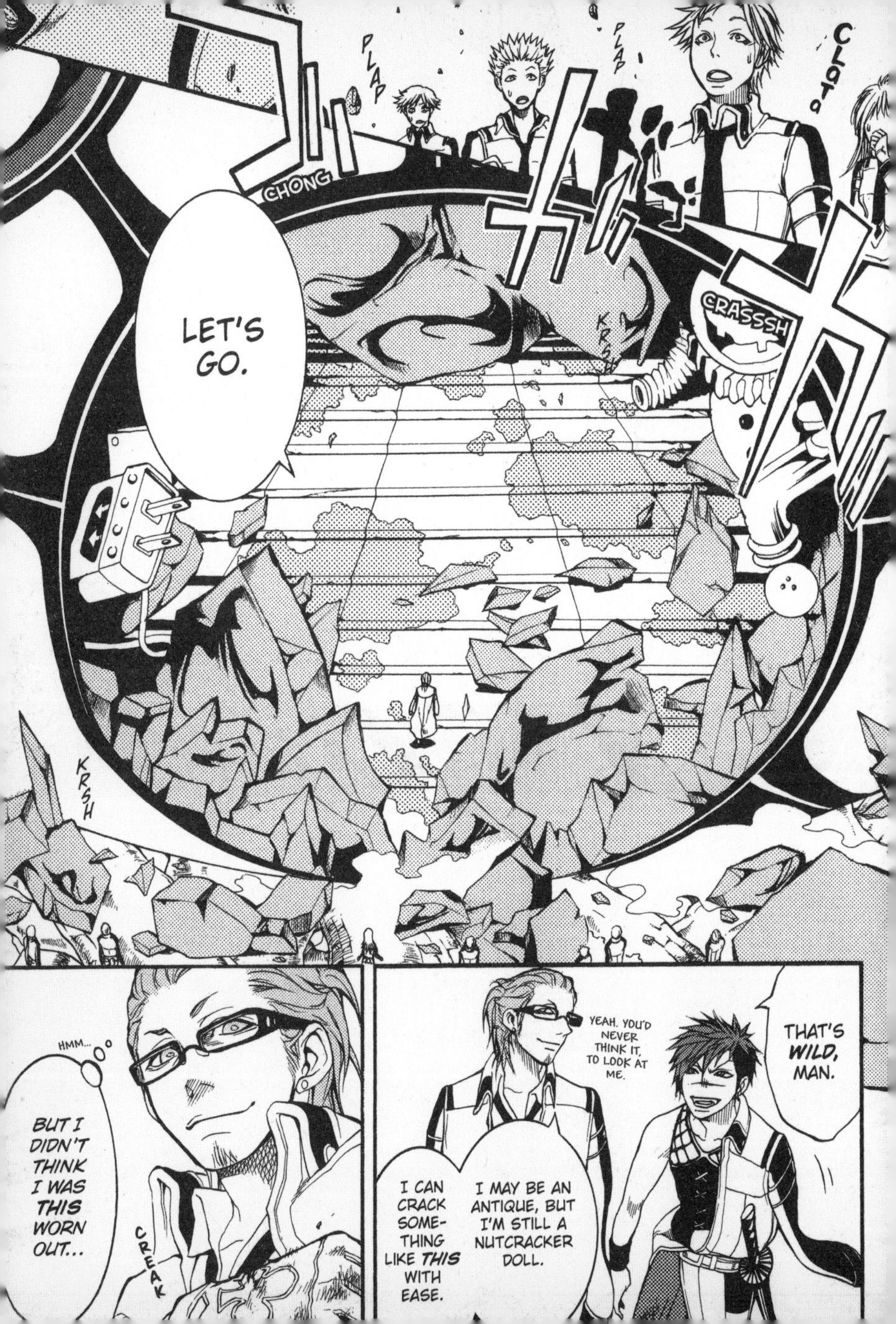
CLOTa
PLAP
PLAP
CRASSSH
KRSH
CHONG
LET'S GO.
KRSH
THAT'S WILD, MAN.
YEAH. YOU'D NEVER THINK IT, TO LOOK AT ME.
I MAY BE AN ANTIQUE, BUT I'M STILL A NUTCRACKER DOLL.
I CAN CRACK SOME-THING LIKE THIS WITH EASE.
HMM...
BUT I DIDN'T THINK I WAS THIS WORN OUT...
CREAK

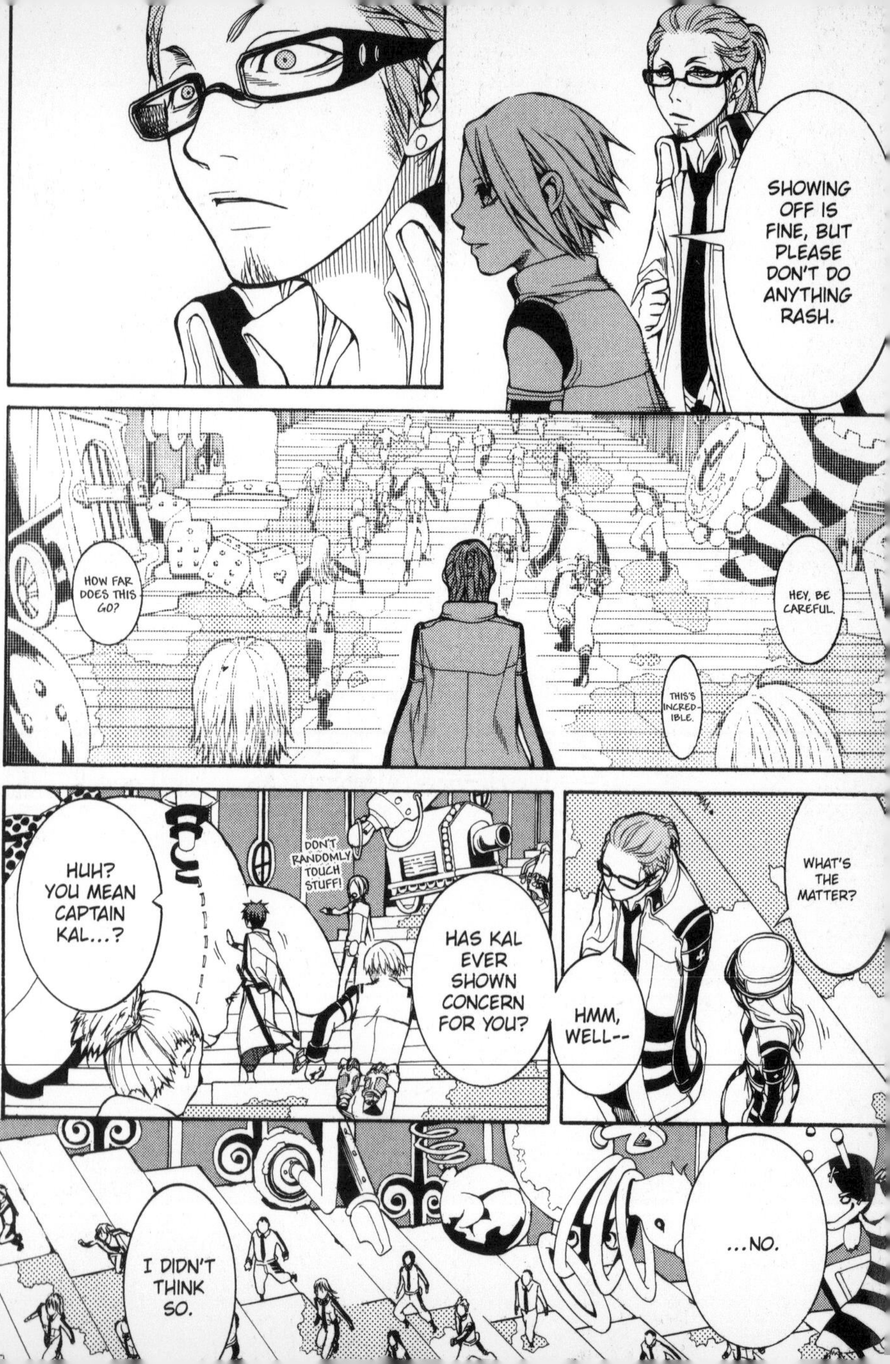

SHOWING OFF IS FINE, BUT PLEASE DON'T DO ANYTHING RASH.
HEY, BE CAREFUL.
HOW FAR DOES THIS GO?
THIS'S INCREDIBLE.
WHAT'S THE MATTER?
HMM, WELL--
HAS KAL EVER SHOWN CONCERN FOR YOU?
DON'T RANDOMLY TOUCH STUFF!
HUH? YOU MEAN CAPTAIN KAL...?
...NO.
I DIDN'T THINK SO.

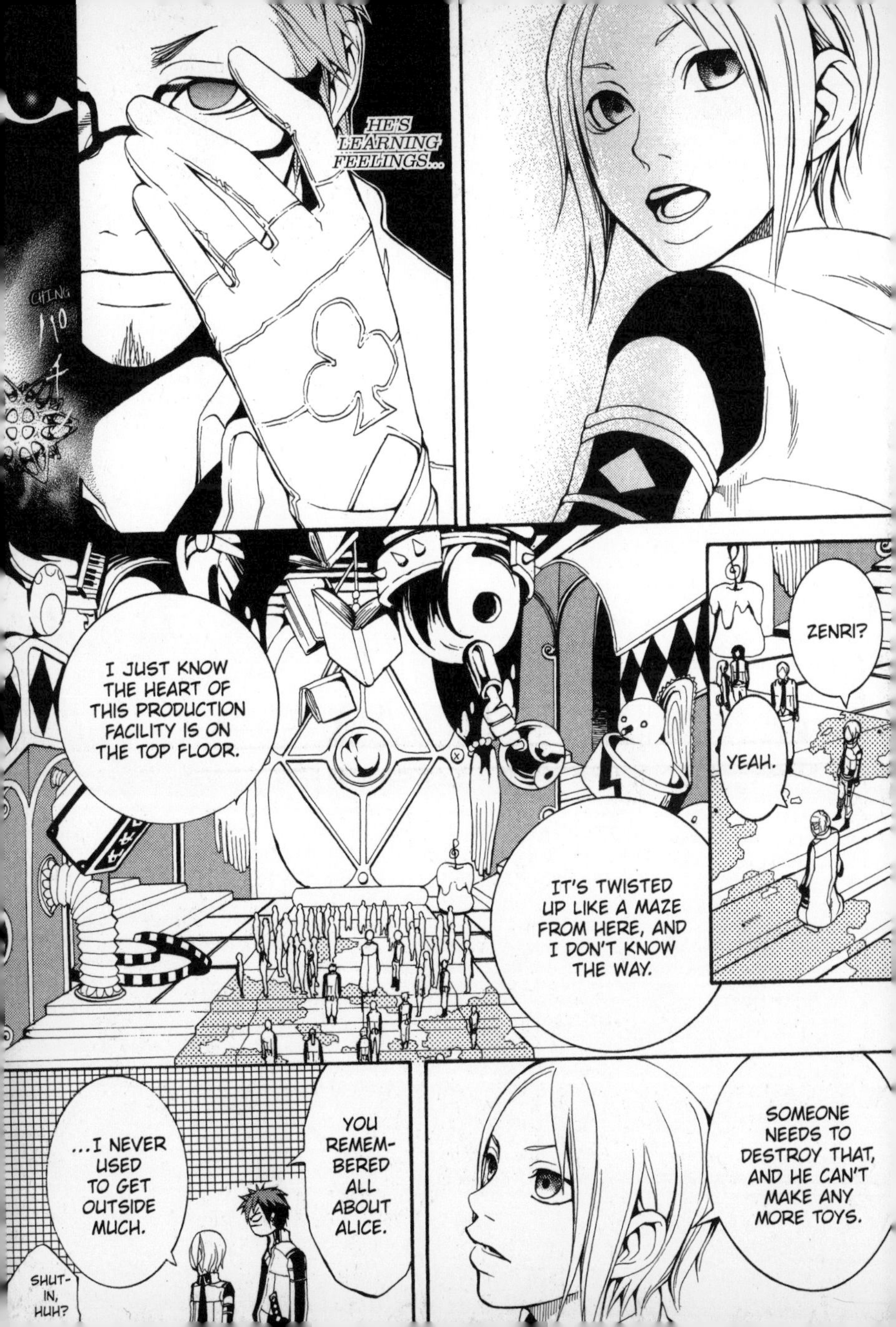
HE'S LEARNING FEELINGS...
CHING
ZENRI?
YEAH.
I JUST KNOW THE HEART OF THIS PRODUCTION FACILITY IS ON THE TOP FLOOR.
IT'S TWISTED UP LIKE A MAZE FROM HERE, AND I DON'T KNOW THE WAY.
SOMEONE NEEDS TO DESTROY THAT, AND HE CAN'T MAKE ANY MORE TOYS.
YOU REMEMBERED ALL ABOUT ALICE.
...I NEVER USED TO GET OUTSIDE MUCH.
SHUT-IN, HUH?

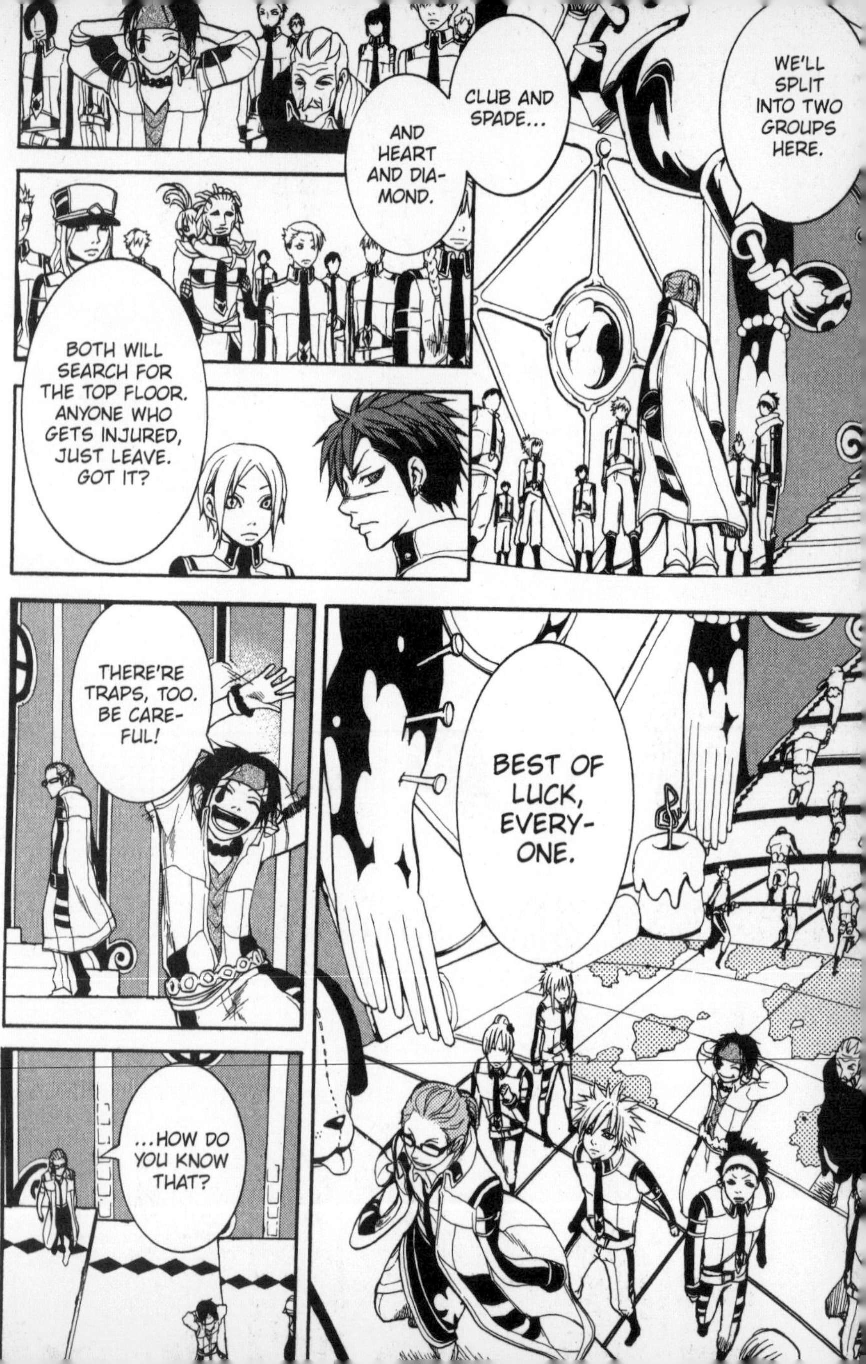
WE'LL SPLIT INTO TWO GROUPS HERE.
CLUB AND SPADE...
AND HEART AND DIA-MOND.
BOTH WILL SEARCH FOR THE TOP FLOOR. ANYONE WHO GETS INJURED, JUST LEAVE. GOT IT?
BEST OF LUCK, EVERY-ONE.
THERE'RE TRAPS, TOO. BE CARE-FUL!
...HOW DO YOU KNOW THAT?

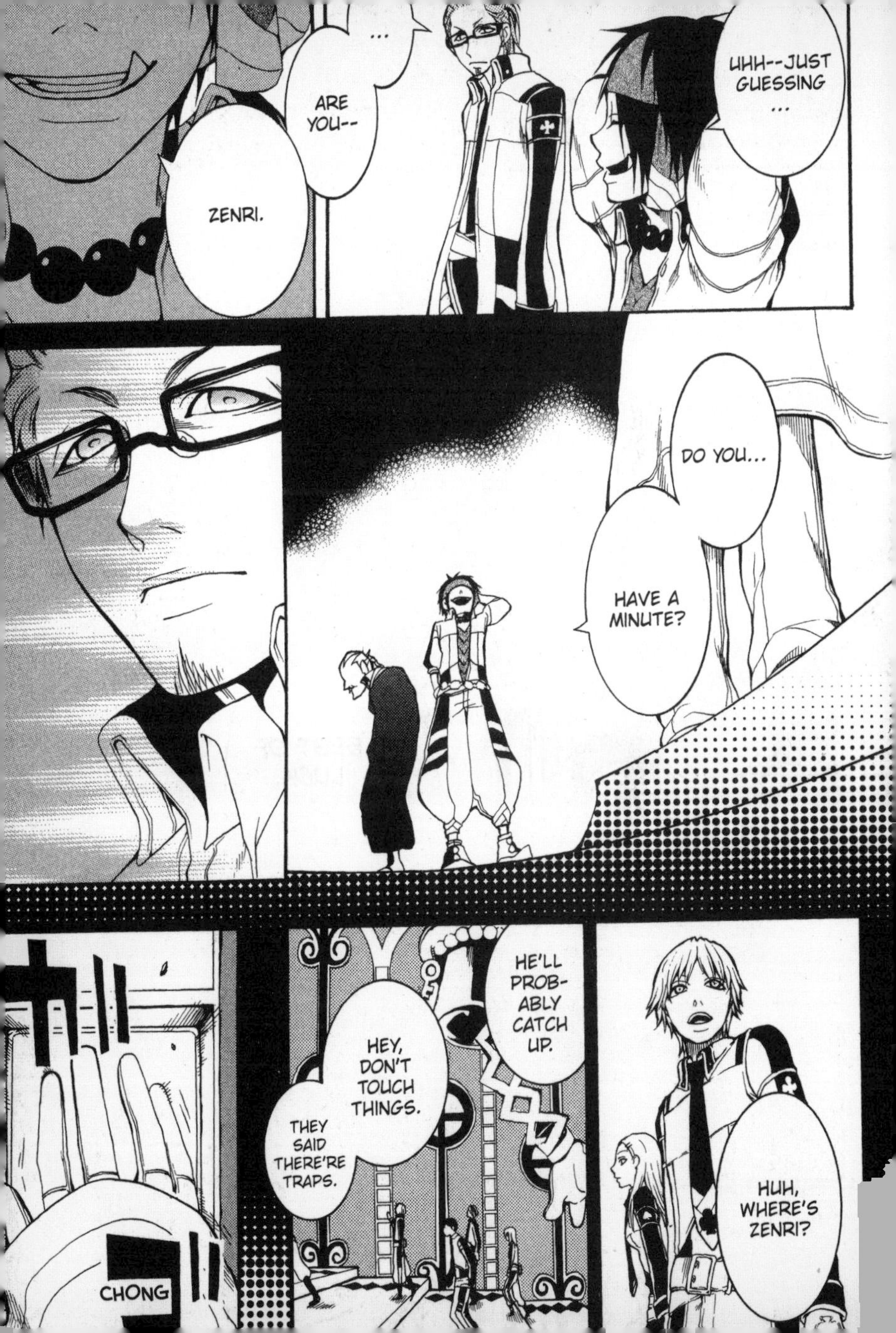

UHH--JUST GUESSING ...
...
ARE YOU--
ZENRI.
DO YOU...
HAVE A MINUTE?
HUH, WHERE'S ZENRI?
HE'LL PROB-ABLY CATCH UP.
HEY, DON'T TOUCH THINGS.
THEY SAID THERE'RE TRAPS.
CHONG

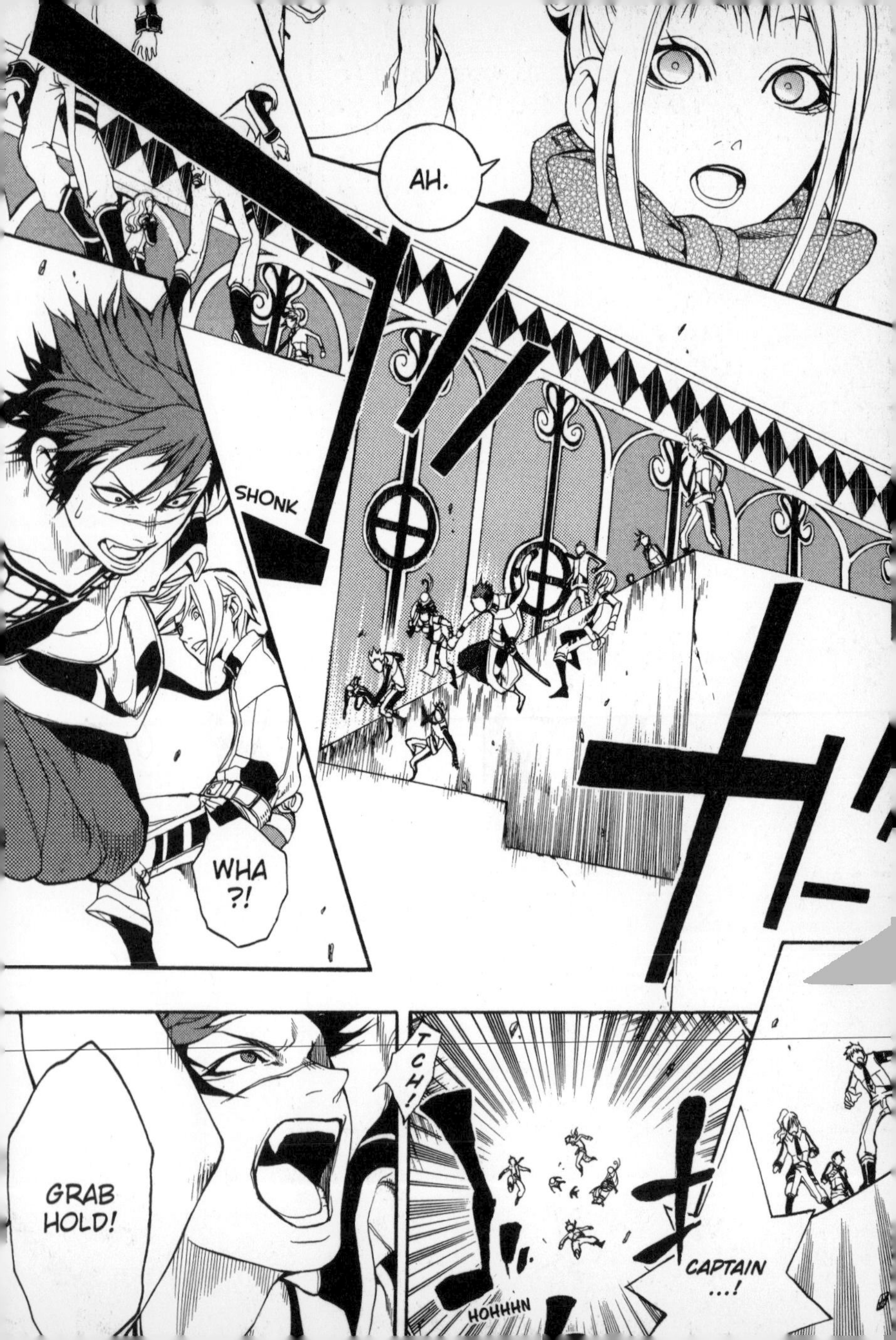
AH.
SHONK
WHA?!
CAPTAIN ...!
TCH!
HOHHHN
GRAB HOLD!

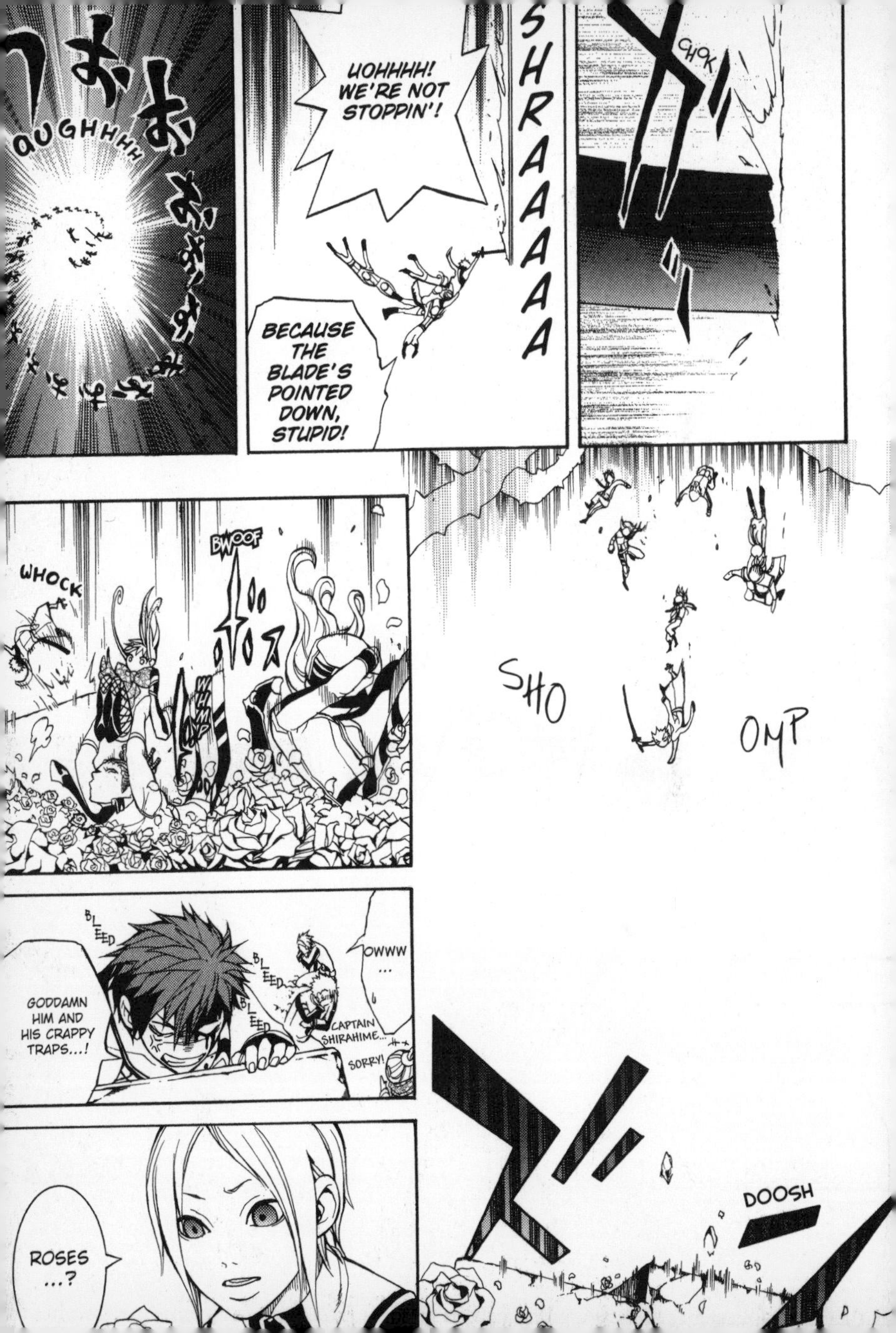

CHOK
UOHHHH! WE'RE NOT STOPPIN'!
SHRAAAAAA
BECAUSE THE BLADE'S POINTED DOWN, STUPID!
AUGHHHH
SHO
OMP
BWOOF
WHOCK
WHUMP
OWWW ...
CAPTAIN SHIRAHIME...
SORRY!
BLEED
BLEED
BLEED
GODDAMN HIM AND HIS CRAPPY TRAPS...!
DOOSH
ROSES ...?

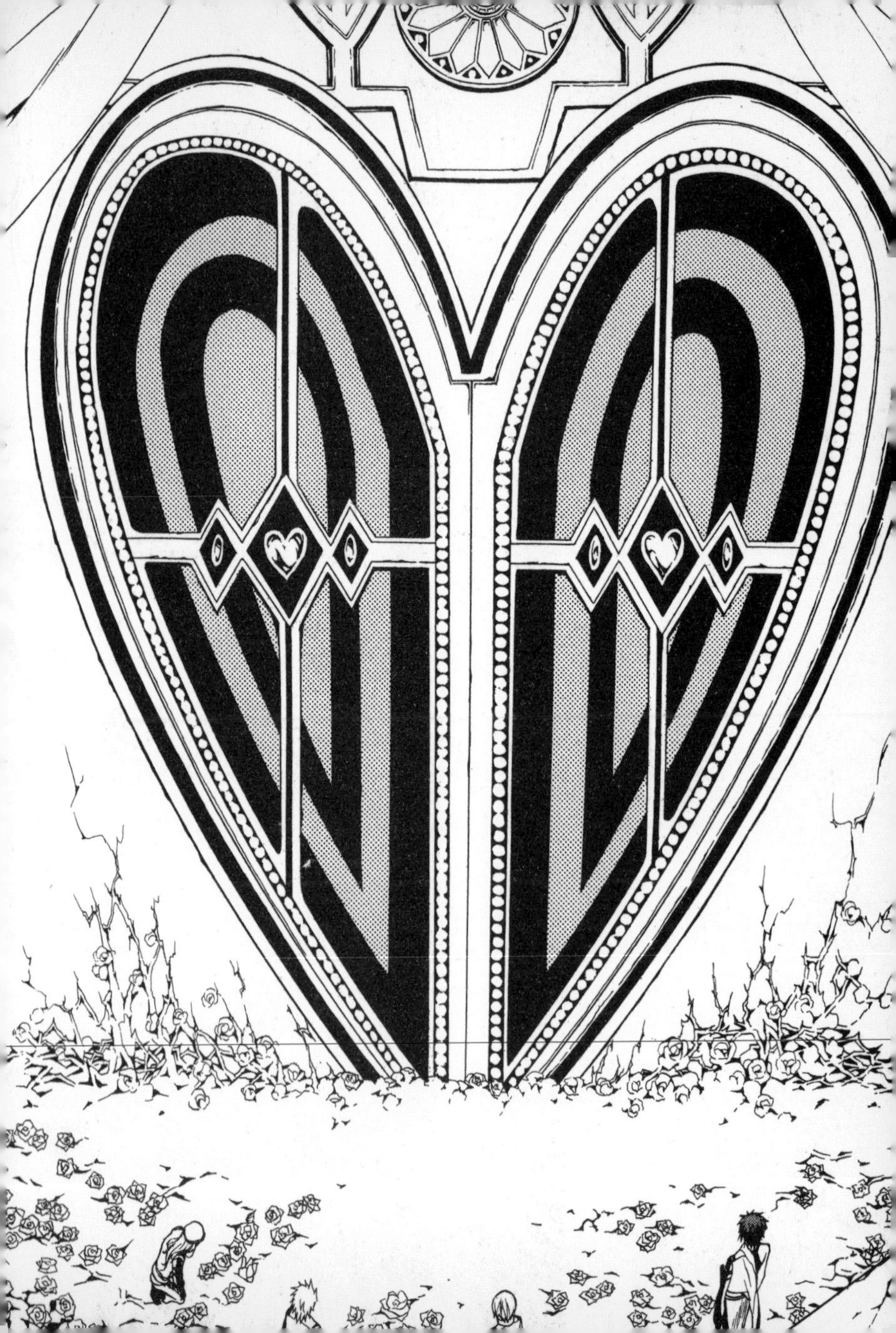

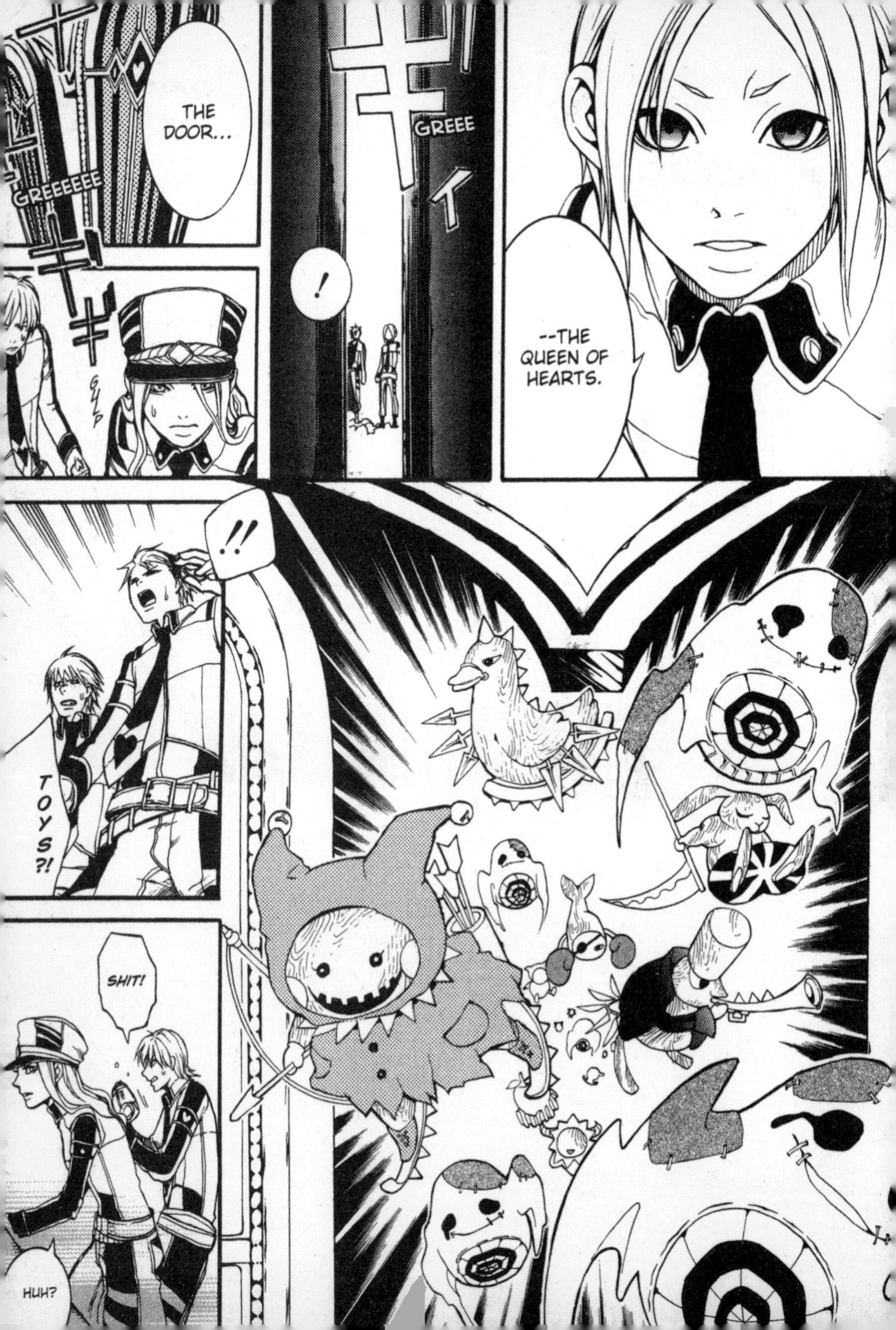
--THE QUEEN OF HEARTS.
GREEE
!
THE DOOR...
GREEEEEEE
GULP
!!
TOYS?!
SHIT!
HUH?

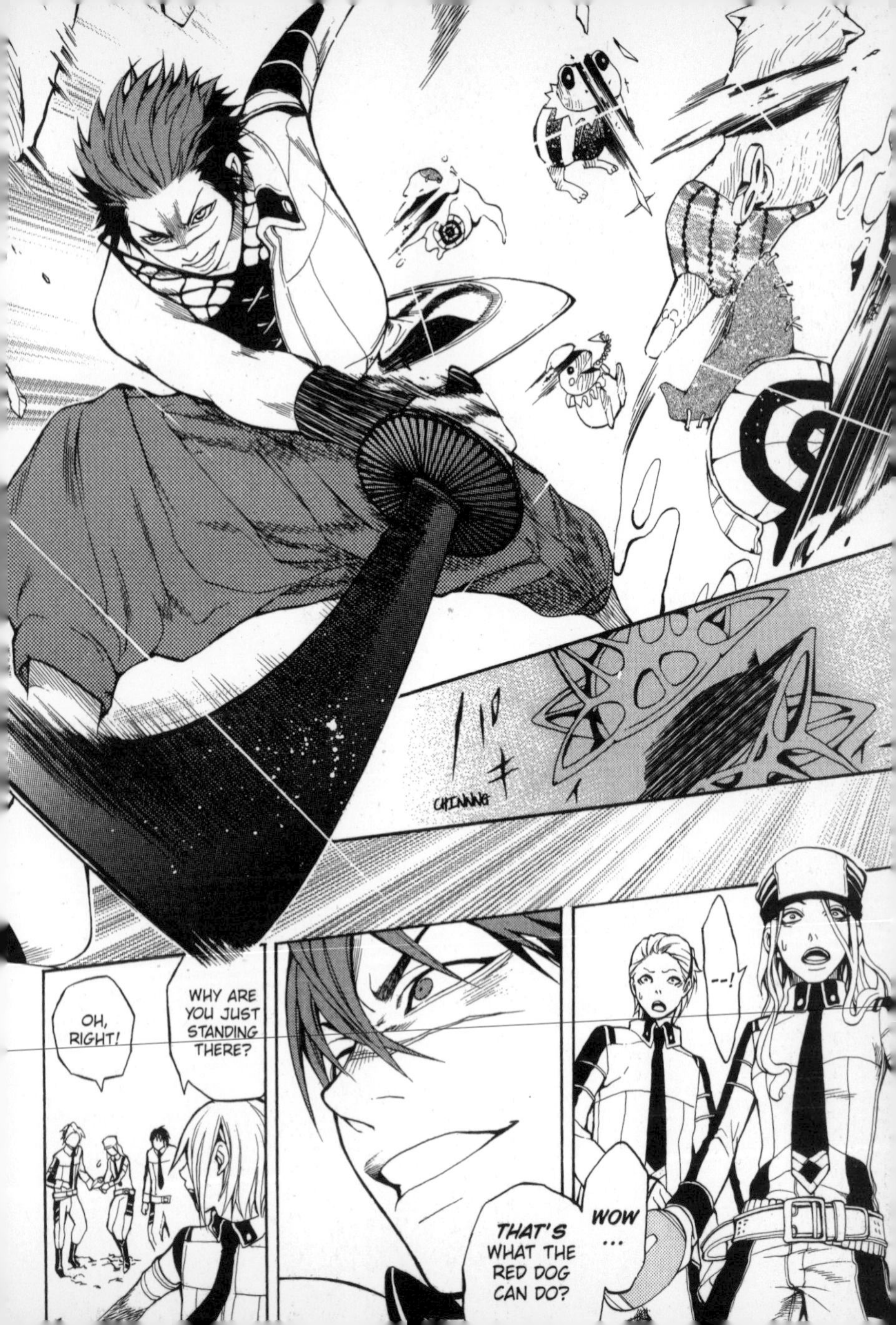
バキ
CHINNNG
--!
WOW ...
THAT'S WHAT THE RED DOG CAN DO?
WHY ARE YOU JUST STANDING THERE?
OH, RIGHT!

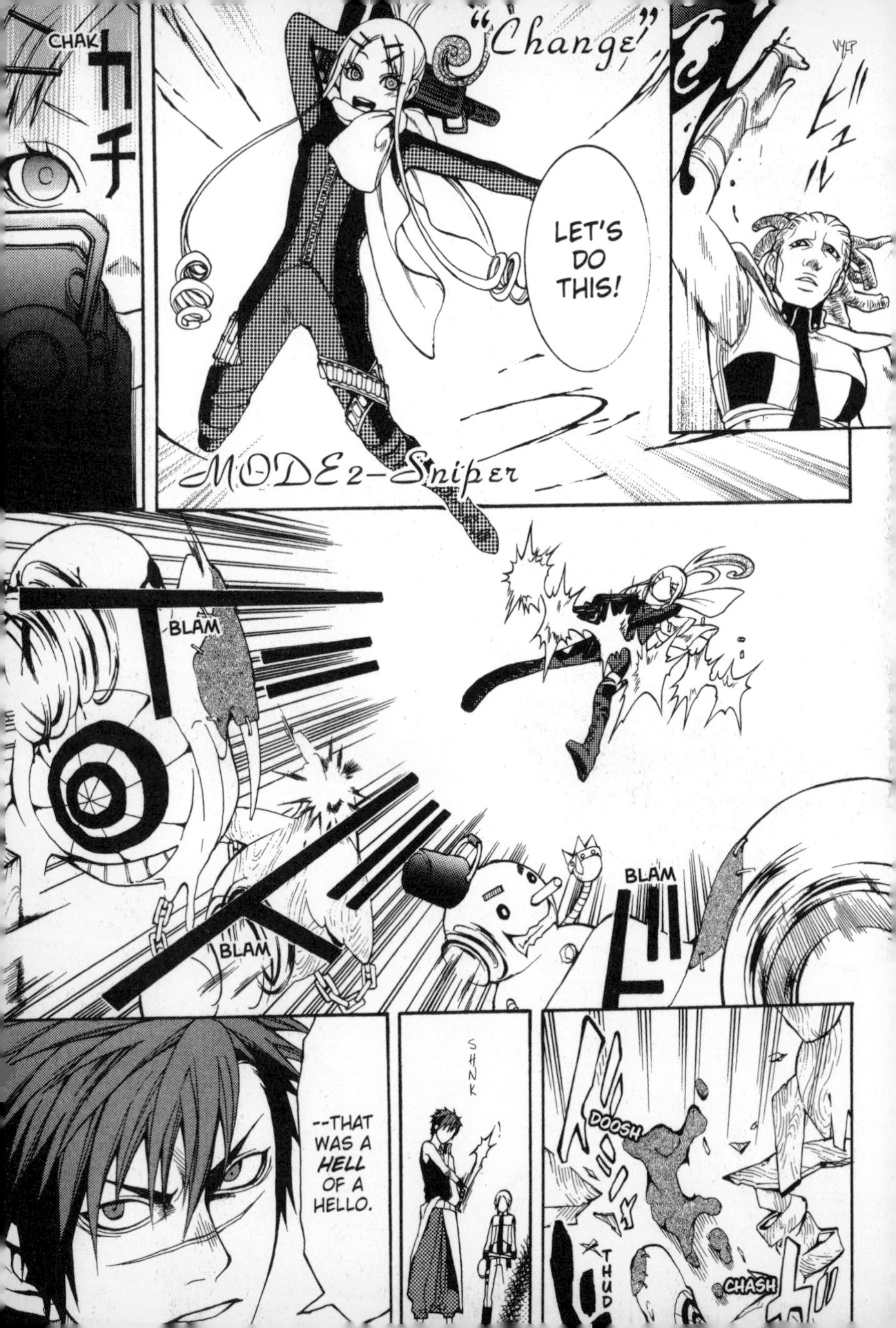
VYLP
"Change"
LET'S DO THIS!
MODE 2-Sniper
CHAK
BLAM
BLAM
BLAM
DOOSH
THUD
CHASH
SHNK
--THAT WAS A *HELL* OF A HELLO.

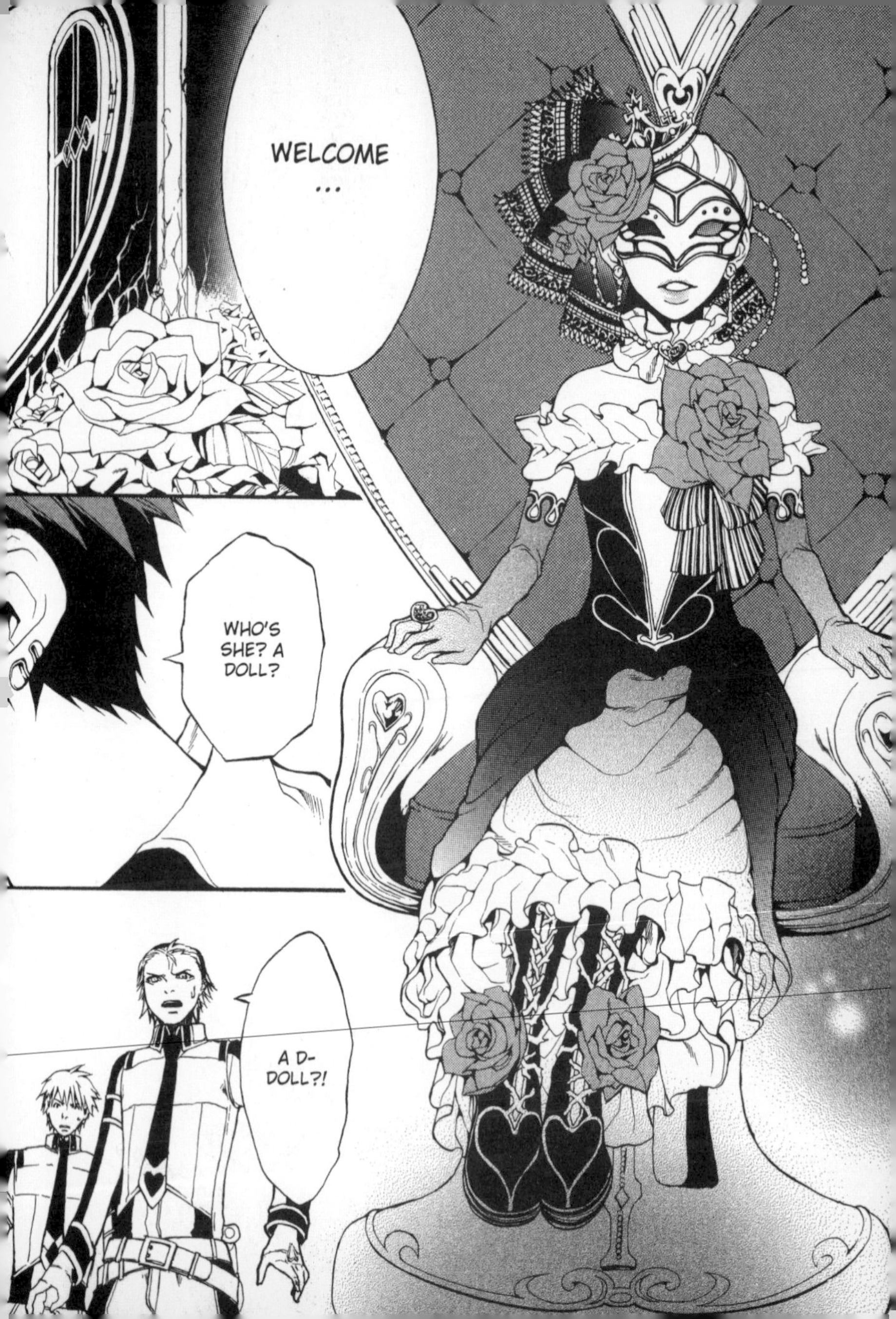
WELCOME ...
WHO'S SHE? A DOLL?
A D-DOLL?!

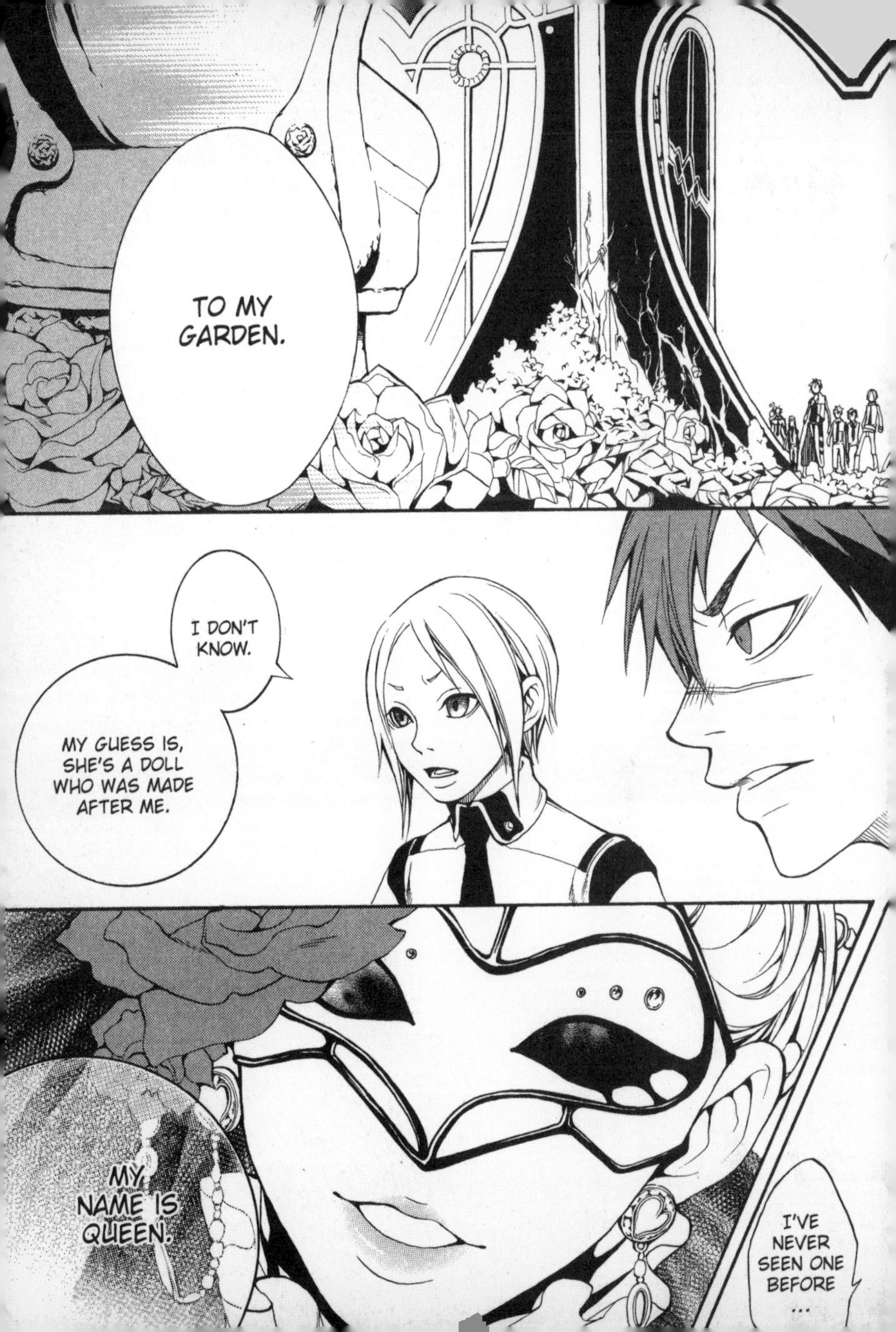
TO MY GARDEN.
I DON'T KNOW.
MY GUESS IS, SHE'S A DOLL WHO WAS MADE AFTER ME.
I'VE NEVER SEEN ONE BEFORE ...
MY NAME IS QUEEN.

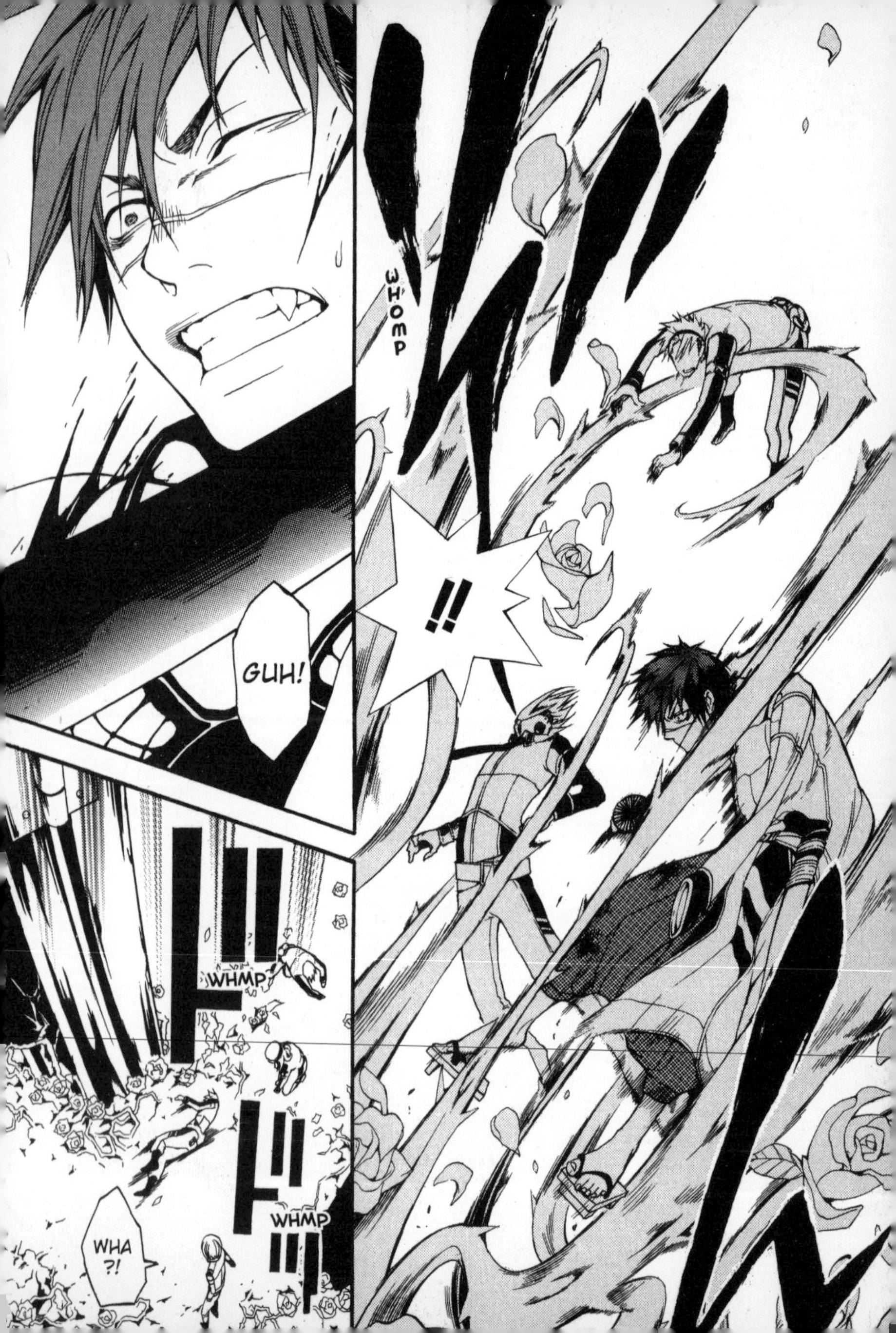
WHOMP
!!
GUH!
WHMP
WHMP
WHA?!

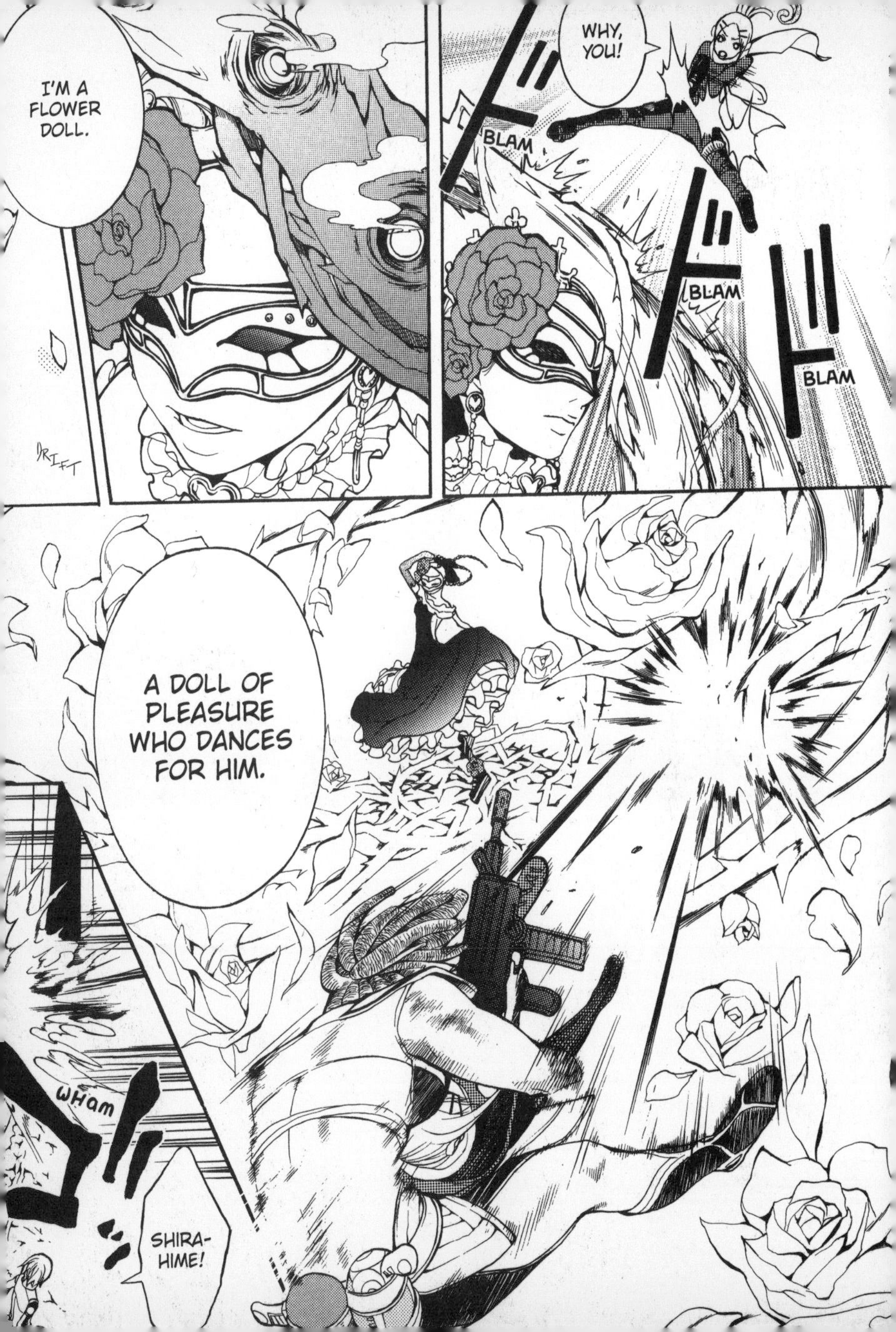
WHY, YOU!
BLAM
BLAM
BLAM
I'M A FLOWER DOLL.
DRIFT
A DOLL OF PLEASURE WHO DANCES FOR HIM.
WHAM
SHIRA-HIME!

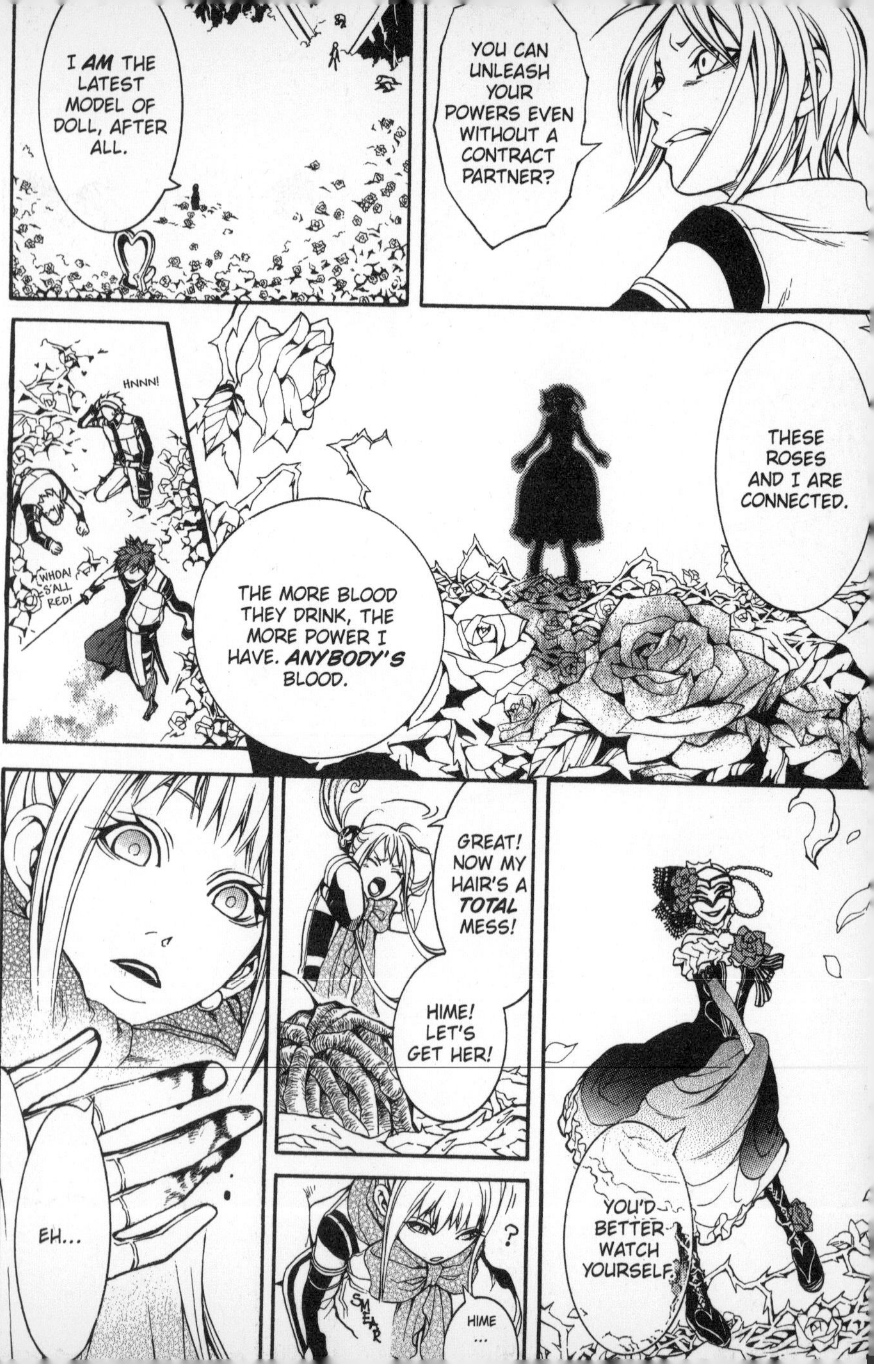

YOU CAN UNLEASH YOUR POWERS EVEN WITHOUT A CONTRACT PARTNER?
I **AM** THE LATEST MODEL OF DOLL, AFTER ALL.
THESE ROSES AND I ARE CONNECTED.
THE MORE BLOOD THEY DRINK, THE MORE POWER I HAVE. ***ANYBODY'S*** BLOOD.
HNNN!
WHOA! S'ALL RED!
YOU'D BETTER WATCH YOURSELF.
GREAT! NOW MY HAIR'S A ***TOTAL*** MESS!
HIME! LET'S GET HER!
?
SMEAR
HIME ...
EH...

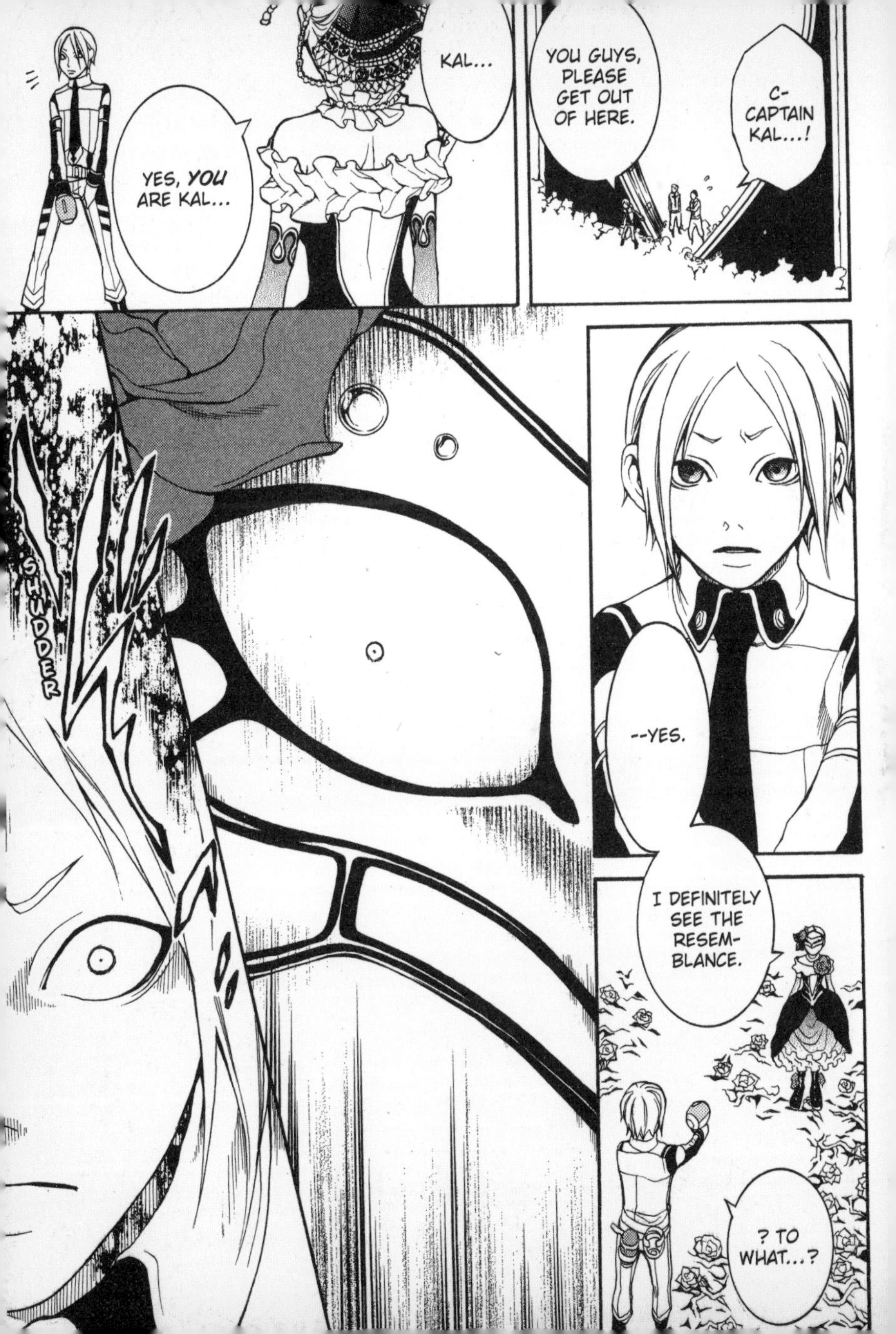
C-CAPTAIN KAL...!
YOU GUYS, PLEASE GET OUT OF HERE.
KAL...
YES, *YOU* ARE KAL...
--YES.
I DEFINITELY SEE THE RESEM-BLANCE.
? TO WHAT...?
SHUDDER

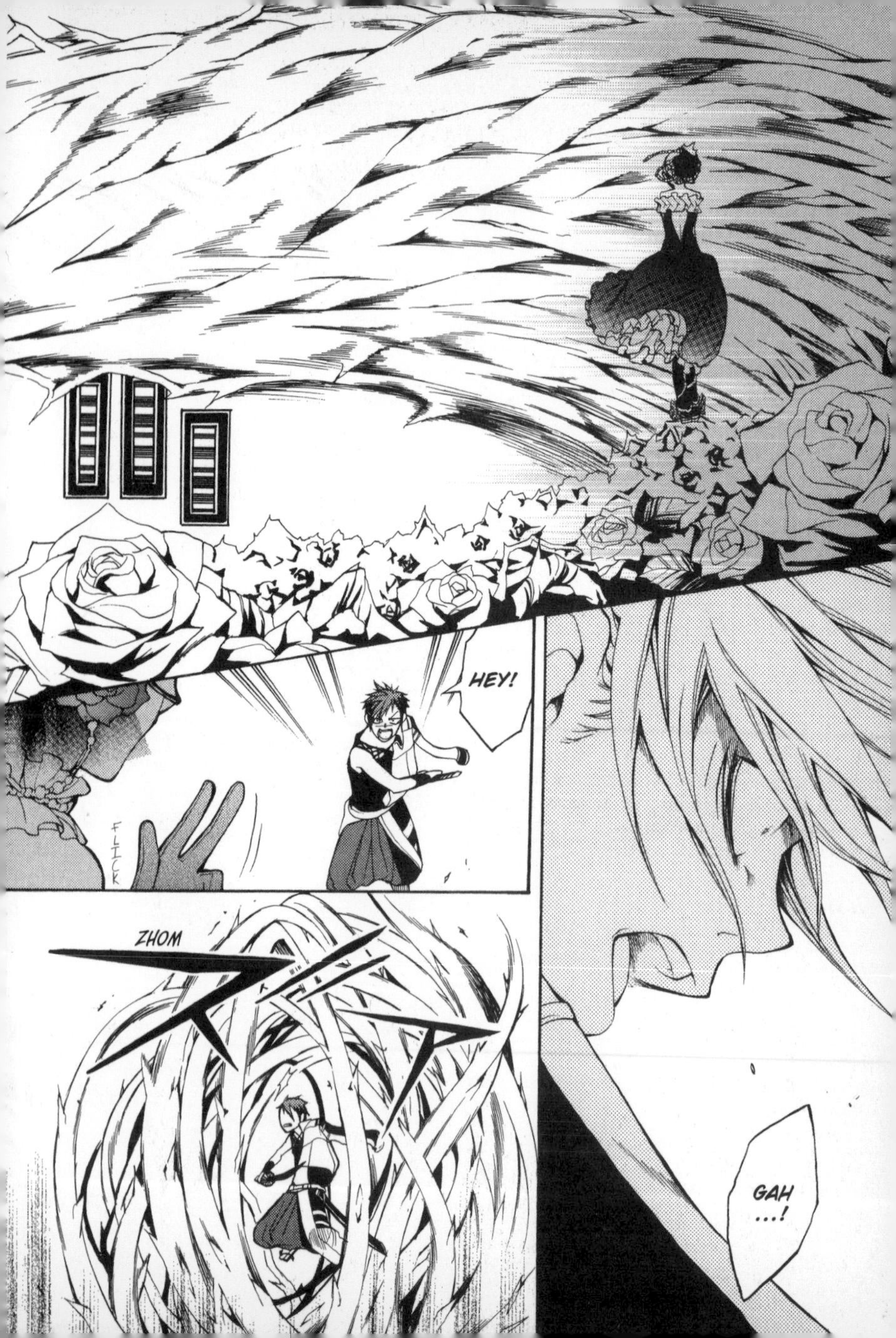
GAH ...!
HEY!
FLICK
ZHOM

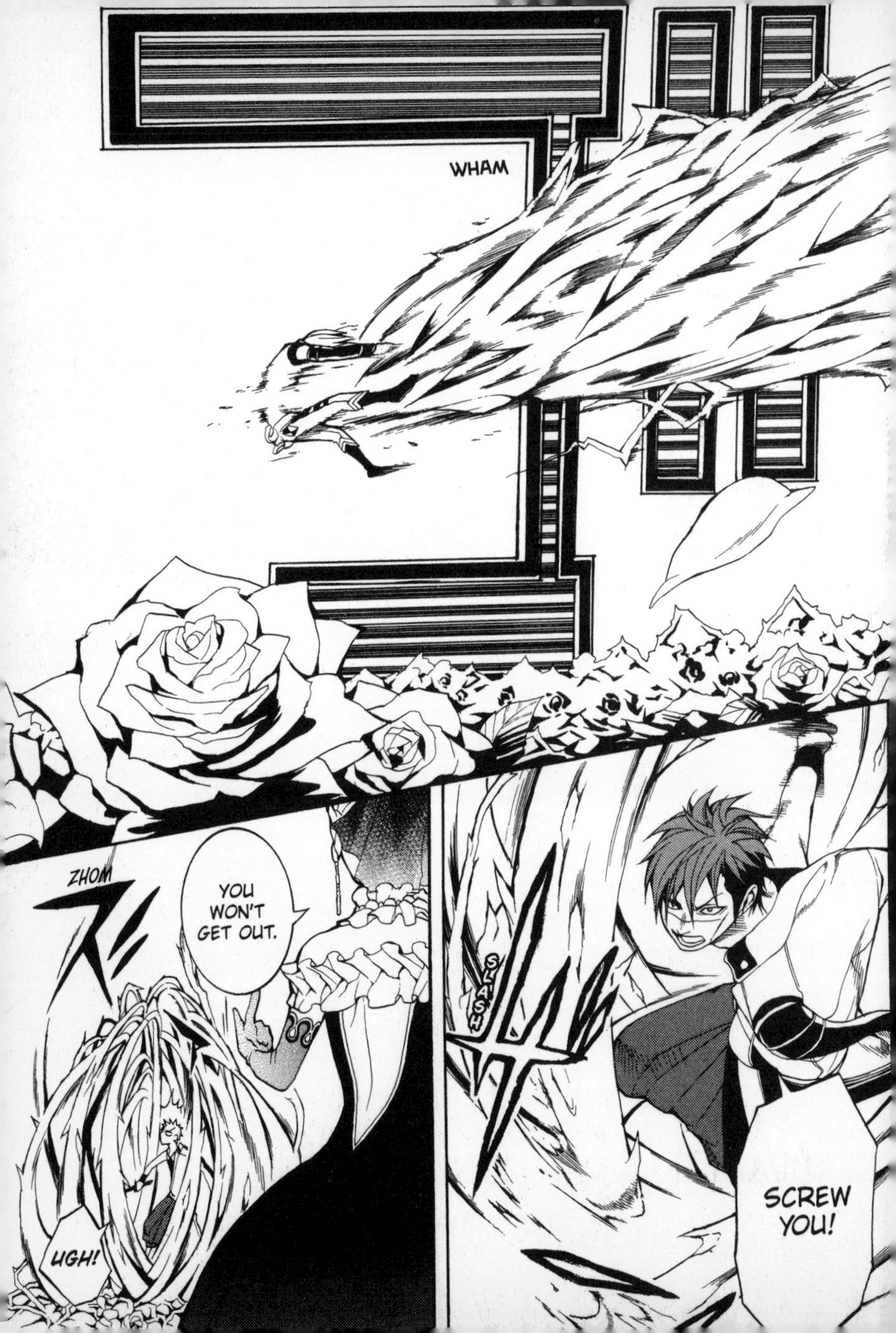
WHAM
SLASH
SCREW YOU!
ZHOM
YOU WON'T GET OUT.
UGH!

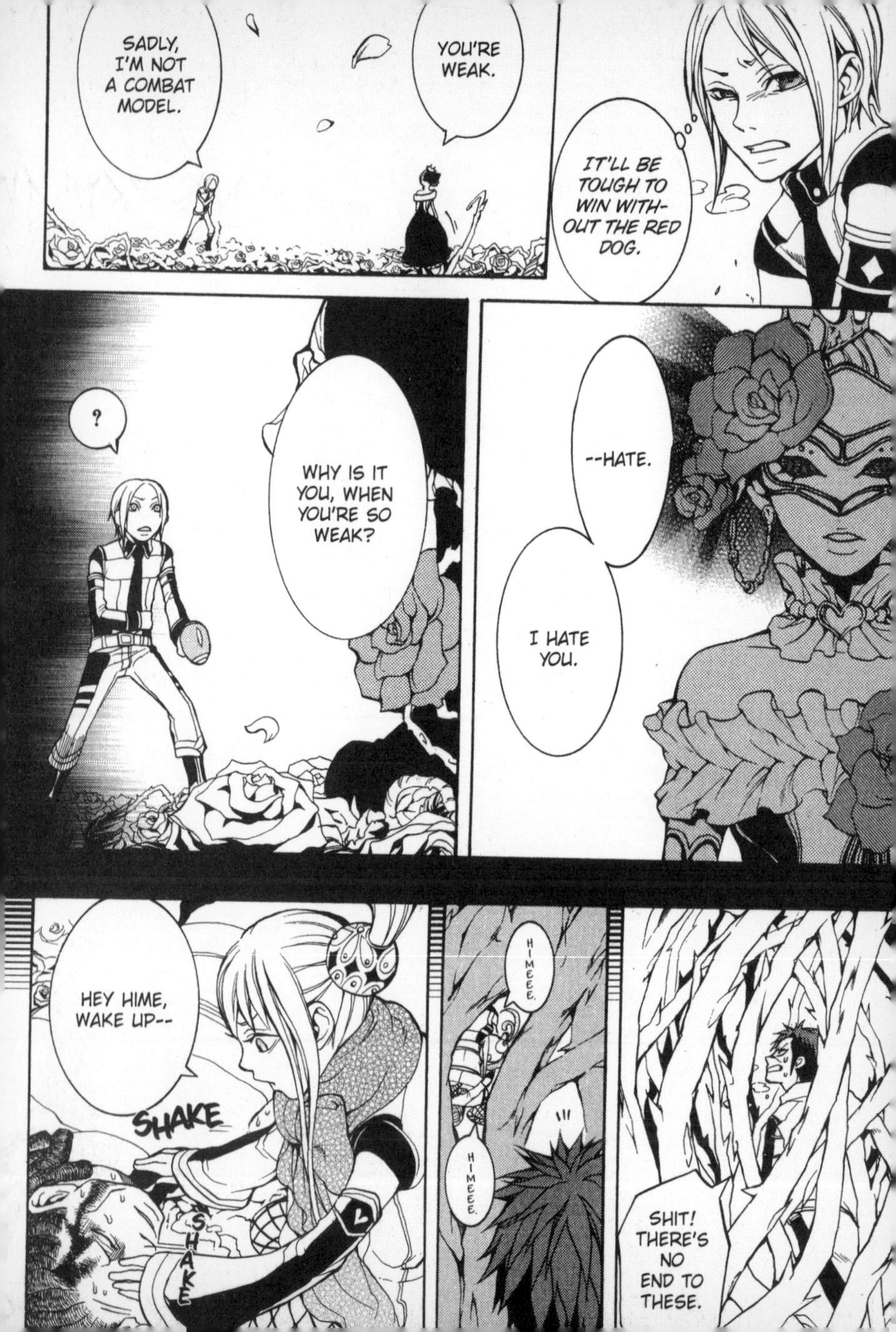
IT'LL BE TOUGH TO WIN WITH-OUT THE RED DOG.
YOU'RE WEAK.
SADLY, I'M NOT A COMBAT MODEL.
--HATE.
I HATE YOU.
WHY IS IT YOU, WHEN YOU'RE SO WEAK?
?
SHIT! THERE'S NO END TO THESE.
HIMEEE.
HIMEEE.
HEY HIME, WAKE UP--
SHAKE
SHAKE

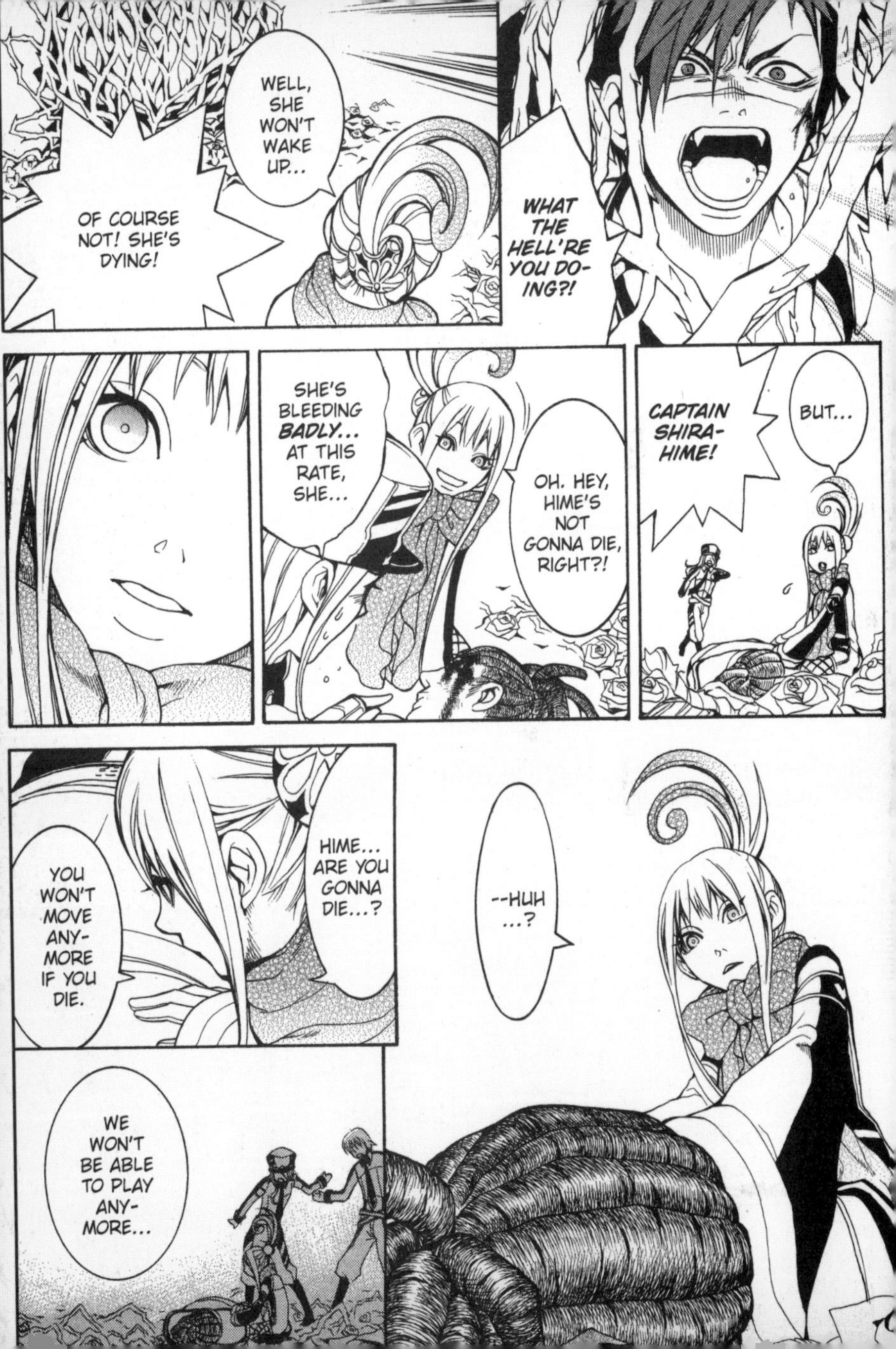
WHAT THE HELL'RE YOU DOING?!
WELL, SHE WON'T WAKE UP...
OF COURSE NOT! SHE'S DYING!
BUT...
CAPTAIN SHIRA-HIME!
OH. HEY, HIME'S NOT GONNA DIE, RIGHT?!
SHE'S BLEEDING BADLY... AT THIS RATE, SHE...
--HUH ...?
HIME... ARE YOU GONNA DIE...?
YOU WON'T MOVE ANY-MORE IF YOU DIE.
WE WON'T BE ABLE TO PLAY ANY-MORE...

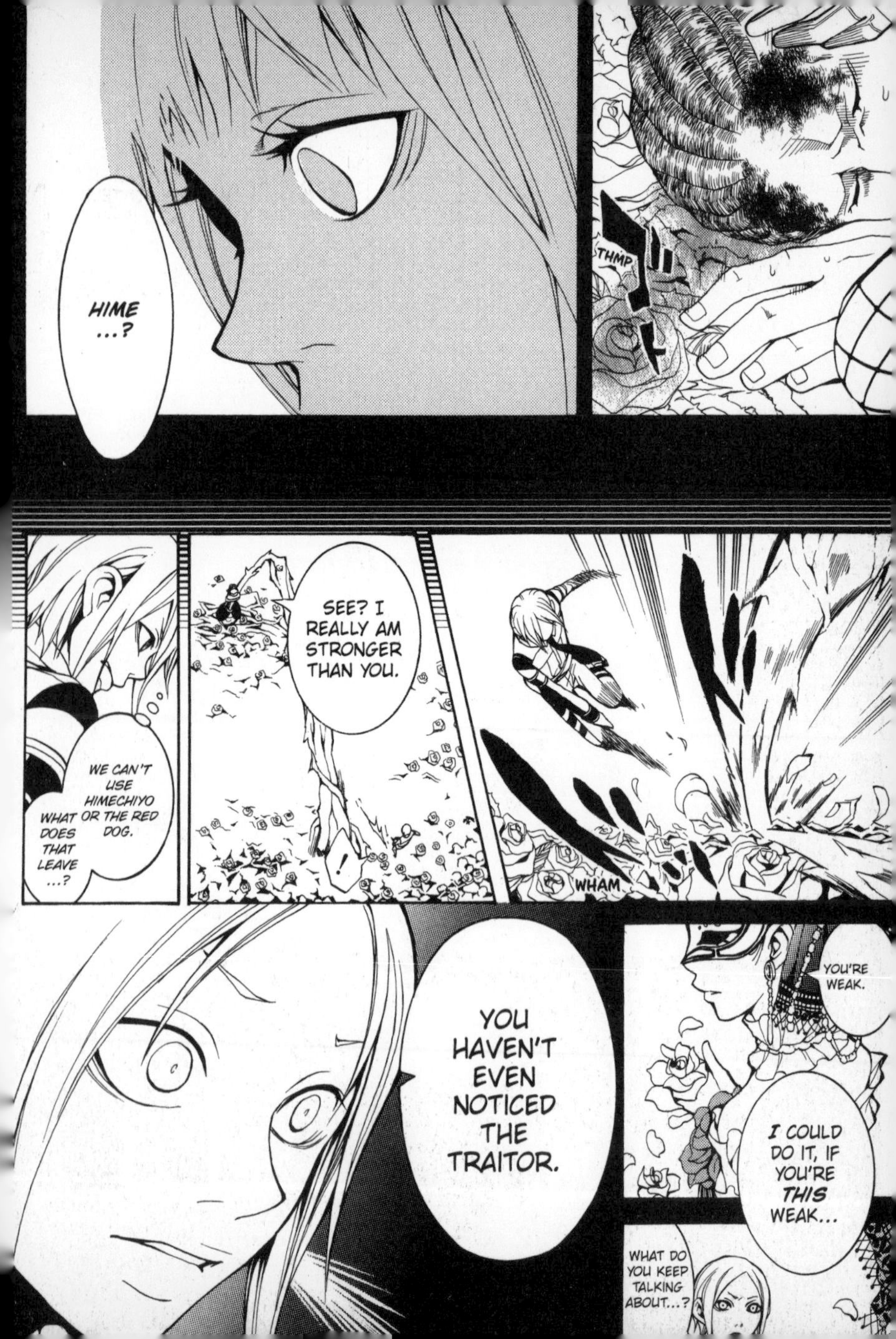
THMP
HIME ...?
WHAM
SEE? I REALLY AM STRONGER THAN YOU.
!
WE CAN'T USE HIMECHIYO OR THE RED DOG.
WHAT DOES THAT LEAVE ...?
YOU'RE WEAK.
I COULD DO IT, IF YOU'RE THIS WEAK...
WHAT DO YOU KEEP TALKING ABOUT...?
YOU HAVEN'T EVEN NOTICED THE TRAITOR.

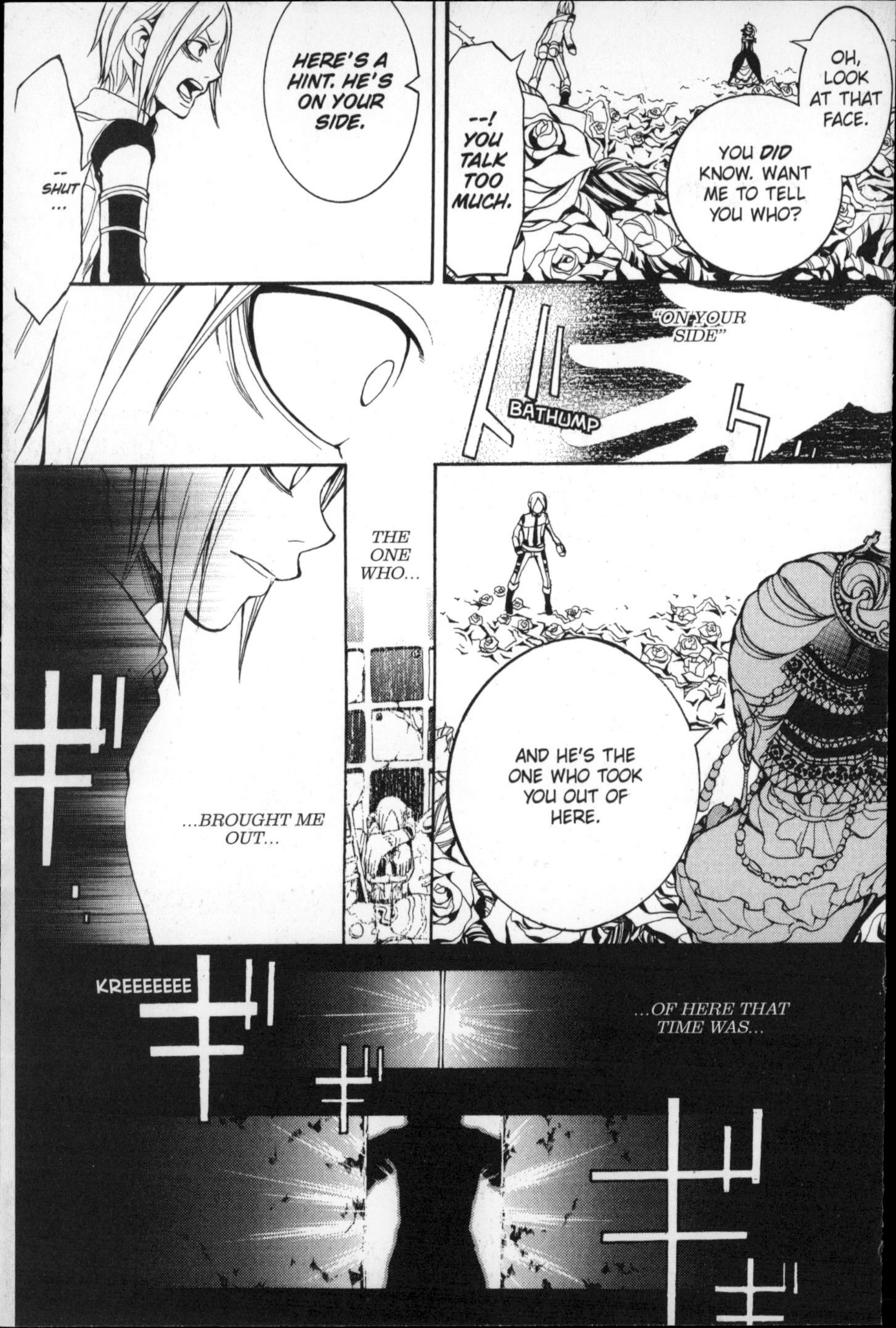

OH, LOOK AT THAT FACE.
YOU DID KNOW. WANT ME TO TELL YOU WHO?
--! YOU TALK TOO MUCH.
HERE'S A HINT. HE'S ON YOUR SIDE.
-- SHUT ...
"ON YOUR SIDE"
BATHUMP
AND HE'S THE ONE WHO TOOK YOU OUT OF HERE.
THE ONE WHO...
...BROUGHT ME OUT...
...OF HERE THAT TIME WAS...
KREEEEEEE

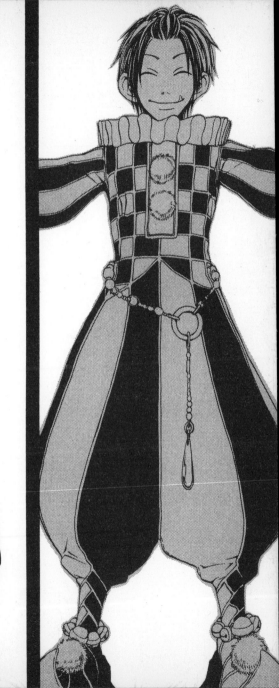

"LET'S
GET OUT
OF THIS
PLACE."

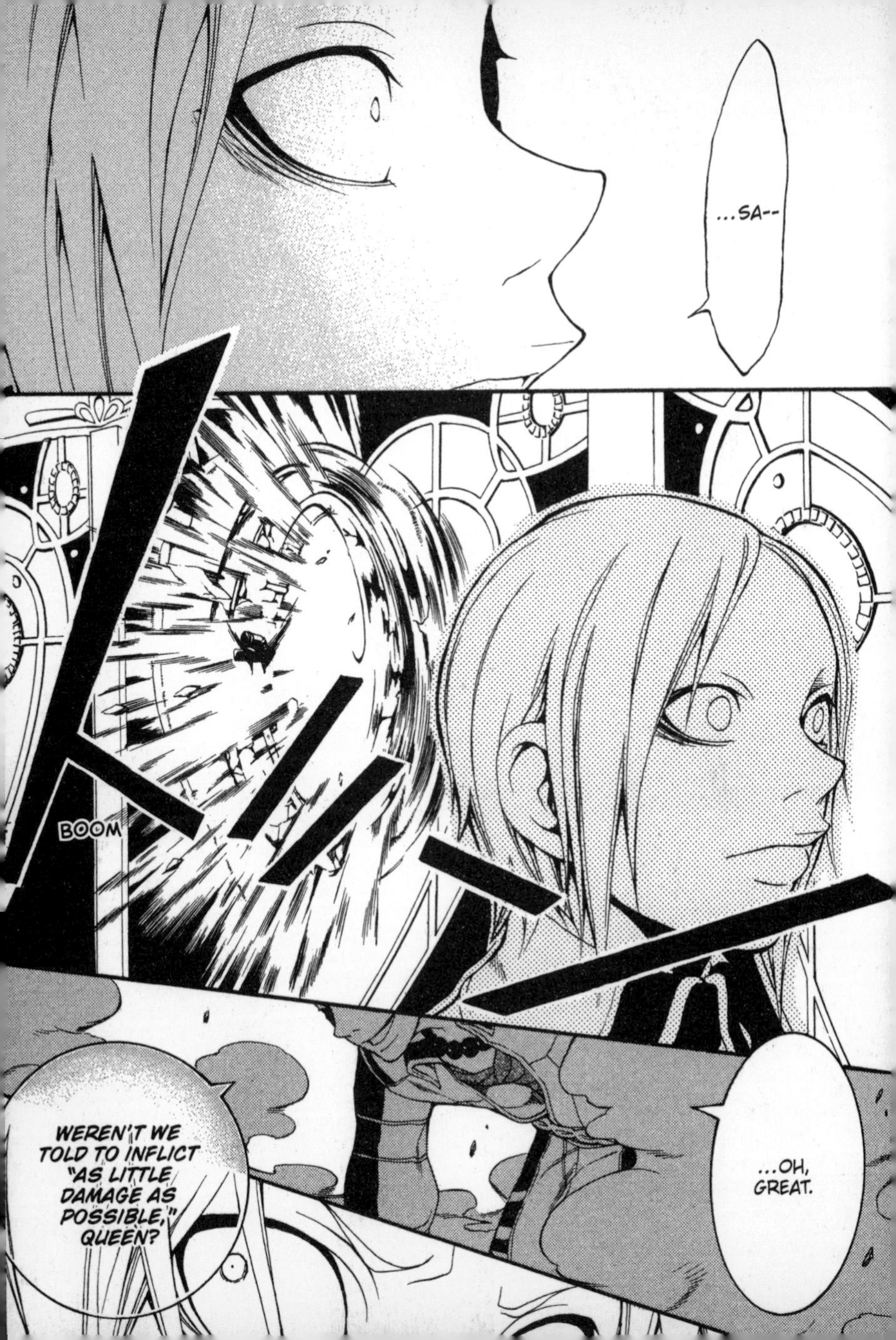
...SA--
BOOM
...OH, GREAT.
WEREN'T WE TOLD TO INFLICT "AS LITTLE DAMAGE AS POSSIBLE," QUEEN?

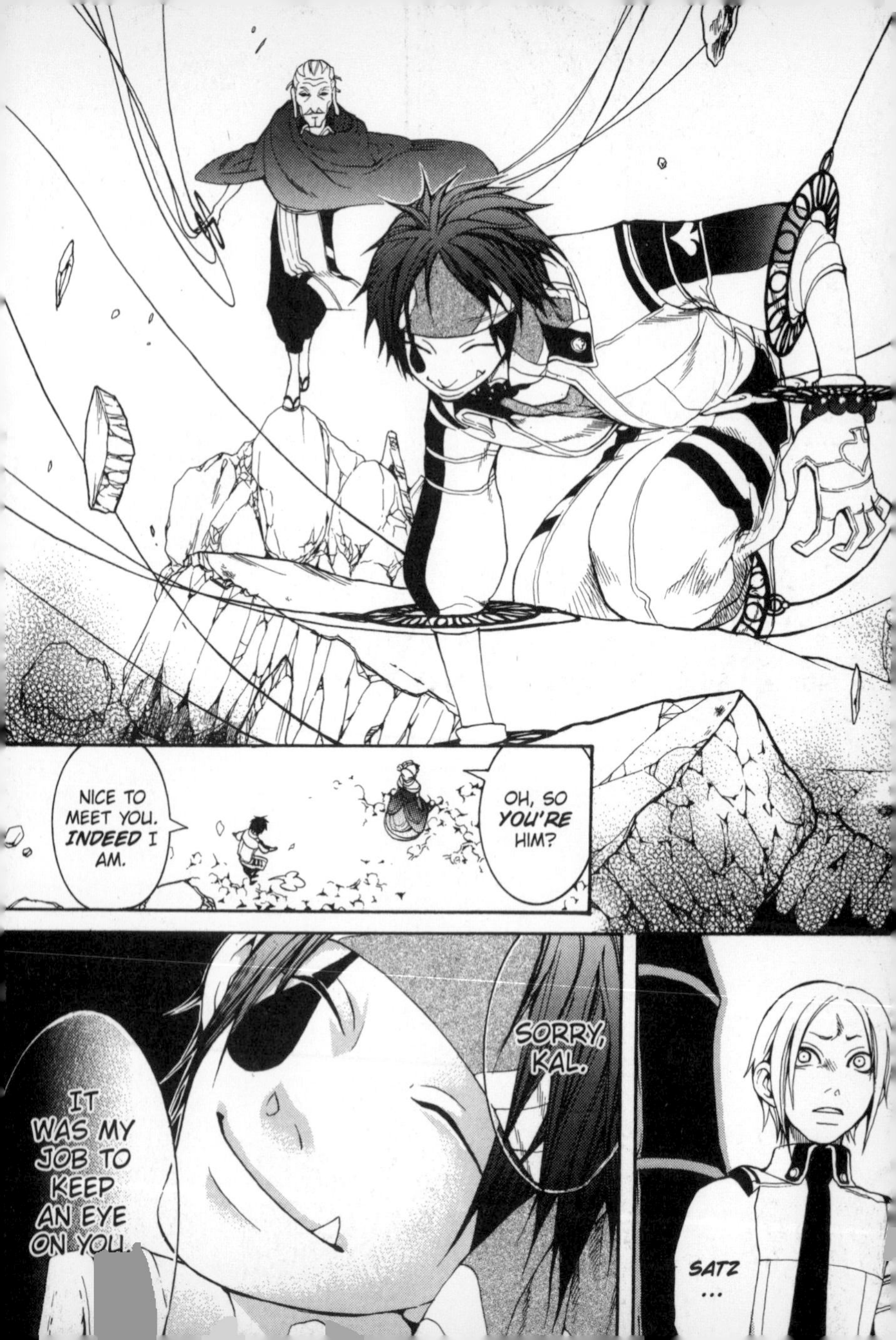
OH, SO *YOU'RE* HIM?
NICE TO MEET YOU. ***INDEED*** I AM.
SATZ ...
SORRY, KAL.
IT WAS MY JOB TO KEEP AN EYE ON YOU.

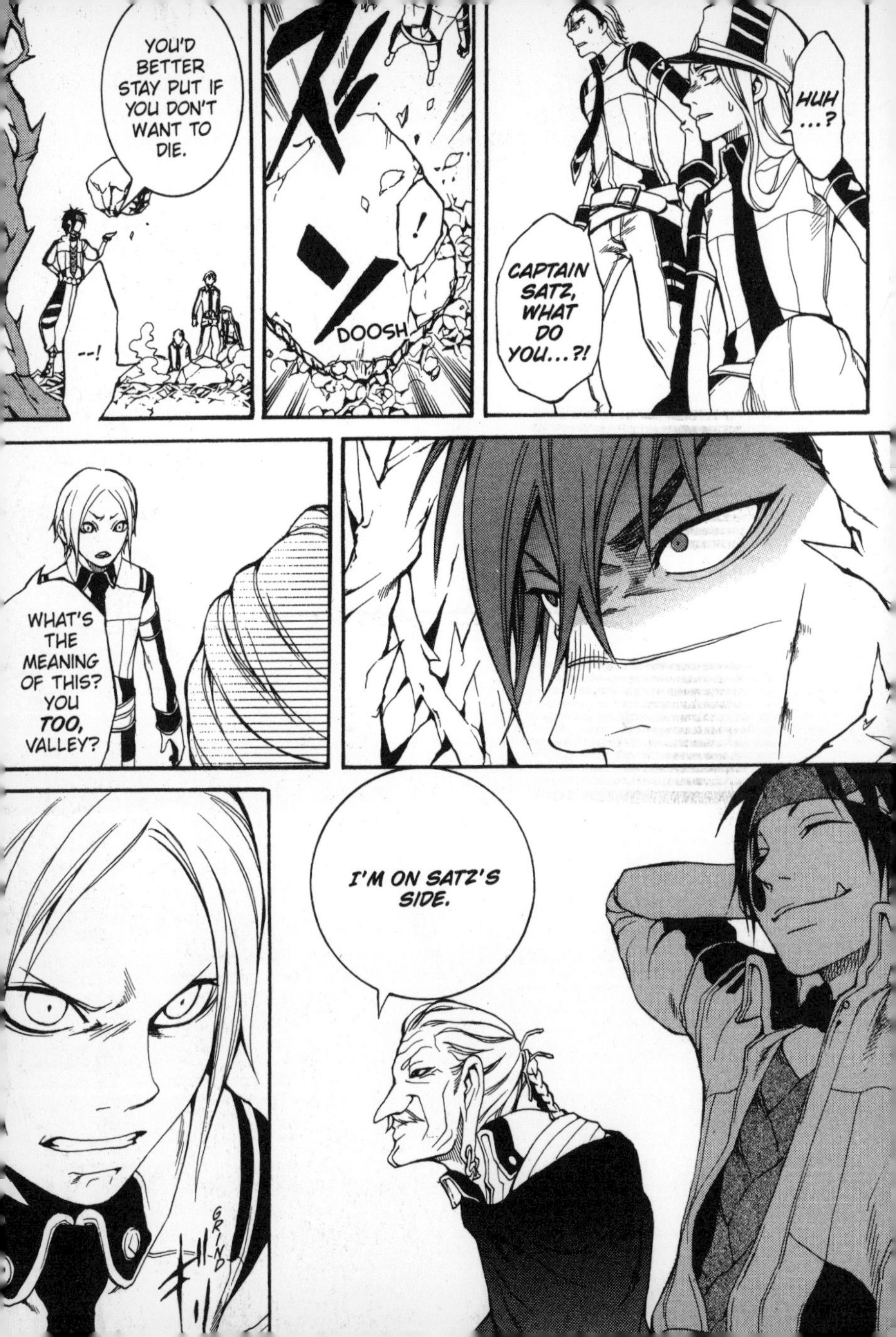
HUH ...?
CAPTAIN SATZ, WHAT DO YOU...?!
ズン
!
DOOSH
YOU'D BETTER STAY PUT IF YOU DON'T WANT TO DIE.
--!
WHAT'S THE MEANING OF THIS? YOU *TOO*, VALLEY?
I'M ON SATZ'S SIDE.
GRIND

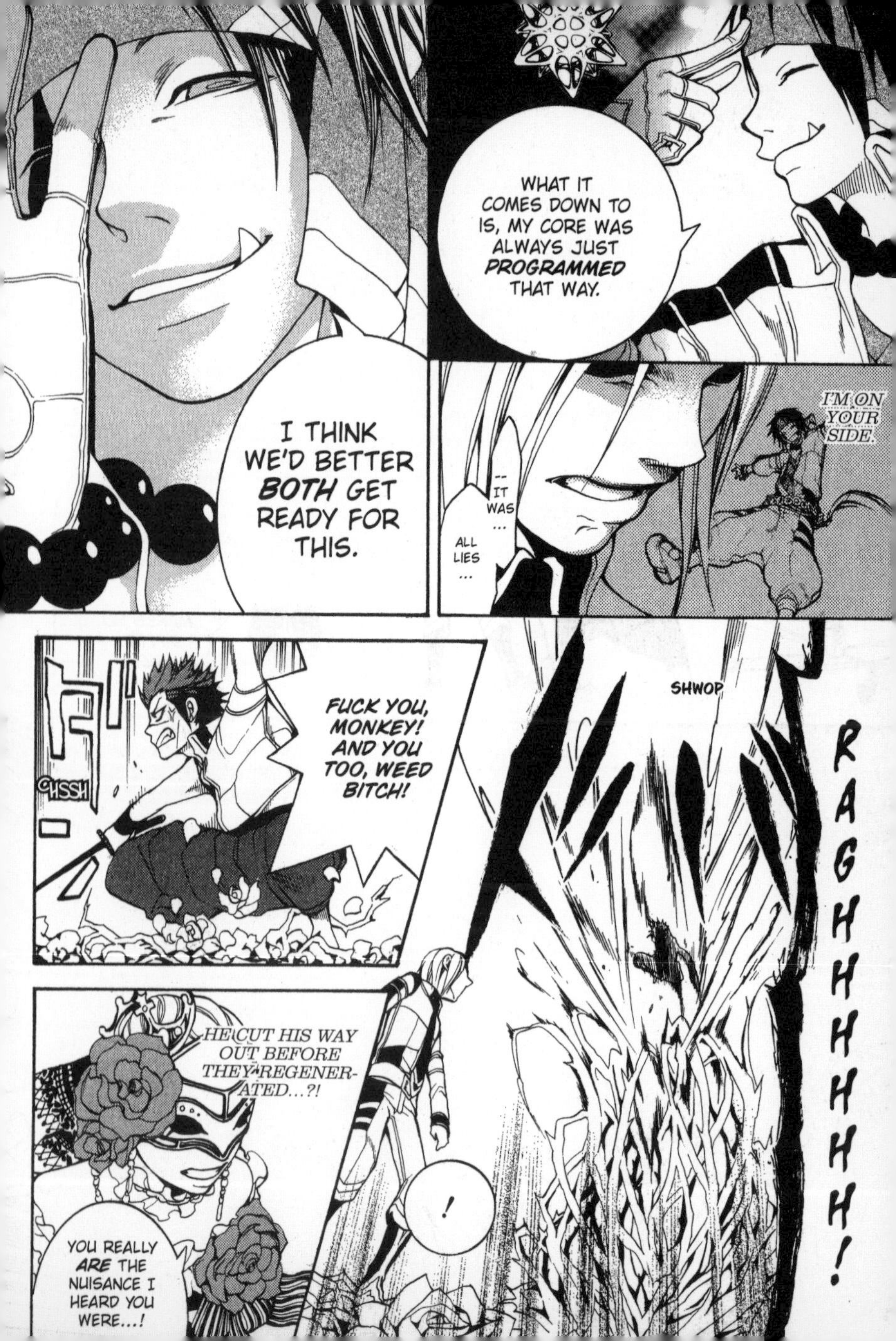
WHAT IT COMES DOWN TO IS, MY CORE WAS ALWAYS JUST PROGRAMMED THAT WAY.
I'M ON YOUR SIDE.
--IT WAS... ALL LIES...
I THINK WE'D BETTER BOTH GET READY FOR THIS.
SHWOP
RAGHHHHHH!
!
FUCK YOU, MONKEY! AND YOU TOO, WEED BITCH!
HSSH
HE CUT HIS WAY OUT BEFORE THEY REGENERATED...?!
YOU REALLY ARE THE NUISANCE I HEARD YOU WERE...!

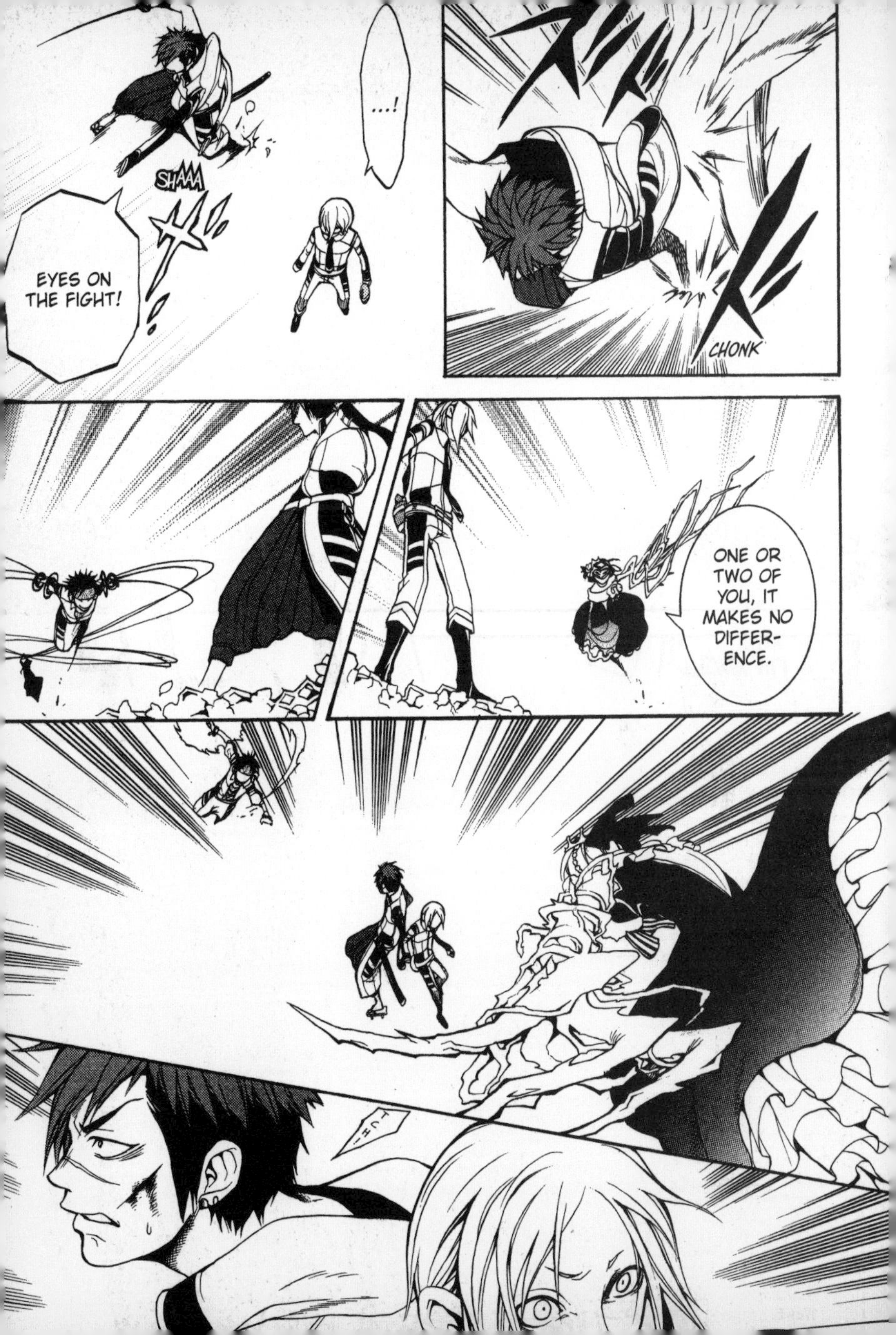
CHONK
...!
SHAAA
EYES ON THE FIGHT!
ONE OR TWO OF YOU, IT MAKES NO DIFFERENCE.
TCH!

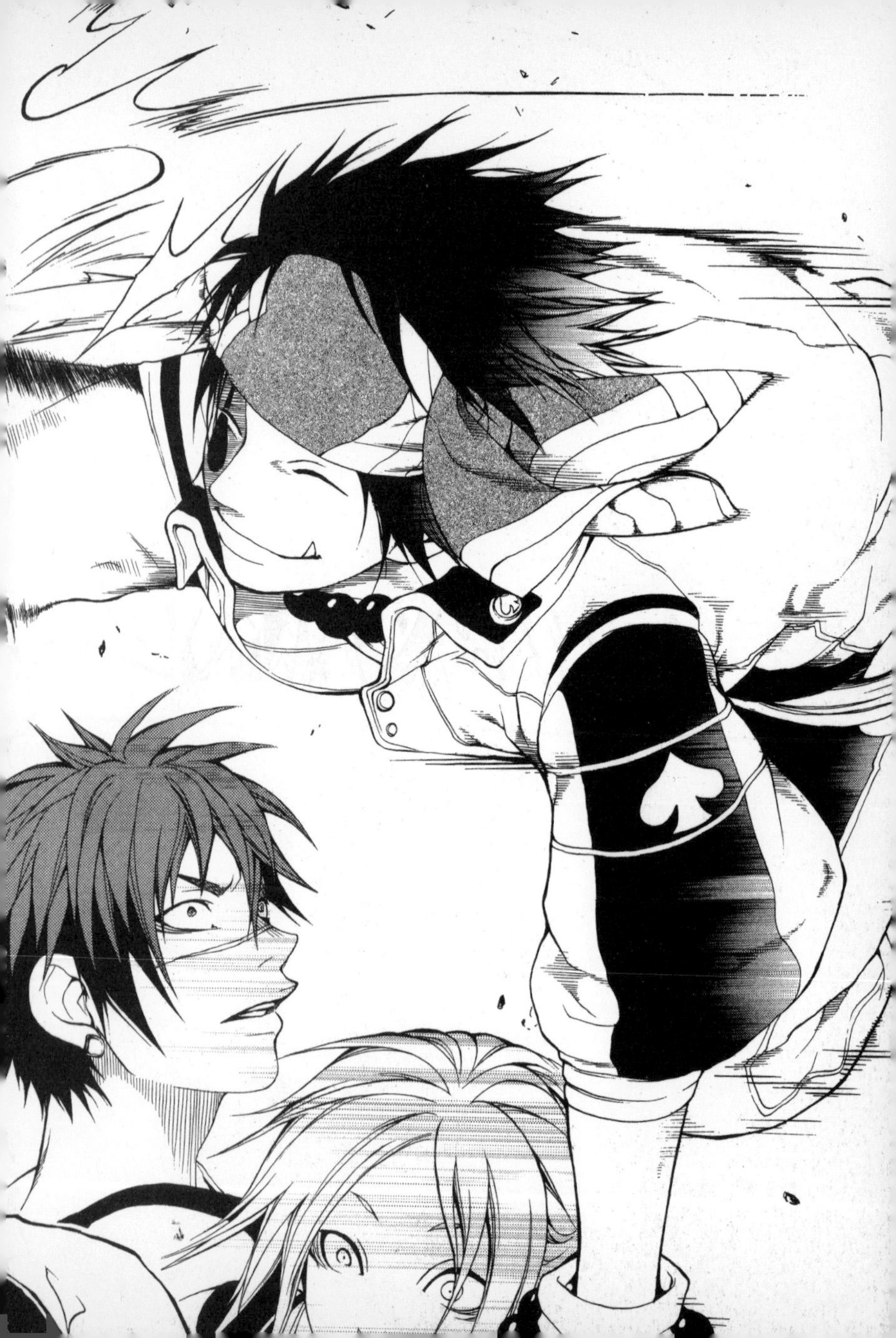

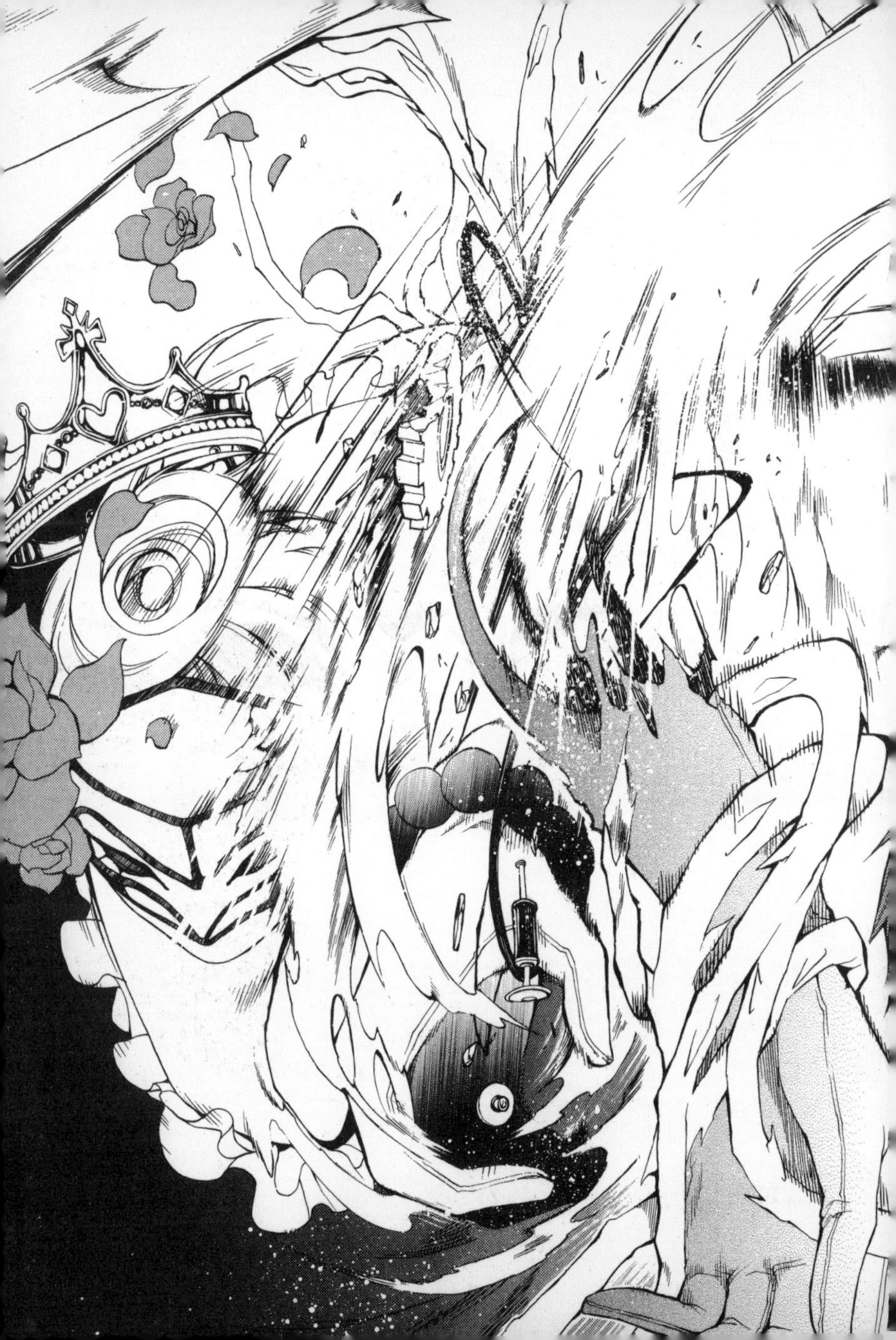

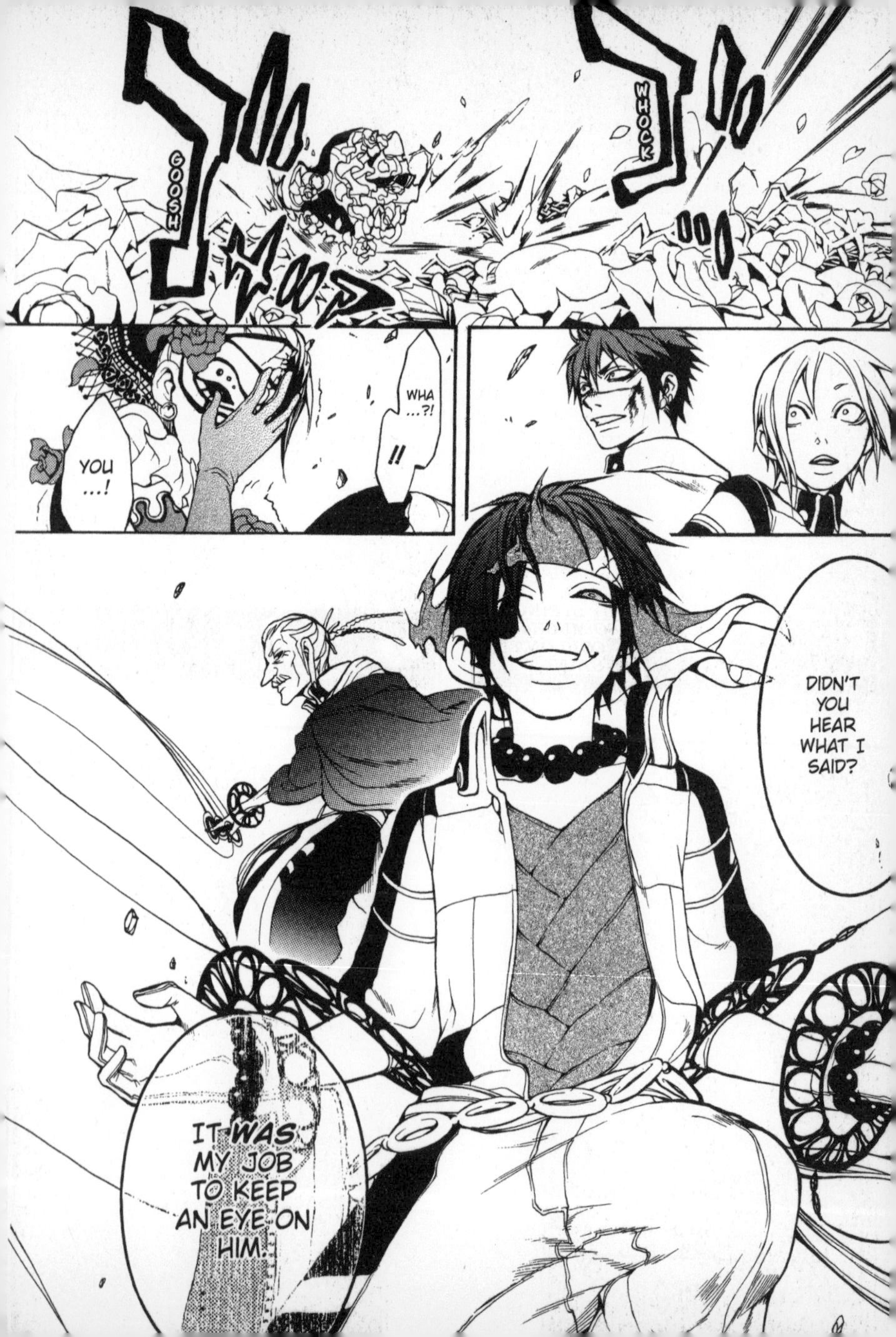
WHOCK
GOOSH
WHA ...?!
!!
YOU ...!
DIDN'T YOU HEAR WHAT I SAID?
IT WAS MY JOB TO KEEP AN EYE ON HIM.

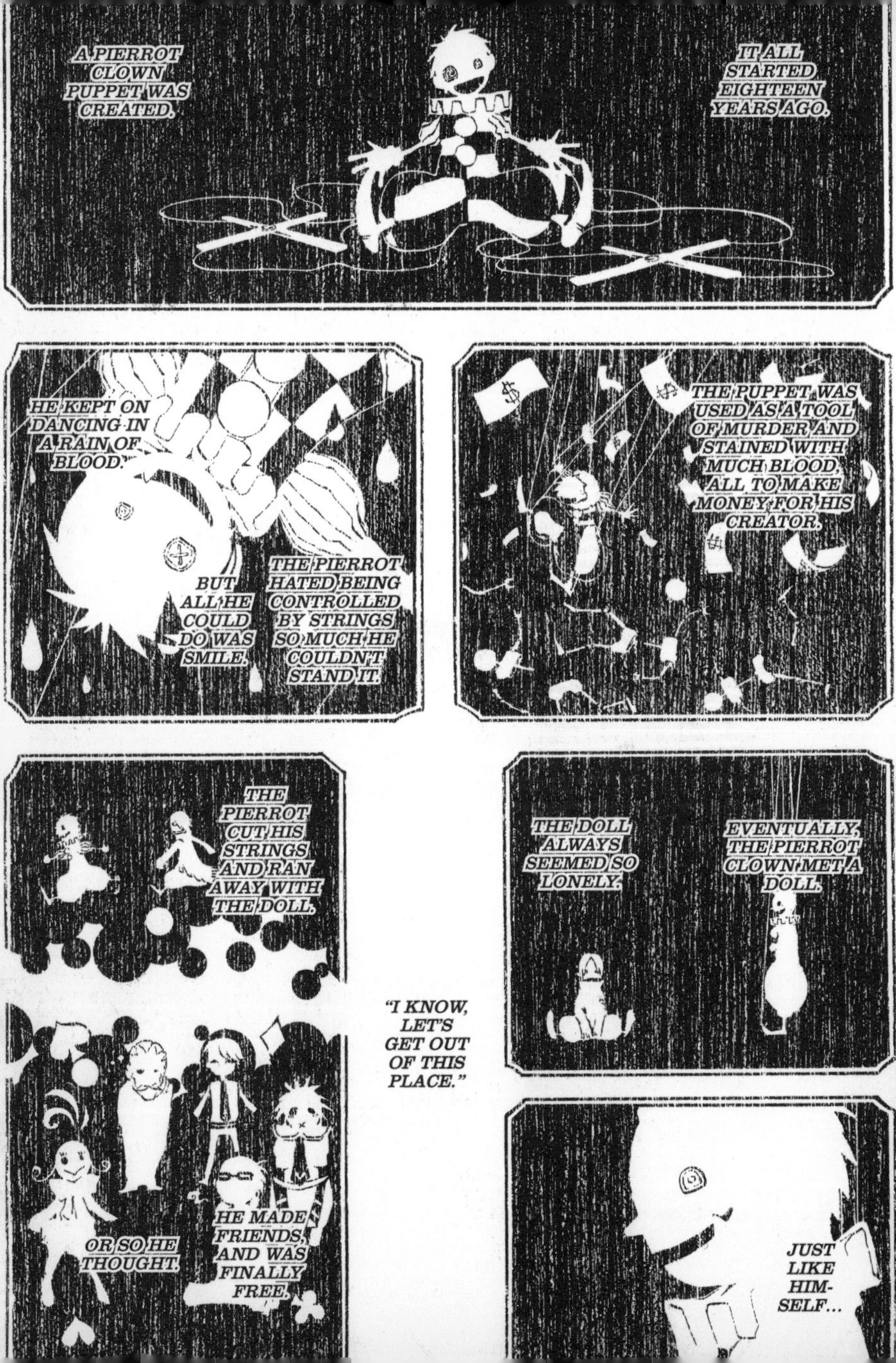
IT ALL STARTED EIGHTEEN YEARS AGO.
A PIERROT CLOWN PUPPET WAS CREATED.
THE PUPPET WAS USED AS A TOOL OF MURDER AND STAINED WITH MUCH BLOOD, ALL TO MAKE MONEY FOR HIS CREATOR.
HE KEPT ON DANCING IN A RAIN OF BLOOD.
THE PIERROT HATED BEING CONTROLLED BY STRINGS SO MUCH HE COULDN'T STAND IT.
BUT ALL HE COULD DO WAS SMILE.
EVENTUALLY, THE PIERROT CLOWN MET A DOLL.
THE DOLL ALWAYS SEEMED SO LONELY.
JUST LIKE HIM-SELF...
"I KNOW, LET'S GET OUT OF THIS PLACE."
THE PIERROT CUT HIS STRINGS AND RAN AWAY WITH THE DOLL.
HE MADE FRIENDS, AND WAS FINALLY FREE.
OR SO HE THOUGHT.

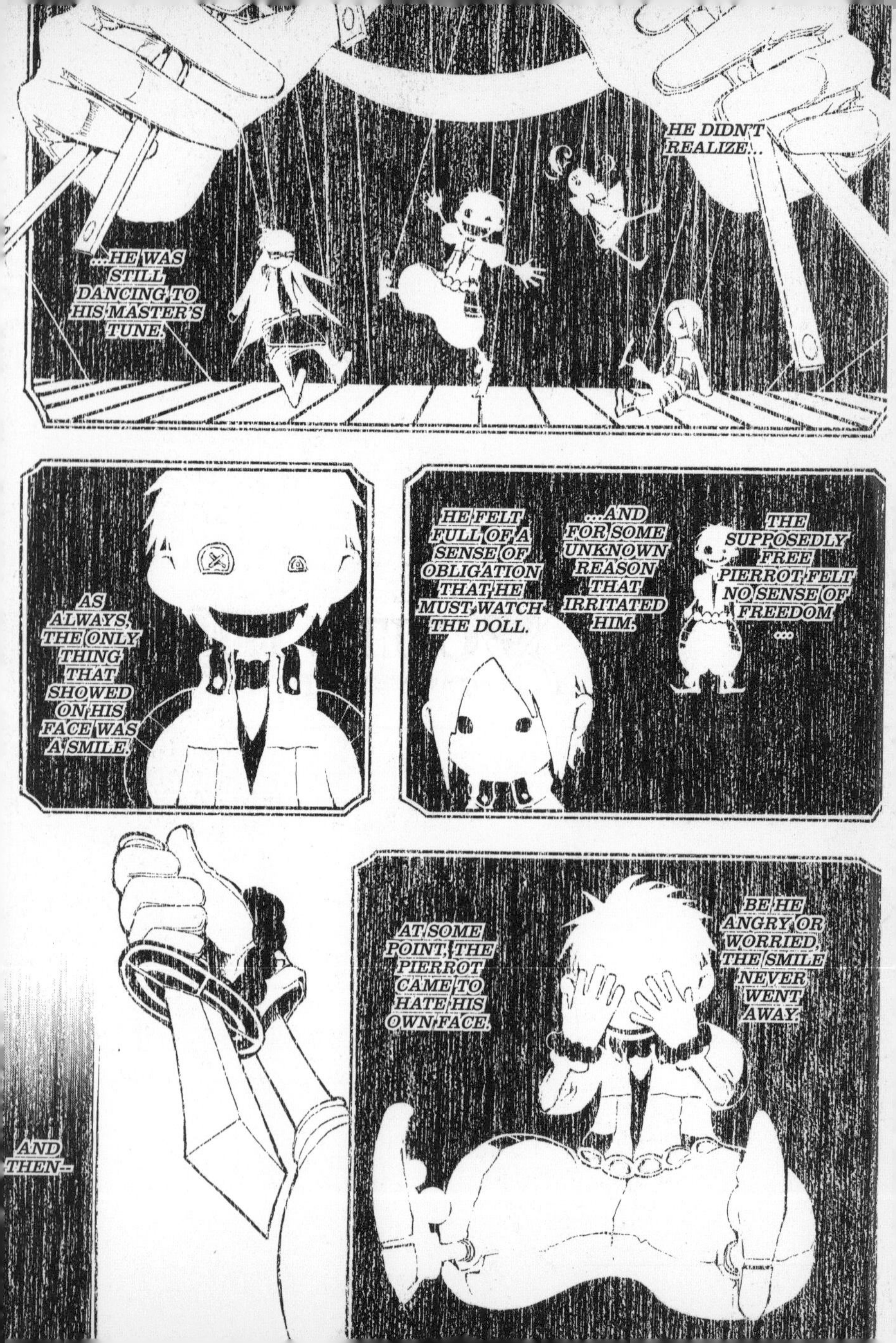
HE DIDN'T REALIZE...
...HE WAS STILL DANCING TO HIS MASTER'S TUNE.
THE SUPPOSEDLY FREE PIERROT FELT NO SENSE OF FREEDOM...
...AND FOR SOME UNKNOWN REASON THAT IRRITATED HIM.
HE FELT FULL OF A SENSE OF OBLIGATION THAT HE MUST WATCH THE DOLL.
AS ALWAYS, THE ONLY THING THAT SHOWED ON HIS FACE WAS A SMILE.
BE HE ANGRY OR WORRIED, THE SMILE NEVER WENT AWAY.
AT SOME POINT, THE PIERROT CAME TO HATE HIS OWN FACE.
AND THEN--

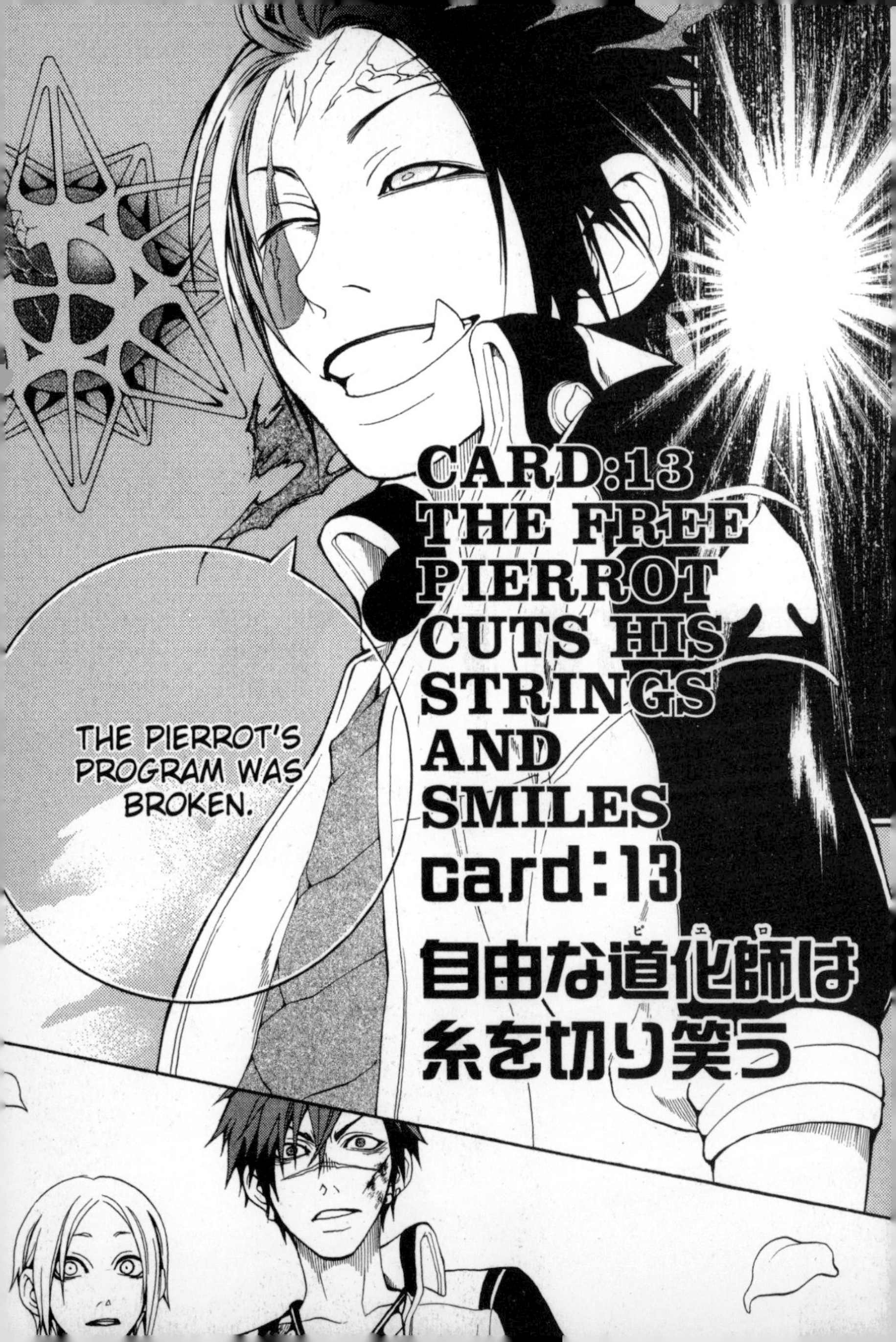
CARD:13 THE FREE PIERROT CUTS HIS STRINGS AND SMILES
card:13
自由な道化師は糸を切り笑う
THE PIERROT'S PROGRAM WAS BROKEN.

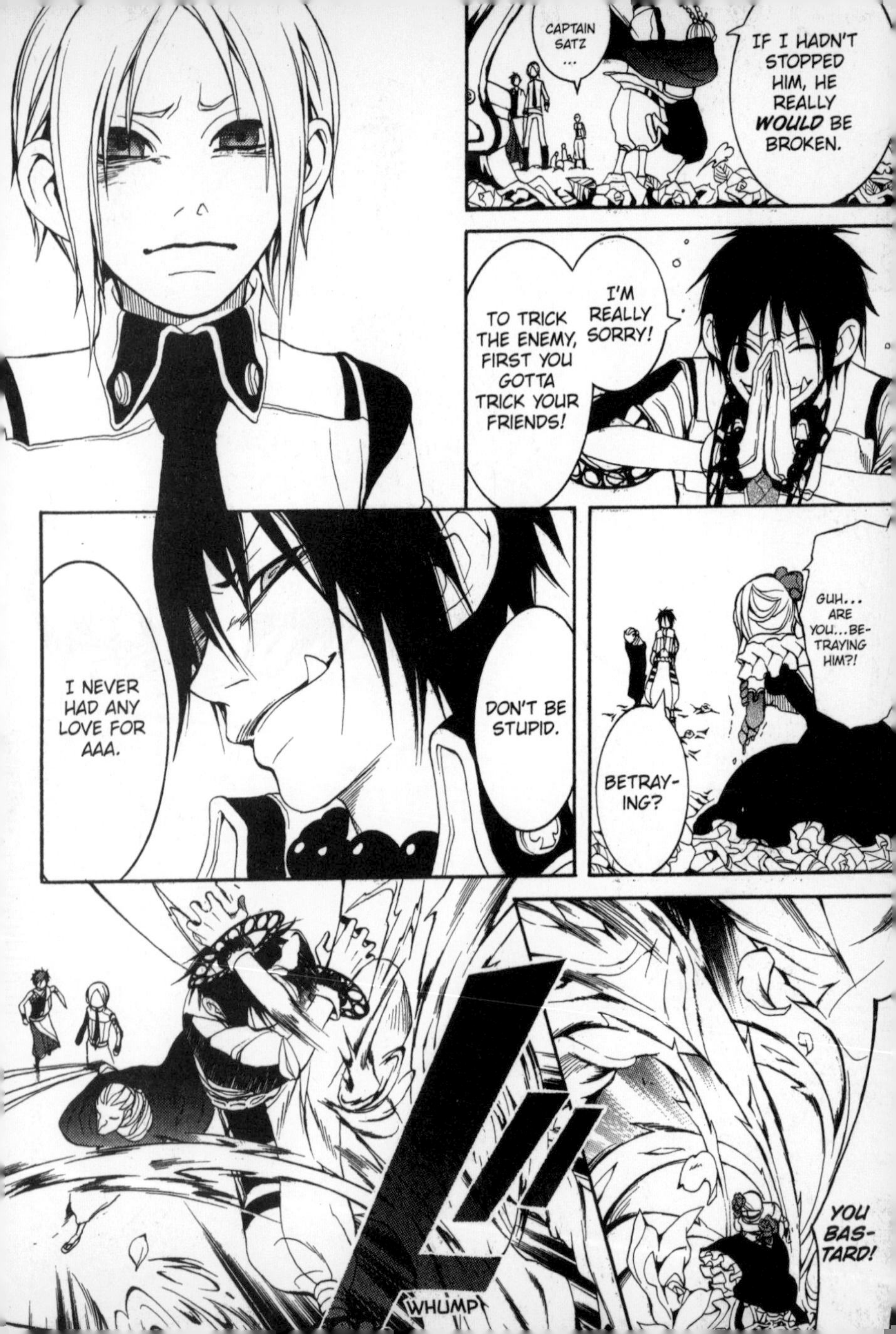

IF I HADN'T STOPPED HIM, HE REALLY *WOULD* BE BROKEN.
CAPTAIN SATZ ...
I'M REALLY SORRY!
TO TRICK THE ENEMY, FIRST YOU GOTTA TRICK YOUR FRIENDS!
GUH... ARE YOU...BE-TRAYING HIM?!
BETRAY-ING?
DON'T BE STUPID.
I NEVER HAD ANY LOVE FOR AAA.
YOU BAS-TARD!
WHUMP

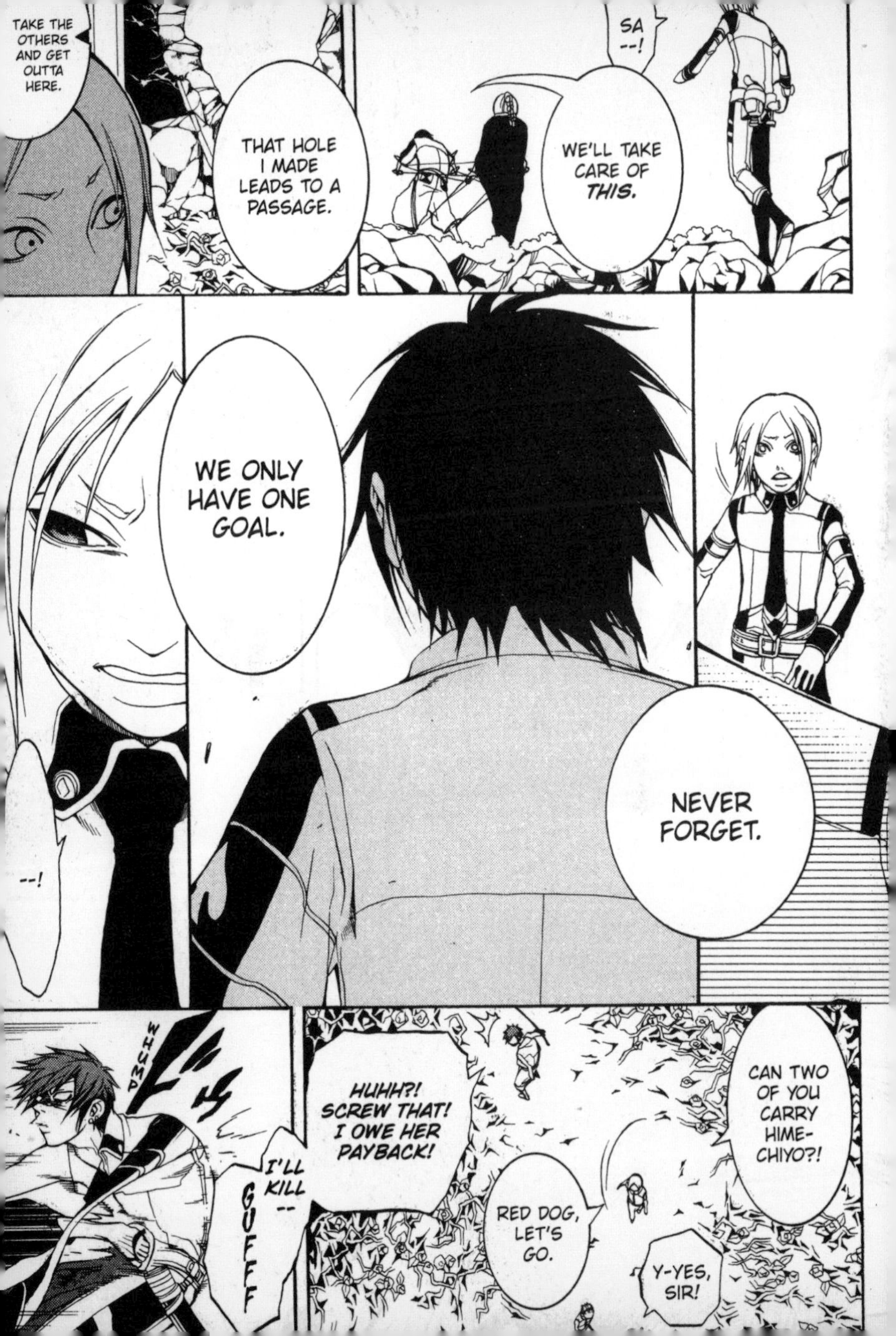
SA --!
WE'LL TAKE CARE OF *THIS.*
THAT HOLE I MADE LEADS TO A PASSAGE.
TAKE THE OTHERS AND GET OUTTA HERE.
WE ONLY HAVE ONE GOAL.
NEVER FORGET.
--!
CAN TWO OF YOU CARRY HIME-CHIYO?!
HUHH?! SCREW THAT! I OWE HER PAYBACK!
RED DOG, LET'S GO.
Y-YES, SIR!
WHUMP
I'LL KILL --
GUFF

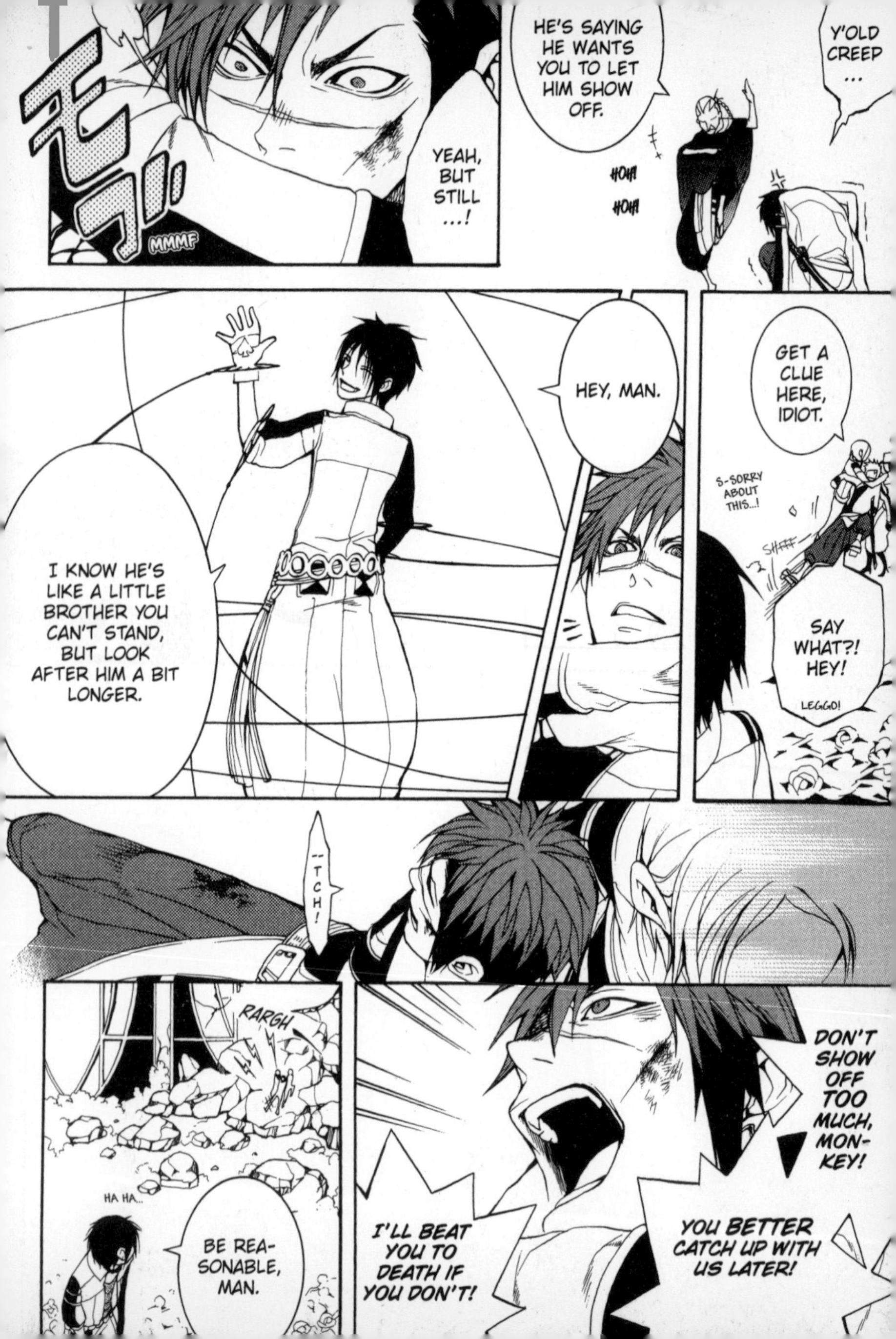
Y'OLD CREEP ...
HE'S SAYING HE WANTS YOU TO LET HIM SHOW OFF.
HOI! HOI!
YEAH, BUT STILL ...!
MMMF
GET A CLUE HERE, IDIOT.
S-SORRY ABOUT THIS...!
SHFFF
SAY WHAT?! HEY!
LEGGO!
HEY, MAN.
I KNOW HE'S LIKE A LITTLE BROTHER YOU CAN'T STAND, BUT LOOK AFTER HIM A BIT LONGER.
--TCH!
DON'T SHOW OFF TOO MUCH, MON-KEY!
YOU BETTER CATCH UP WITH US LATER!
I'LL BEAT YOU TO DEATH IF YOU DON'T!
RARGH
HA HA...
BE REA-SONABLE, MAN.

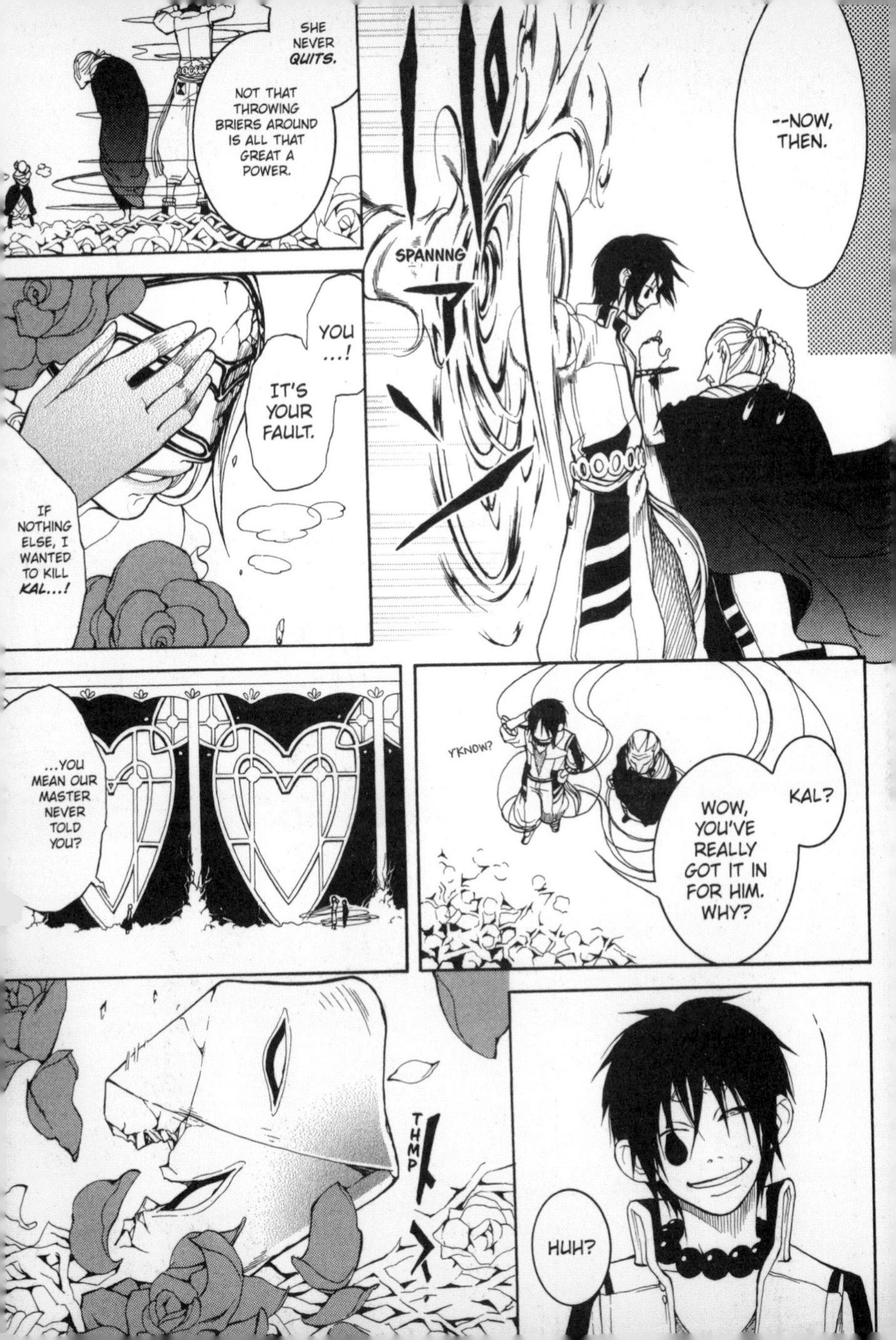
--NOW, THEN.
SPANNNG
SHE NEVER QUITS.
NOT THAT THROWING BRIERS AROUND IS ALL THAT GREAT A POWER.
YOU ...!
IT'S YOUR FAULT.
IF NOTHING ELSE, I WANTED TO KILL KAL...!
KAL?
WOW, YOU'VE REALLY GOT IT IN FOR HIM. WHY?
Y'KNOW?
...YOU MEAN OUR MASTER NEVER TOLD YOU?
HUH?
THMP

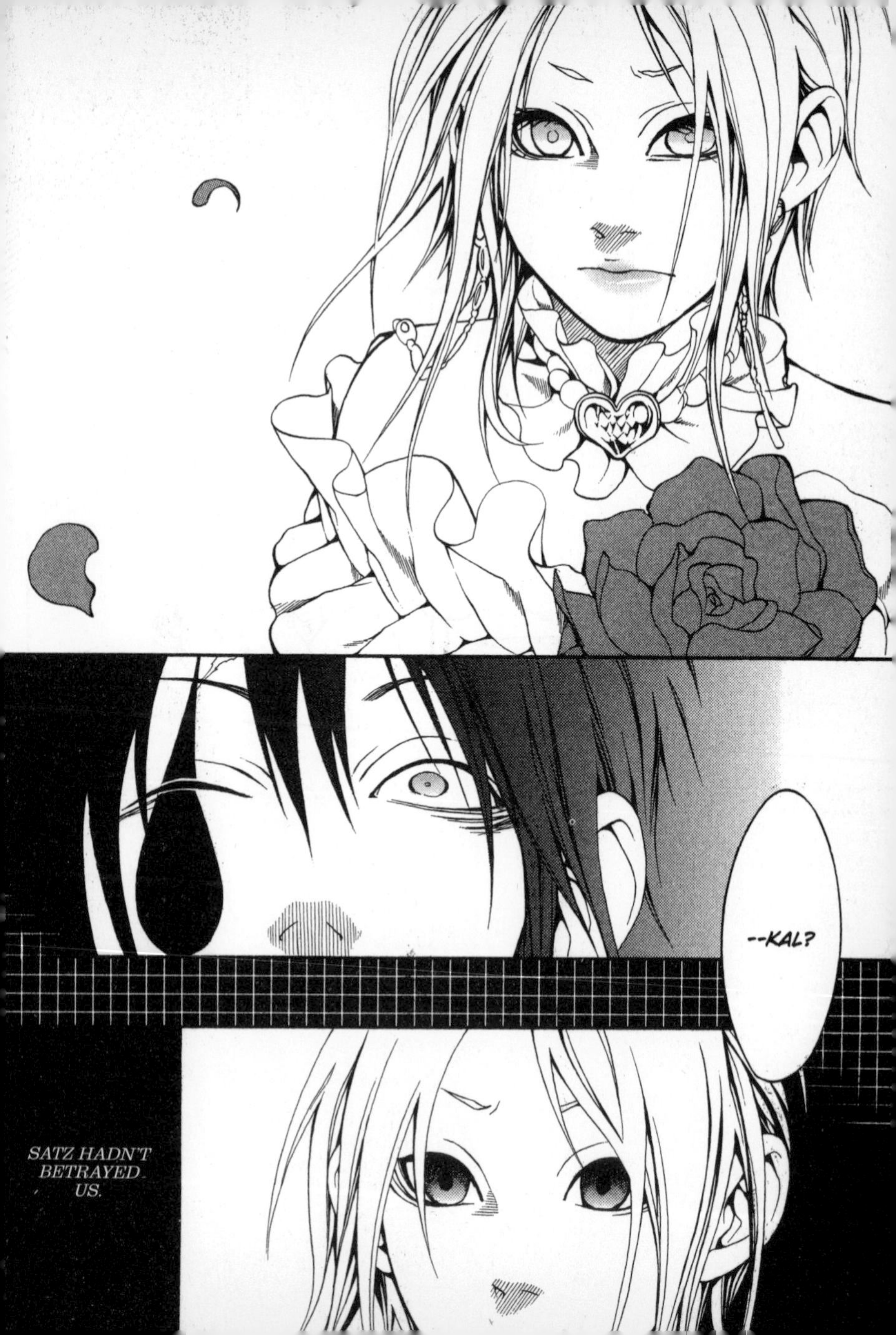
--KAL?
SATZ HADN'T BETRAYED US.

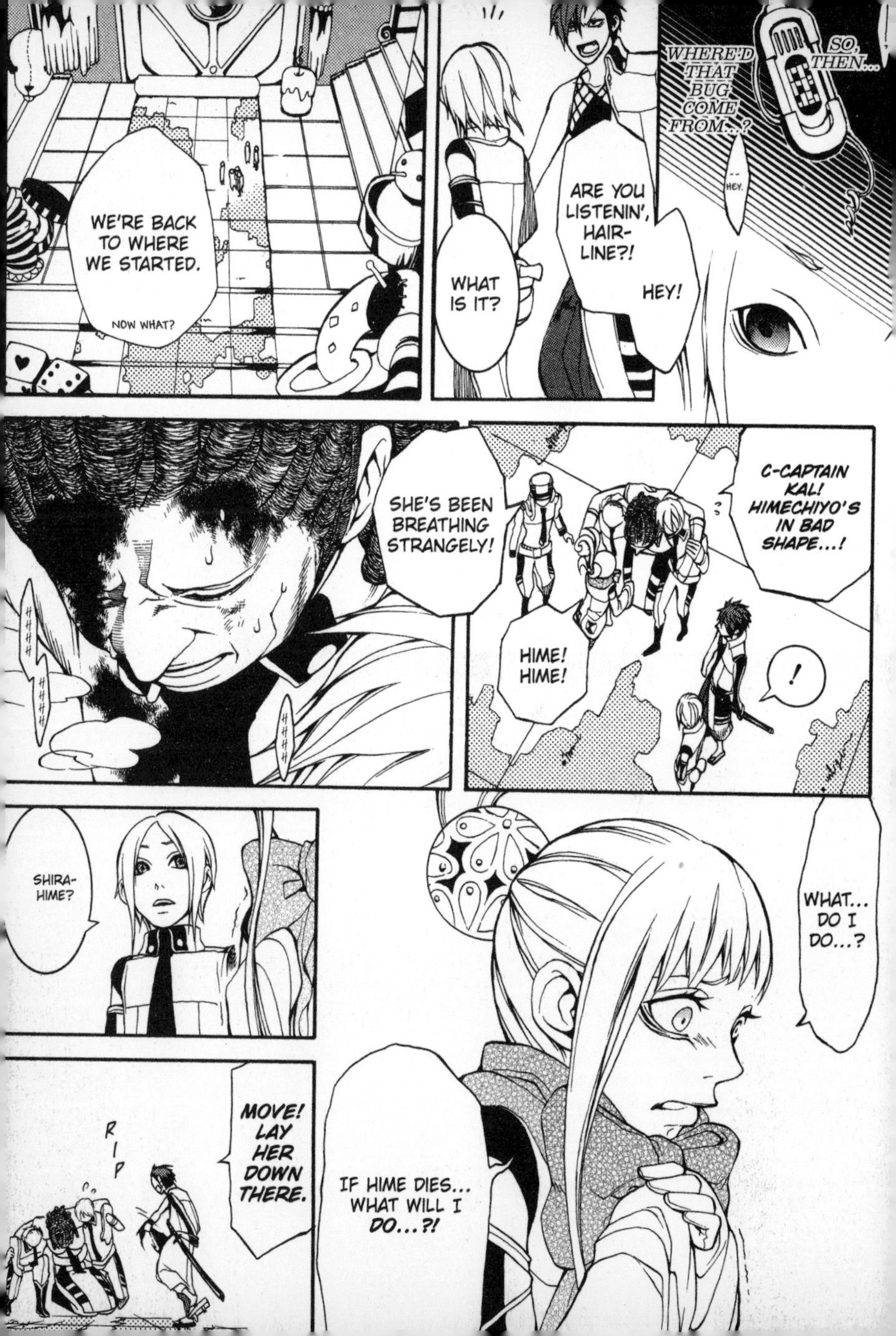
SO, THEN...
WHERE'D THAT BUG COME FROM...?
--HEY.
HEY!
ARE YOU LISTENIN', HAIR-LINE?!
WHAT IS IT?
WE'RE BACK TO WHERE WE STARTED.
NOW WHAT?
C-CAPTAIN KAL! HIMECHIYO'S IN BAD SHAPE...!
SHE'S BEEN BREATHING STRANGELY!
HIME! HIME!
!
WHAT... DO I DO...?
IF HIME DIES... WHAT WILL I DO...?!
SHIRA-HIME?
MOVE! LAY HER DOWN THERE.
RIP

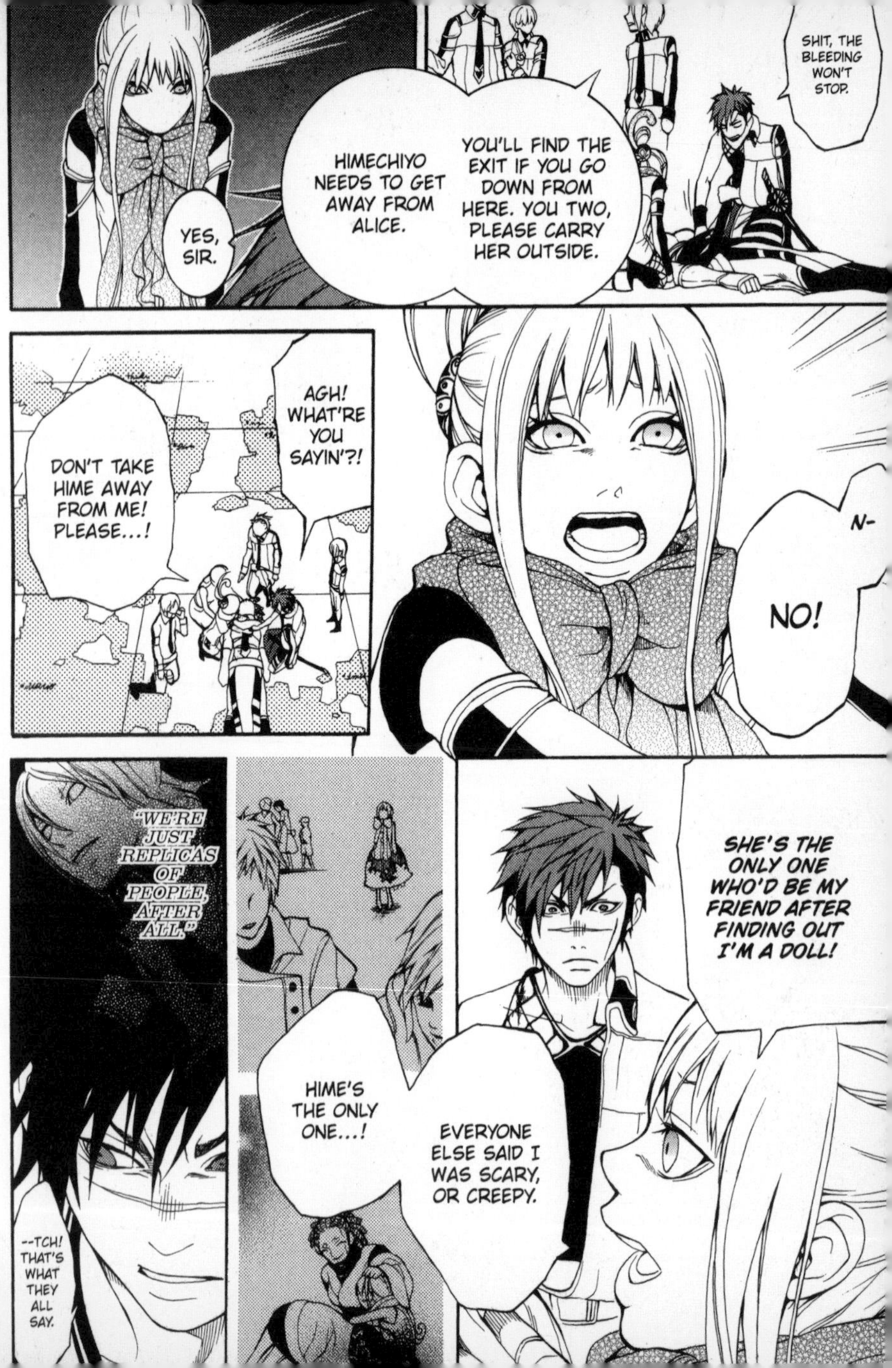
SHIT, THE BLEEDING WON'T STOP.
YOU'LL FIND THE EXIT IF YOU GO DOWN FROM HERE. YOU TWO, PLEASE CARRY HER OUTSIDE.
HIMECHIYO NEEDS TO GET AWAY FROM ALICE.
YES, SIR.
N-
NO!
AGH! WHAT'RE YOU SAYIN'?!
DON'T TAKE HIME AWAY FROM ME! PLEASE...!
SHE'S THE ONLY ONE WHO'D BE MY FRIEND AFTER FINDING OUT I'M A DOLL!
EVERYONE ELSE SAID I WAS SCARY, OR CREEPY.
HIME'S THE ONLY ONE...!
"WE'RE JUST REPLICAS OF PEOPLE, AFTER ALL."
--TCH! THAT'S WHAT THEY ALL SAY.

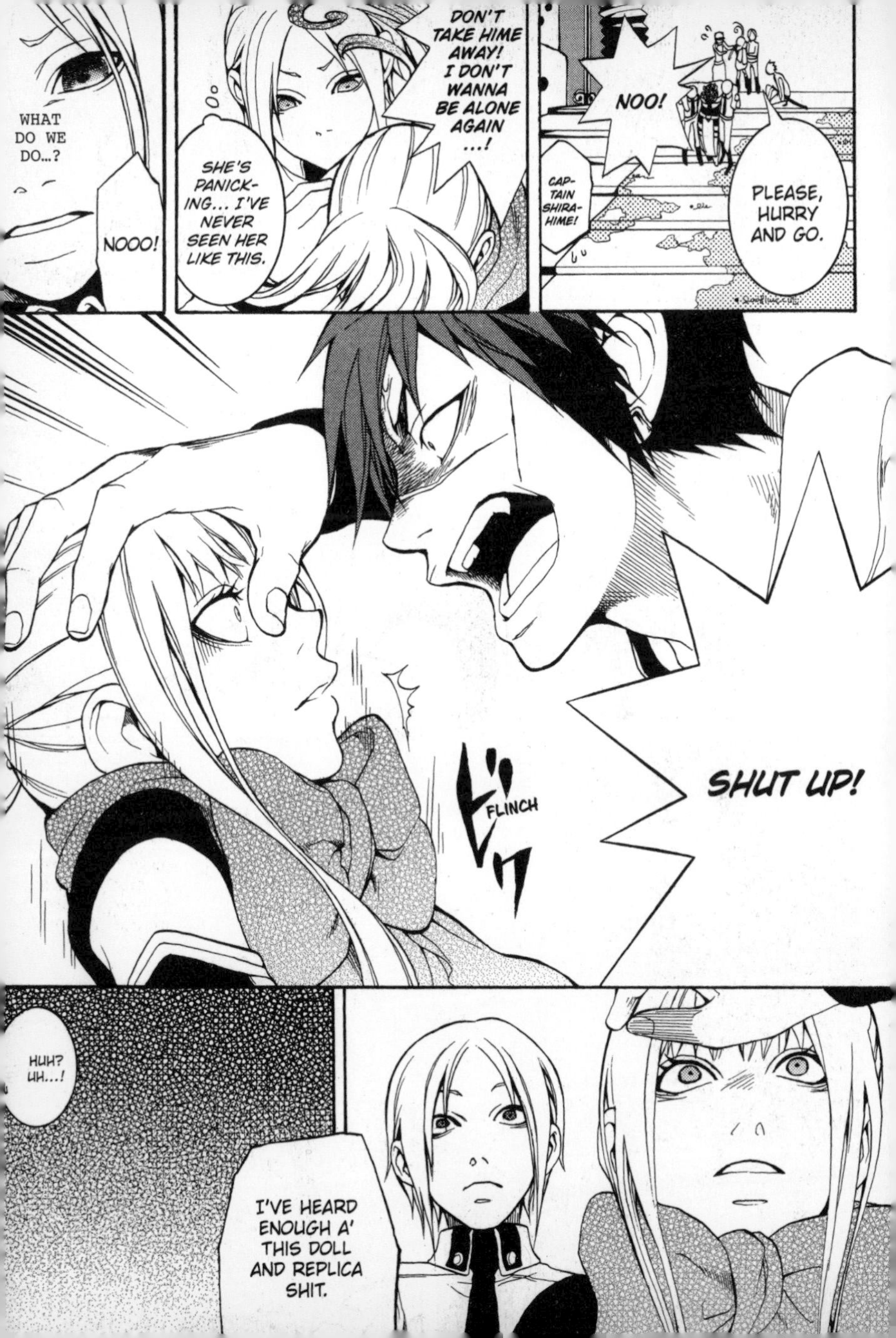
NOO!
PLEASE, HURRY AND GO.
CAP-TAIN SHIRA-HIME!
DON'T TAKE HIME AWAY! I DON'T WANNA BE ALONE AGAIN ...!
SHE'S PANICK-ING... I'VE NEVER SEEN HER LIKE THIS.
WHAT DO WE DO...?
NOOO!
SHUT UP!
FLINCH
I'VE HEARD ENOUGH A' THIS DOLL AND REPLICA SHIT.
HUH? UH...!

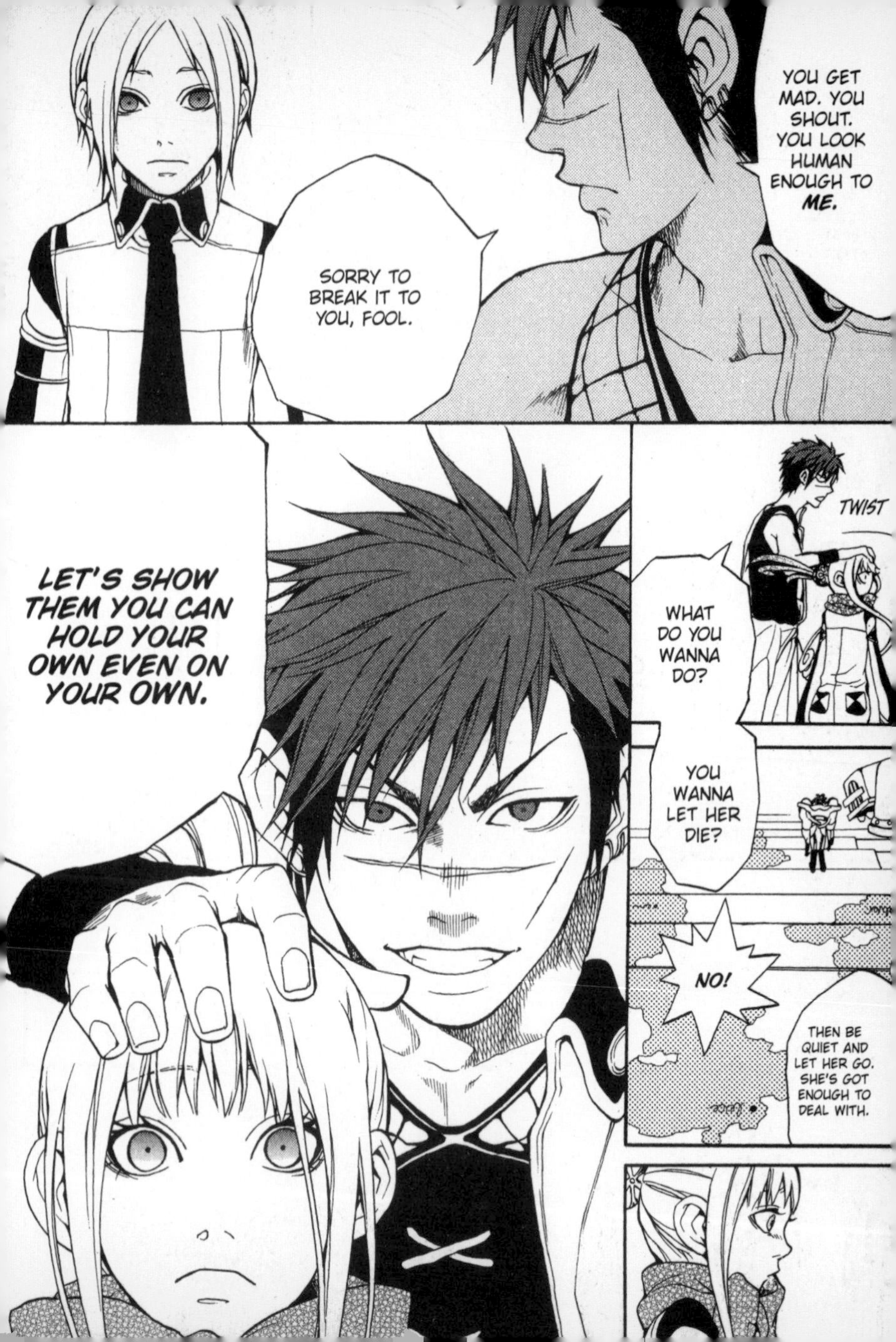
YOU GET MAD. YOU SHOUT. YOU LOOK HUMAN ENOUGH TO *ME.*
SORRY TO BREAK IT TO YOU, FOOL.
TWIST
WHAT DO YOU WANNA DO?
YOU WANNA LET HER DIE?
NO!
THEN BE QUIET AND LET HER GO. SHE'S GOT ENOUGH TO DEAL WITH.
LET'S SHOW THEM YOU CAN HOLD YOUR OWN EVEN ON YOUR OWN.

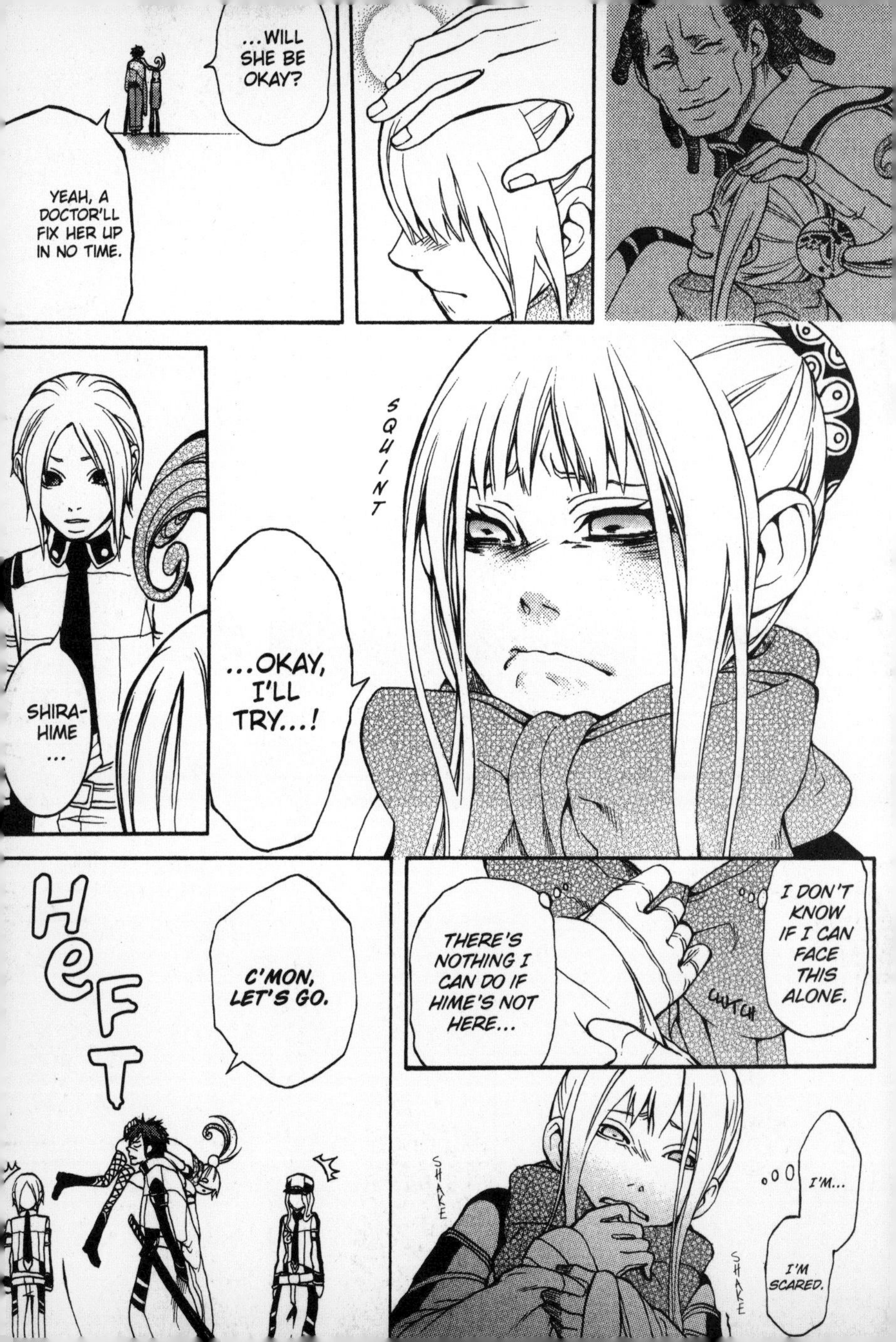
...WILL SHE BE OKAY?
YEAH, A DOCTOR'LL FIX HER UP IN NO TIME.
SQUINT
...OKAY, I'LL TRY...!
SHIRA-HIME ...
I DON'T KNOW IF I CAN FACE THIS ALONE.
THERE'S NOTHING I CAN DO IF HIME'S NOT HERE...
CLUTCH
I'M...
I'M SCARED.
SHAKE
SHAKE
C'MON, LET'S GO.
HEFT

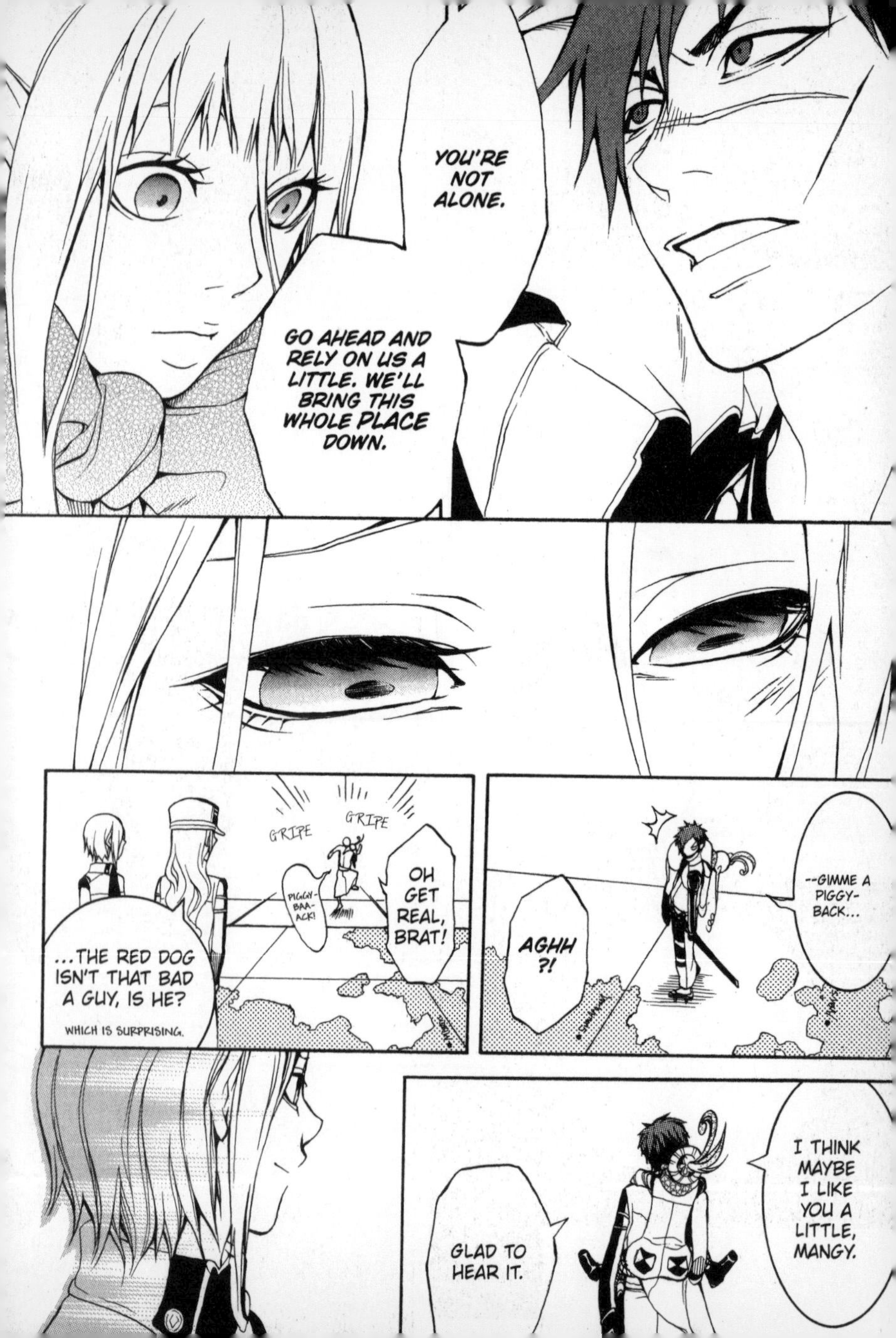
YOU'RE NOT ALONE.
GO AHEAD AND RELY ON US A LITTLE. WE'LL BRING THIS WHOLE PLACE DOWN.
--GIMME A PIGGY-BACK...
AGHH ?!
GRIPE
GRIPE
OH GET REAL, BRAT!
PIGGY-BAA-ACK!
...THE RED DOG ISN'T THAT BAD A GUY, IS HE?
WHICH IS SURPRISING.
I THINK MAYBE I LIKE YOU A LITTLE, MANGY.
GLAD TO HEAR IT.

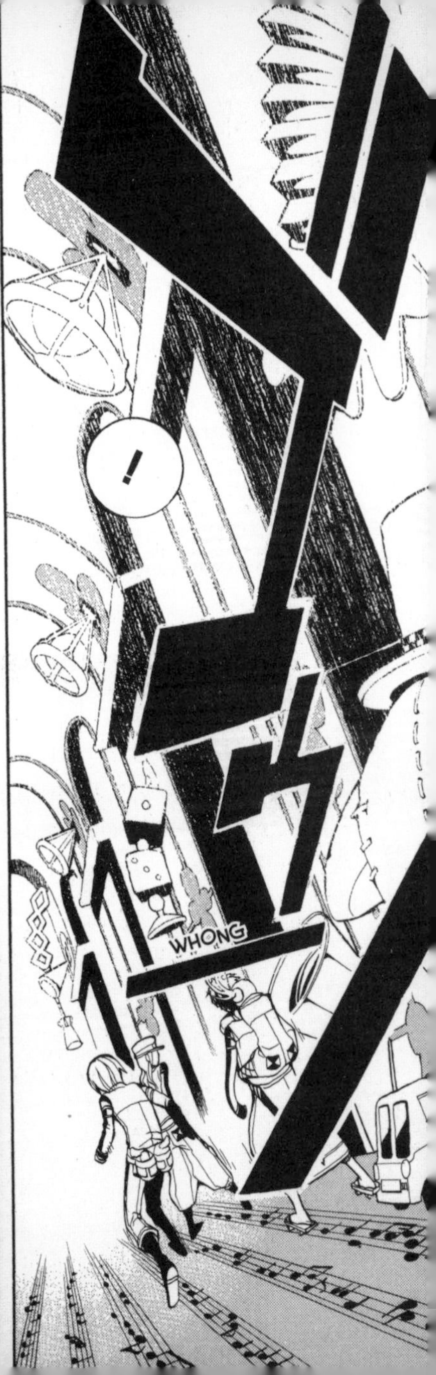
!
WHONG
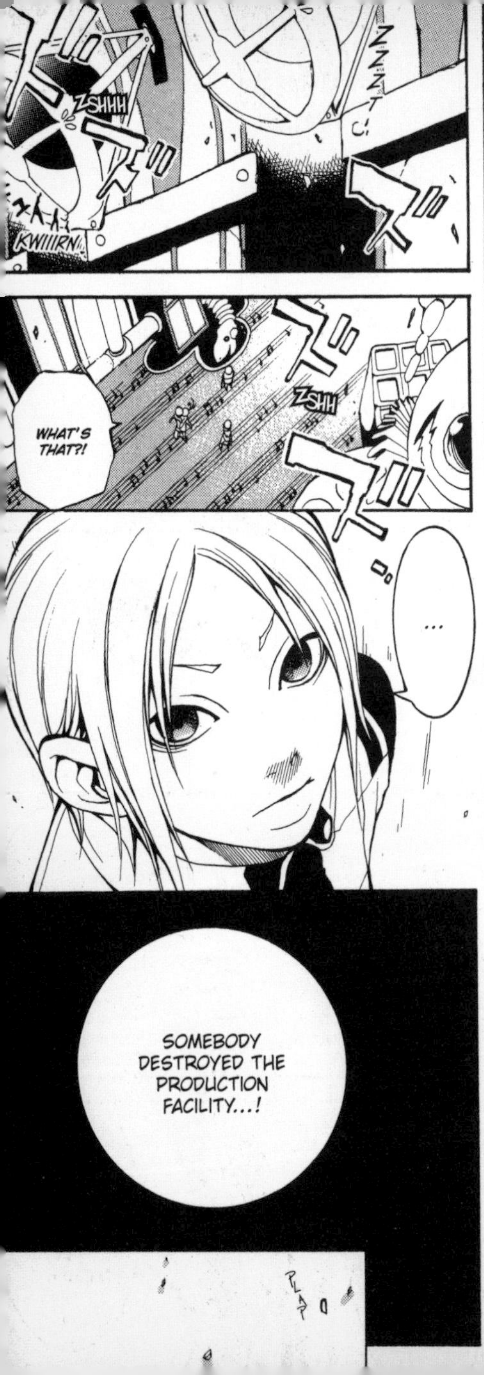
ZZZT
ZSHHH
KWIIIRN
ZSHH
WHAT'S THAT?!
...
SOMEBODY DESTROYED THE PRODUCTION FACILITY...!
PLAP

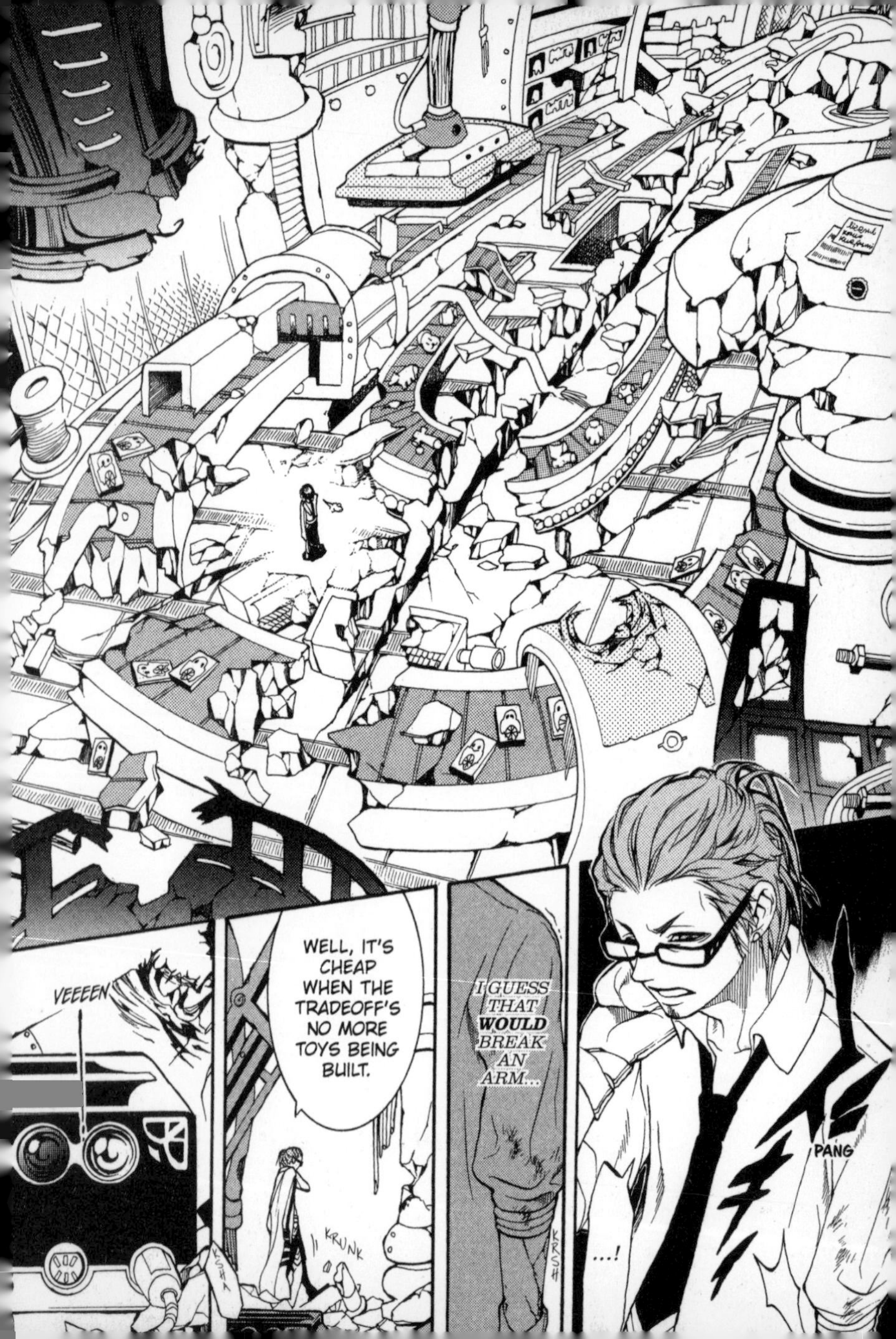
PANG
...!
I GUESS THAT WOULD BREAK AN ARM...
KRSH
WELL, IT'S CHEAP WHEN THE TRADEOFF'S NO MORE TOYS BEING BUILT.
KRUNK
KSHA
VEEEEN

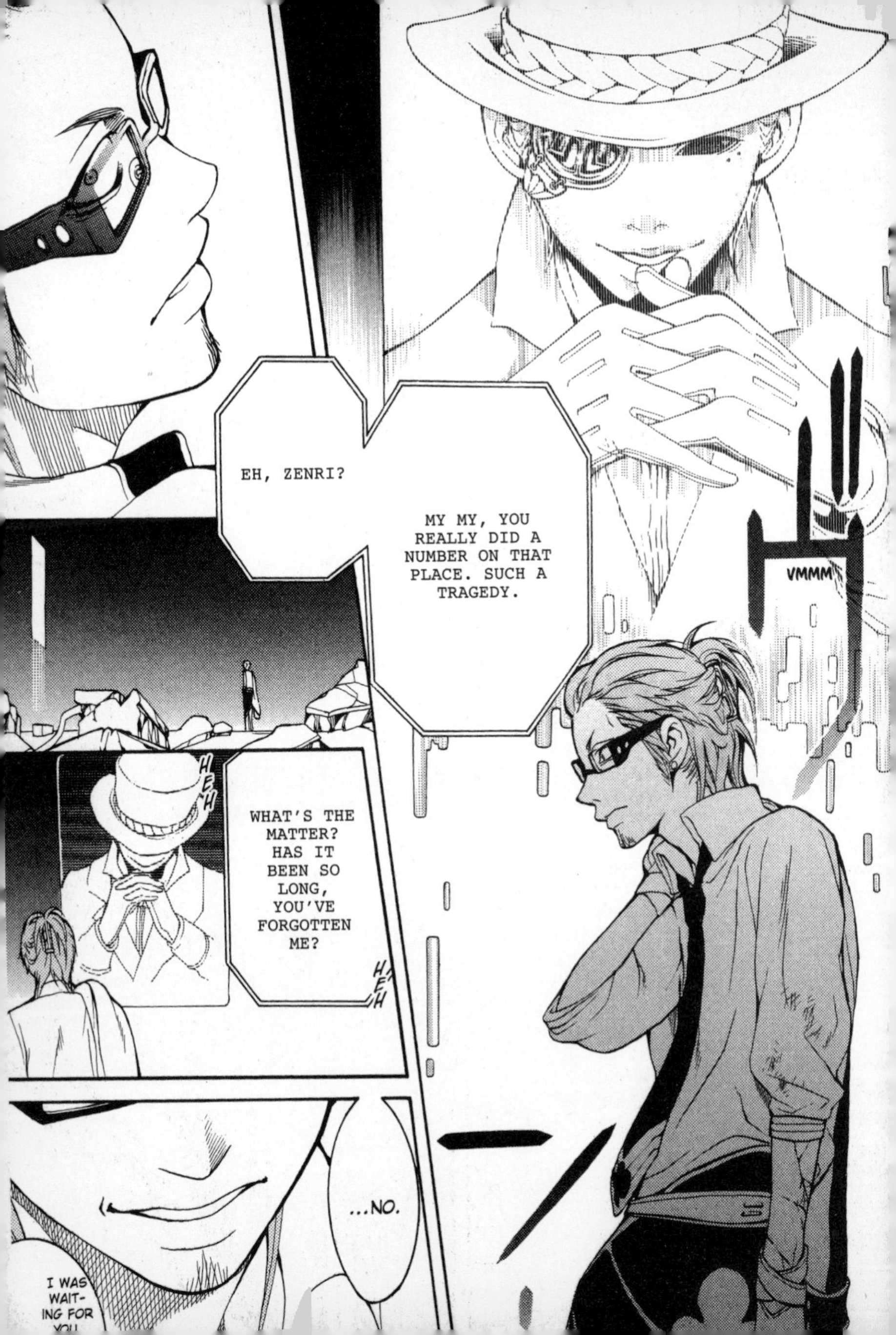
EH, ZENRI?
MY MY, YOU REALLY DID A NUMBER ON THAT PLACE. SUCH A TRAGEDY.
VMMM
HEH
WHAT'S THE MATTER? HAS IT BEEN SO LONG, YOU'VE FORGOTTEN ME?
HEH
...NO.
I WAS WAIT- ING FOR

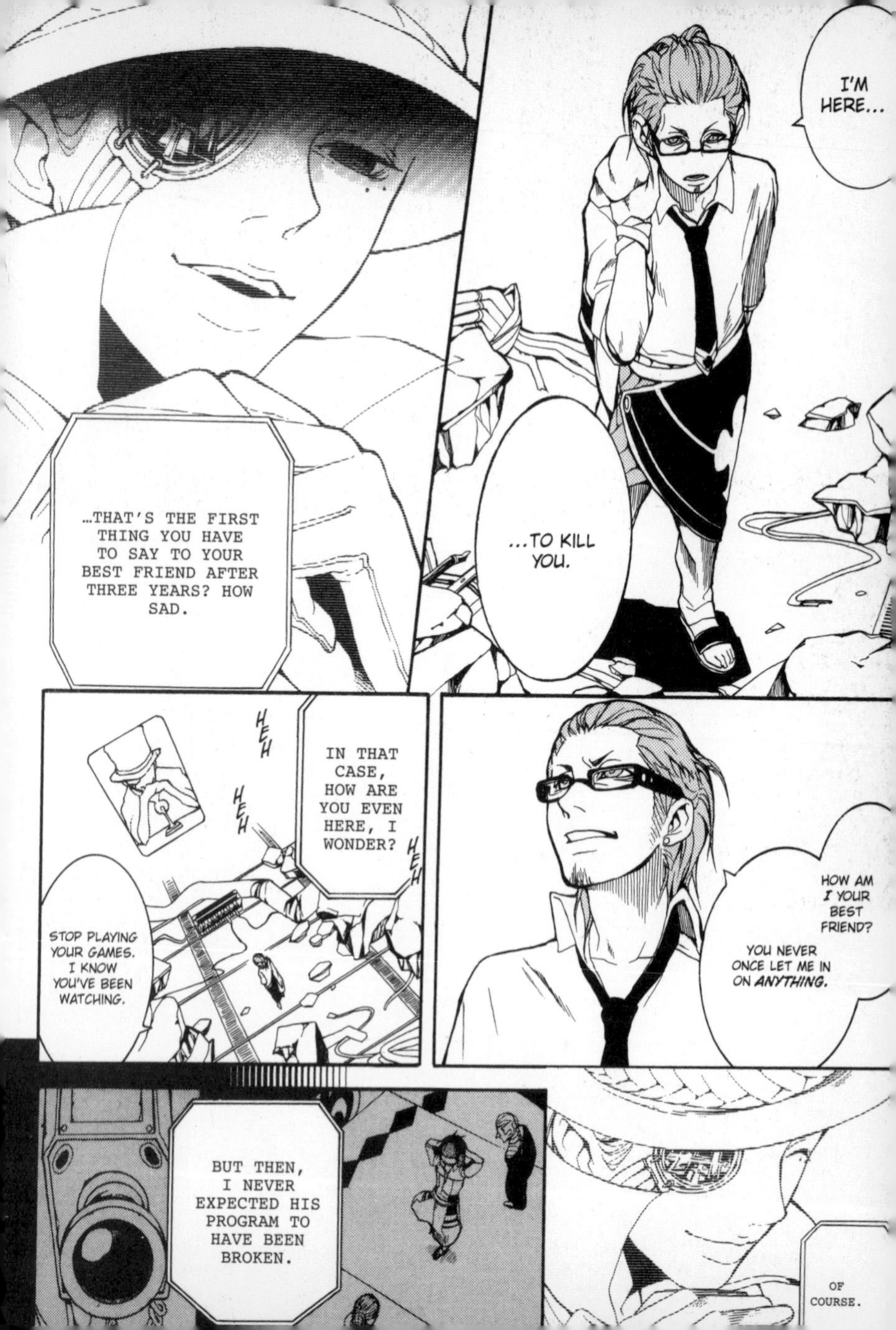
I'M HERE...
...TO KILL YOU.
...THAT'S THE FIRST THING YOU HAVE TO SAY TO YOUR BEST FRIEND AFTER THREE YEARS? HOW SAD.
HOW AM *I* YOUR BEST FRIEND?
YOU NEVER ONCE LET ME IN ON *ANYTHING*.
IN THAT CASE, HOW ARE YOU EVEN HERE, I WONDER?
HEH
HEH
HEH
STOP PLAYING YOUR GAMES. I KNOW YOU'VE BEEN WATCHING.
OF COURSE.
BUT THEN, I NEVER EXPECTED HIS PROGRAM TO HAVE BEEN BROKEN.

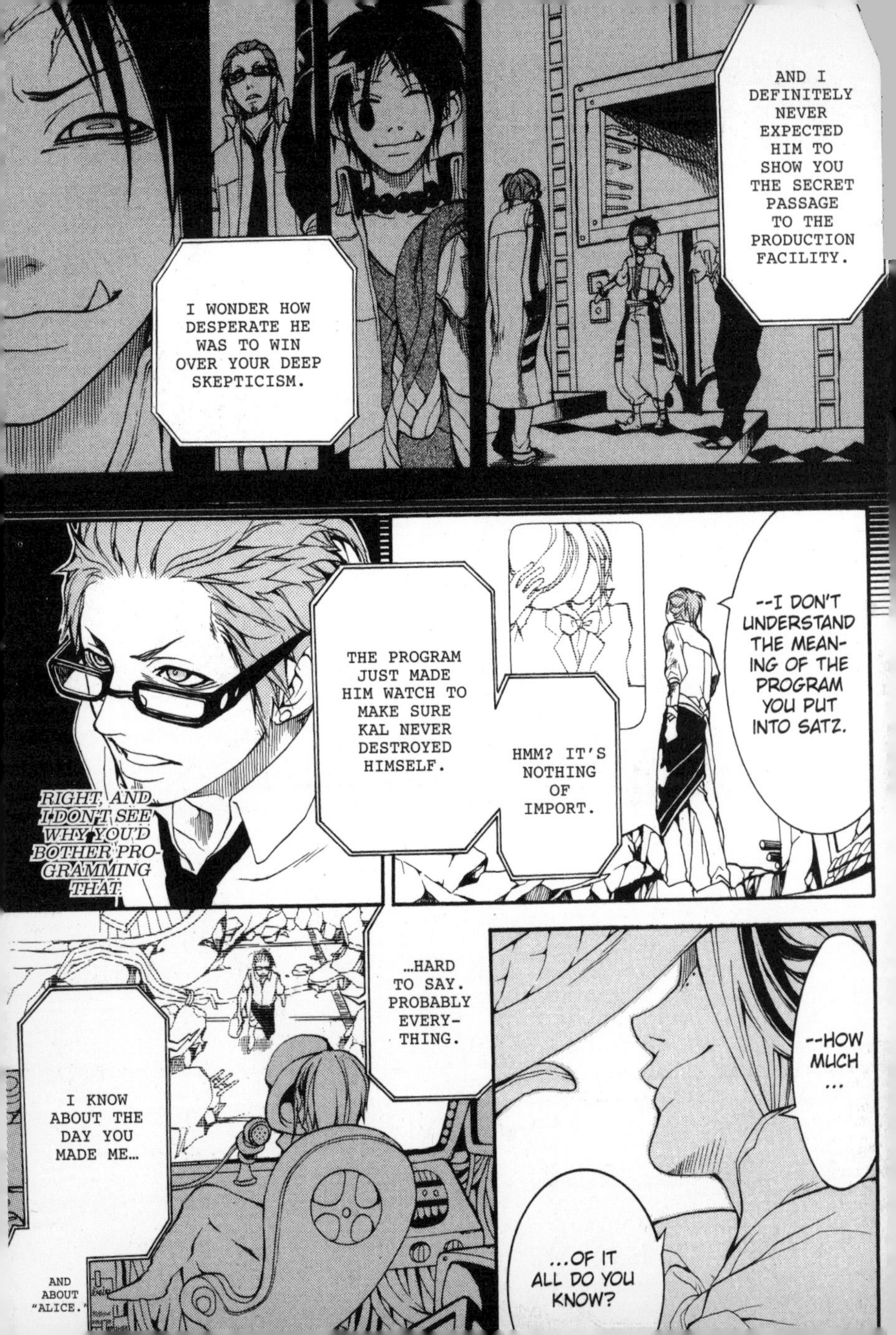

AND I DEFINITELY NEVER EXPECTED HIM TO SHOW YOU THE SECRET PASSAGE TO THE PRODUCTION FACILITY.
I WONDER HOW DESPERATE HE WAS TO WIN OVER YOUR DEEP SKEPTICISM.
--I DON'T UNDERSTAND THE MEANING OF THE PROGRAM YOU PUT INTO SATZ.
HMM? IT'S NOTHING OF IMPORT.
THE PROGRAM JUST MADE HIM WATCH TO MAKE SURE KAL NEVER DESTROYED HIMSELF.
RIGHT, AND I DON'T SEE WHY YOU'D BOTHER PROGRAMMING THAT.
--HOW MUCH ...
...OF IT ALL DO YOU KNOW?
...HARD TO SAY. PROBABLY EVERYTHING.
I KNOW ABOUT THE DAY YOU MADE ME...
AND ABOUT "ALICE."

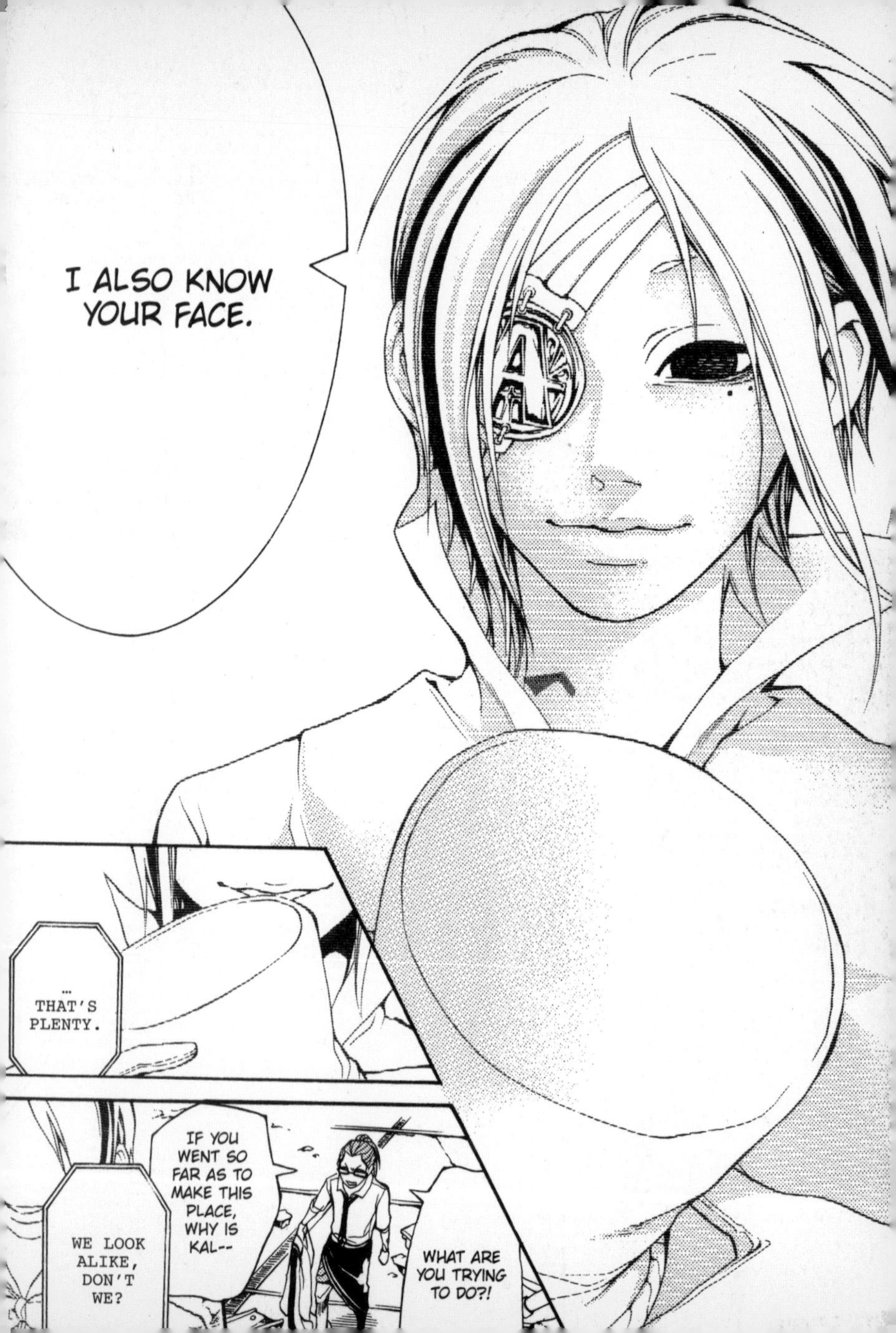
I ALSO KNOW YOUR FACE.
... THAT'S PLENTY.
WHAT ARE YOU TRYING TO DO?!
IF YOU WENT SO FAR AS TO MAKE THIS PLACE, WHY IS KAL--
WE LOOK ALIKE, DON'T WE?

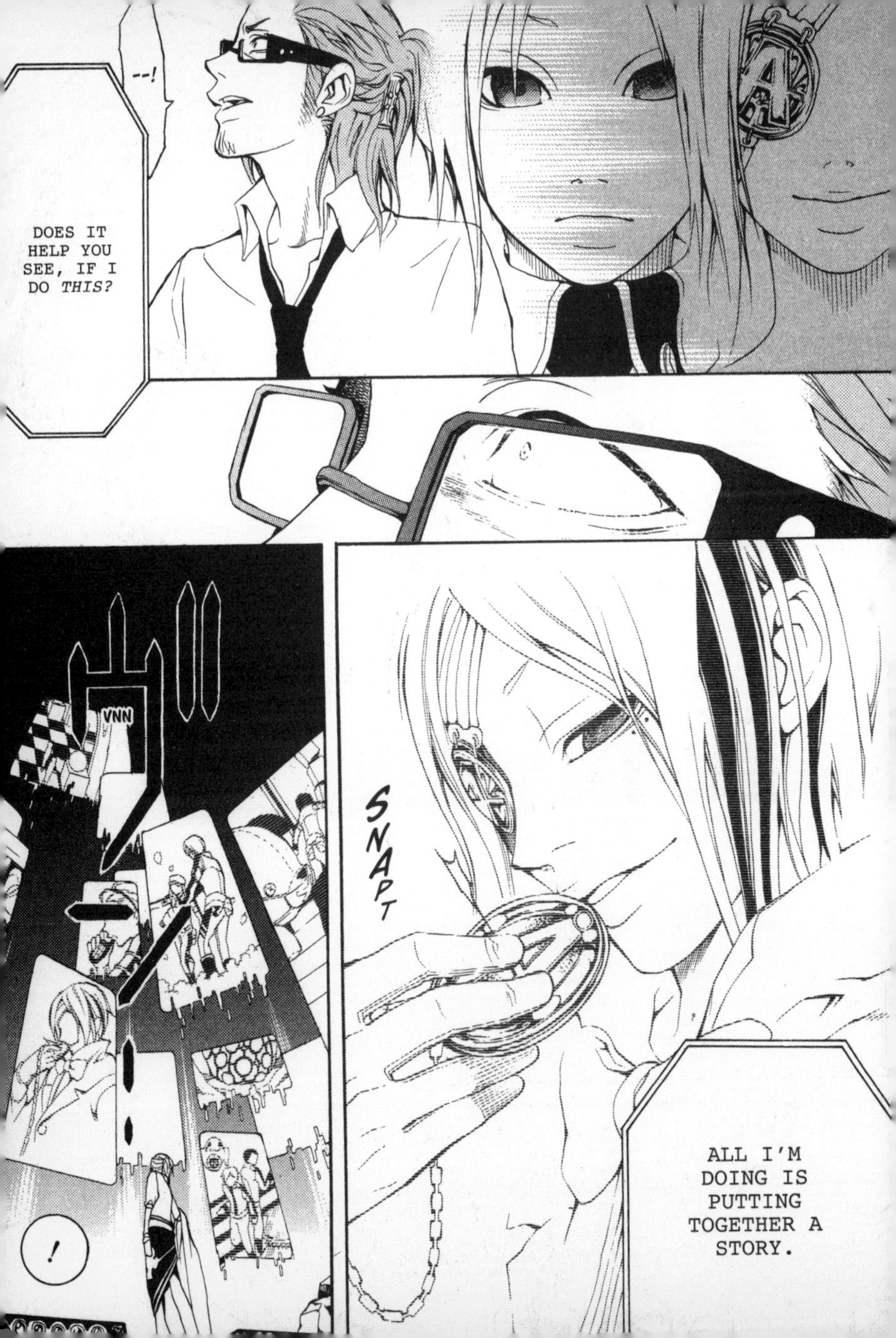
--!
DOES IT HELP YOU SEE, IF I DO THIS?
SNAPT
ALL I'M DOING IS PUTTING TOGETHER A STORY.
VNN
!

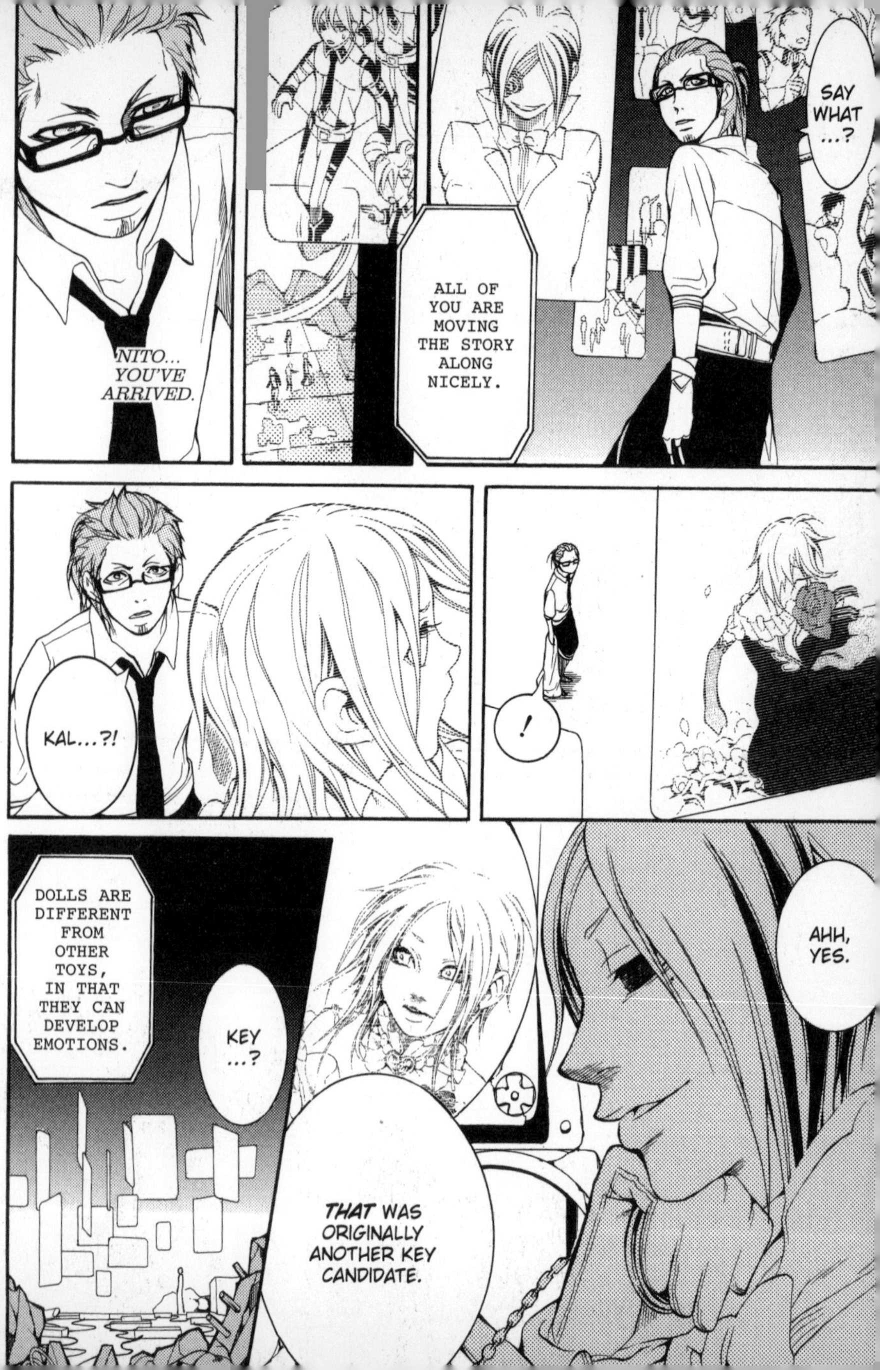
SAY WHAT ...?
ALL OF YOU ARE MOVING THE STORY ALONG NICELY.
NITO... YOU'VE ARRIVED.
!
KAL...?!
AHH, YES.
THAT WAS ORIGINALLY ANOTHER KEY CANDIDATE.
KEY ...?
DOLLS ARE DIFFERENT FROM OTHER TOYS, IN THAT THEY CAN DEVELOP EMOTIONS.

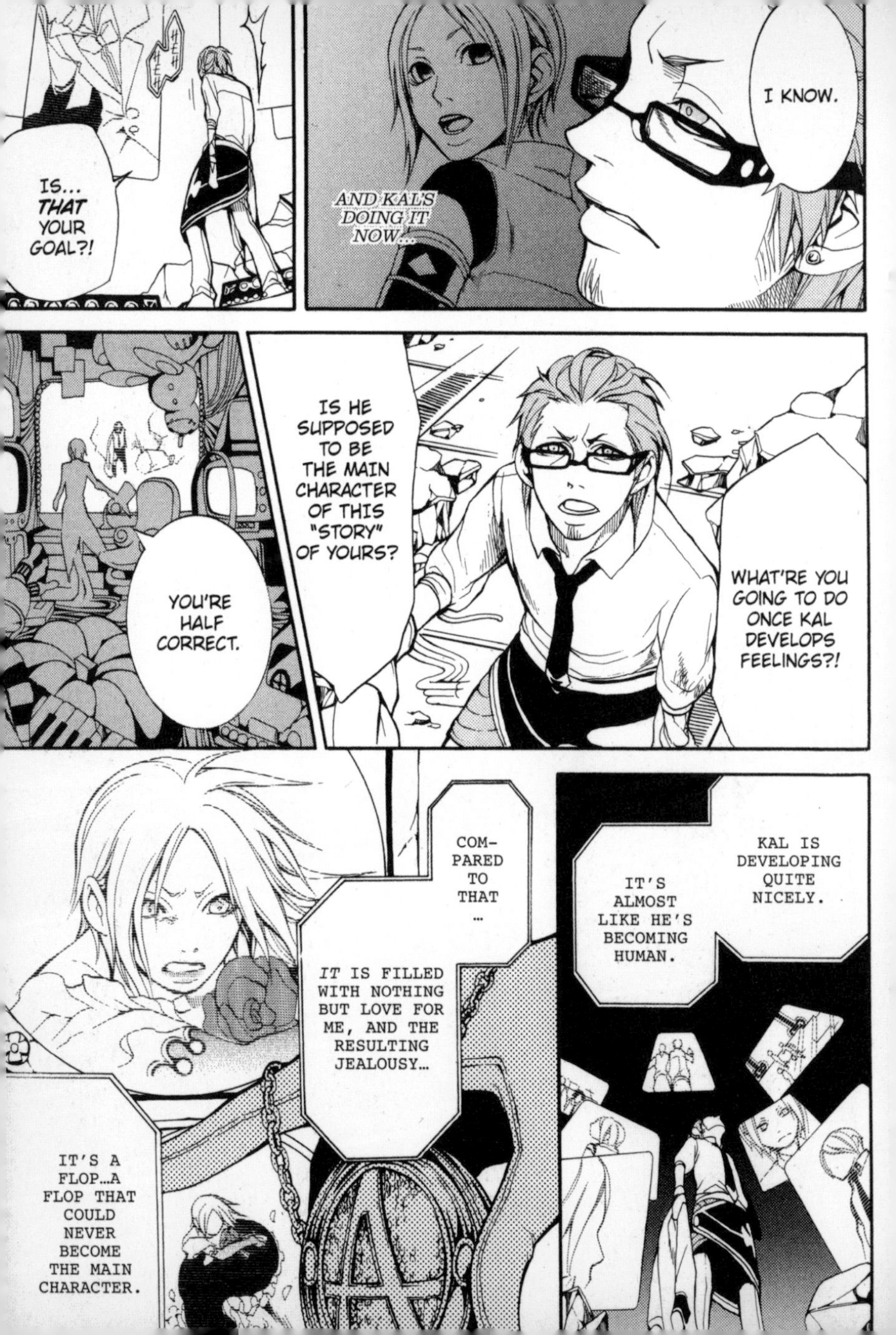
I KNOW.
AND KAL'S DOING IT NOW...
HEH HEH
IS... *THAT* YOUR GOAL?!
WHAT'RE YOU GOING TO DO ONCE KAL DEVELOPS FEELINGS?!
IS HE SUPPOSED TO BE THE MAIN CHARACTER OF THIS "STORY" OF YOURS?
YOU'RE HALF CORRECT.
KAL IS DEVELOPING QUITE NICELY.
IT'S ALMOST LIKE HE'S BECOMING HUMAN.
COM-PARED TO THAT ...
IT IS FILLED WITH NOTHING BUT LOVE FOR ME, AND THE RESULTING JEALOUSY...
IT'S A FLOP...A FLOP THAT COULD NEVER BECOME THE MAIN CHARACTER.

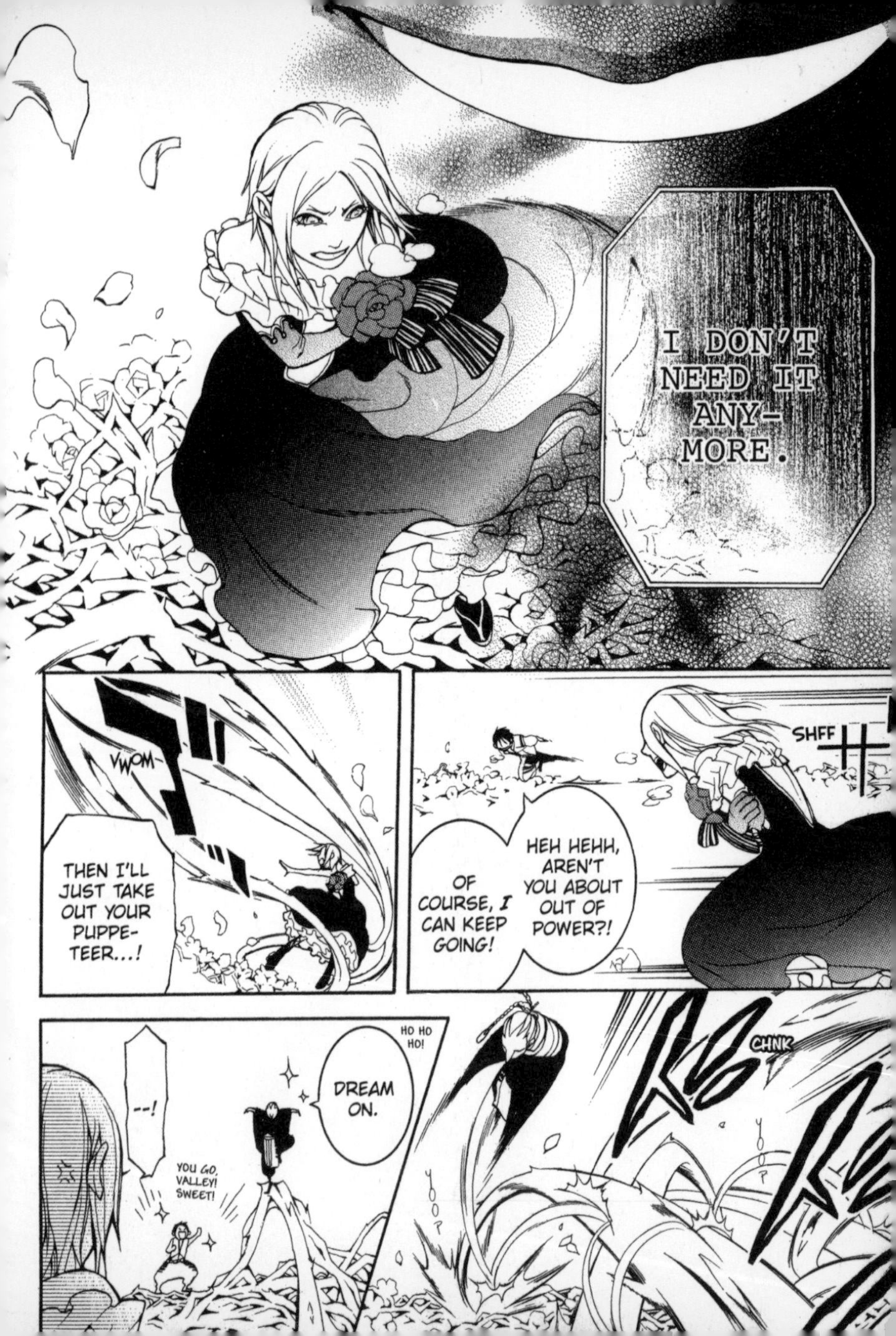

I DON'T NEED IT ANY-MORE.
SHFF
HEH HEHH, AREN'T YOU ABOUT OUT OF POWER?!
OF COURSE, I CAN KEEP GOING!
VWOM-
THEN I'LL JUST TAKE OUT YOUR PUPPE-TEER...!
CHNK
YOOP
YOOP
HO HO HO!
DREAM ON.
--!
YOU GO, VALLEY! SWEET!

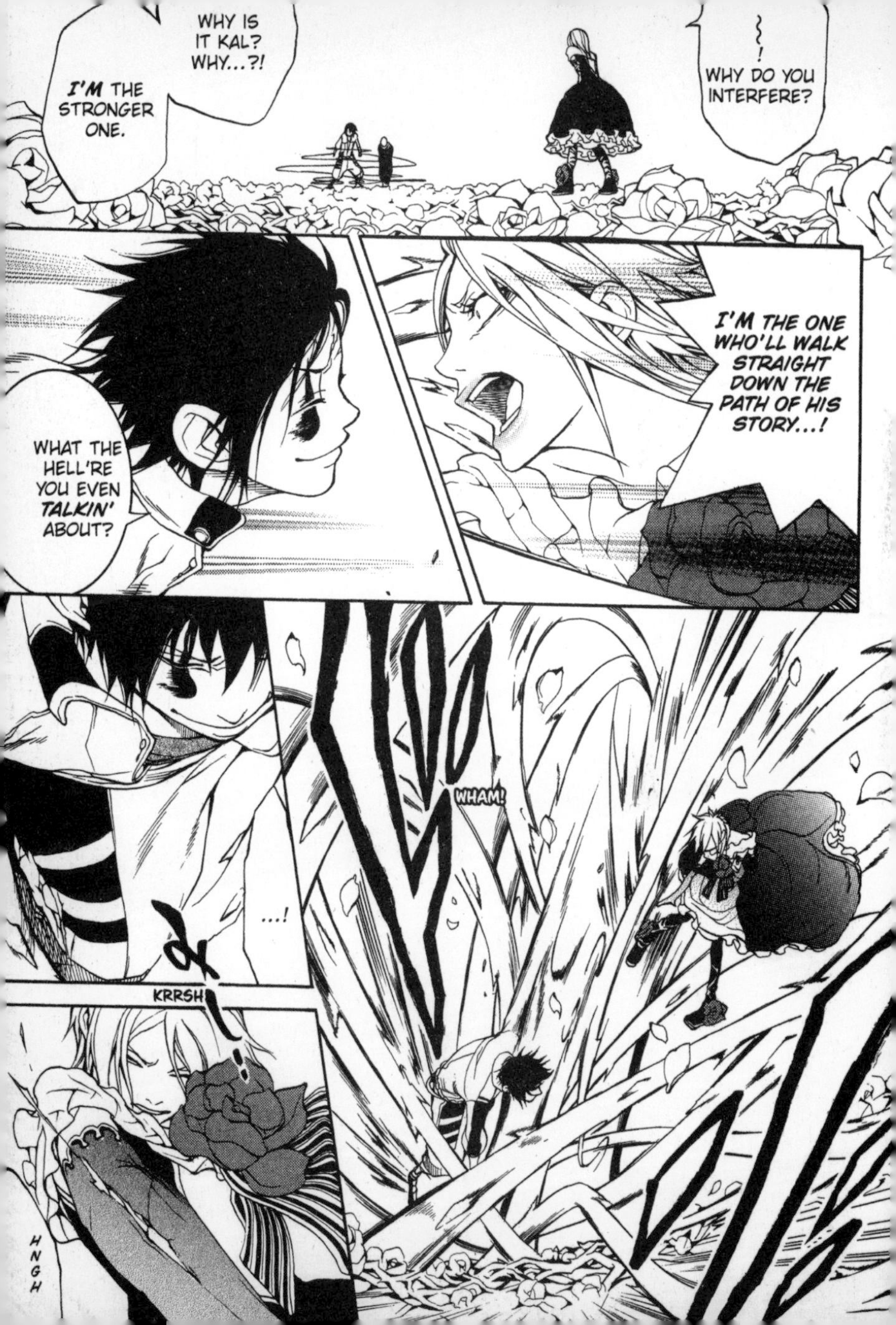

WHY DO YOU INTERFERE?
WHY IS IT KAL? WHY...?!
I'M THE STRONGER ONE.
I'M THE ONE WHO'LL WALK STRAIGHT DOWN THE PATH OF HIS STORY...!
WHAT THE HELL'RE YOU EVEN TALKIN' ABOUT?
WHAM!
...!
KRRSH
HNGH

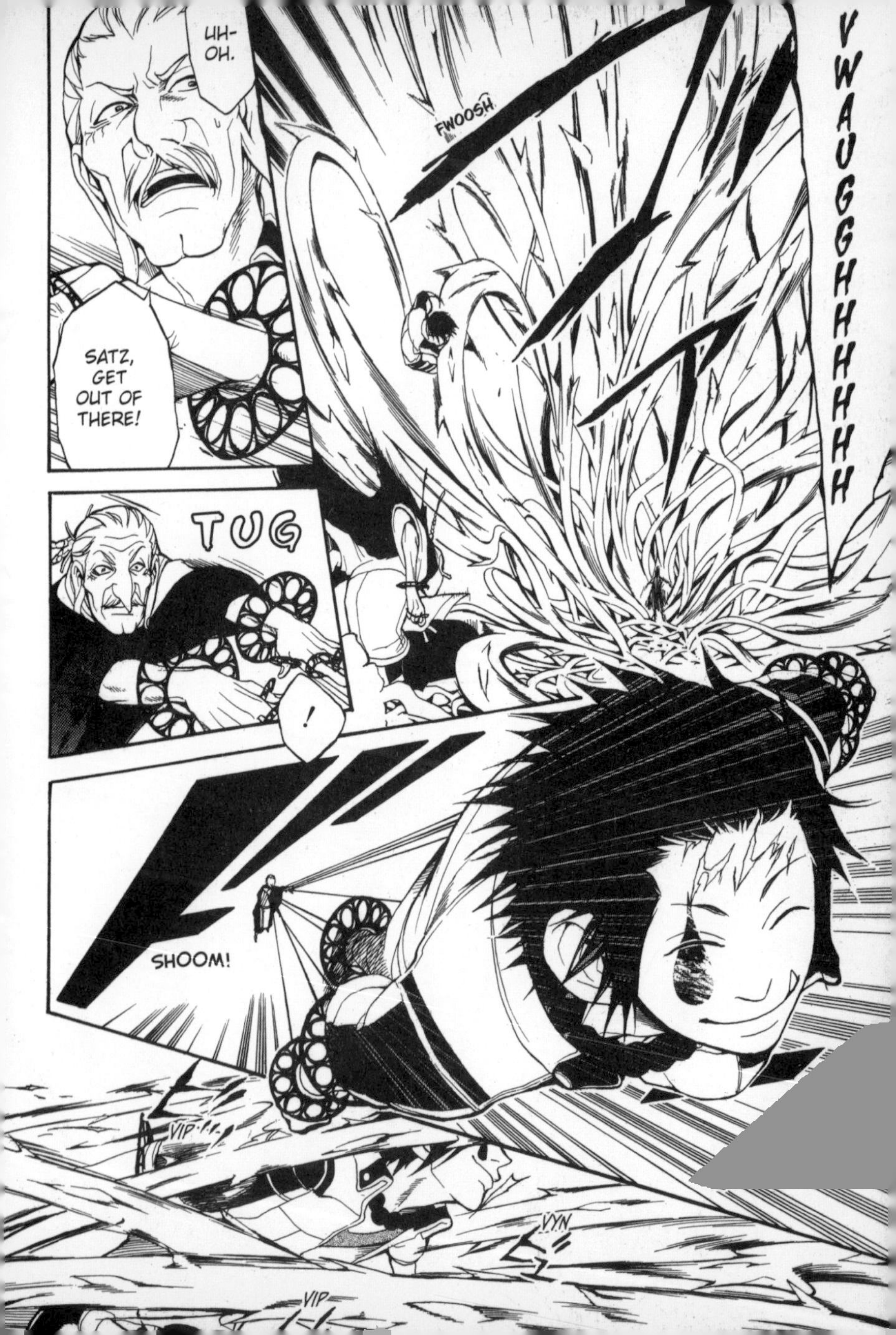
VWAUGGHHHHHHH
FWOOSH
UH-OH.
SATZ, GET OUT OF THERE!
TUG
!
SHOOM!
VIP
VYN
VIP

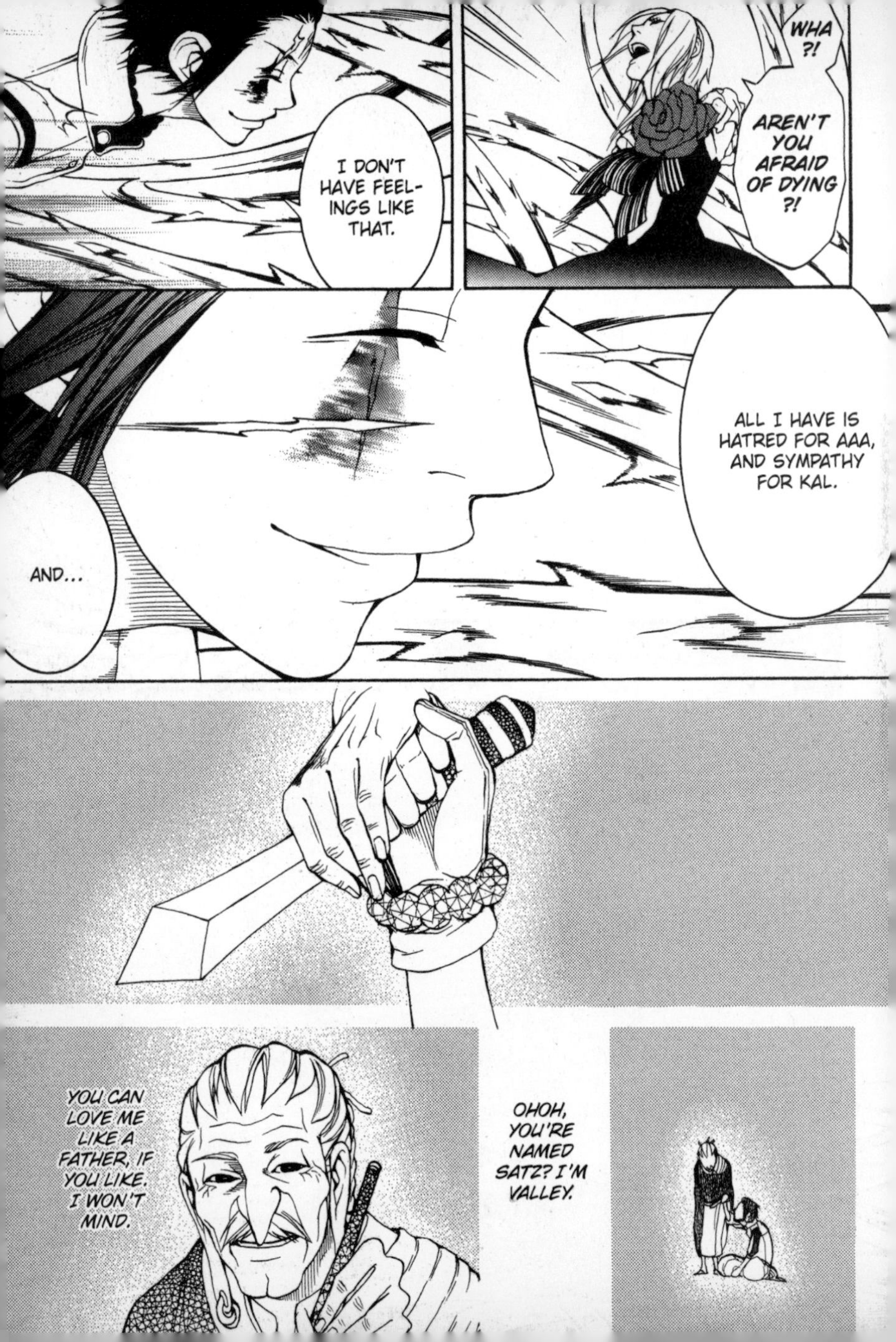
WHA ?!
AREN'T YOU AFRAID OF DYING ?!
I DON'T HAVE FEEL-INGS LIKE THAT.
ALL I HAVE IS HATRED FOR AAA, AND SYMPATHY FOR KAL.
AND...
OHOH, YOU'RE NAMED SATZ? I'M VALLEY.
YOU CAN LOVE ME LIKE A FATHER, IF YOU LIKE. I WON'T MIND.

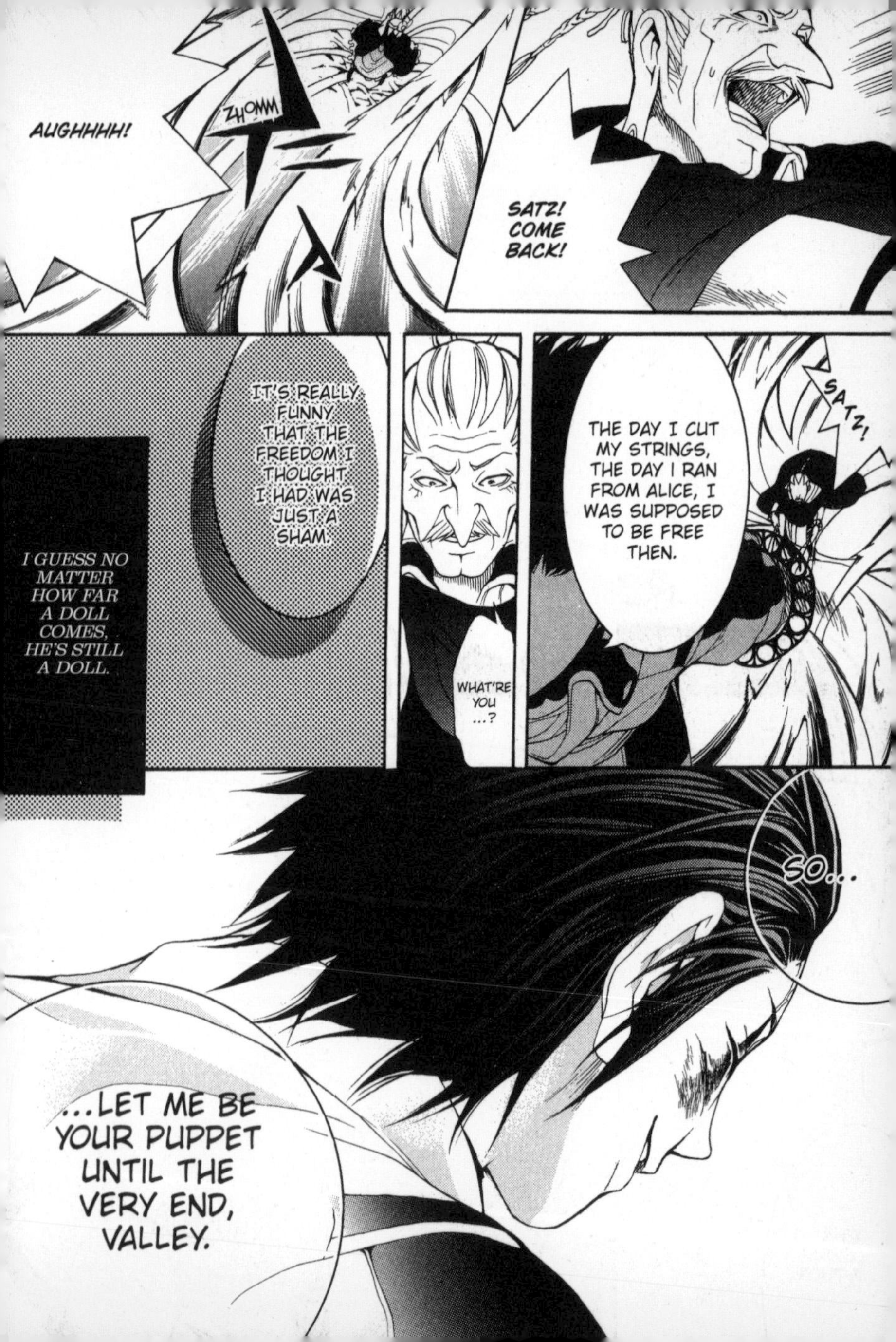
SATZ! COME BACK!
ZHOMM
AUGHHHH!
SATZ!
THE DAY I CUT MY STRINGS, THE DAY I RAN FROM ALICE, I WAS SUPPOSED TO BE FREE THEN.
WHAT'RE YOU ...?
IT'S REALLY FUNNY THAT THE FREEDOM I THOUGHT I HAD WAS JUST A SHAM.
I GUESS NO MATTER HOW FAR A DOLL COMES, HE'S STILL A DOLL.
SO...
...LET ME BE YOUR PUPPET UNTIL THE VERY END, VALLEY.

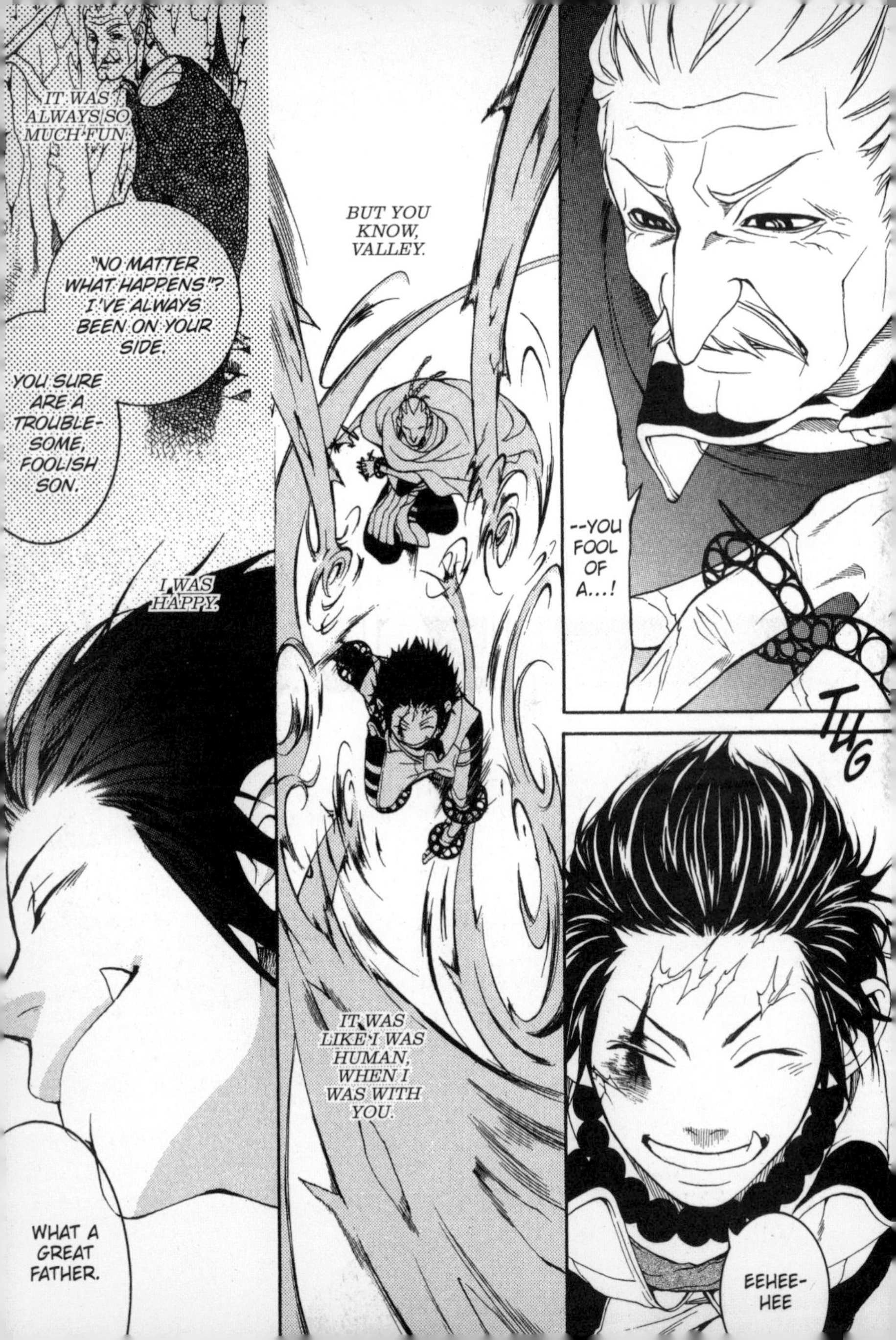
--YOU FOOL OF A...!
TUG
EEHEE-HEE
BUT YOU KNOW, VALLEY.
IT WAS LIKE I WAS HUMAN, WHEN I WAS WITH YOU.
IT WAS ALWAYS SO MUCH FUN.
"NO MATTER WHAT HAPPENS"? I'VE ALWAYS BEEN ON YOUR SIDE.
YOU SURE ARE A TROUBLE-SOME, FOOLISH SON.
I WAS HAPPY.
WHAT A GREAT FATHER.

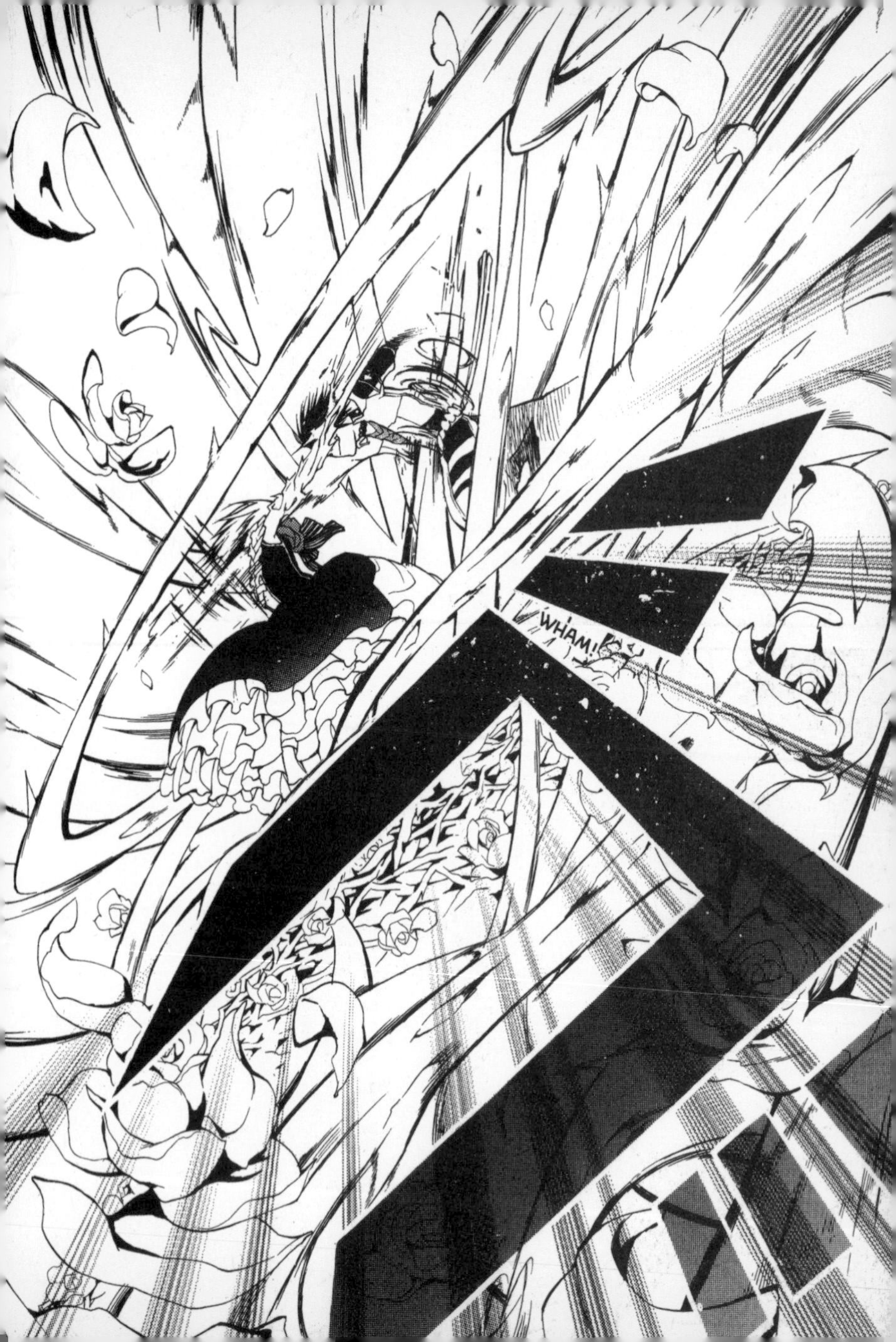
WHAM!

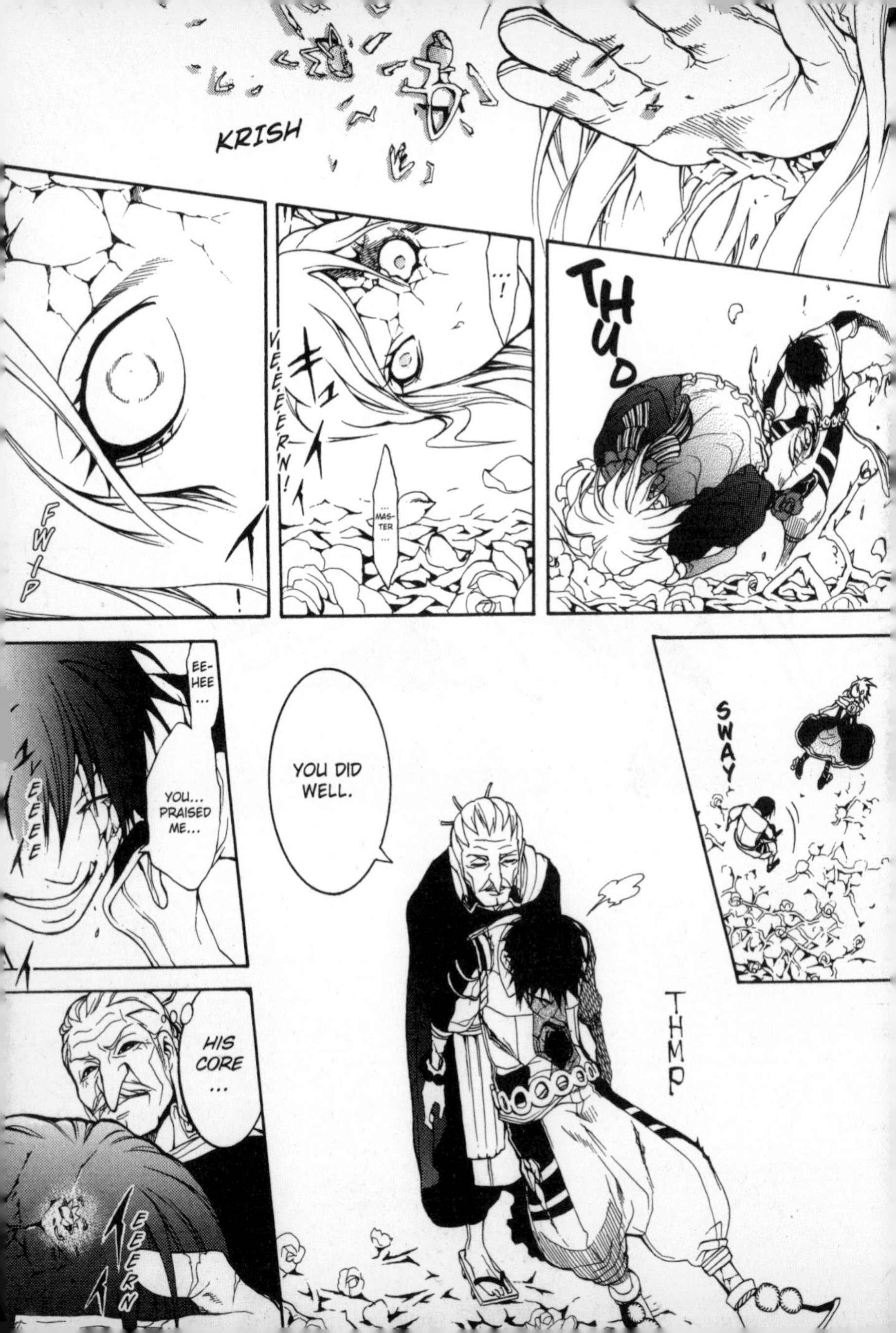

KRISH
THUD
...!
...MASTER...
VEEEERN!
FWIP
SWAY
THMP
YOU DID WELL.
EE-HEE...
YOU... PRAISED ME...
VEEEEE
HIS CORE...
EEERN

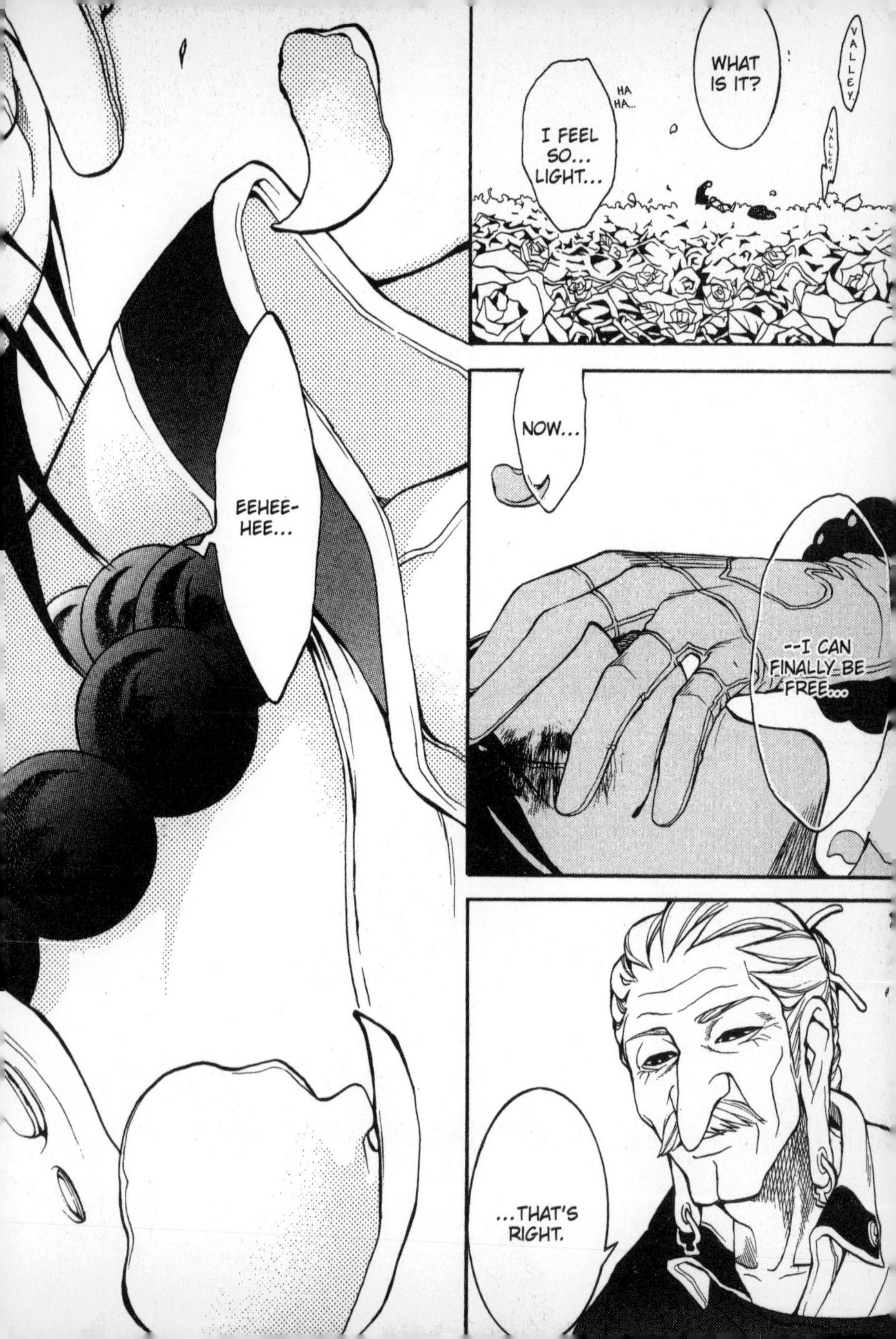
VALLEY.
WHAT IS IT?
VALLEY.
HA HA..
I FEEL SO... LIGHT...
NOW...
--I CAN FINALLY BE FREE...
...THAT'S RIGHT.
EEHEE-HEE...

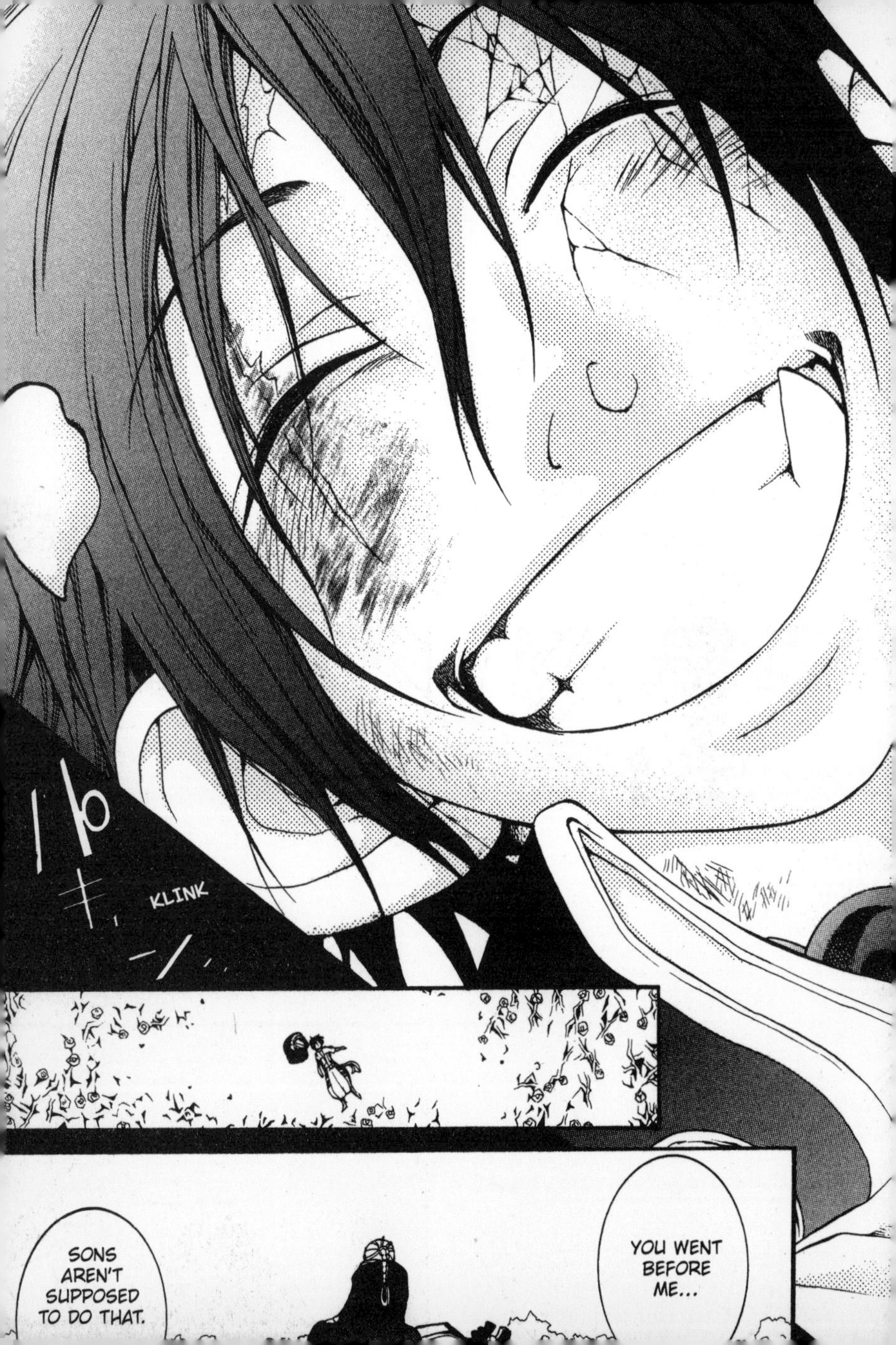
KLINK
YOU WENT BEFORE ME...
SONS AREN'T SUPPOSED TO DO THAT.

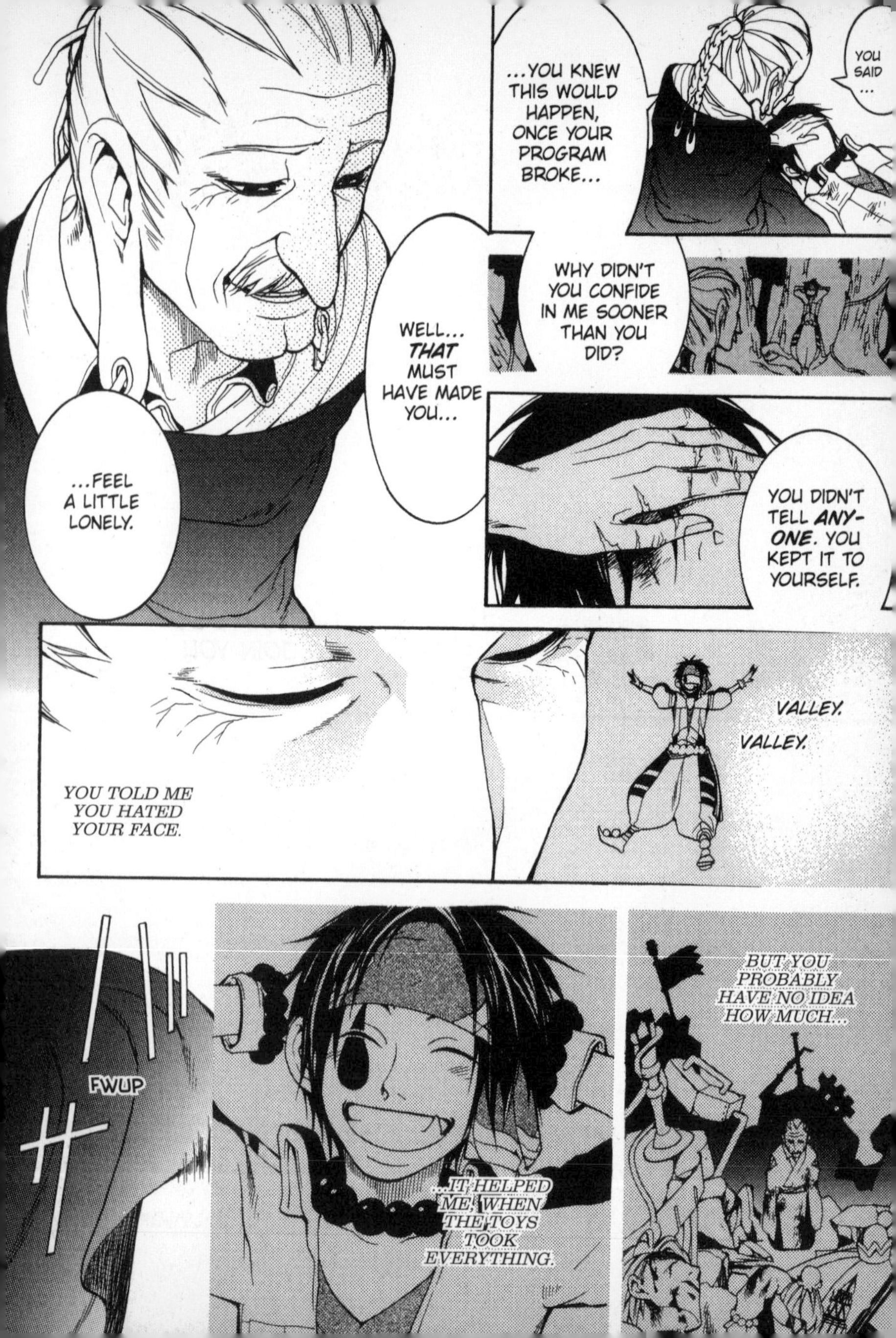
YOU SAID ...
...YOU KNEW THIS WOULD HAPPEN, ONCE YOUR PROGRAM BROKE...
WHY DIDN'T YOU CONFIDE IN ME SOONER THAN YOU DID?
YOU DIDN'T TELL ANY-ONE. YOU KEPT IT TO YOURSELF.
WELL... THAT MUST HAVE MADE YOU...
...FEEL A LITTLE LONELY.
VALLEY.
VALLEY.
YOU TOLD ME YOU HATED YOUR FACE.
BUT YOU PROBABLY HAVE NO IDEA HOW MUCH...
...IT HELPED ME, WHEN THE TOYS TOOK EVERYTHING.
FWUP

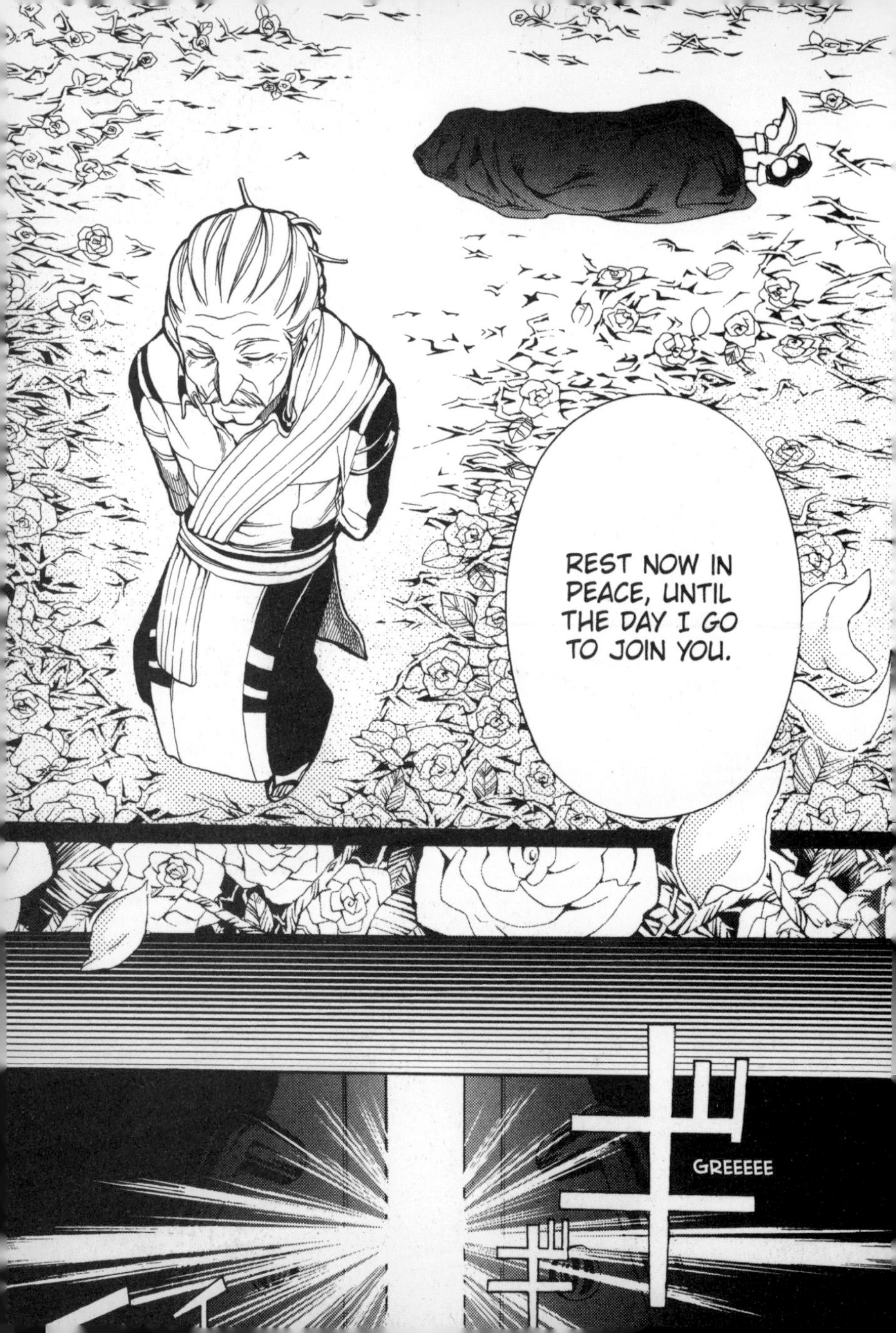
REST NOW IN PEACE, UNTIL THE DAY I GO TO JOIN YOU.
GREEEEE

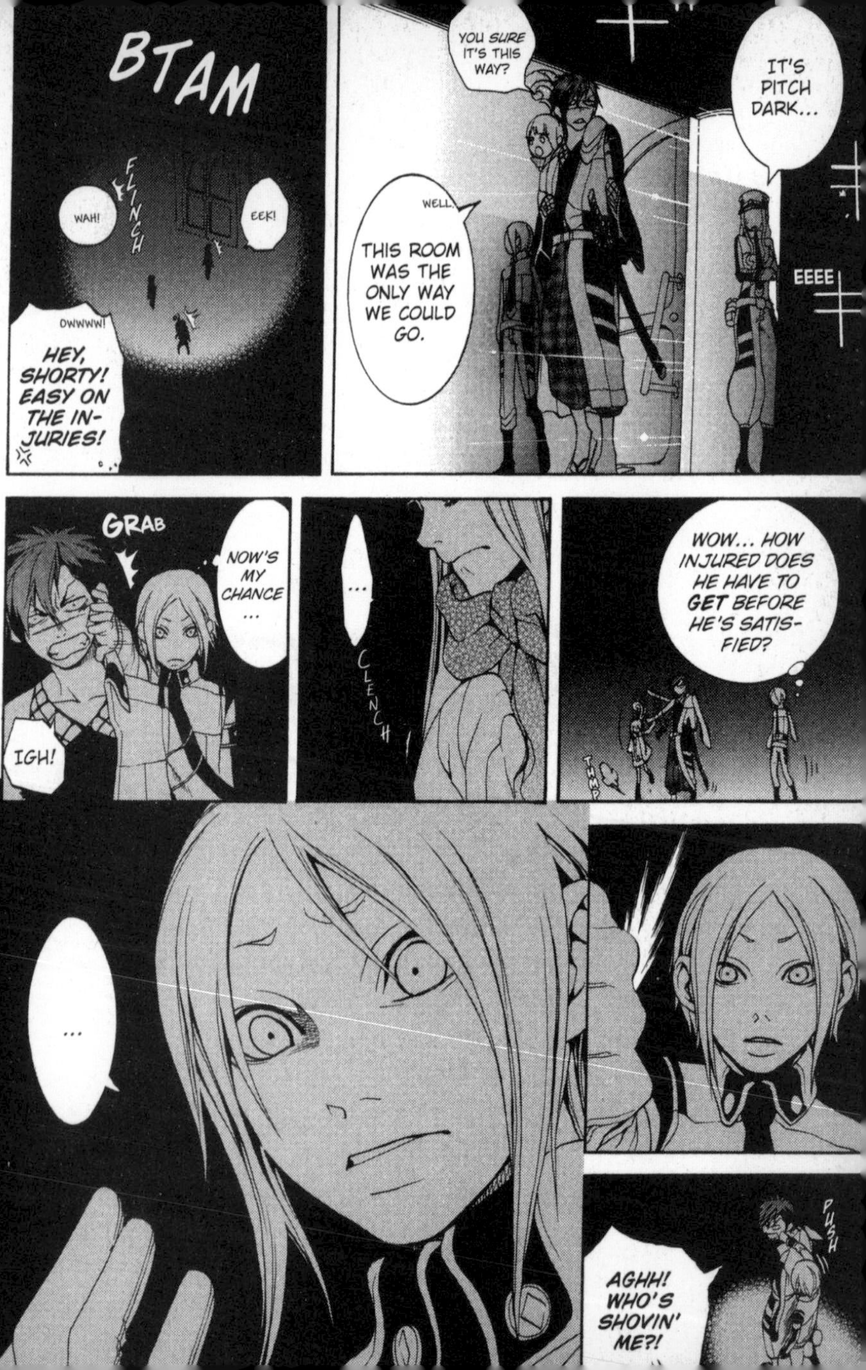

IT'S PITCH DARK...
YOU SURE IT'S THIS WAY?
EEEE
WELL.
THIS ROOM WAS THE ONLY WAY WE COULD GO.
BTAM
FLINCH
EEK!
WAH!
OWWWW!
HEY, SHORTY! EASY ON THE IN-JURIES!
WOW... HOW INJURED DOES HE HAVE TO GET BEFORE HE'S SATIS-FIED?
THMP
...
CLENCH
GRAB
NOW'S MY CHANCE...
IGH!
PUSH
AGHH! WHO'S SHOVIN' ME?!
...

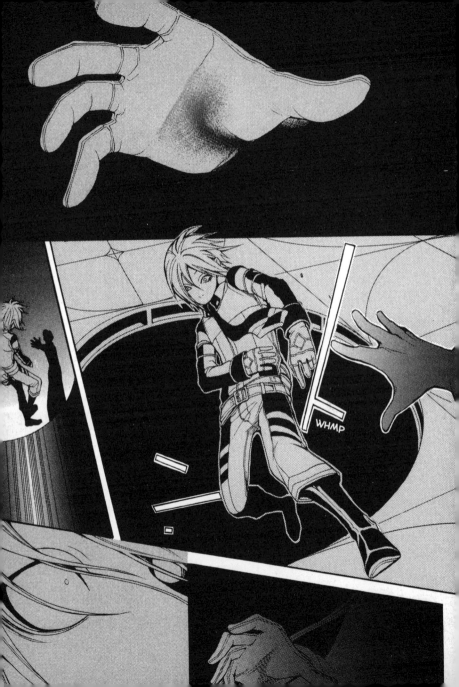

WHMP

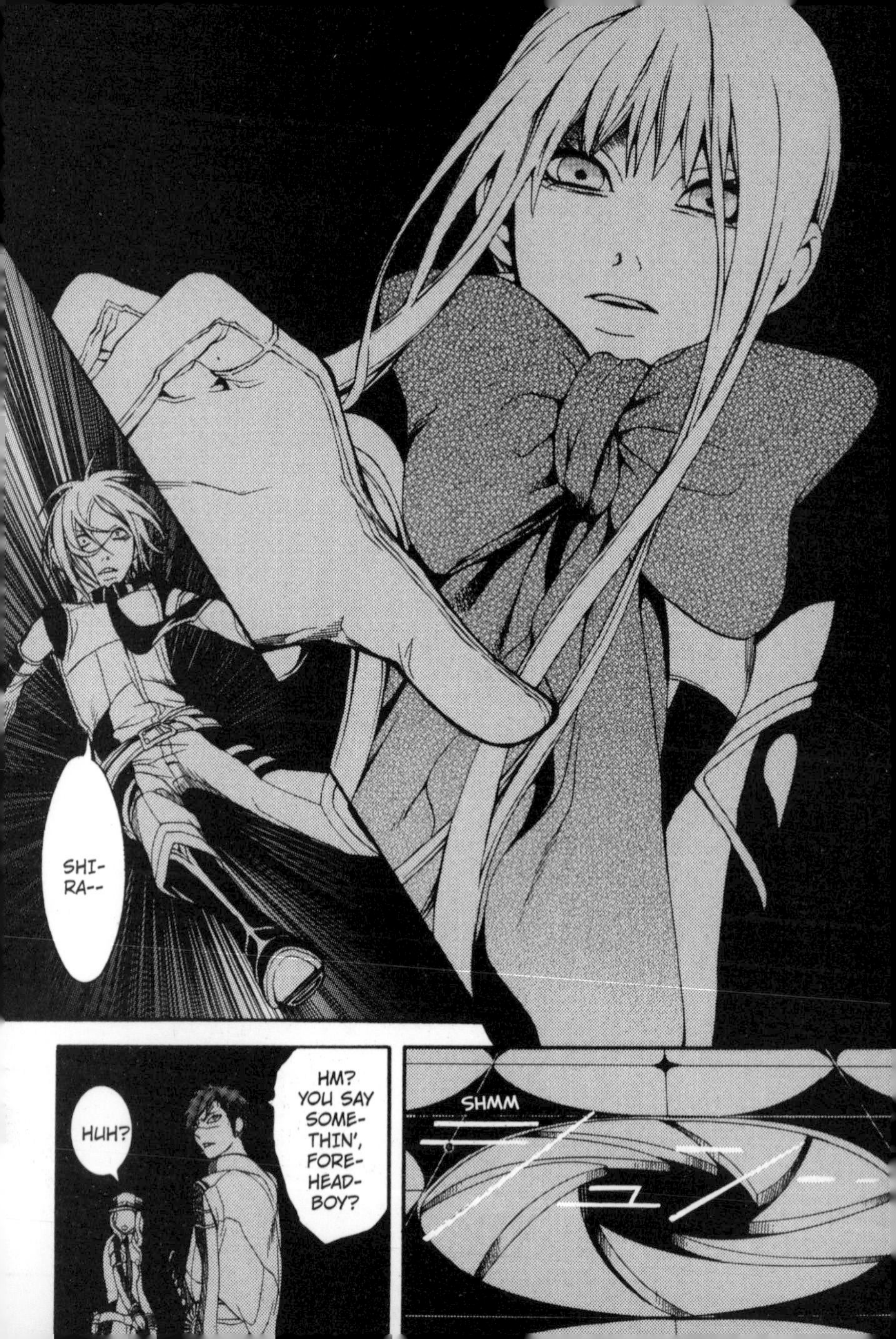
SHI-RA--
SHMM
HM? YOU SAY SOMETHIN', FORE-HEAD-BOY?
HUH?

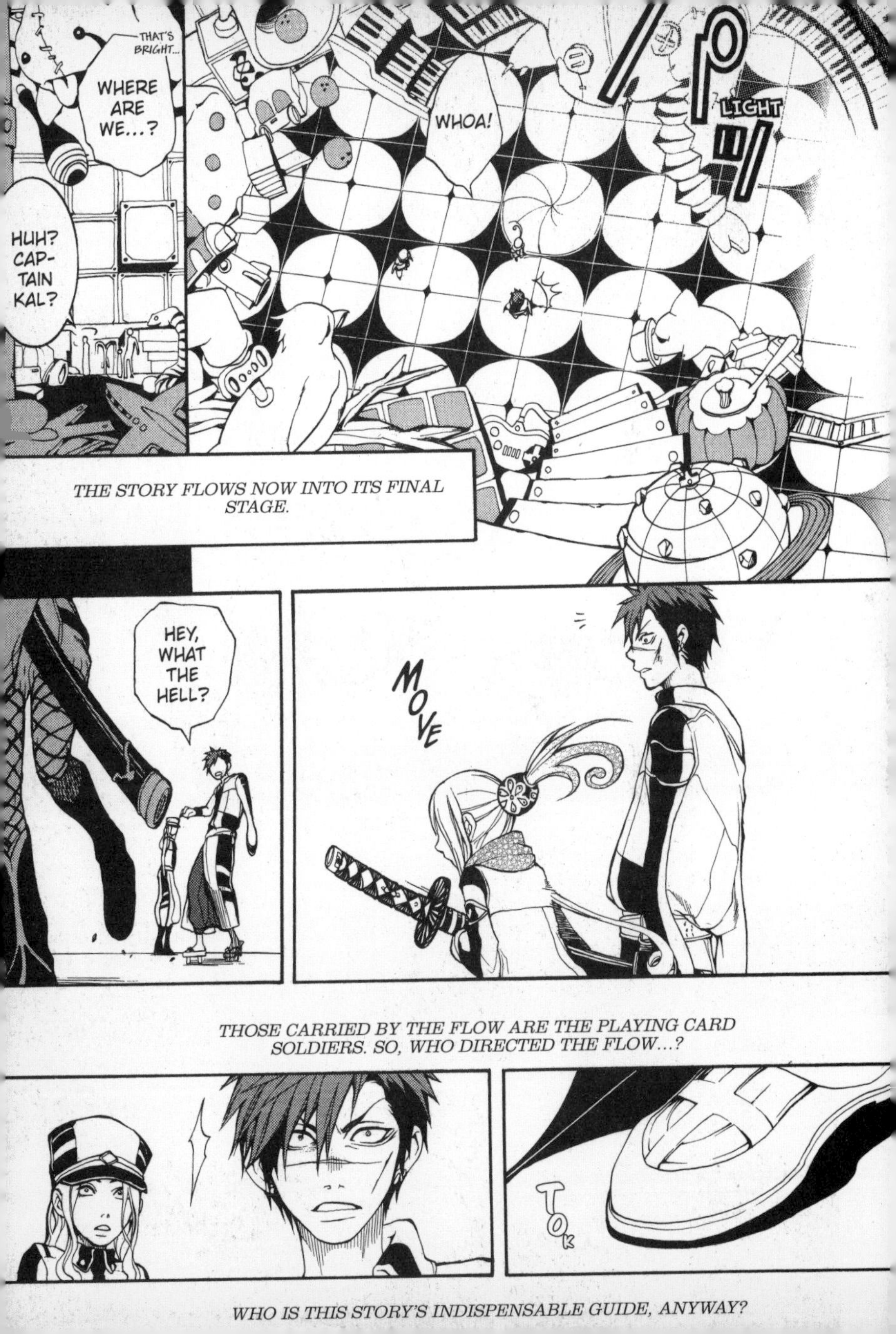

WHOA!
LIGHT
THE STORY FLOWS NOW INTO ITS FINAL STAGE.
THAT'S BRIGHT...
WHERE ARE WE...?
HUH? CAP-TAIN KAL?
MOVE
HEY, WHAT THE HELL?
THOSE CARRIED BY THE FLOW ARE THE PLAYING CARD SOLDIERS. SO, WHO DIRECTED THE FLOW...?
TOK
WHO IS THIS STORY'S INDISPENSABLE GUIDE, ANYWAY?

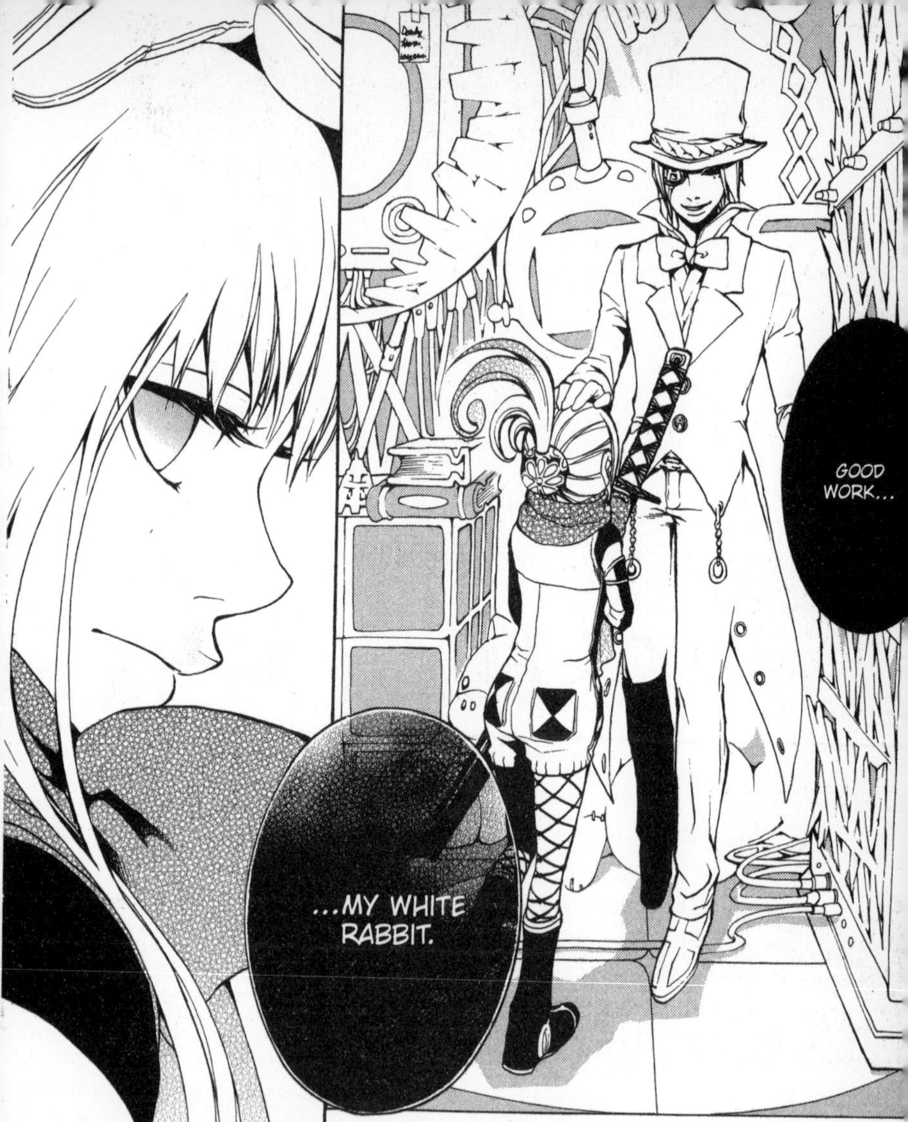
GOOD WORK...
...MY WHITE RABBIT.

THE ENDING HAD BEEN PLANNED EVER SINCE THE START.

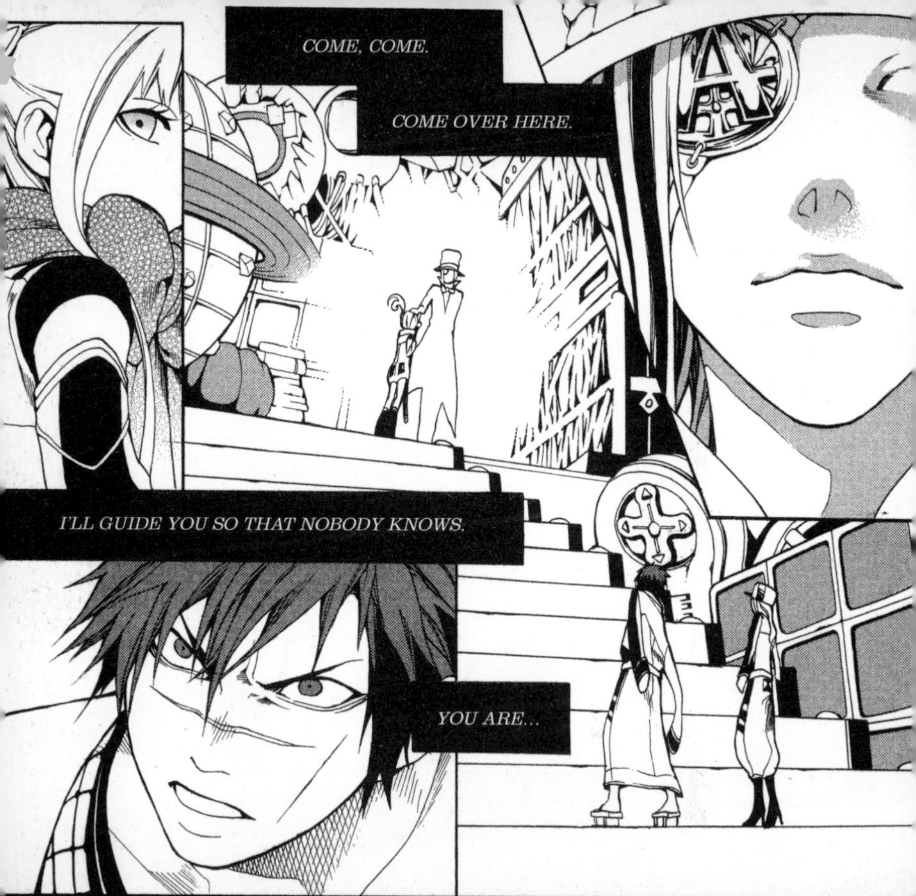
COME, COME.
COME OVER HERE.
I'LL GUIDE YOU SO THAT NOBODY KNOWS.
YOU ARE...

CARD 14: A JOB FOR THE WHITE RABBIT

card:14 白うさぎのお仕事

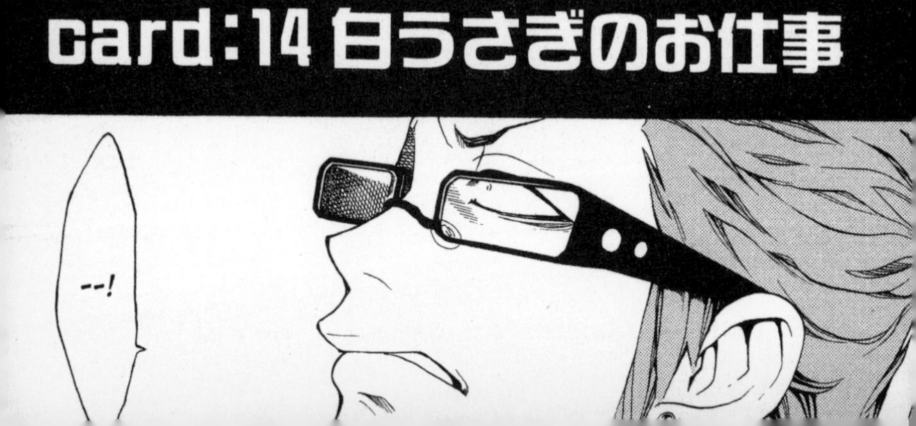
--!

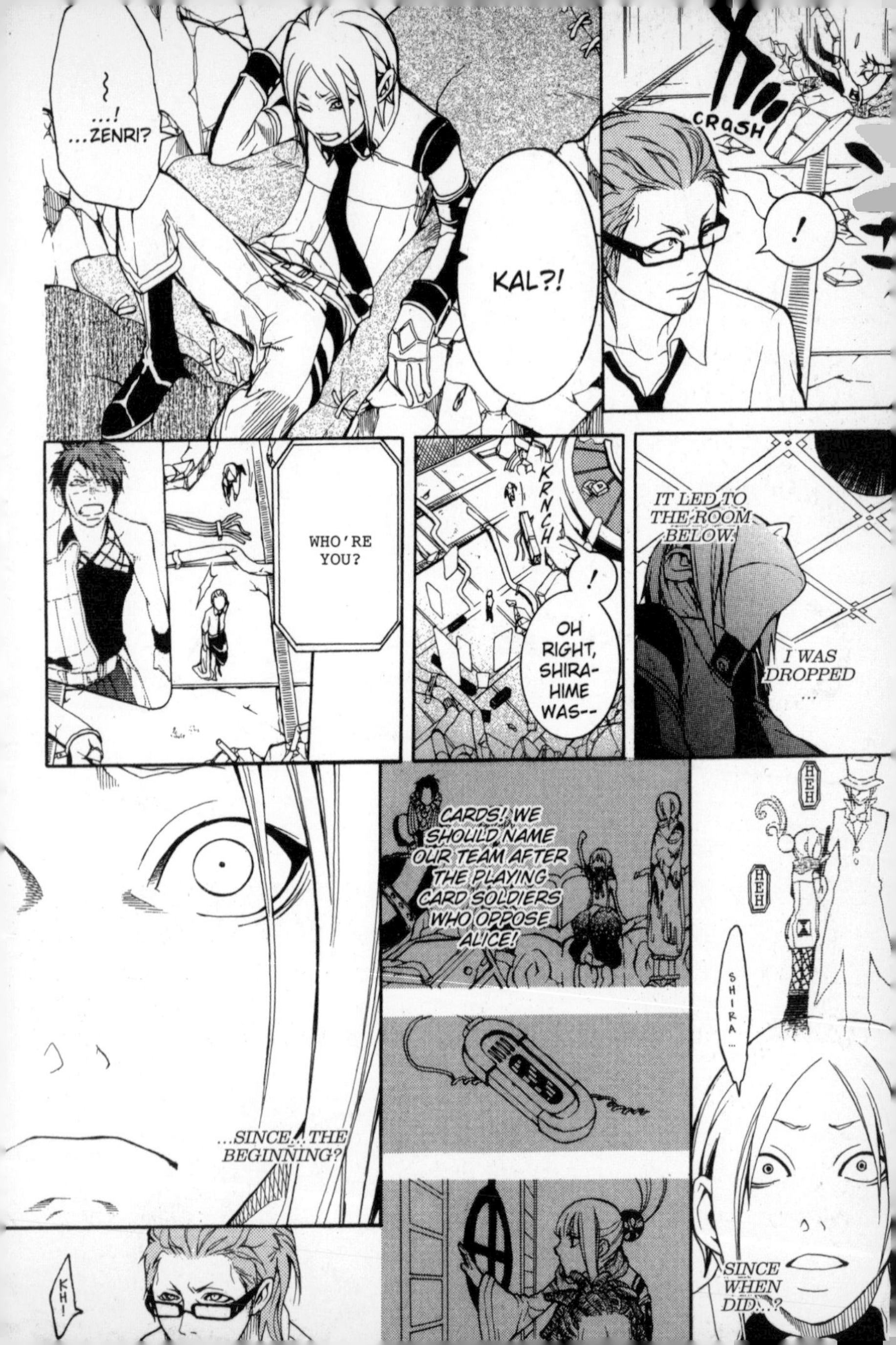
CRASH
!
KAL?!
...!
...ZENRI?
IT LED TO THE ROOM BELOW.
I WAS DROPPED...
KRNCH
!
OH RIGHT, SHIRAHIME WAS--
WHO'RE YOU?
HEH
HEH
SHIRA...
SINCE WHEN DID...?
CARDS! WE SHOULD NAME OUR TEAM AFTER THE PLAYING CARD SOLDIERS WHO OPPOSE ALICE!
...SINCE... THE BEGINNING?
KH!

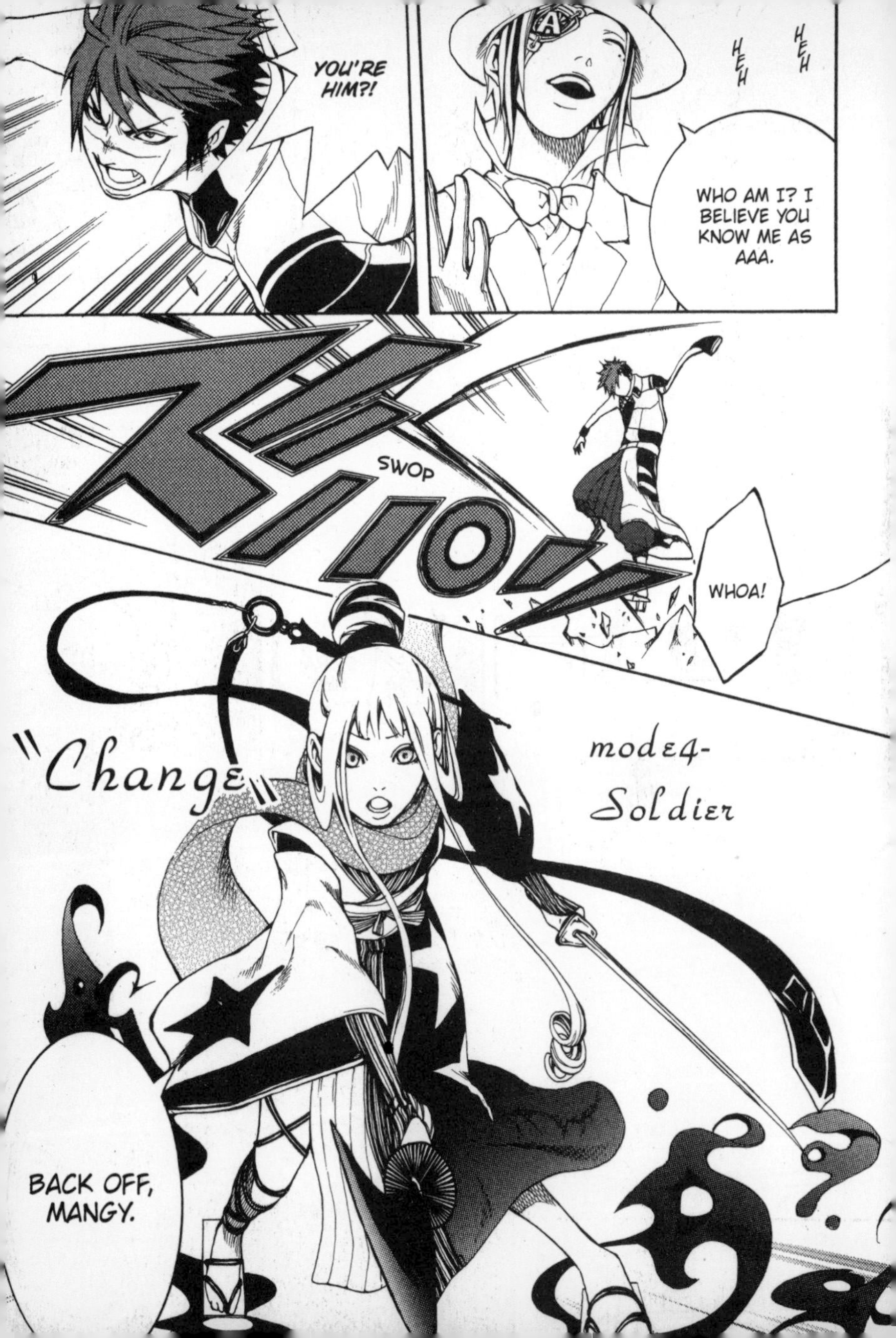
HEH HEH
WHO AM I? I BELIEVE YOU KNOW ME AS AAA.
YOU'RE HIM?!
WHOA!
SWOP
mode4- Soldier
"Change"
BACK OFF, MANGY.

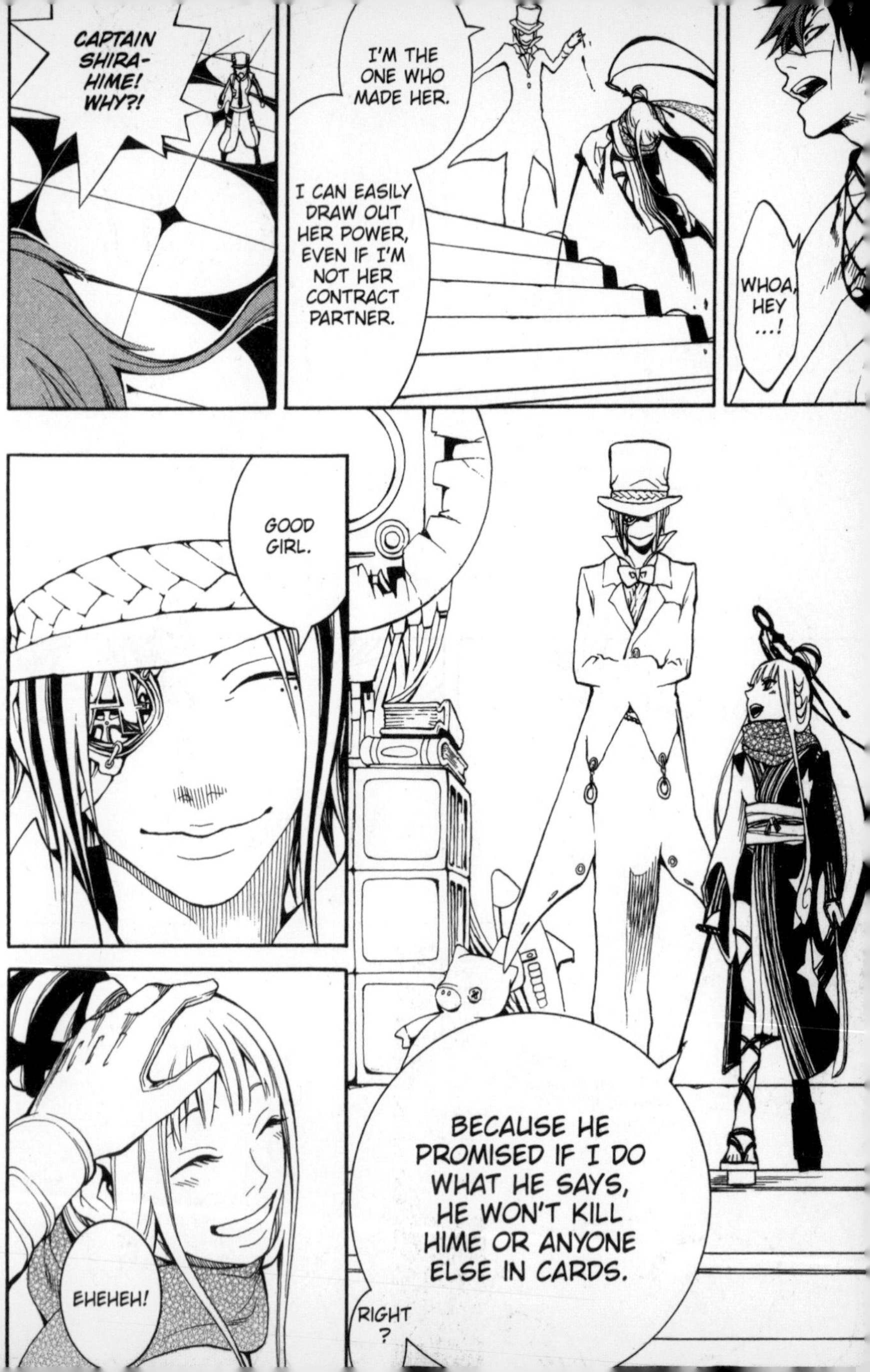
WHOA, HEY ...!
I'M THE ONE WHO MADE HER.
I CAN EASILY DRAW OUT HER POWER, EVEN IF I'M NOT HER CONTRACT PARTNER.
CAPTAIN SHIRA-HIME! WHY?!
BECAUSE HE PROMISED IF I DO WHAT HE SAYS, HE WON'T KILL HIME OR ANYONE ELSE IN CARDS.
RIGHT?
GOOD GIRL.
EHEHEH!

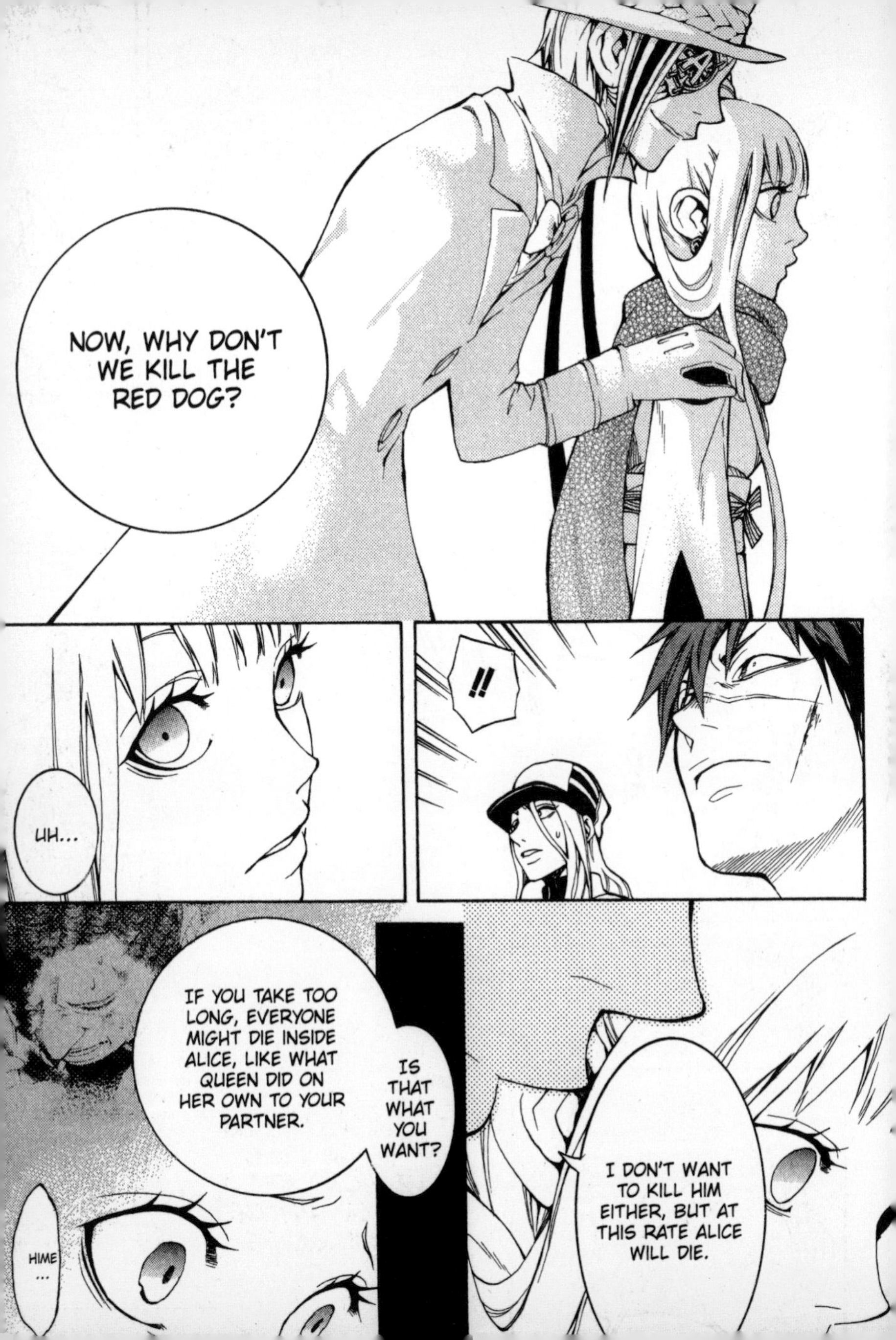
NOW, WHY DON'T WE KILL THE RED DOG?
!!
UH...
I DON'T WANT TO KILL HIM EITHER, BUT AT THIS RATE ALICE WILL DIE.
IF YOU TAKE TOO LONG, EVERYONE MIGHT DIE INSIDE ALICE, LIKE WHAT QUEEN DID ON HER OWN TO YOUR PARTNER.
IS THAT WHAT YOU WANT?
HIME ...

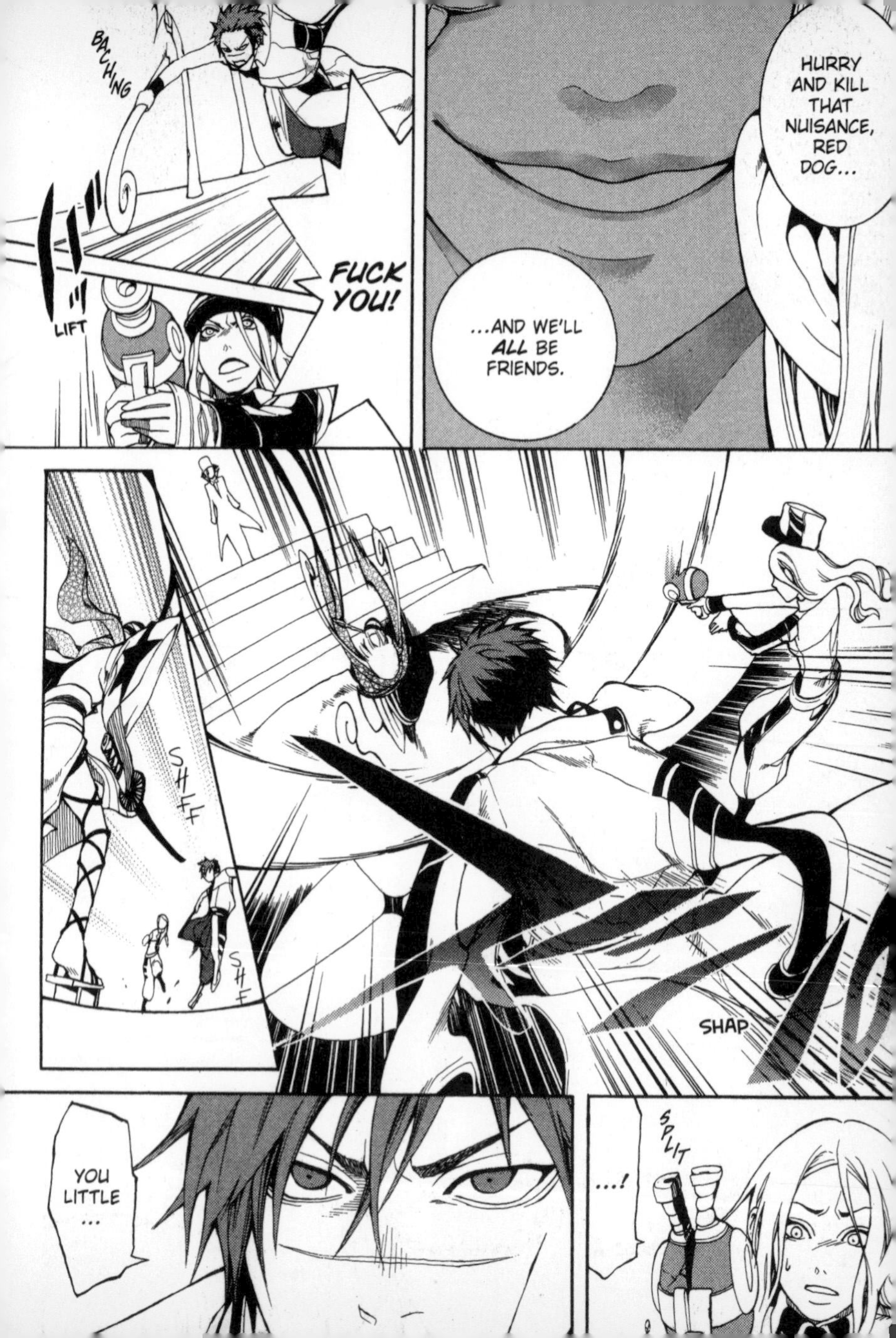
HURRY AND KILL THAT NUISANCE, RED DOG...
...AND WE'LL ALL BE FRIENDS.
BACHING
FUCK YOU!
LIFT
SHAP
SHFF
SHF
SPLIT
...!
YOU LITTLE ...

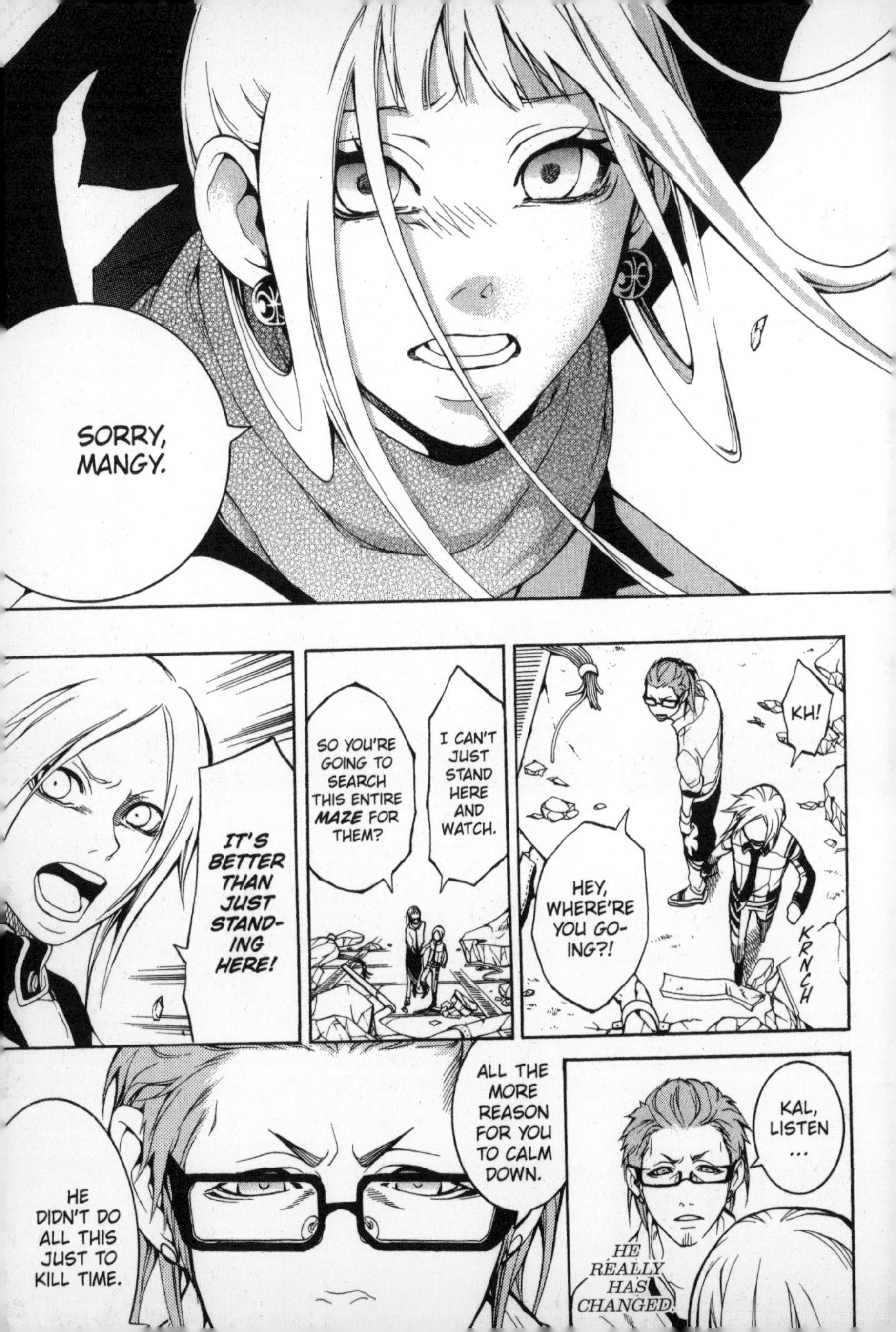
SORRY, MANGY.
KH!
HEY, WHERE'RE YOU GO-ING?!
KRNCH
I CAN'T JUST STAND HERE AND WATCH.
SO YOU'RE GOING TO SEARCH THIS ENTIRE *MAZE* FOR THEM?
IT'S BETTER THAN JUST STAND-ING HERE!
KAL, LISTEN ...
HE REALLY HAS CHANGED.
ALL THE MORE REASON FOR YOU TO CALM DOWN.
HE DIDN'T DO ALL THIS JUST TO KILL TIME.

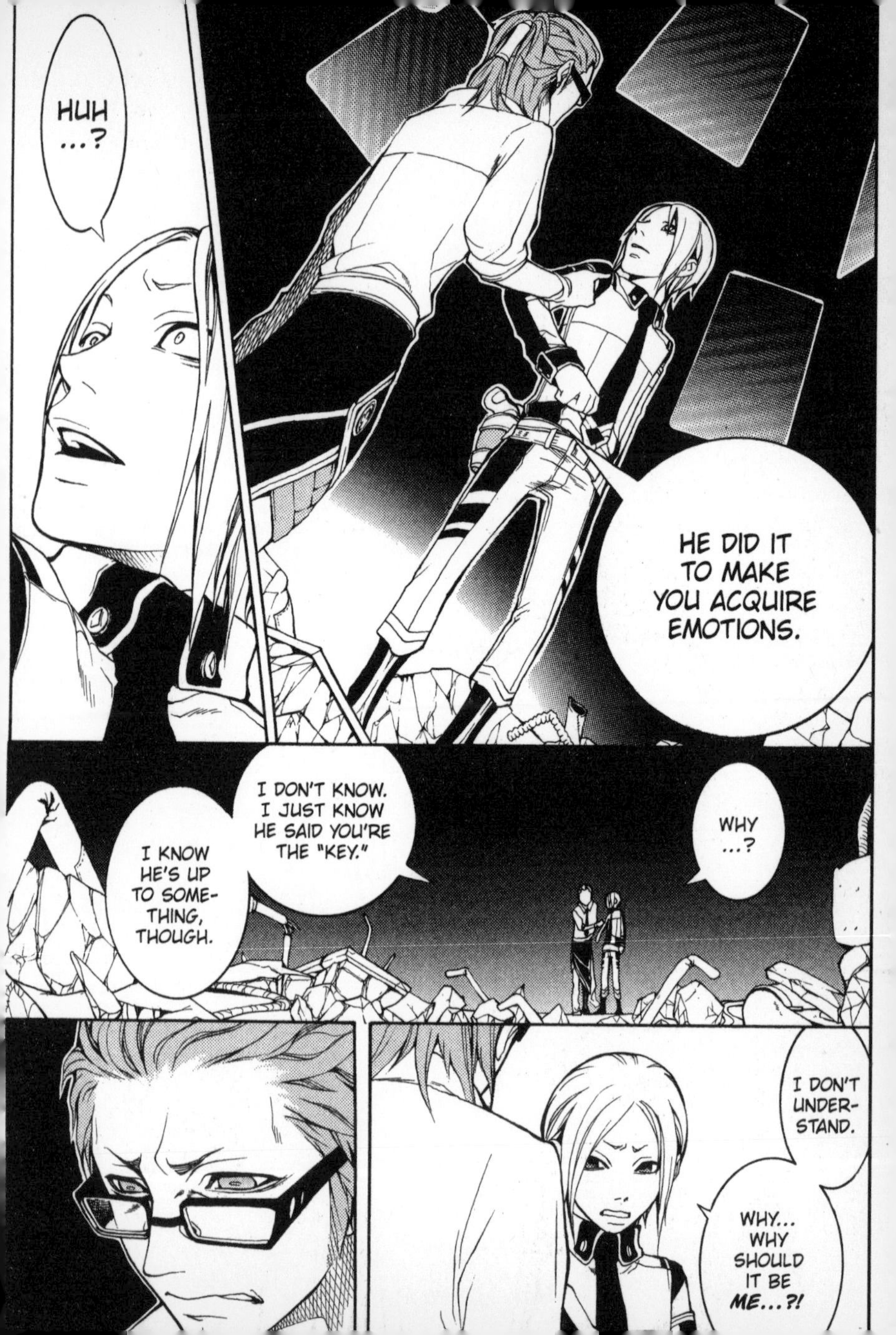
HE DID IT TO MAKE YOU ACQUIRE EMOTIONS.
HUH ...?
WHY ...?
I DON'T KNOW. I JUST KNOW HE SAID YOU'RE THE "KEY."
I KNOW HE'S UP TO SOME-THING, THOUGH.
I DON'T UNDER-STAND.
WHY... WHY SHOULD IT BE *ME...?!*

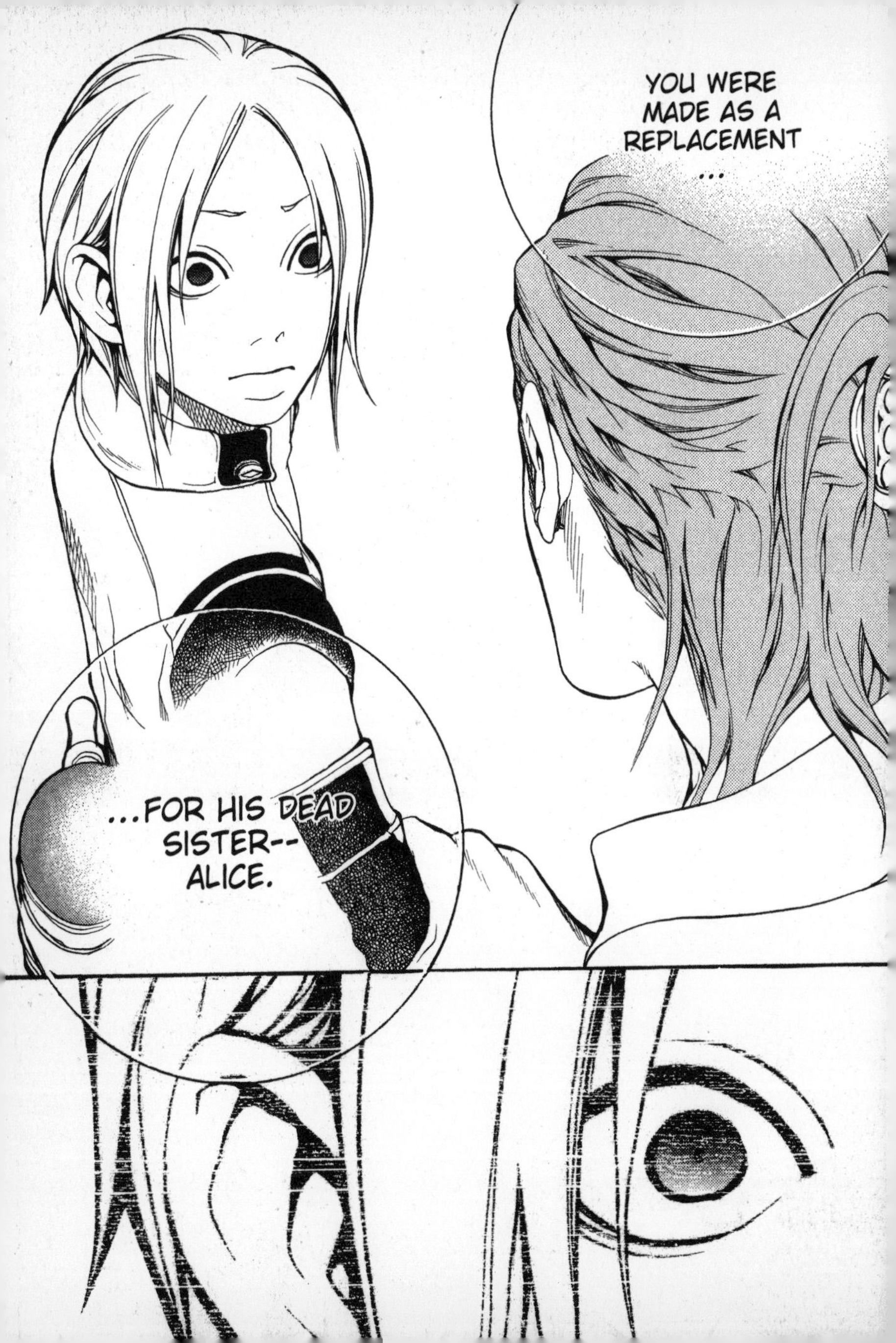
YOU WERE MADE AS A REPLACEMENT ...
...FOR HIS DEAD SISTER-- ALICE.

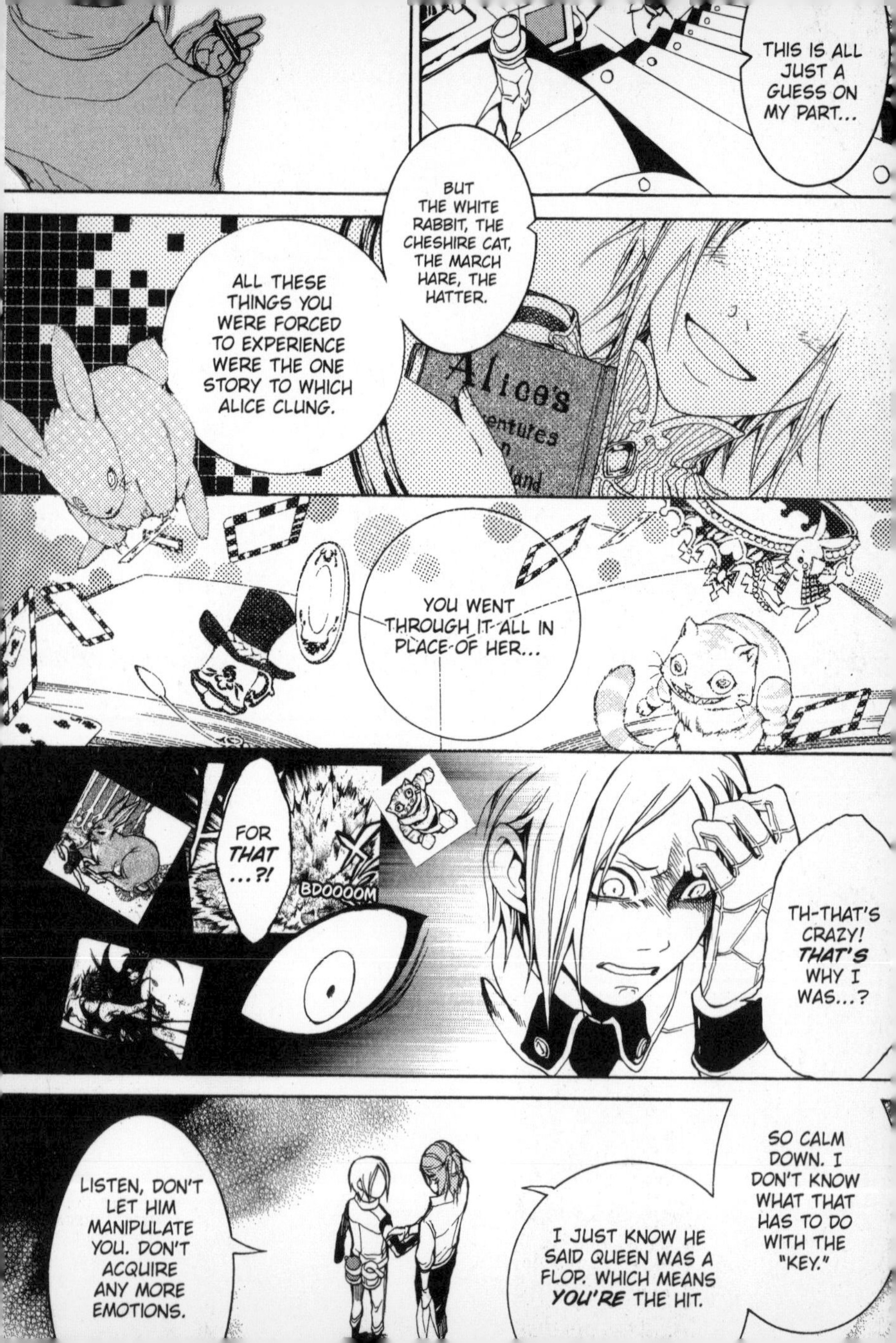
THIS IS ALL JUST A GUESS ON MY PART...
BUT THE WHITE RABBIT, THE CHESHIRE CAT, THE MARCH HARE, THE HATTER.
ALL THESE THINGS YOU WERE FORCED TO EXPERIENCE WERE THE ONE STORY TO WHICH ALICE CLUNG.
Alice's Adventures in Wonderland
YOU WENT THROUGH IT ALL IN PLACE OF HER...
TH-THAT'S CRAZY! ***THAT'S*** WHY I WAS...?
FOR ***THAT***...?!
BDOOOOM
SO CALM DOWN. I DON'T KNOW WHAT THAT HAS TO DO WITH THE "KEY."
I JUST KNOW HE SAID QUEEN WAS A FLOP. WHICH MEANS ***YOU'RE*** THE HIT.
LISTEN, DON'T LET HIM MANIPULATE YOU. DON'T ACQUIRE ANY MORE EMOTIONS.

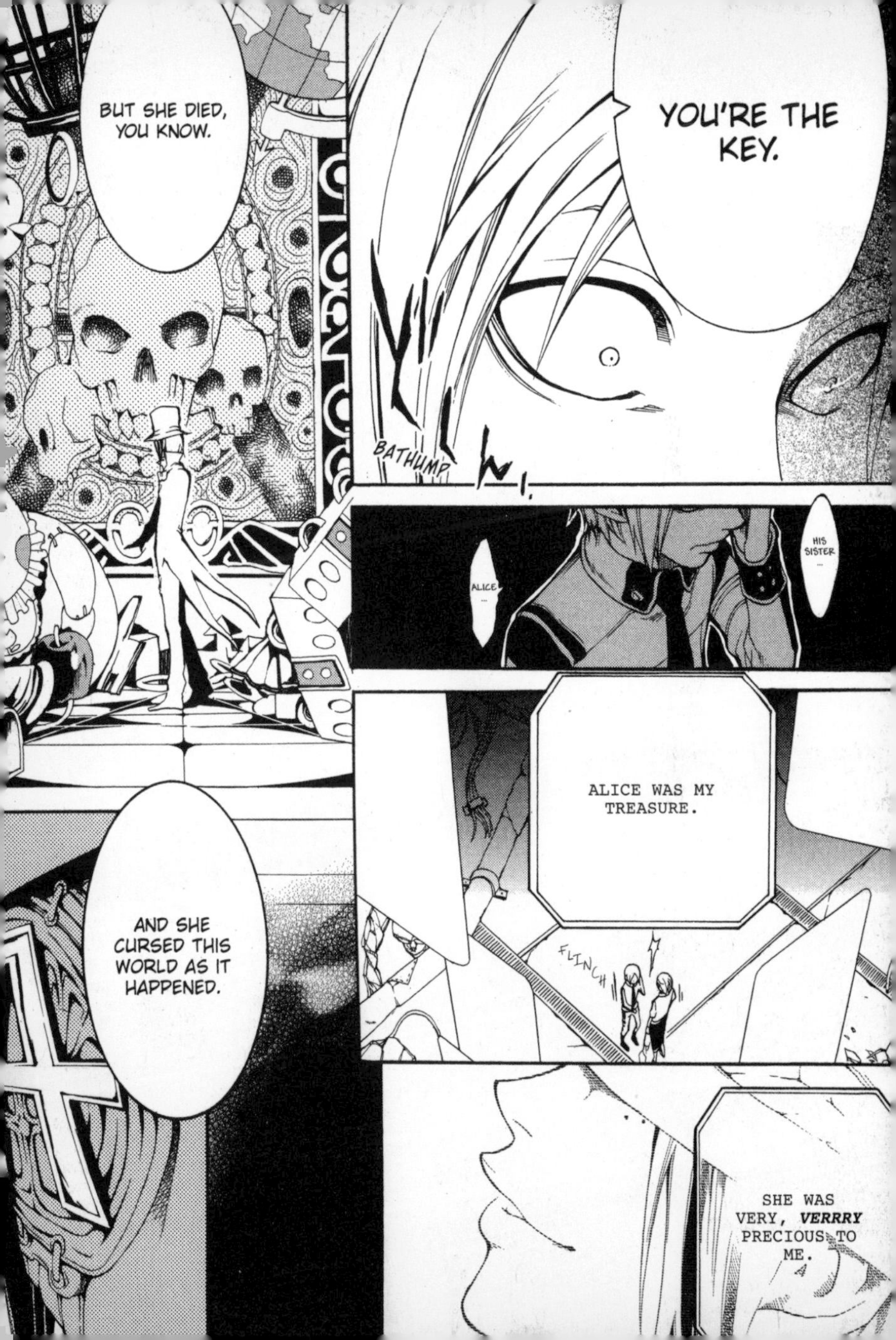
YOU'RE THE KEY.
BATHUMP
HIS SISTER ...
ALICE ...
ALICE WAS MY TREASURE.
FLINCH
SHE WAS VERY, ***VERRRY*** PRECIOUS TO ME.
BUT SHE DIED, YOU KNOW.
AND SHE CURSED THIS WORLD AS IT HAPPENED.

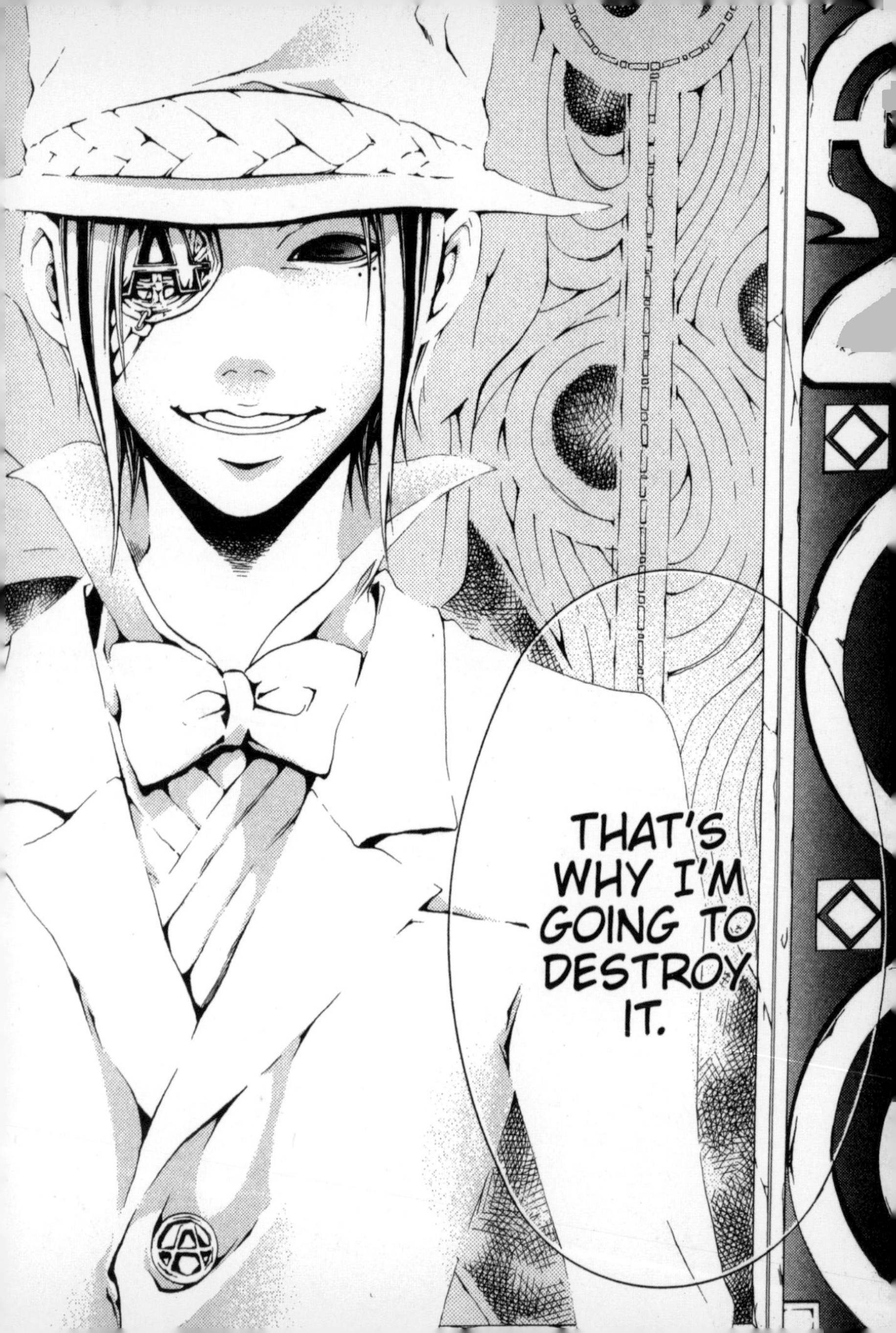
THAT'S WHY I'M GOING TO DESTROY IT.

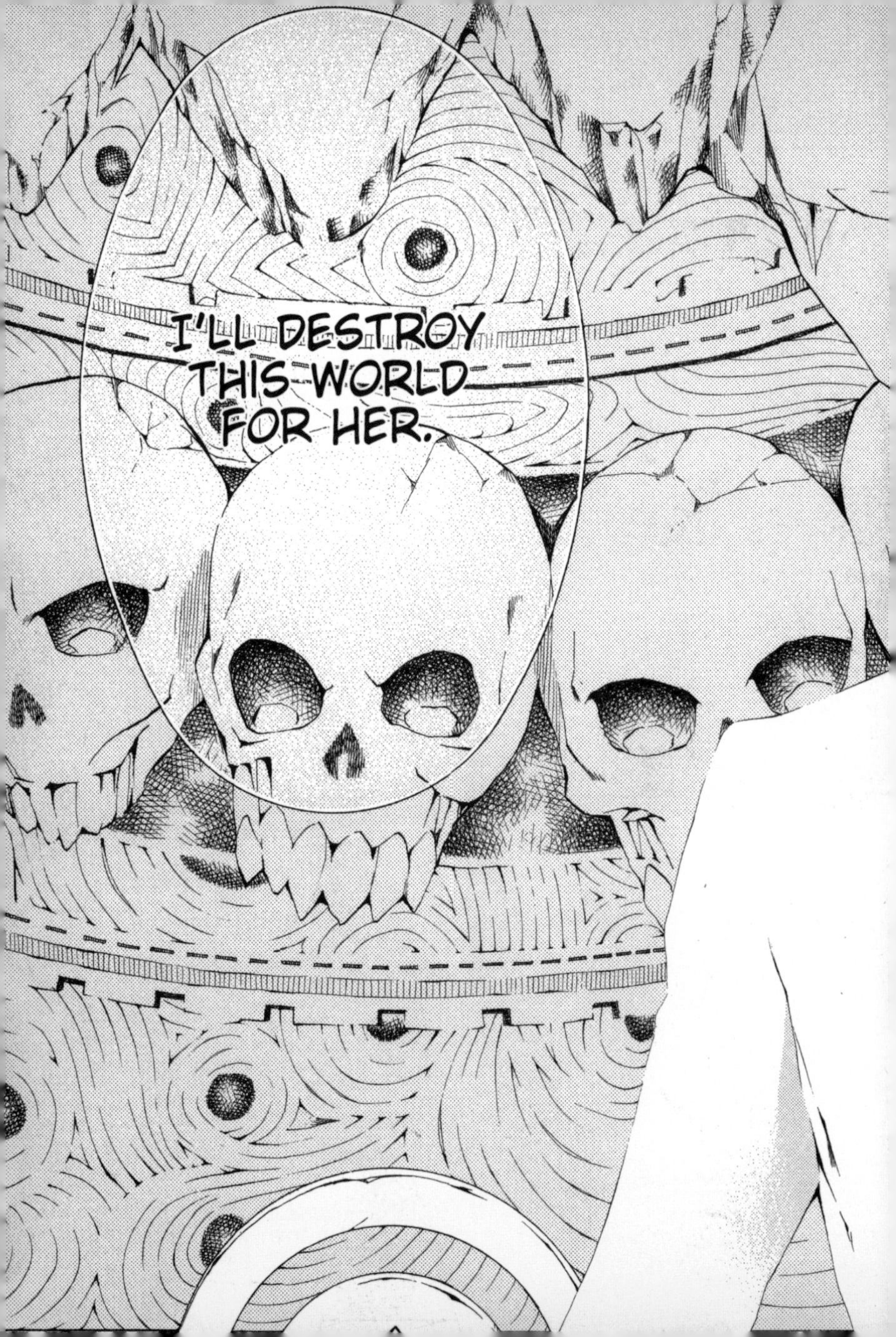
I'LL DESTROY THIS WORLD FOR HER.

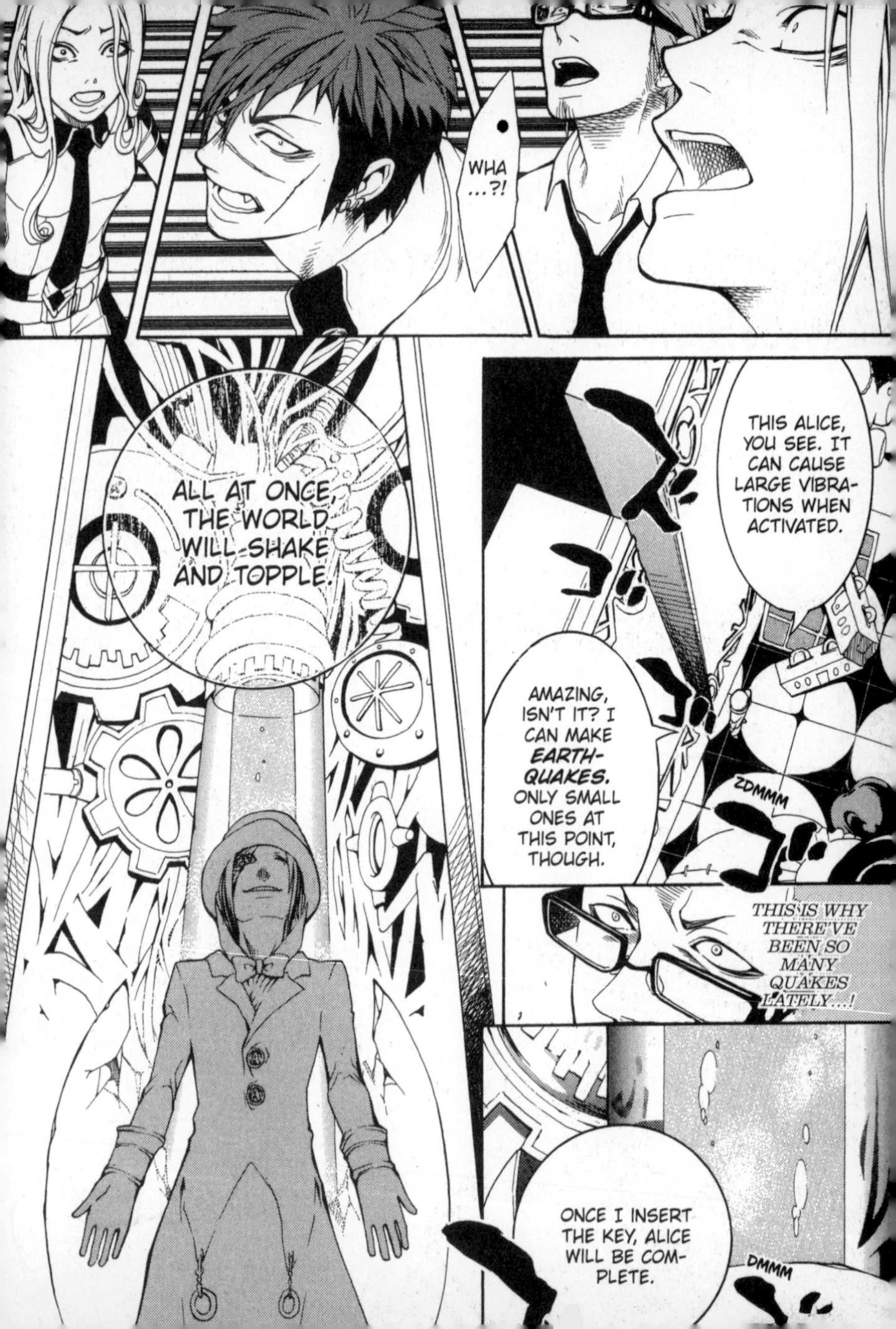
WHA ...?!
THIS ALICE, YOU SEE. IT CAN CAUSE LARGE VIBRATIONS WHEN ACTIVATED.
AMAZING, ISN'T IT? I CAN MAKE EARTHQUAKES. ONLY SMALL ONES AT THIS POINT, THOUGH.
ZDMMM
THIS IS WHY THERE'VE BEEN SO MANY QUAKES LATELY...!
ONCE I INSERT THE KEY, ALICE WILL BE COMPLETE.
DMMM
ALL AT ONCE, THE WORLD WILL SHAKE AND TOPPLE.

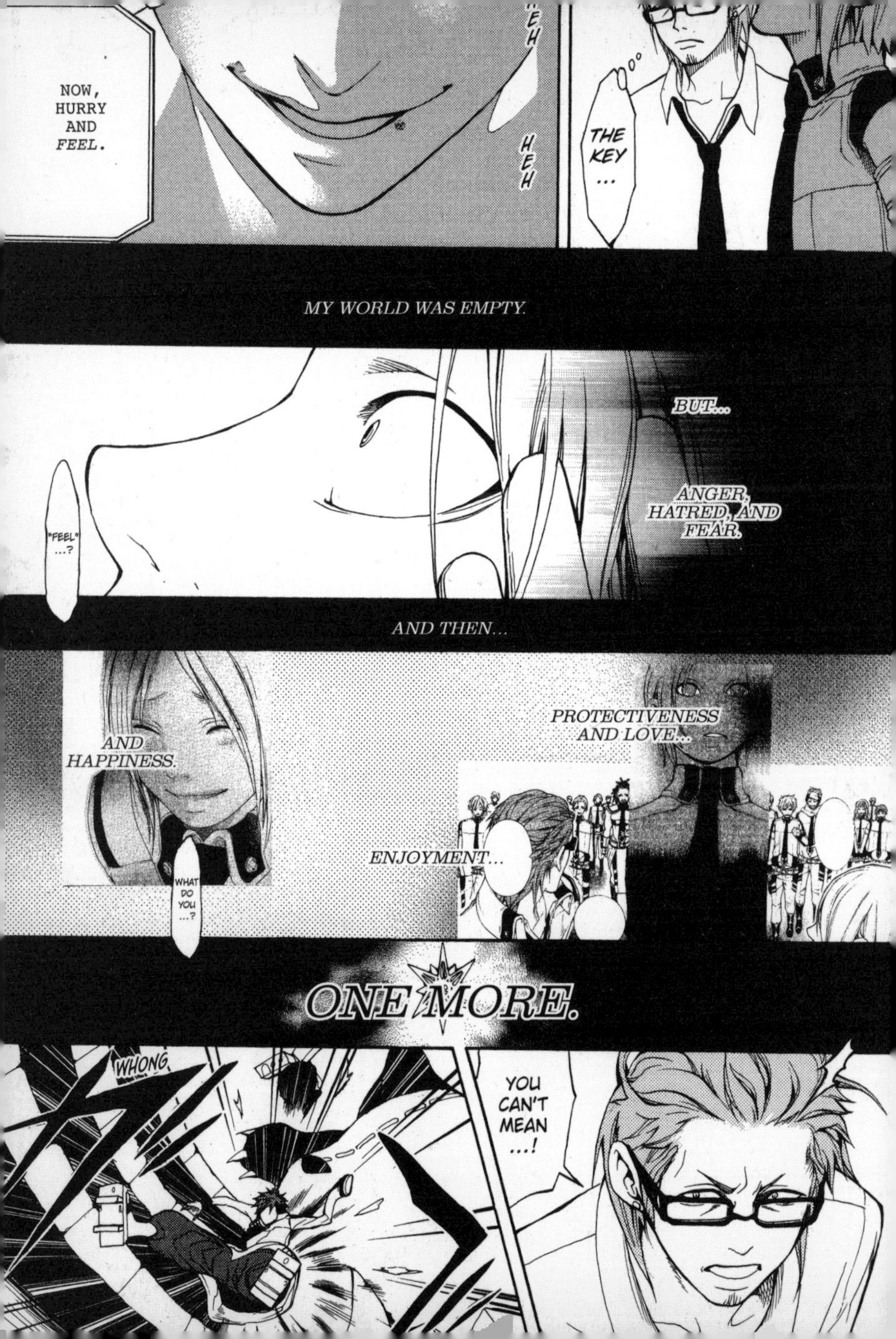
THE KEY ...
HEH HEH
NOW, HURRY AND FEEL.
MY WORLD WAS EMPTY.
BUT...
ANGER, HATRED, AND FEAR.
"FEEL" ...?
AND THEN...
PROTECTIVENESS AND LOVE...
ENJOYMENT...
AND HAPPINESS.
WHAT DO YOU ...?
ONE MORE.
YOU CAN'T MEAN ...!
WHONG

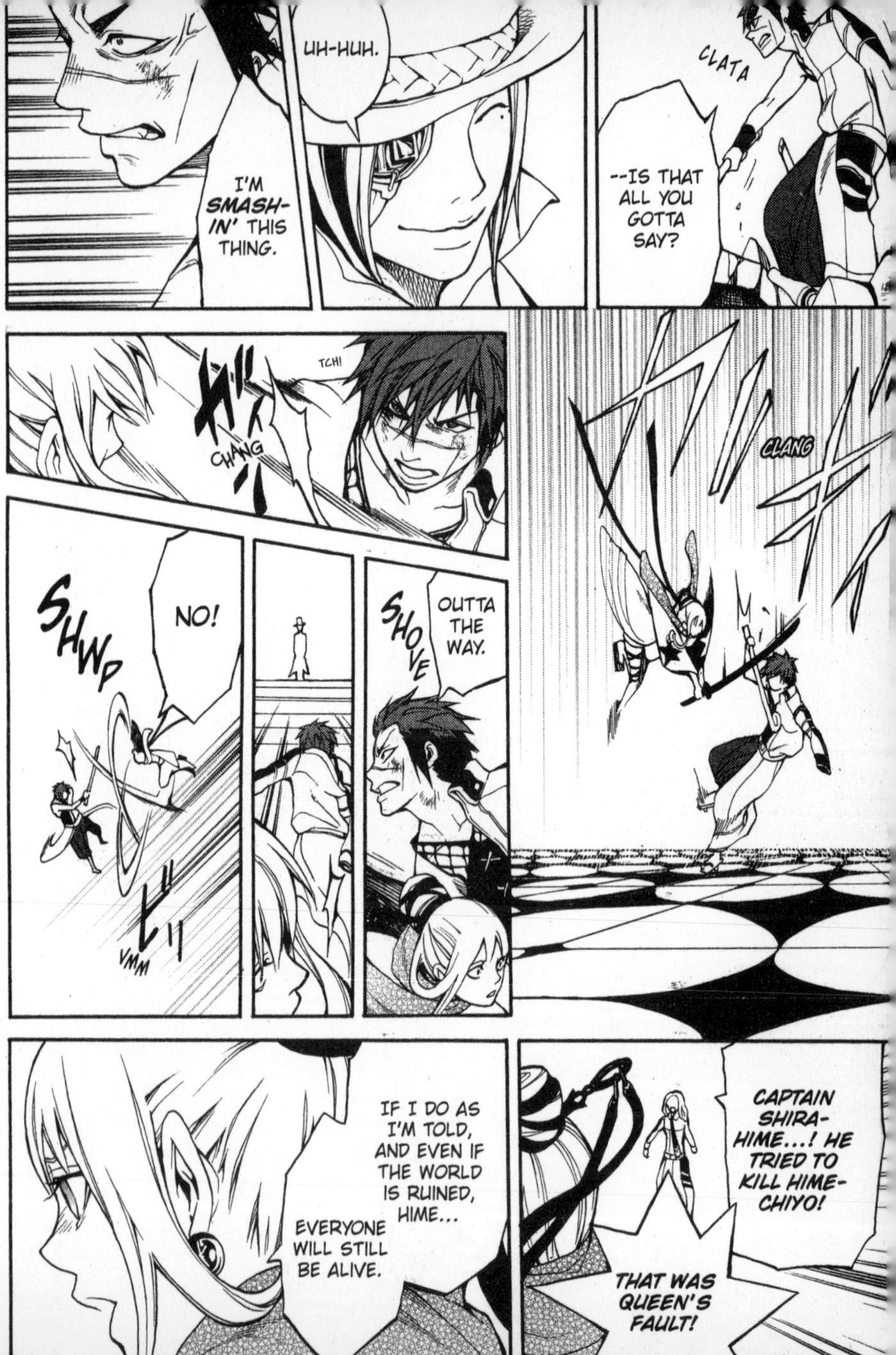
CLATA
--IS THAT ALL YOU GOTTA SAY?
UH-HUH.
I'M SMASHIN' THIS THING.
CLANG
TCH!
CHANG
SHOVE
OUTTA THE WAY.
NO!
SHWP
VMM
CAPTAIN SHIRA-HIME...! HE TRIED TO KILL HIME-CHIYO!
THAT WAS QUEEN'S FAULT!
IF I DO AS I'M TOLD, AND EVEN IF THE WORLD IS RUINED, HIME...
EVERYONE WILL STILL BE ALIVE.

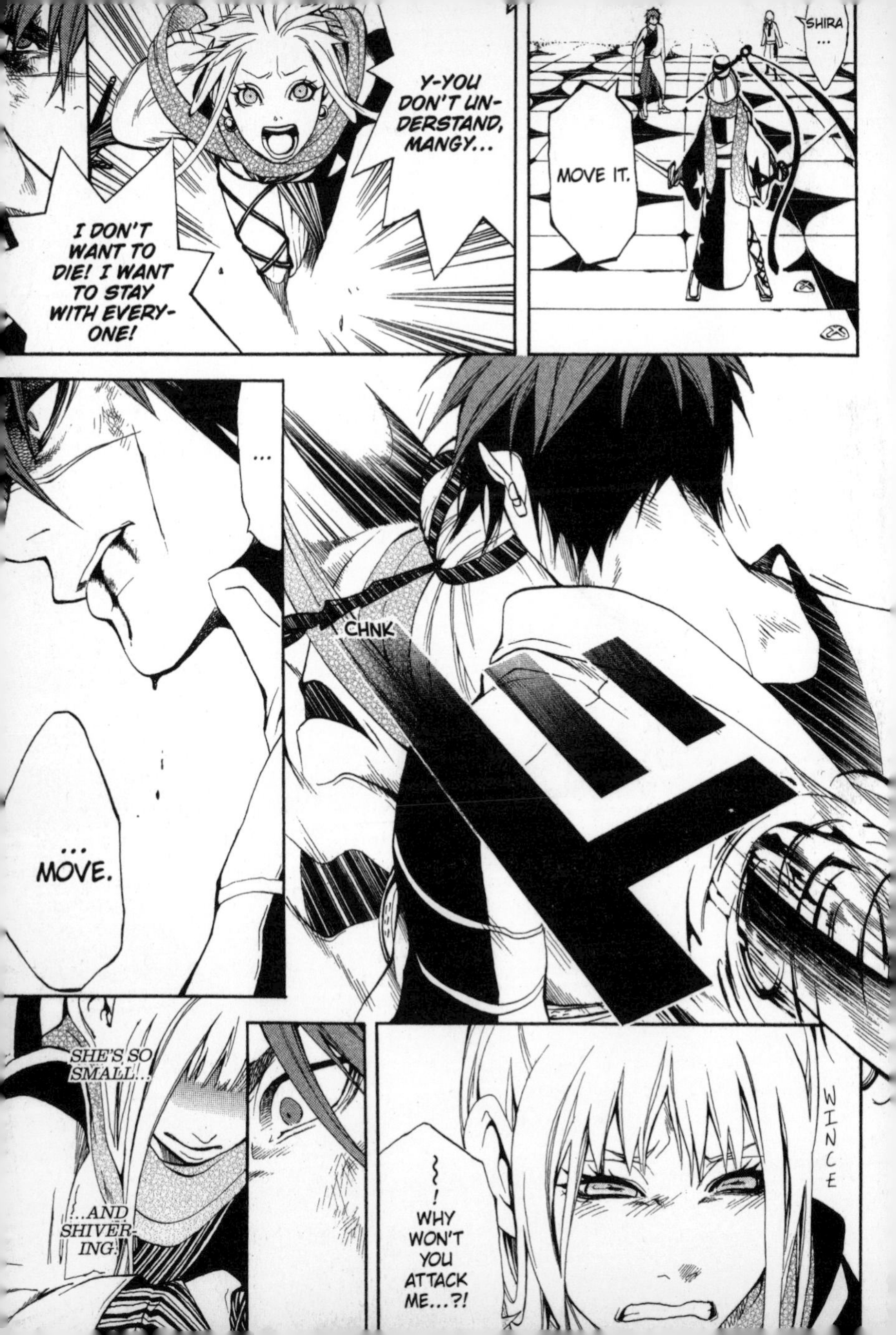
SHIRA ...
MOVE IT.
Y-YOU DON'T UNDERSTAND, MANGY...
I DON'T WANT TO DIE! I WANT TO STAY WITH EVERYONE!
CHNK
...
... MOVE.
WINCE
~~! WHY WON'T YOU ATTACK ME...?!
SHE'S SO SMALL...
...AND SHIVERING.

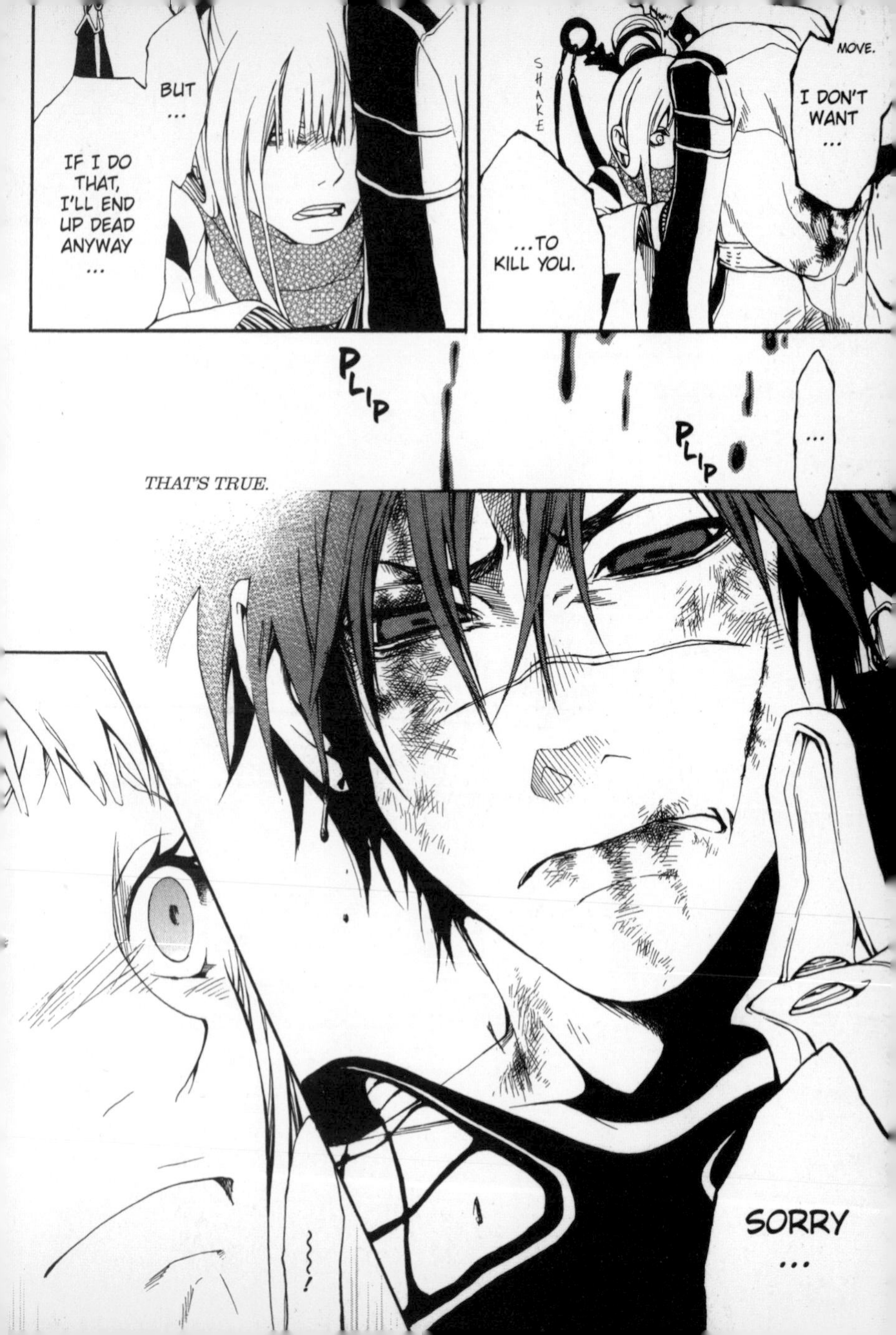
MOVE.
I DON'T WANT ...
...TO KILL YOU.
SHAKE
BUT ...
IF I DO THAT, I'LL END UP DEAD ANYWAY ...
...
PLIP
PLIP
THAT'S TRUE.
SORRY ...

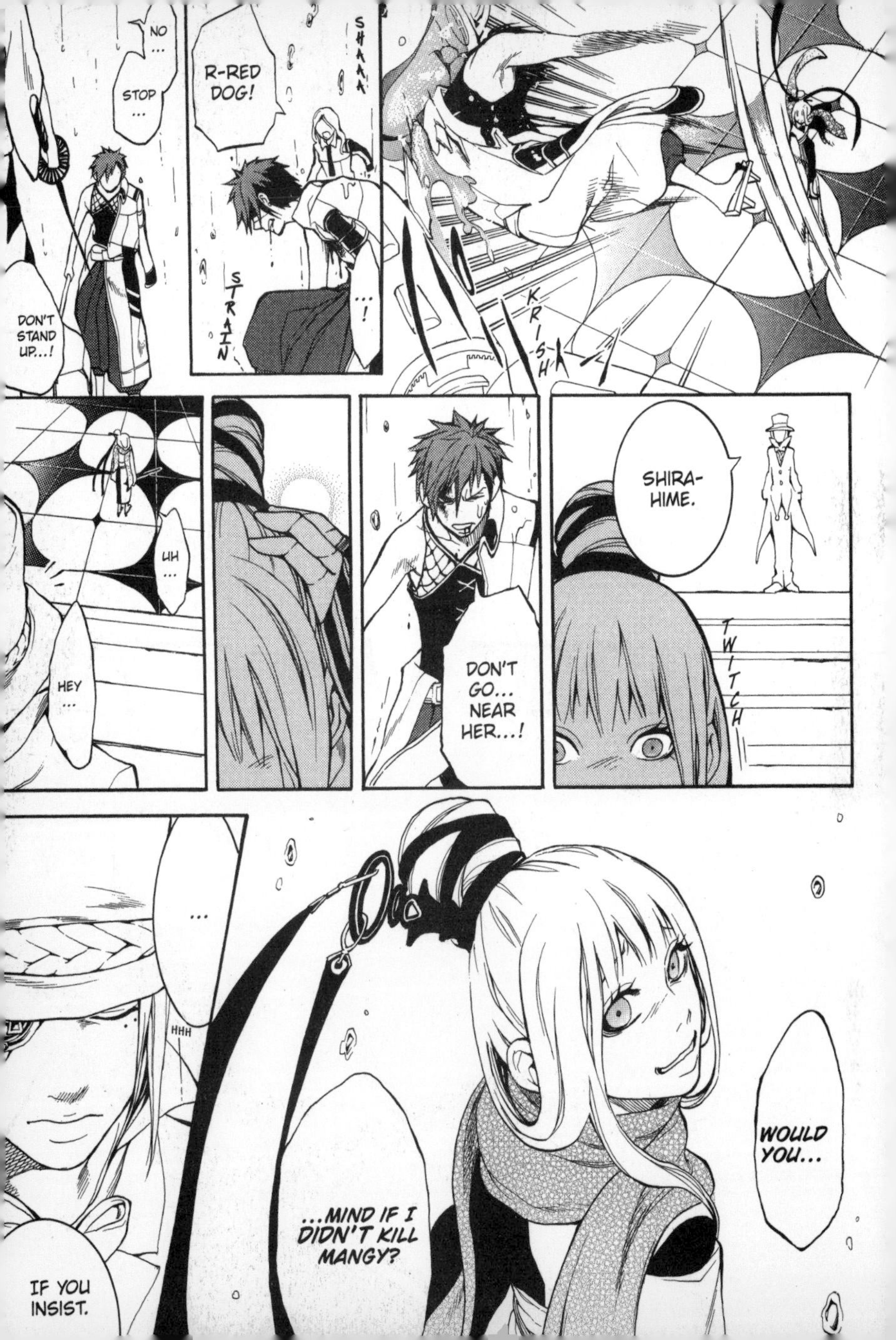
KRISHA
SHAAA
R-RED DOG!
...!
STRAIN
NO ...
STOP ...
DON'T STAND UP...!
SHIRA-HIME.
TWITCH
DON'T GO... NEAR HER...!
UH ...
HEY ...
WOULD YOU...
...MIND IF I DIDN'T KILL MANGY?
...
HHH
IF YOU INSIST.

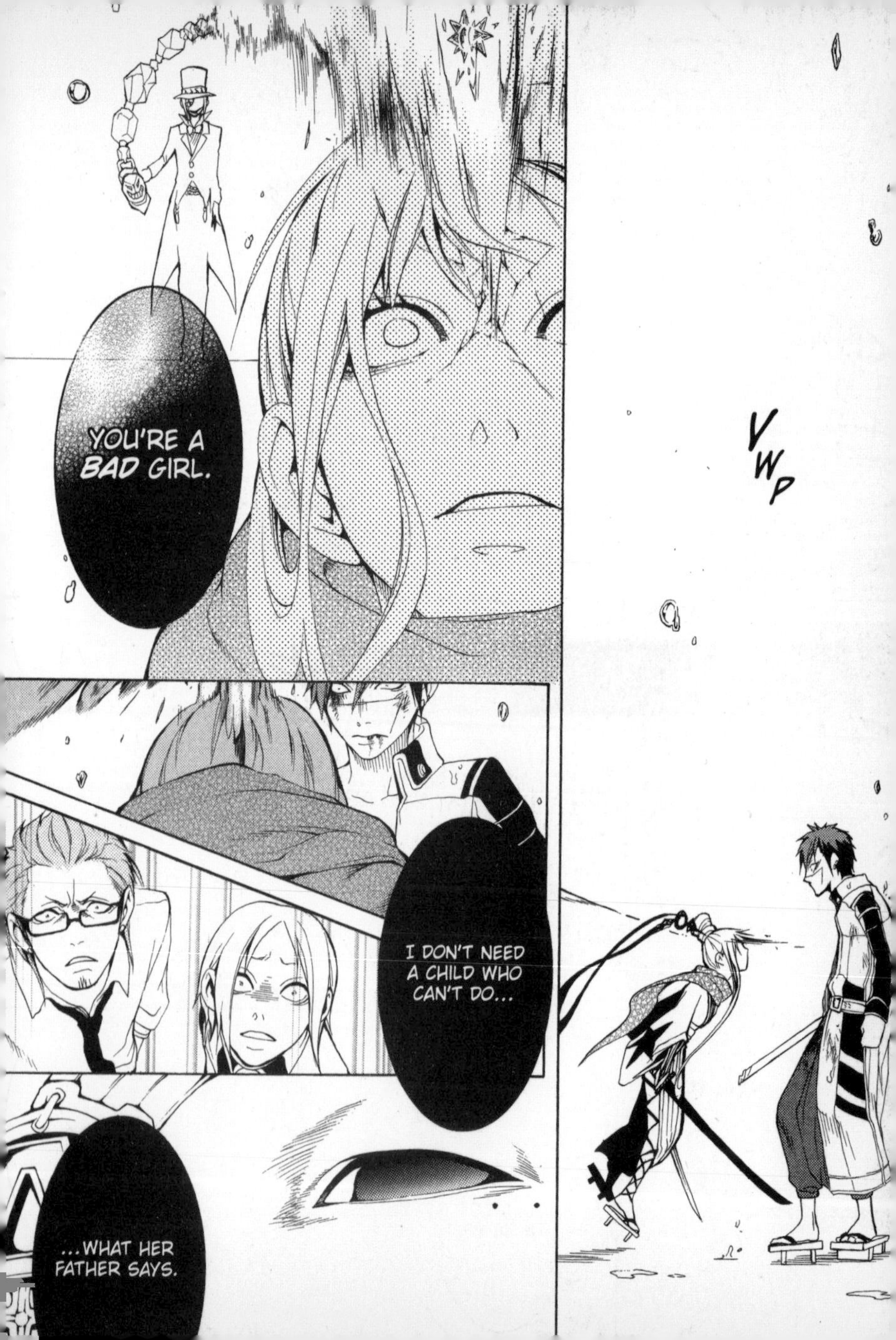
VWP
YOU'RE A BAD GIRL.
I DON'T NEED A CHILD WHO CAN'T DO...
...WHAT HER FATHER SAYS.

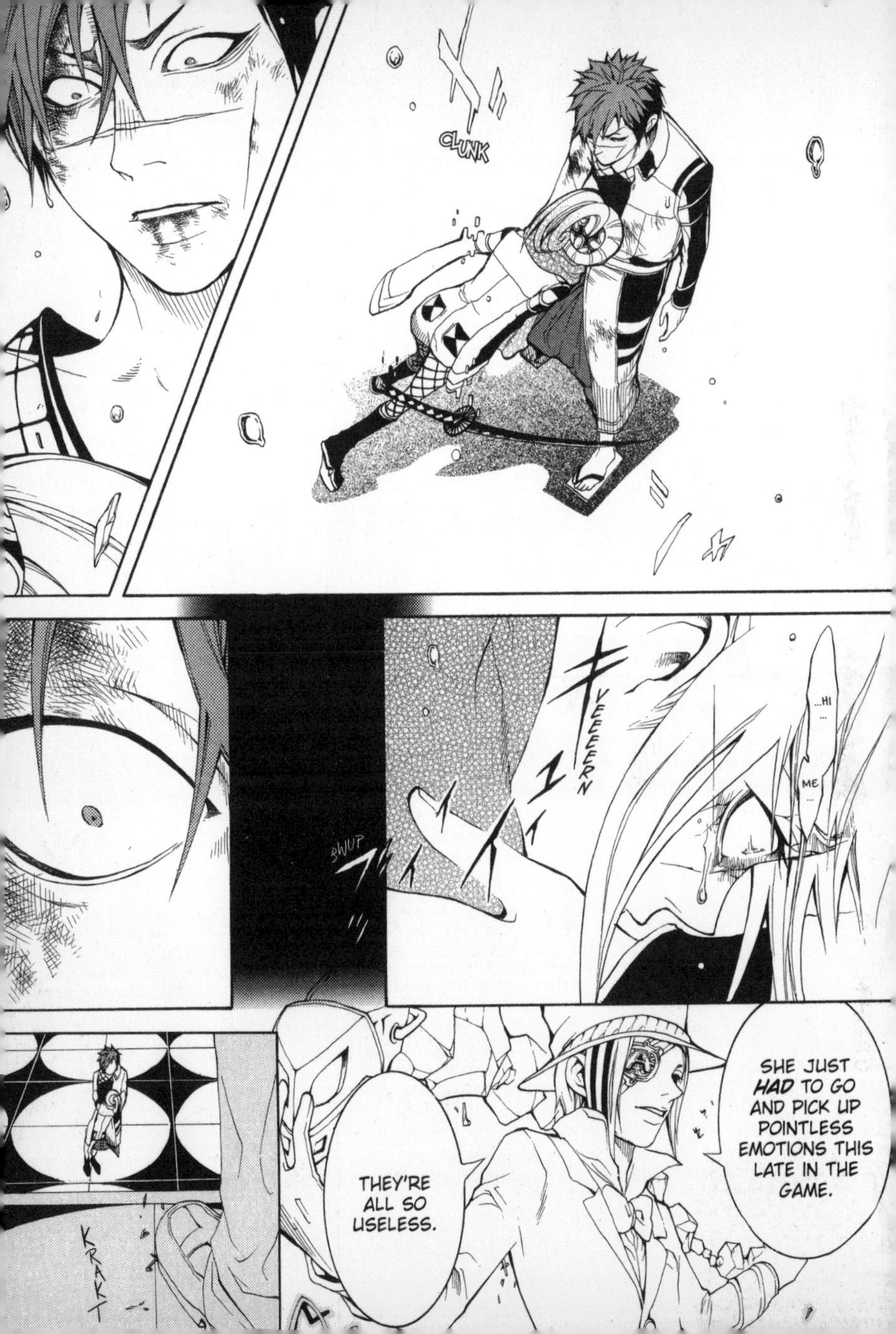

CLUNK
VEEEERN
...HI ... ME ...
BWUP
SHE JUST HAD TO GO AND PICK UP POINTLESS EMOTIONS THIS LATE IN THE GAME.
THEY'RE ALL SO USELESS.
KRAKT

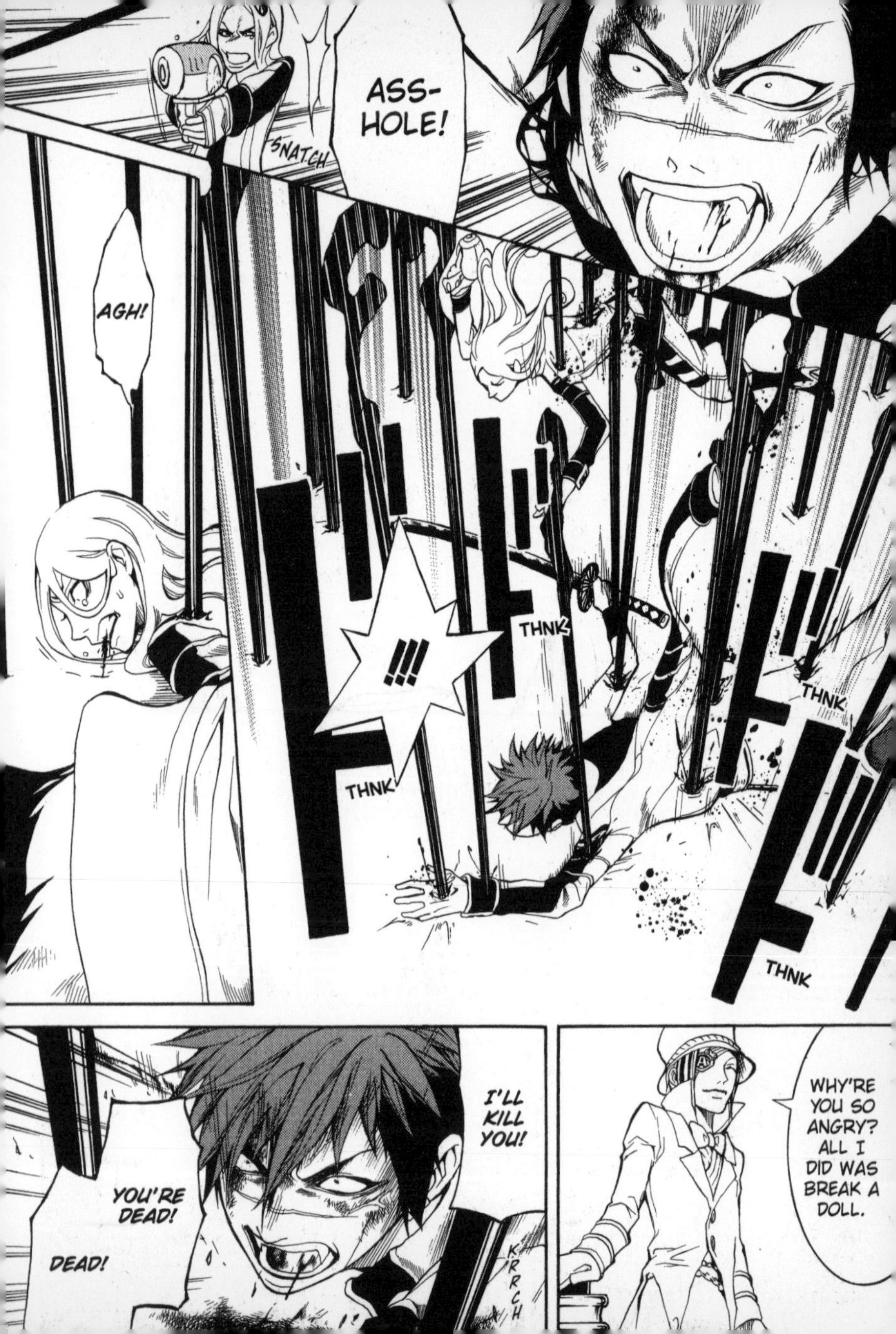
ASS-HOLE!
SNATCH
AGH!
THNK
THNK
!!!!
THNK
THNK
THNK
WHY'RE YOU SO ANGRY? ALL I DID WAS BREAK A DOLL.
I'LL KILL YOU!
KRRCH
YOU'RE DEAD!
DEAD!

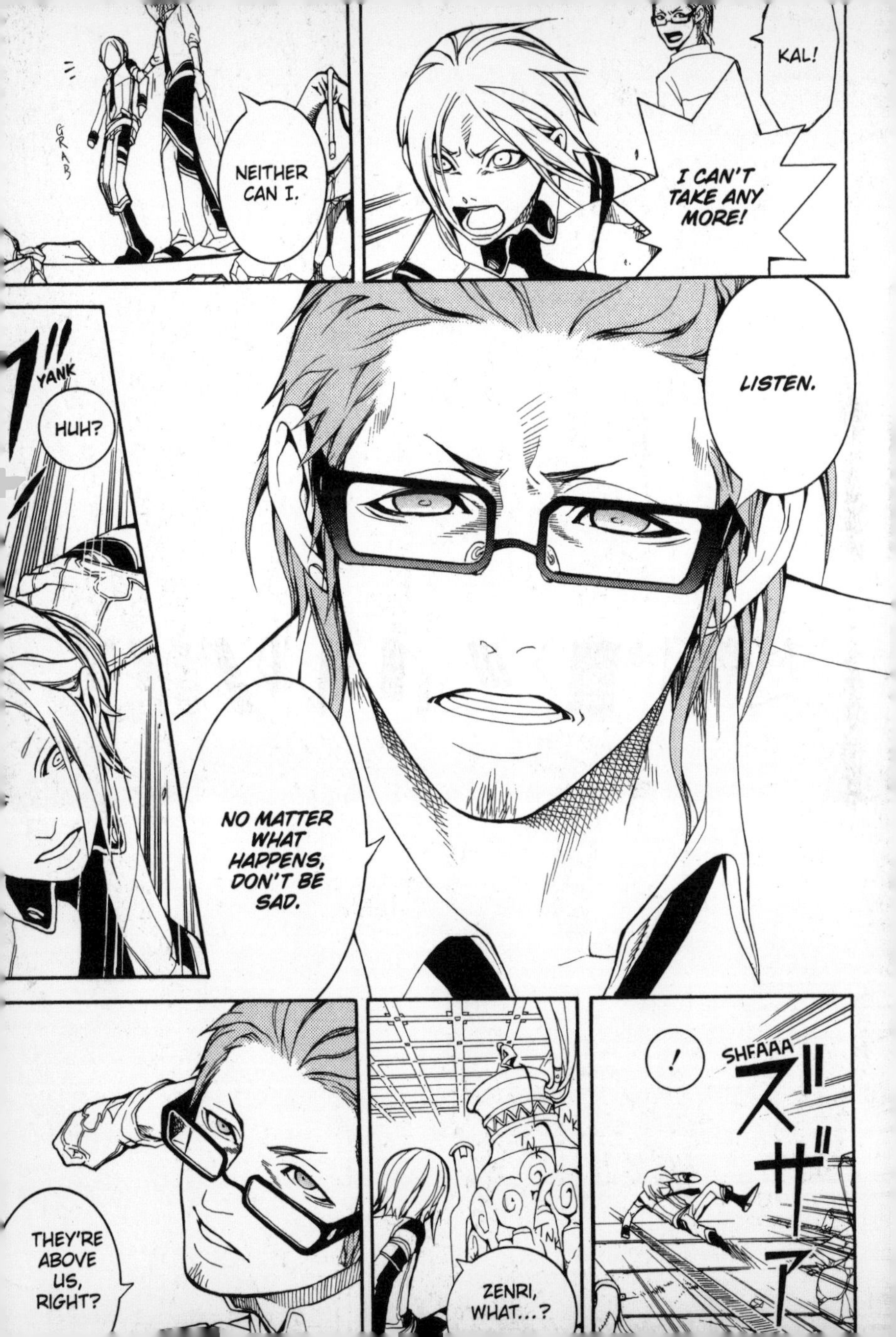
KAL!
I CAN'T TAKE ANY MORE!
GRAB
NEITHER CAN I.
LISTEN.
NO MATTER WHAT HAPPENS, DON'T BE SAD.
YANK
HUH?
!
SHFAAA
TNK
TNK
TNK
ZENRI, WHAT...?
THEY'RE ABOVE US, RIGHT?

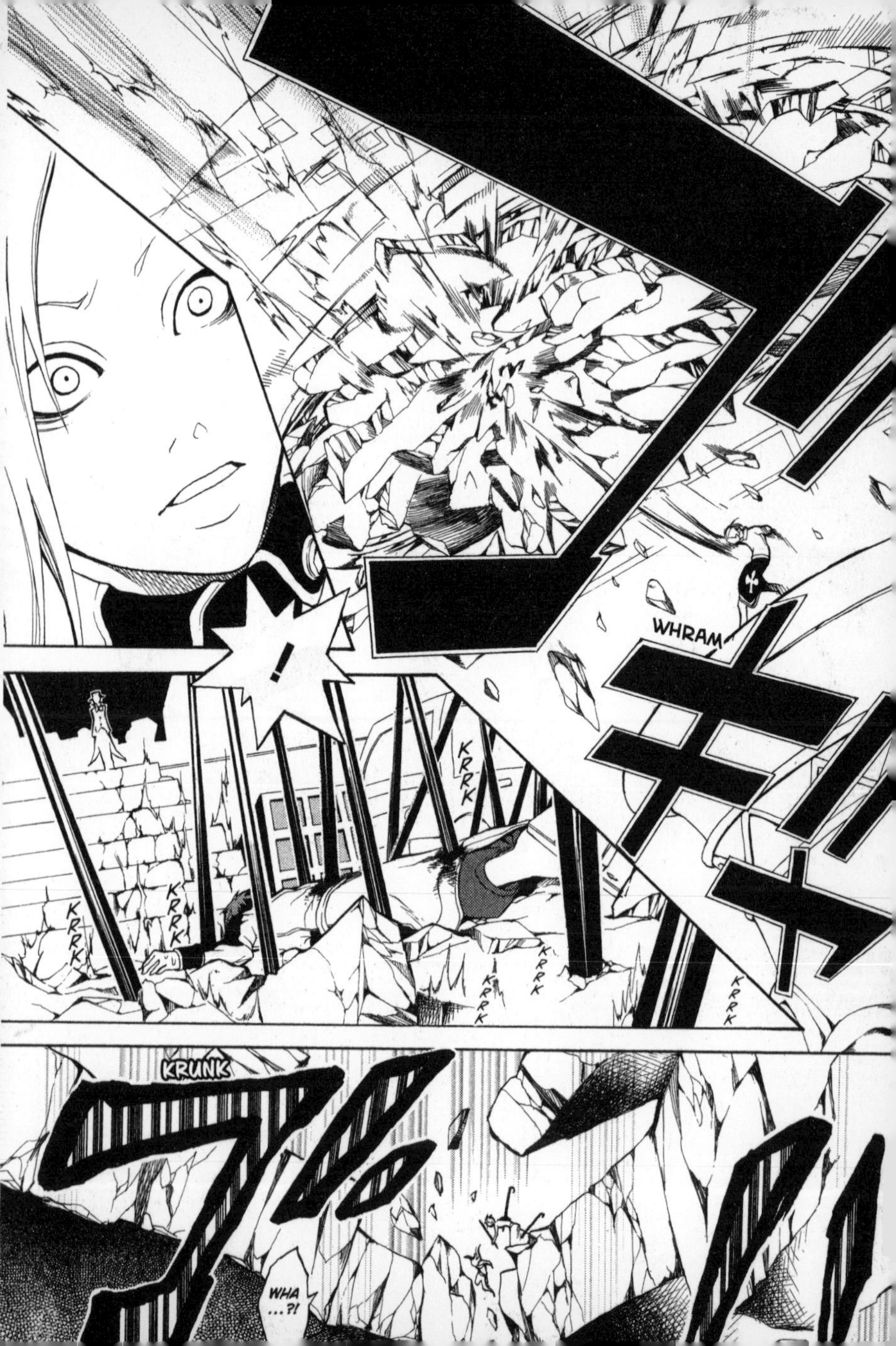

WHRAM
!
KRRK
KRRK
KRRK
KRRK
KRRK
KRRK
KRUNK
WHA ...?!

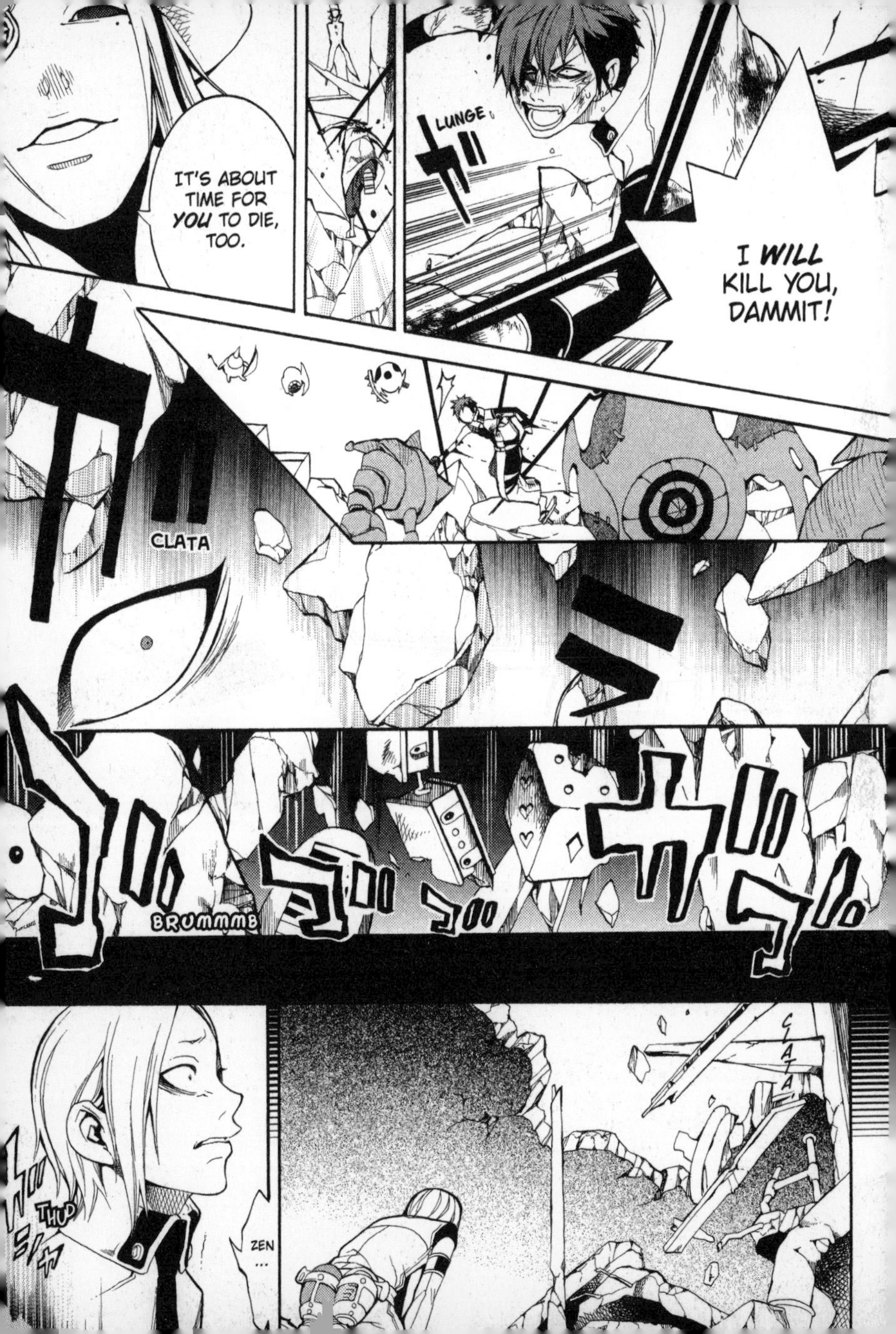
I WILL KILL YOU, DAMMIT!
LUNGE
IT'S ABOUT TIME FOR YOU TO DIE, TOO.
CLATA
BRUMMMB
CLATA
THUD
ZEN ...

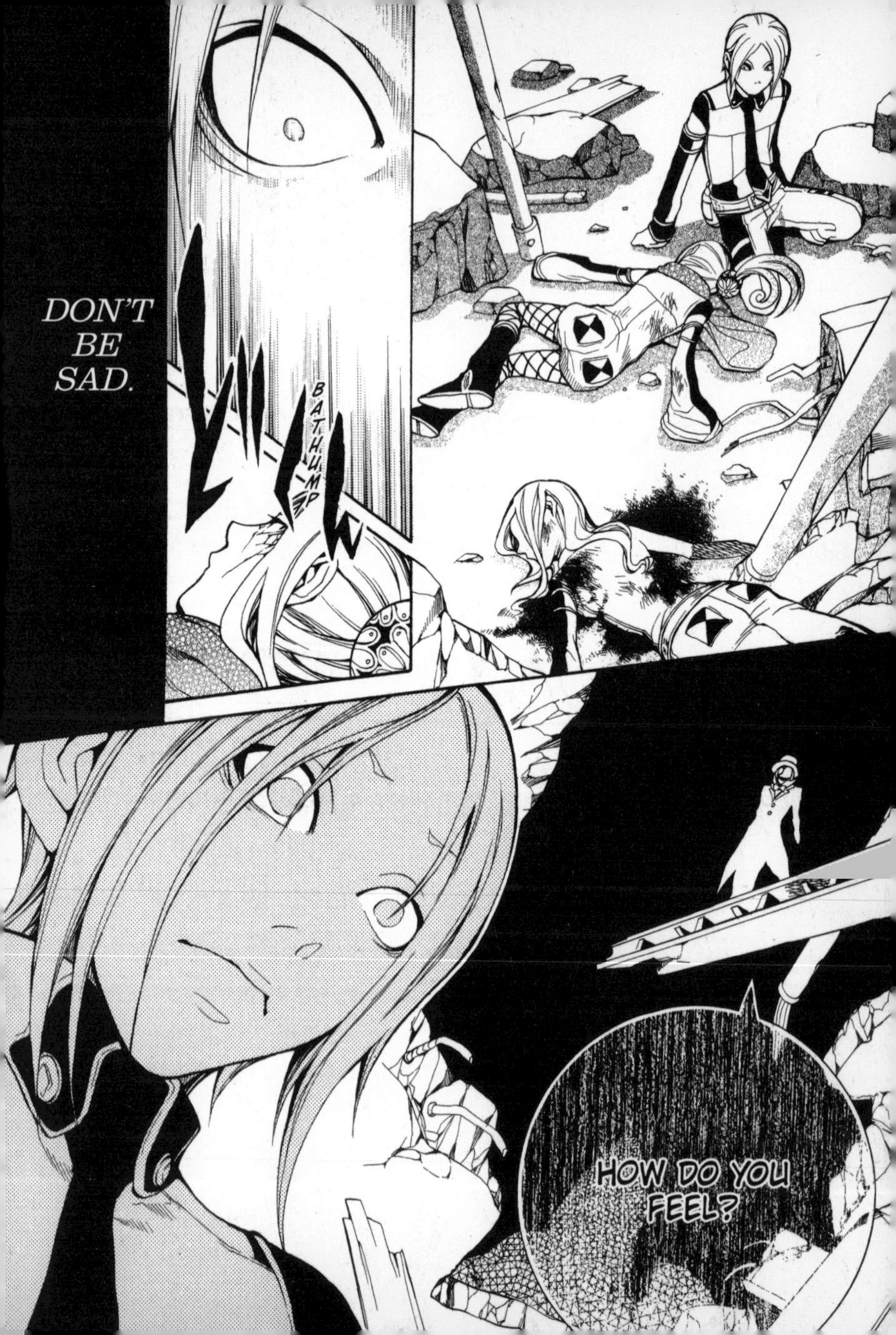
BATHUMP
DON'T BE SAD.
HOW DO YOU FEEL?

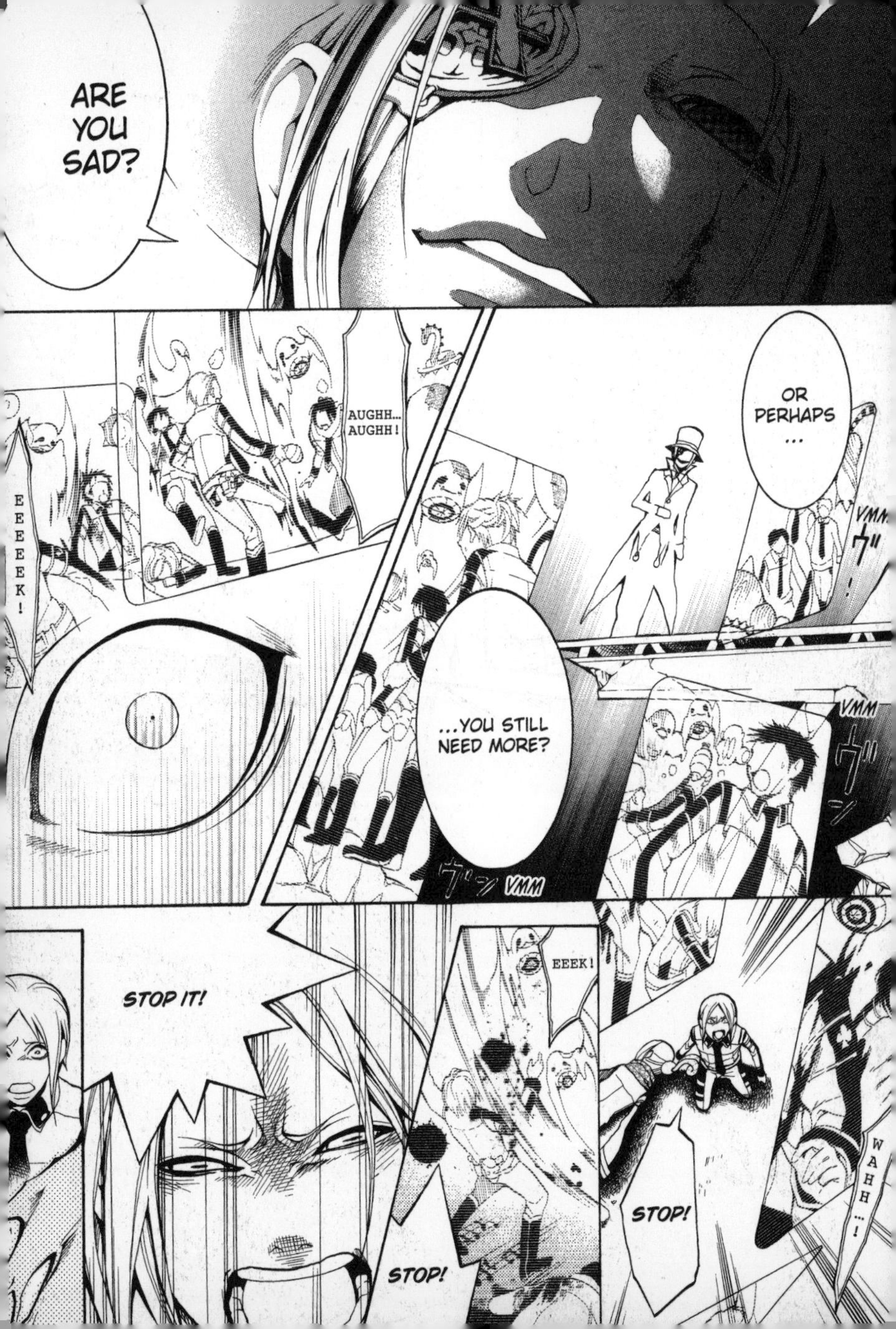
ARE YOU SAD?
OR PERHAPS ...
VMM
...YOU STILL NEED MORE?
VMM
VMM
AUGHH... AUGHH!
EEEEEK!
WAHH...!
STOP!
EEEK!
STOP!
STOP IT!

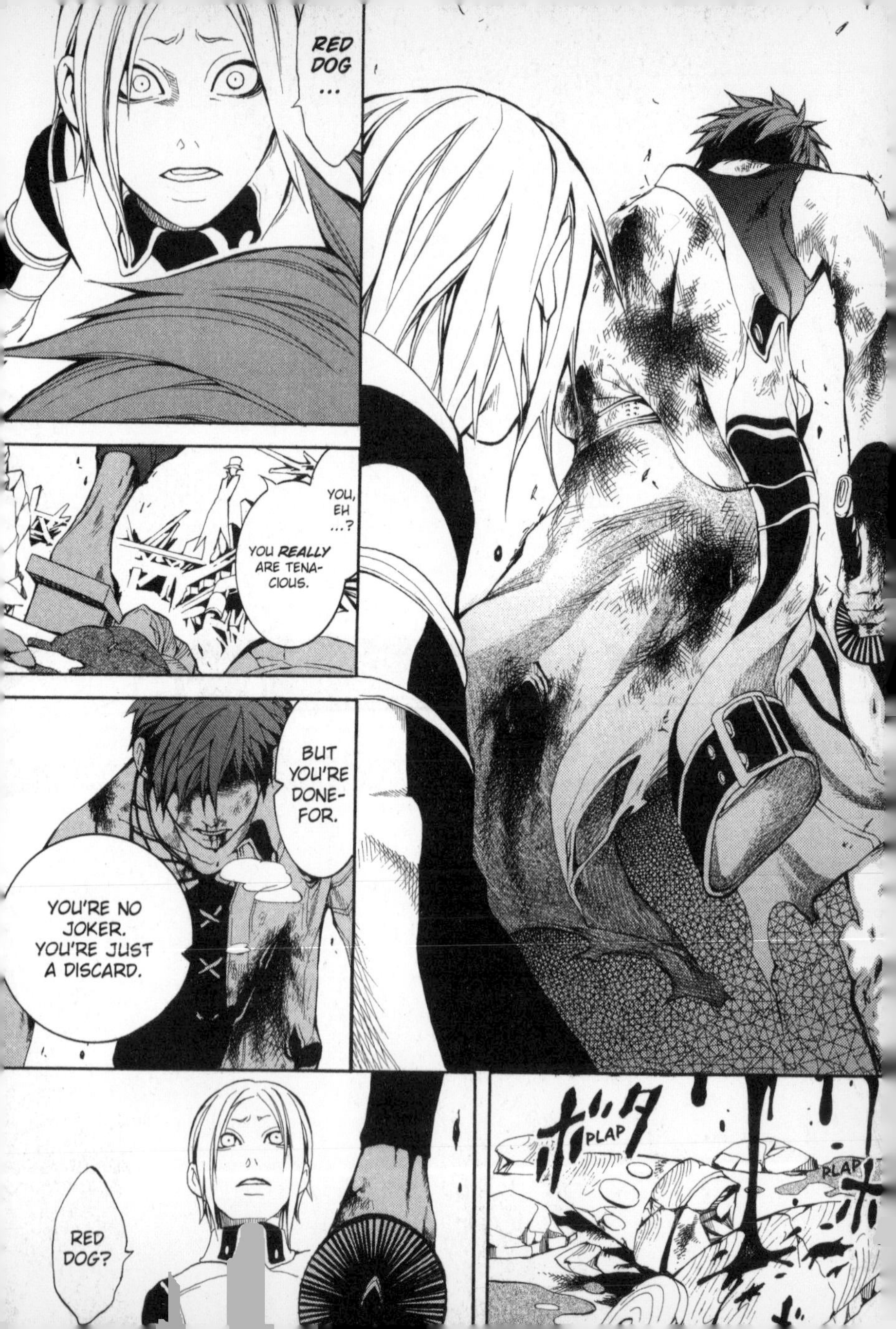

RED DOG ...
YOU, EH ...?
YOU REALLY ARE TENACIOUS.
BUT YOU'RE DONE-FOR.
YOU'RE NO JOKER. YOU'RE JUST A DISCARD.
PLAP
PLAP
RED DOG?

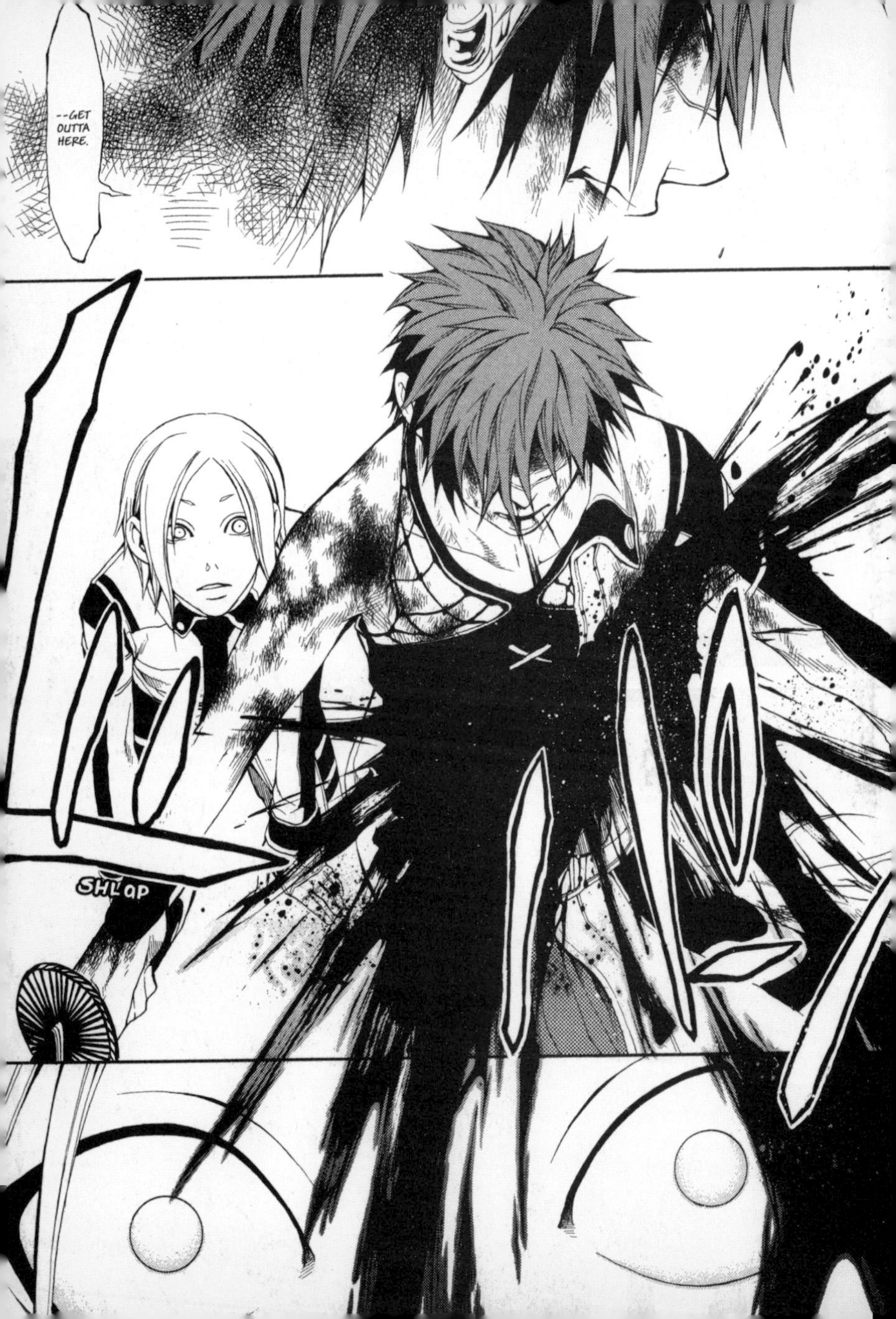
--GET OUTTA HERE.
SHLap

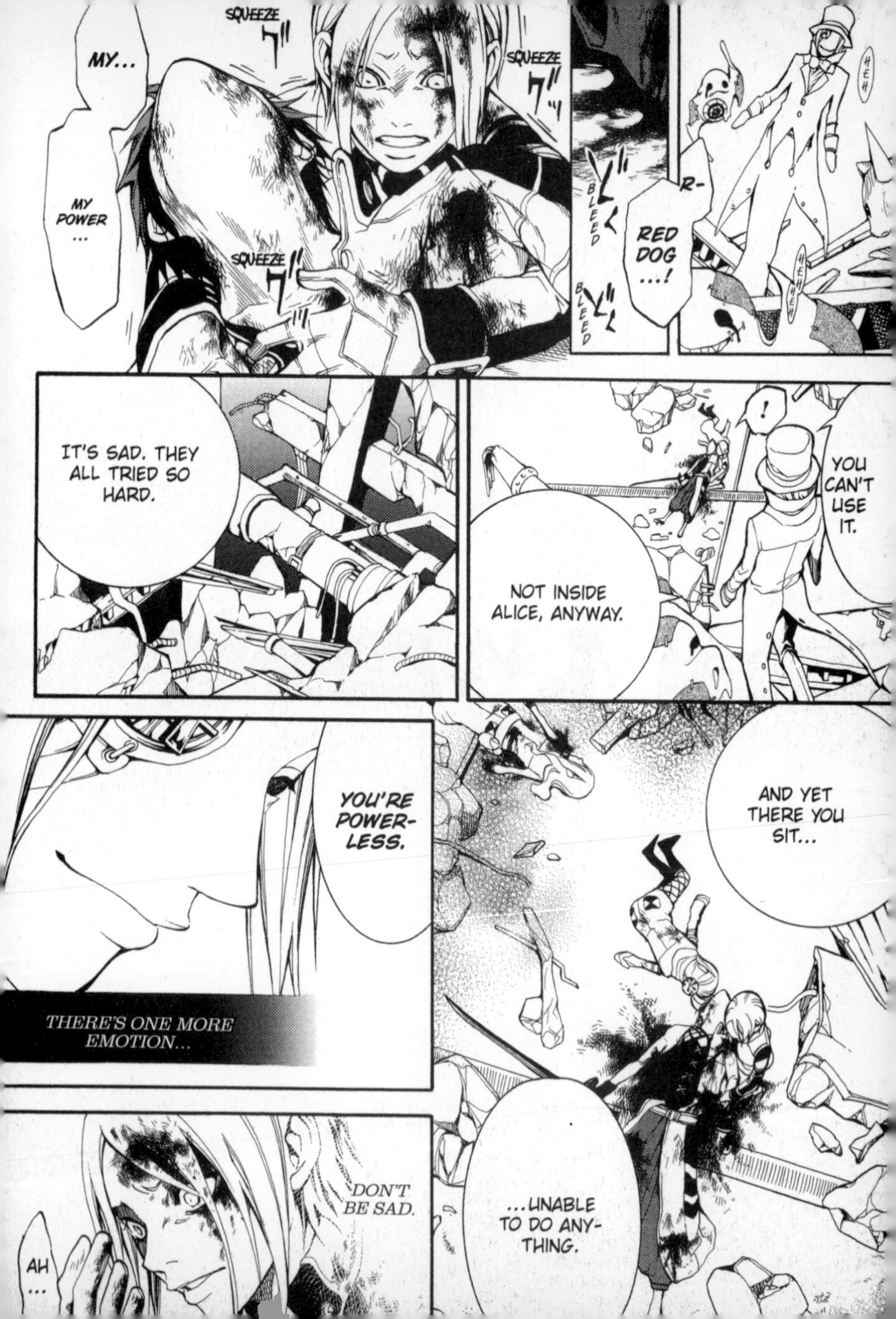
HEH HEH
HEHEHEH
R-
RED DOG...!
BLEED
BLEED
SQUEEZE
SQUEEZE
MY...
MY POWER...
SQUEEZE
YOU CAN'T USE IT.
NOT INSIDE ALICE, ANYWAY.
IT'S SAD. THEY ALL TRIED SO HARD.
AND YET THERE YOU SIT...
...UNABLE TO DO ANY-THING.
YOU'RE POWER-LESS.
THERE'S ONE MORE EMOTION...
DON'T BE SAD.
AH...

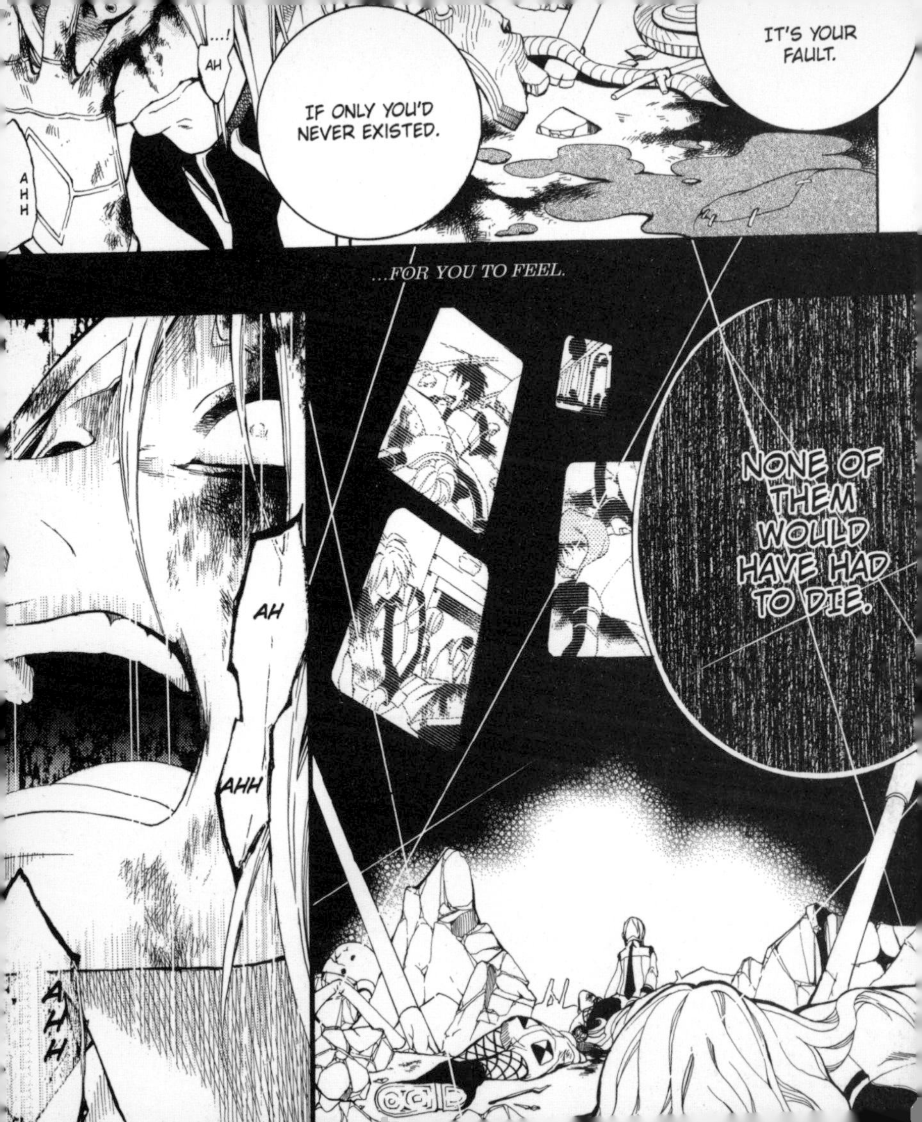
IT'S YOUR FAULT.
IF ONLY YOU'D NEVER EXISTED.
...!
AH
AHH
...FOR YOU TO FEEL.
NONE OF THEM WOULD HAVE HAD TO DIE.
AH
AHH
AHH

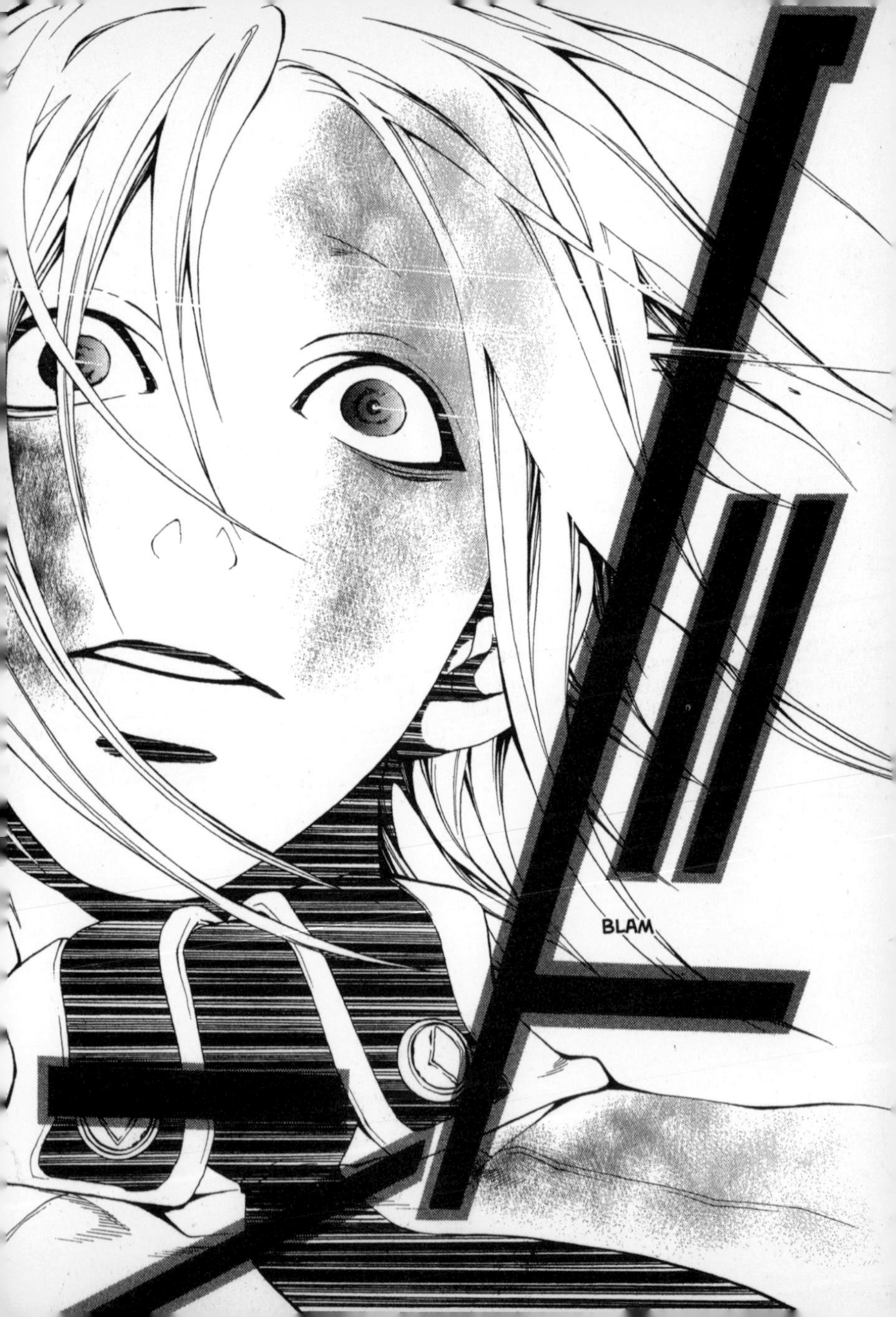
BLAM

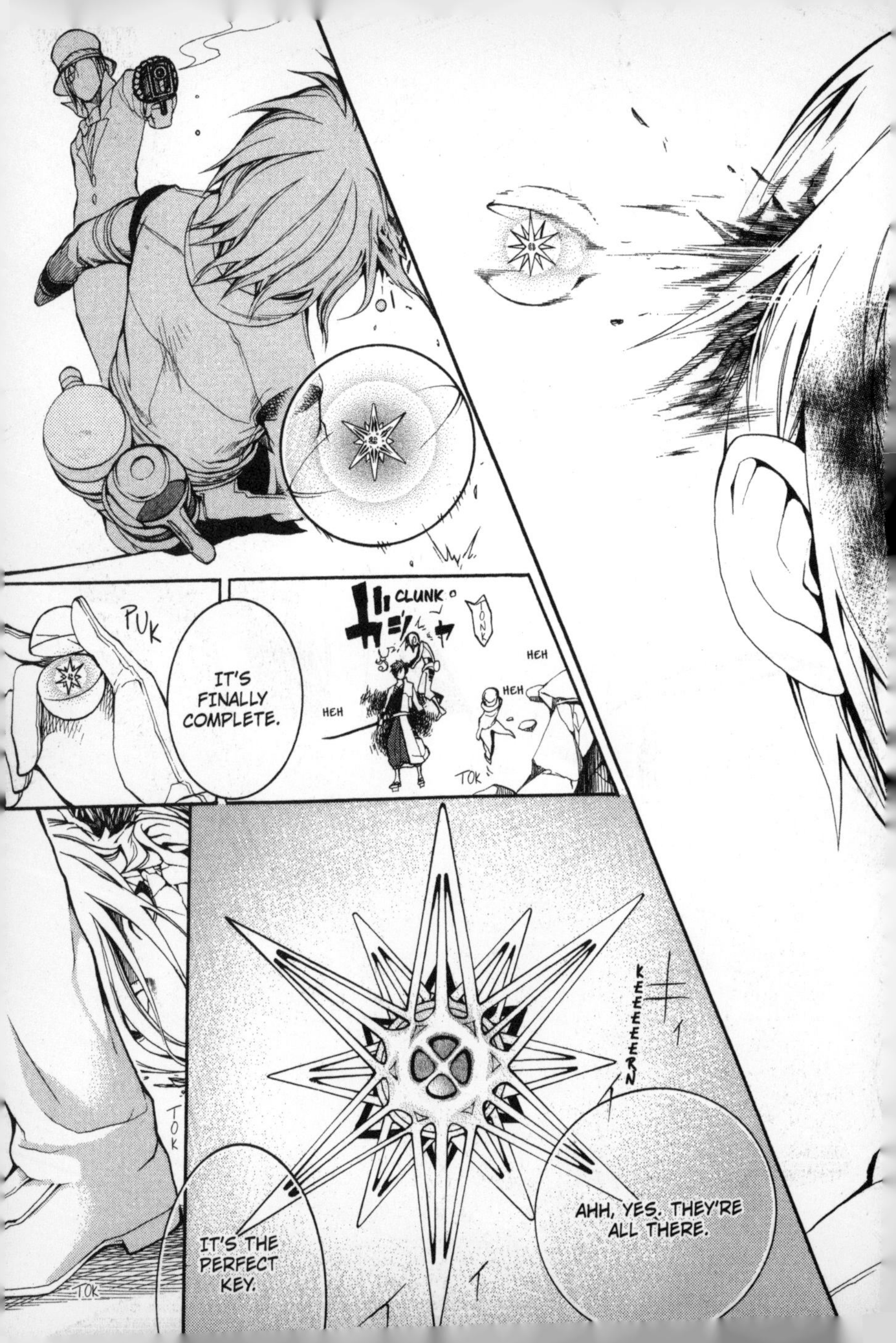
CLUNK
TONK
HEH
HEH
HEH
TOK
PUK
IT'S FINALLY COMPLETE.
KEEEERN
AHH, YES. THEY'RE ALL THERE.
IT'S THE PERFECT KEY.
TOK
TOK

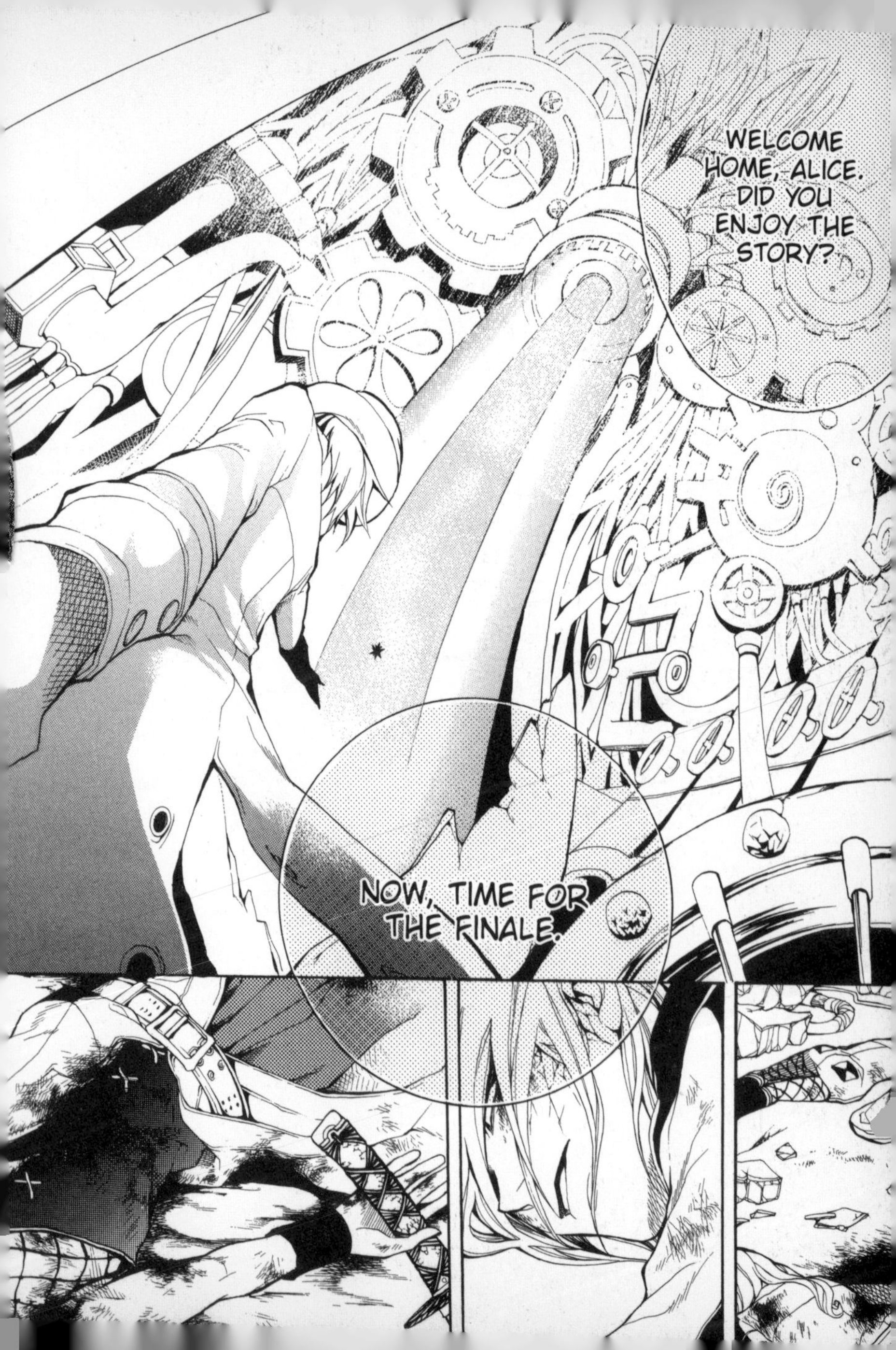
WELCOME HOME, ALICE. DID YOU ENJOY THE STORY?
NOW, TIME FOR THE FINALE.

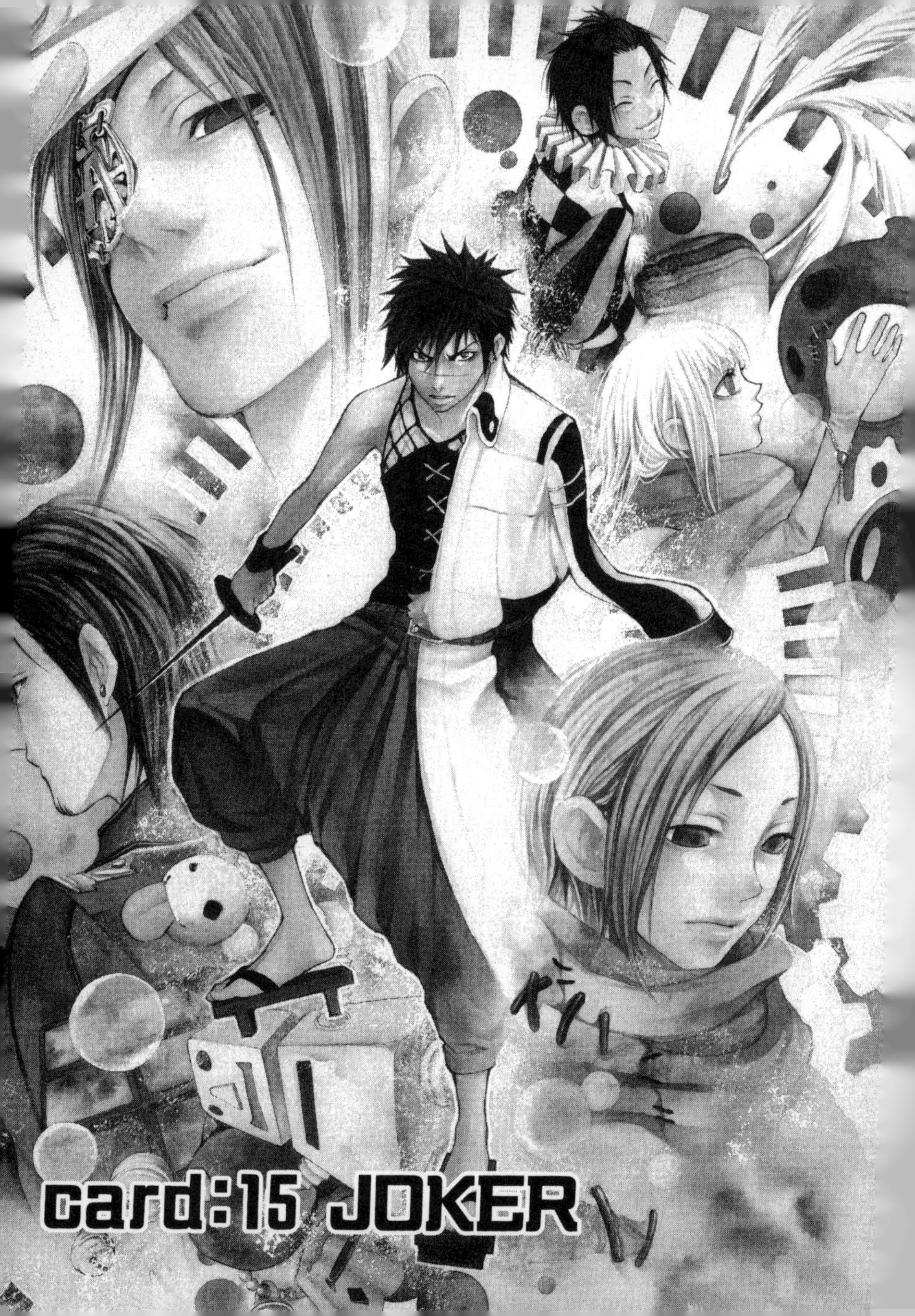
card:15 JOKER

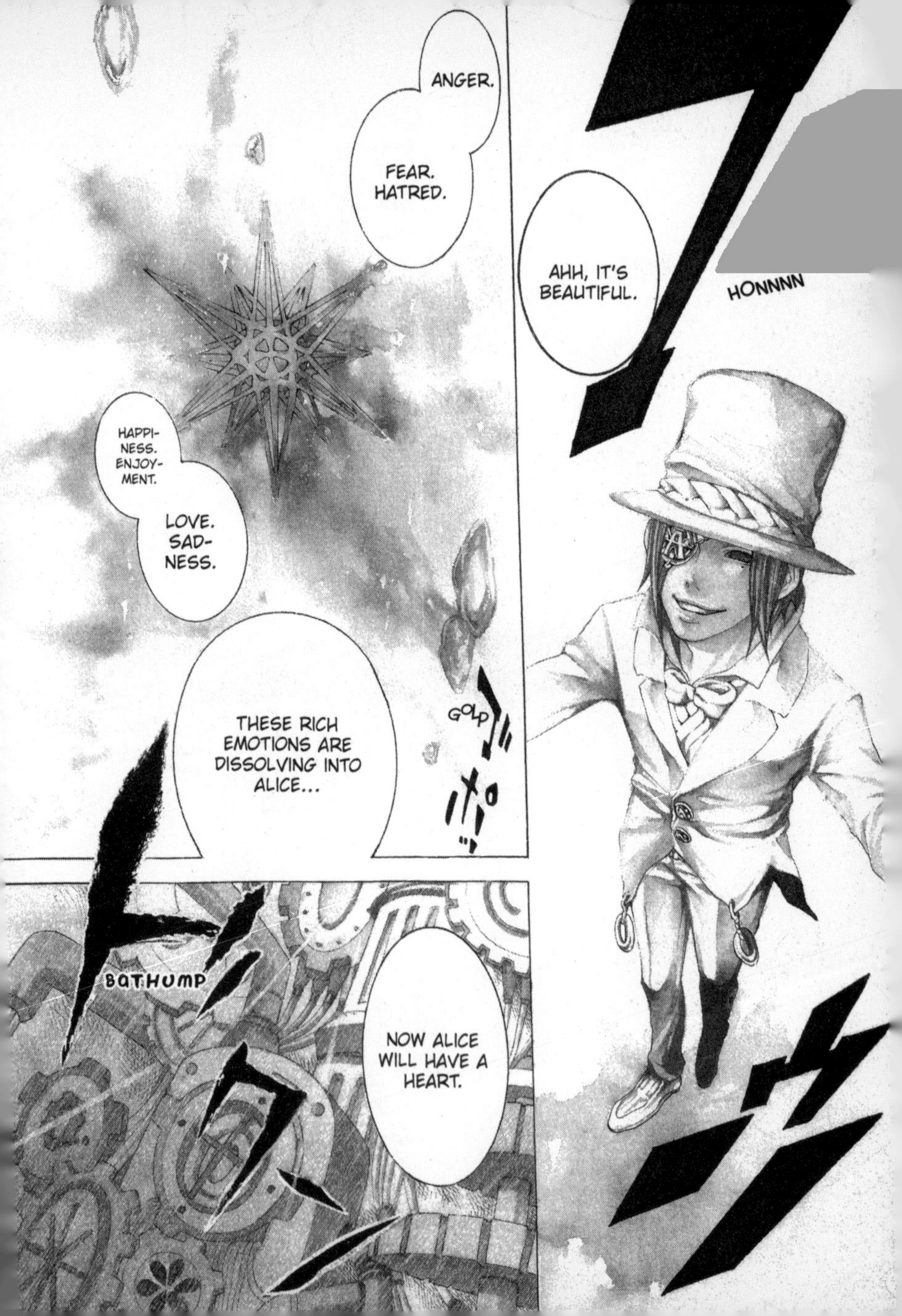
HONNNN
AHH, IT'S BEAUTIFUL.
ANGER.
FEAR. HATRED.
HAPPI-NESS. ENJOY-MENT.
LOVE. SAD-NESS.
THESE RICH EMOTIONS ARE DISSOLVING INTO ALICE...
GOLP
BATHUMP
NOW ALICE WILL HAVE A HEART.

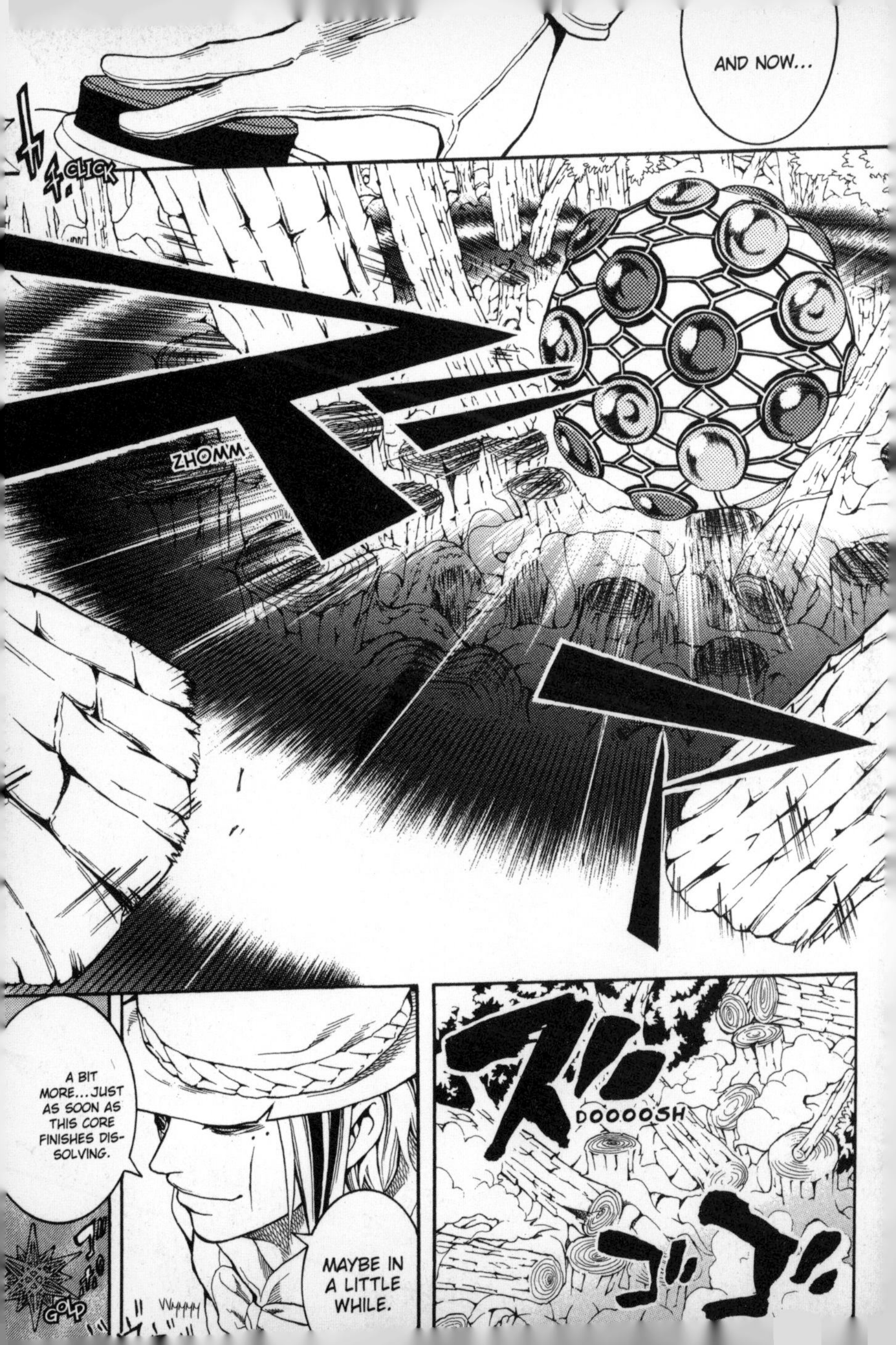
AND NOW...
CLICK
ZHOMM
DOOOOSH
A BIT MORE... JUST AS SOON AS THIS CORE FINISHES DIS-SOLVING.
MAYBE IN A LITTLE WHILE.
GOLP
VVMMMM

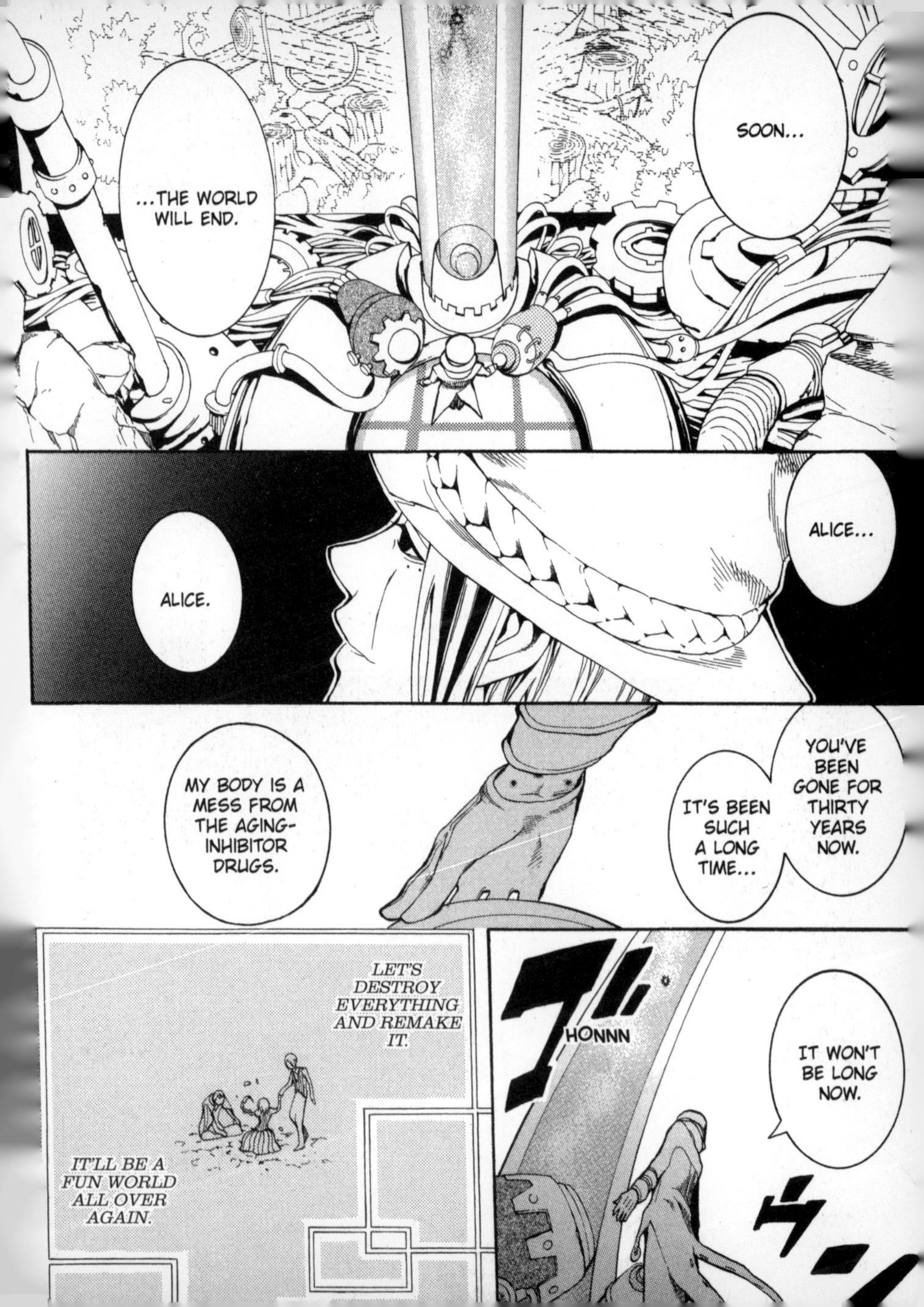
SOON...
...THE WORLD WILL END.
ALICE...
ALICE.
YOU'VE BEEN GONE FOR THIRTY YEARS NOW.
IT'S BEEN SUCH A LONG TIME...
MY BODY IS A MESS FROM THE AGING-INHIBITOR DRUGS.
HONNN
IT WON'T BE LONG NOW.
LET'S DESTROY EVERYTHING AND REMAKE IT.
IT'LL BE A FUN WORLD ALL OVER AGAIN.

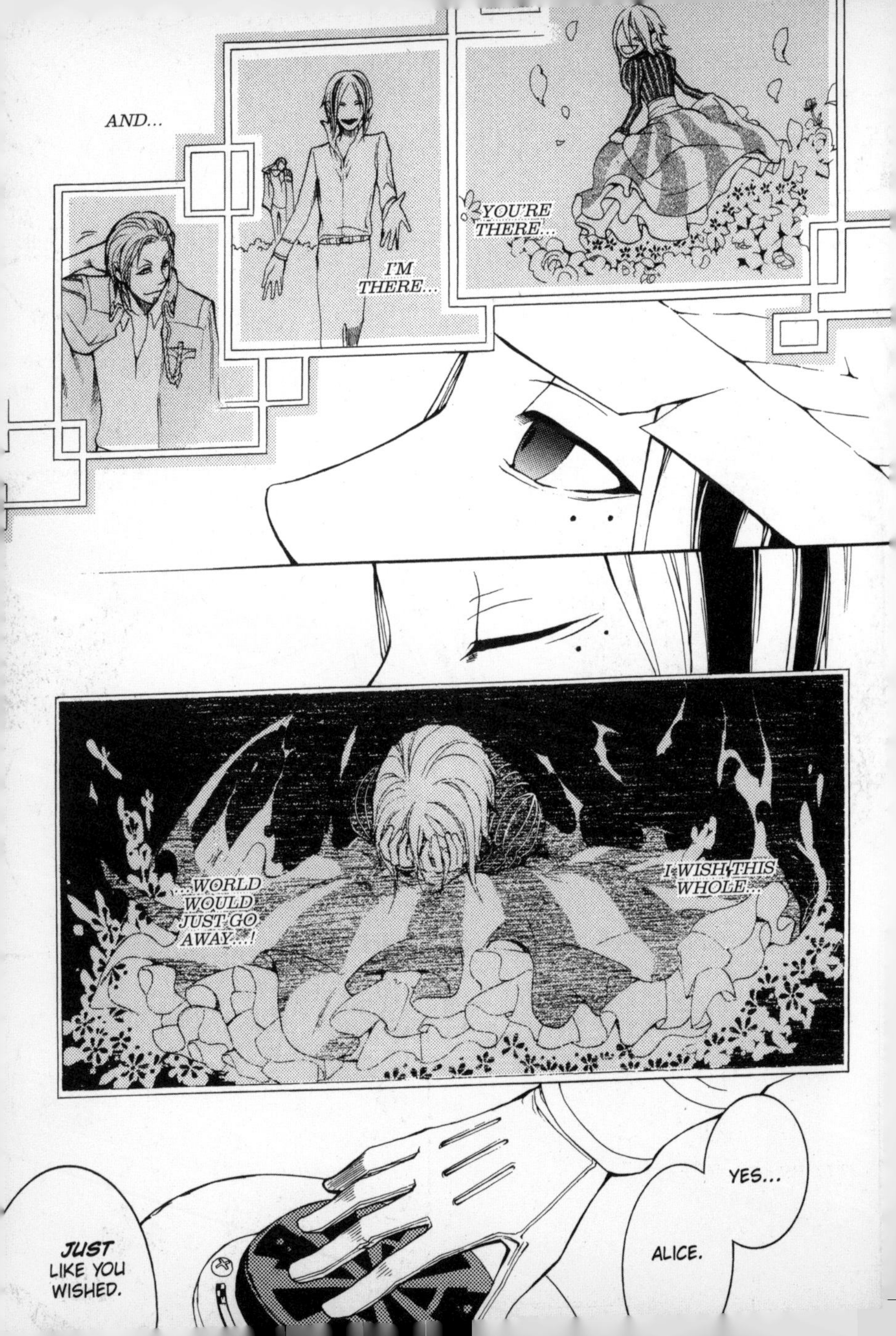
YOU'RE THERE...
I'M THERE...
AND...
I WISH THIS WHOLE...
...WORLD WOULD JUST GO AWAY...!
YES...
ALICE.
JUST LIKE YOU WISHED.

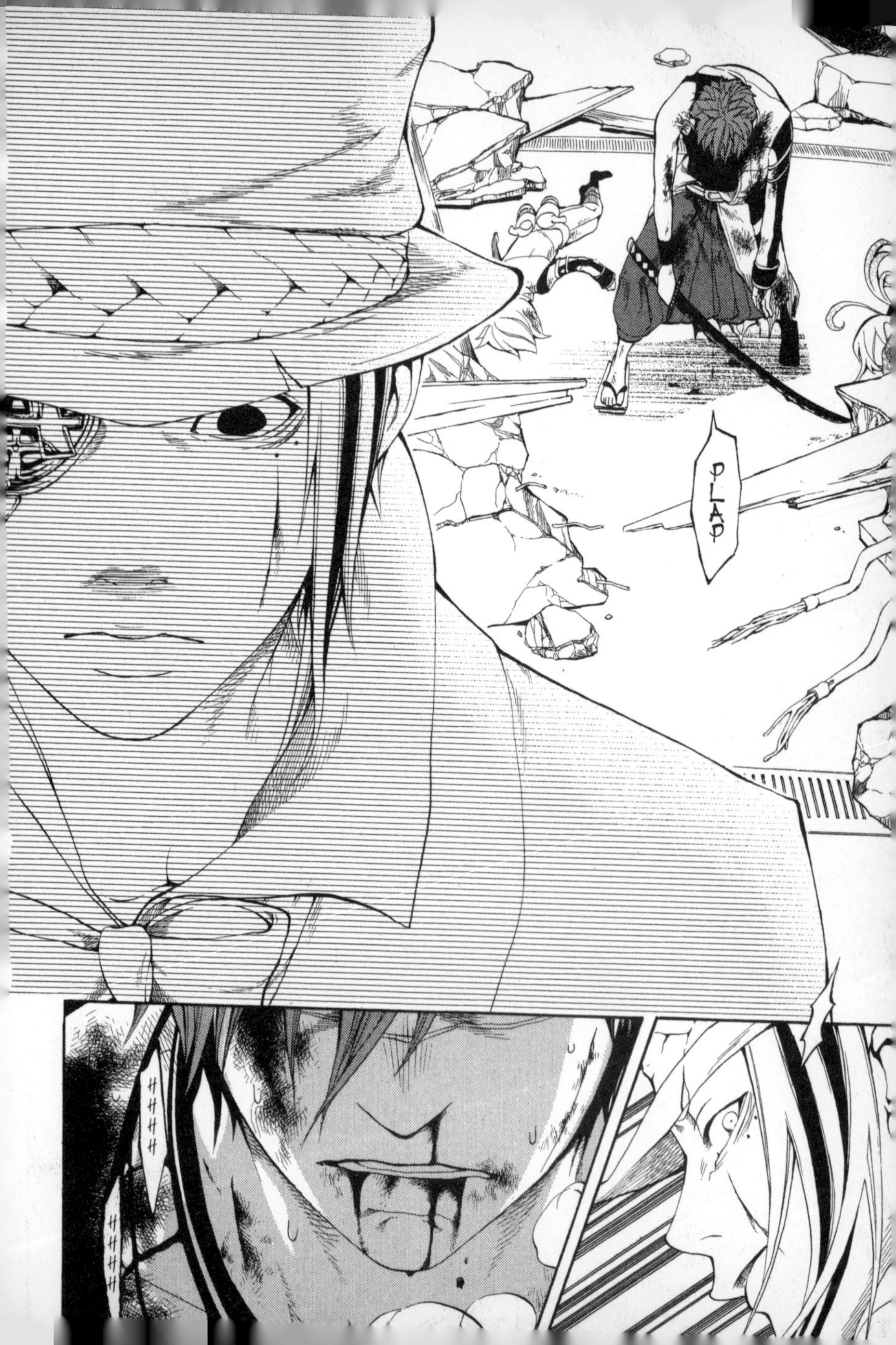
PLAP
HHHH
HHHH

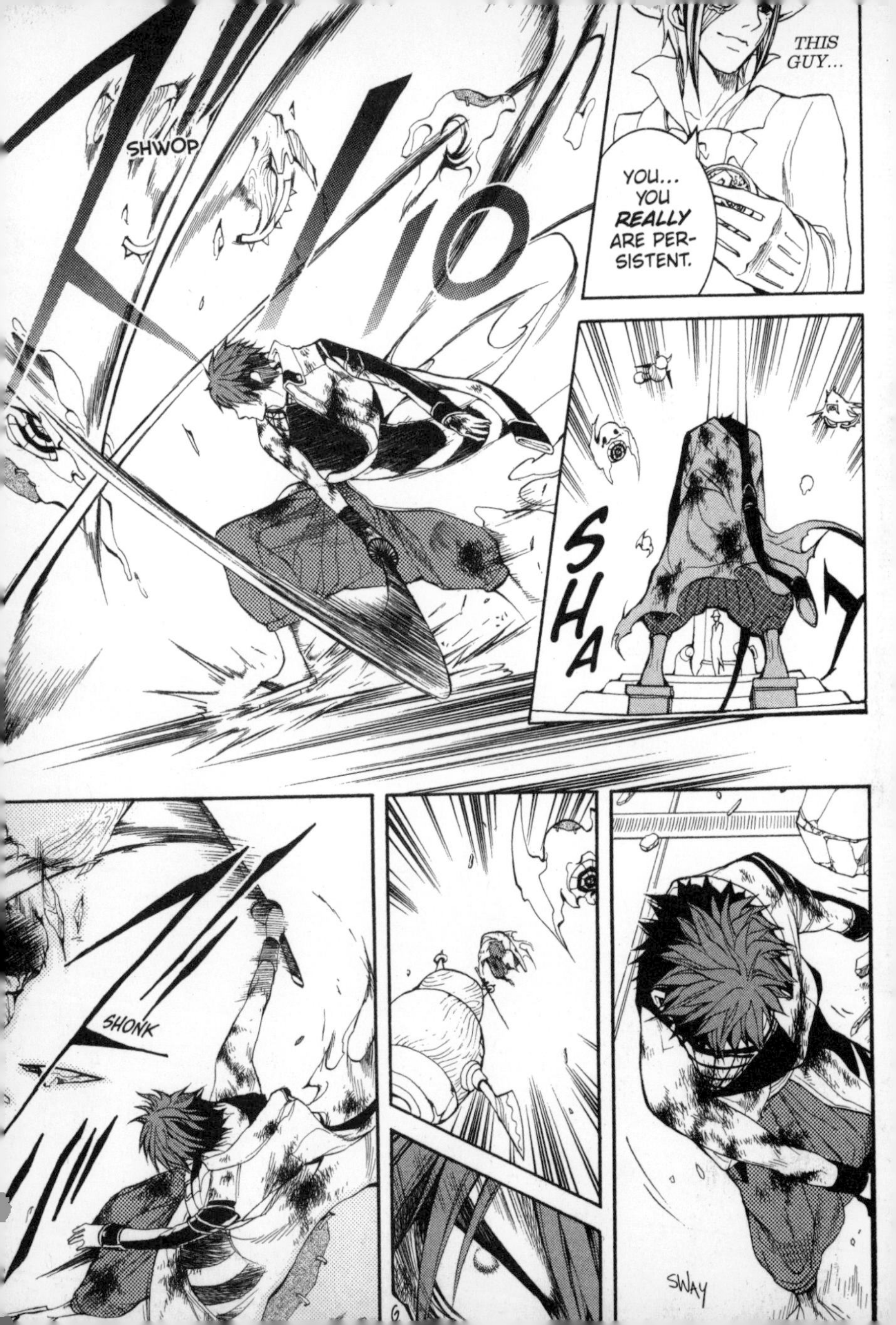
THIS GUY...
YOU... YOU REALLY ARE PER-SISTENT.
SHA
SHWOP
SWAY
SHONK

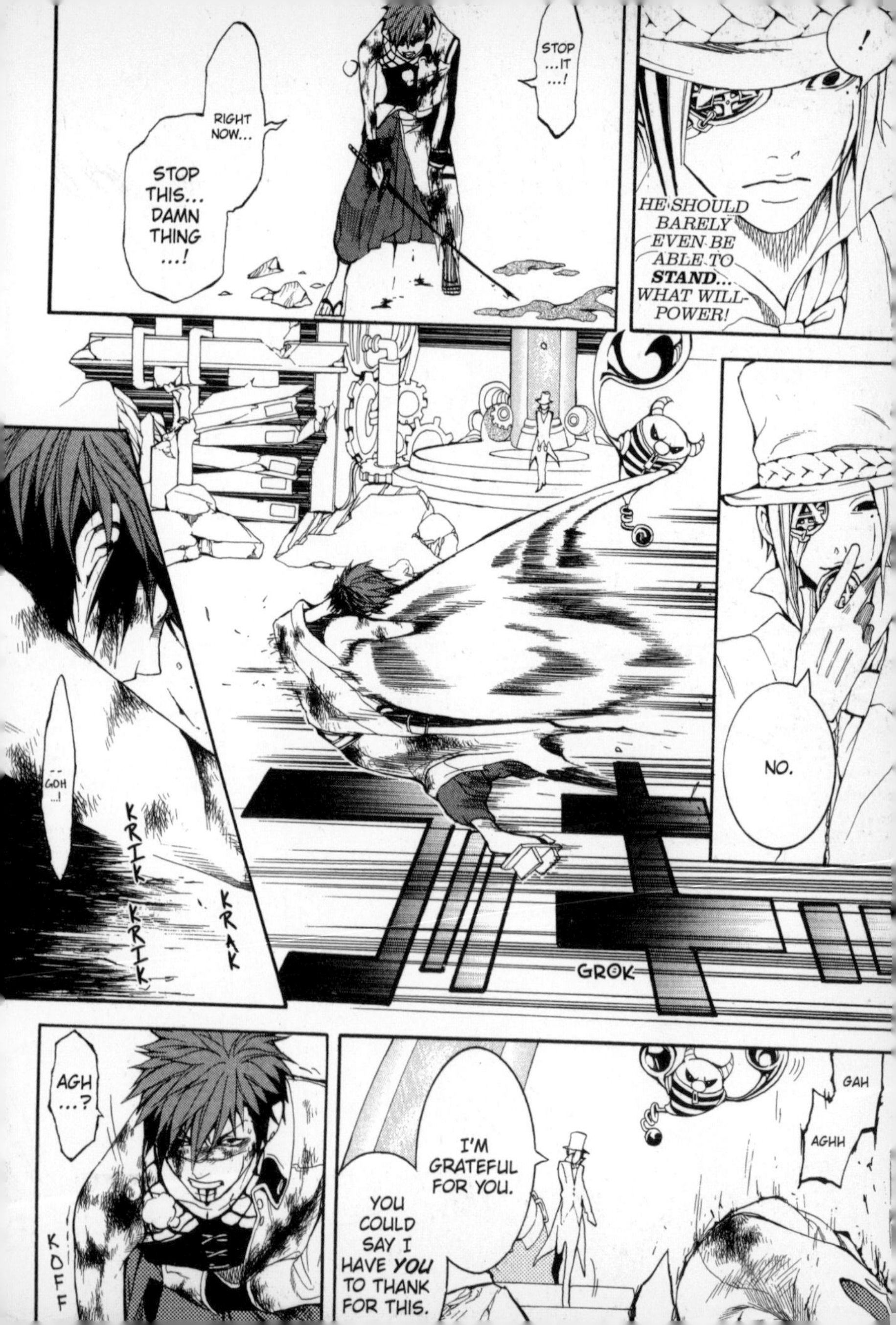
!
HE SHOULD BARELY EVEN BE ABLE TO **STAND**... WHAT WILL-POWER!
STOP ...IT ...!
RIGHT NOW...
STOP THIS... DAMN THING ...!
NO.
GROK
-- GOH ...!
KRIK KRIK
KRAK
GAH
AGHH
I'M GRATEFUL FOR YOU.
YOU COULD SAY I HAVE *YOU* TO THANK FOR THIS.
AGH ...?
KOFF

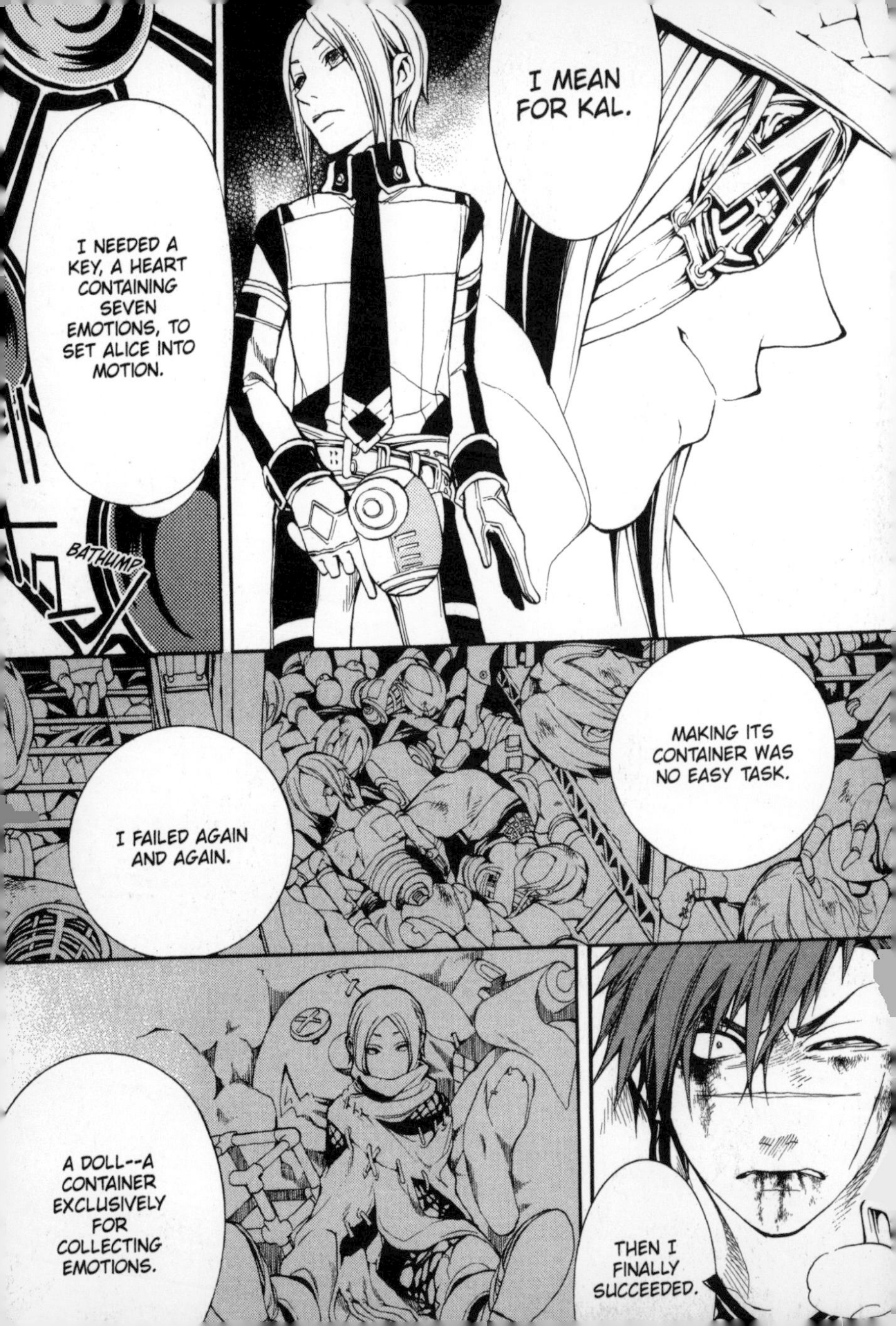
I MEAN FOR KAL.
I NEEDED A KEY, A HEART CONTAINING SEVEN EMOTIONS, TO SET ALICE INTO MOTION.
BATHUMP
MAKING ITS CONTAINER WAS NO EASY TASK.
I FAILED AGAIN AND AGAIN.
THEN I FINALLY SUCCEEDED.
A DOLL--A CONTAINER EXCLUSIVELY FOR COLLECTING EMOTIONS.

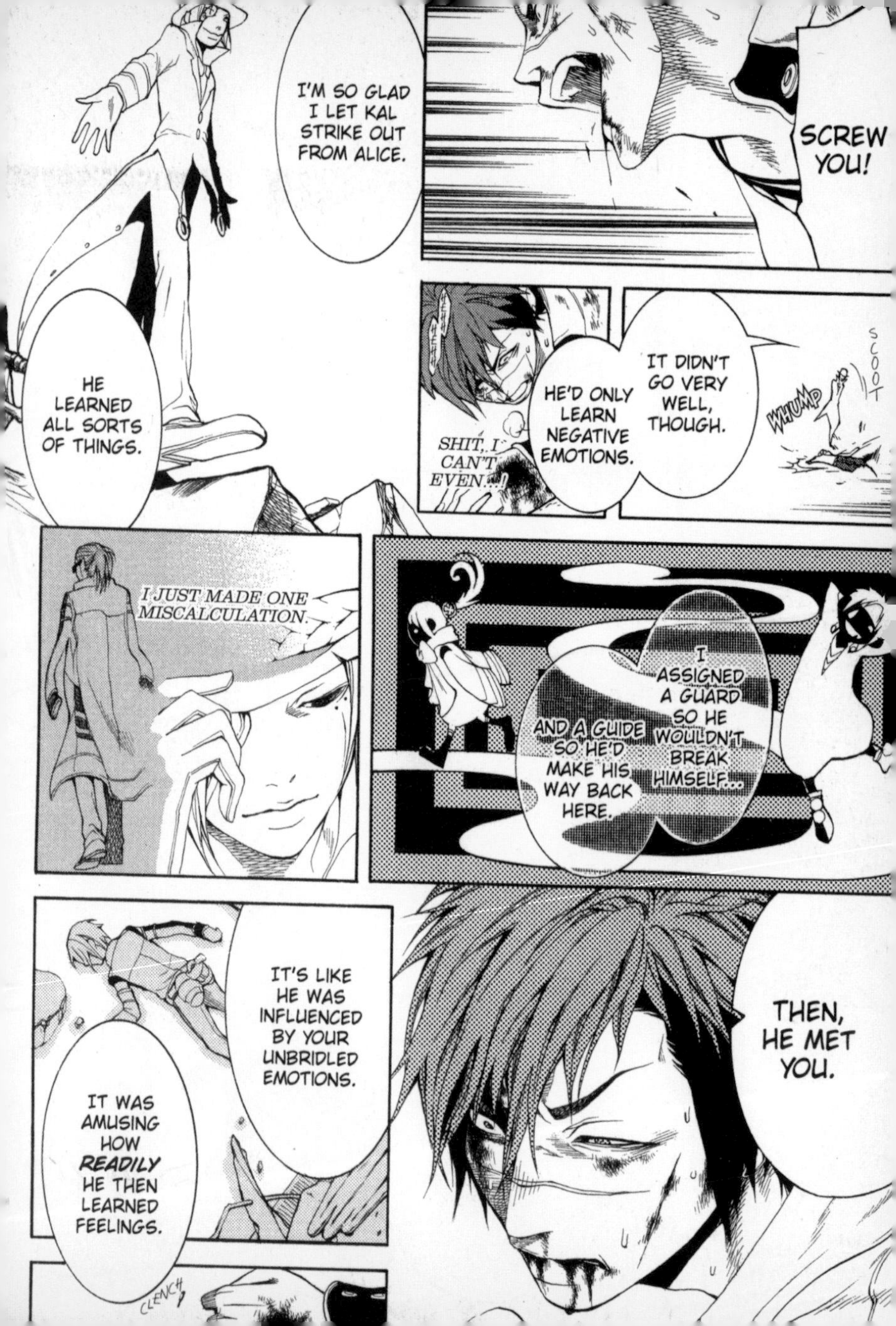
SCREW YOU!
SCOOT
WHUMP
IT DIDN'T GO VERY WELL, THOUGH.
HE'D ONLY LEARN NEGATIVE EMOTIONS.
SHIT, I CAN'T EVEN...!
I'M SO GLAD I LET KAL STRIKE OUT FROM ALICE.
HE LEARNED ALL SORTS OF THINGS.
I ASSIGNED A GUARD SO HE WOULDN'T BREAK HIMSELF...
AND A GUIDE SO HE'D MAKE HIS WAY BACK HERE.
I JUST MADE ONE MISCALCULATION.
THEN, HE MET YOU.
IT'S LIKE HE WAS INFLUENCED BY YOUR UNBRIDLED EMOTIONS.
IT WAS AMUSING HOW READILY HE THEN LEARNED FEELINGS.
CLENCH

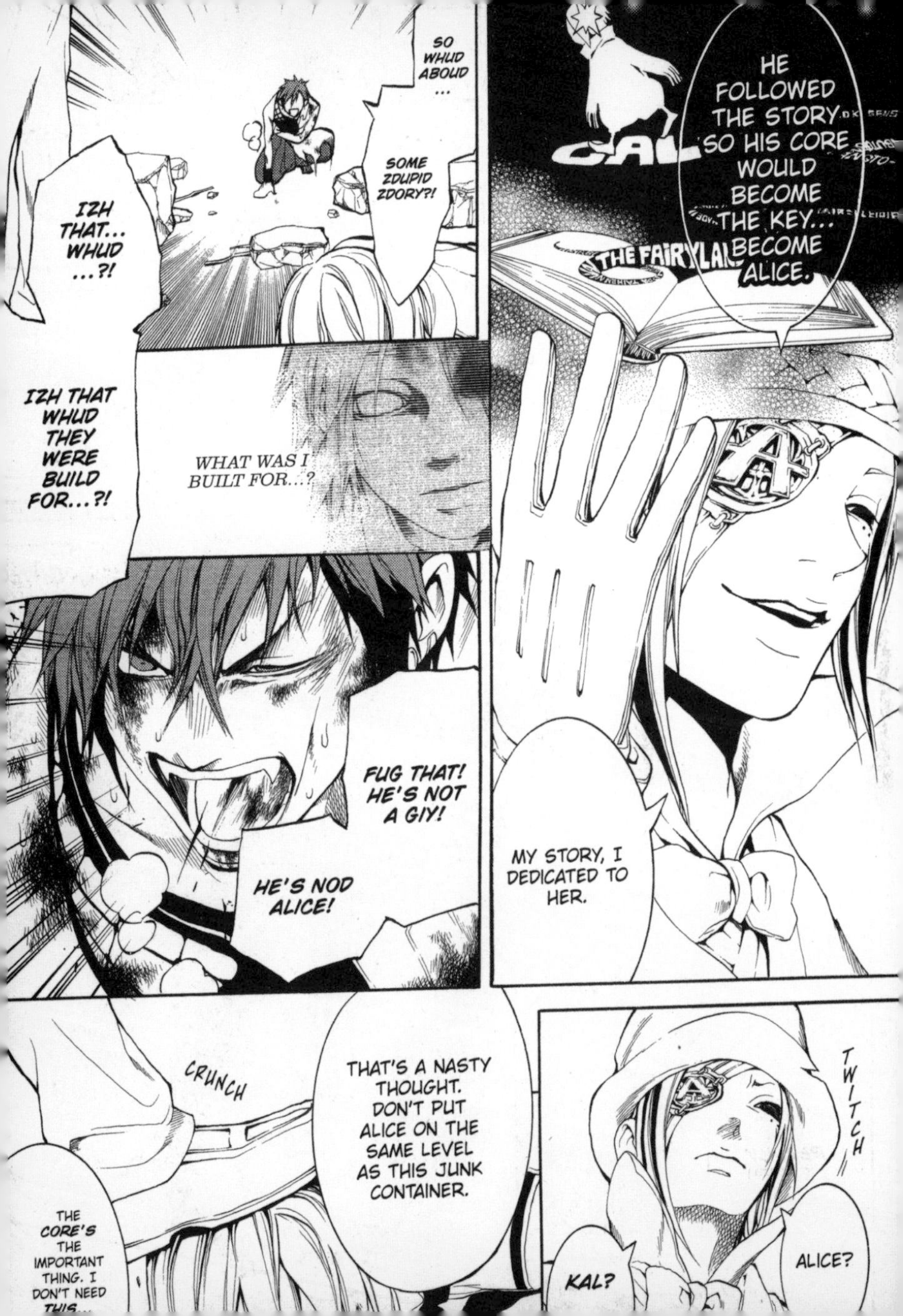
HE FOLLOWED THE STORY SO HIS CORE WOULD BECOME THE KEY... BECOME ALICE.
MY STORY, I DEDICATED TO HER.
SO WHUD ABOUD ...
SOME ZDUPID ZDORY?!
IZH THAT... WHUD ...?!
WHAT WAS I BUILT FOR...?
IZH THAT WHUD THEY WERE BUILD FOR...?!
FUG THAT! HE'S NOT A GIY!
HE'S NOD ALICE!
TWITCH
ALICE?
KAL?
THAT'S A NASTY THOUGHT. DON'T PUT ALICE ON THE SAME LEVEL AS THIS JUNK CONTAINER.
CRUNCH
THE CORE'S THE IMPORTANT THING. I DON'T NEED THIS...

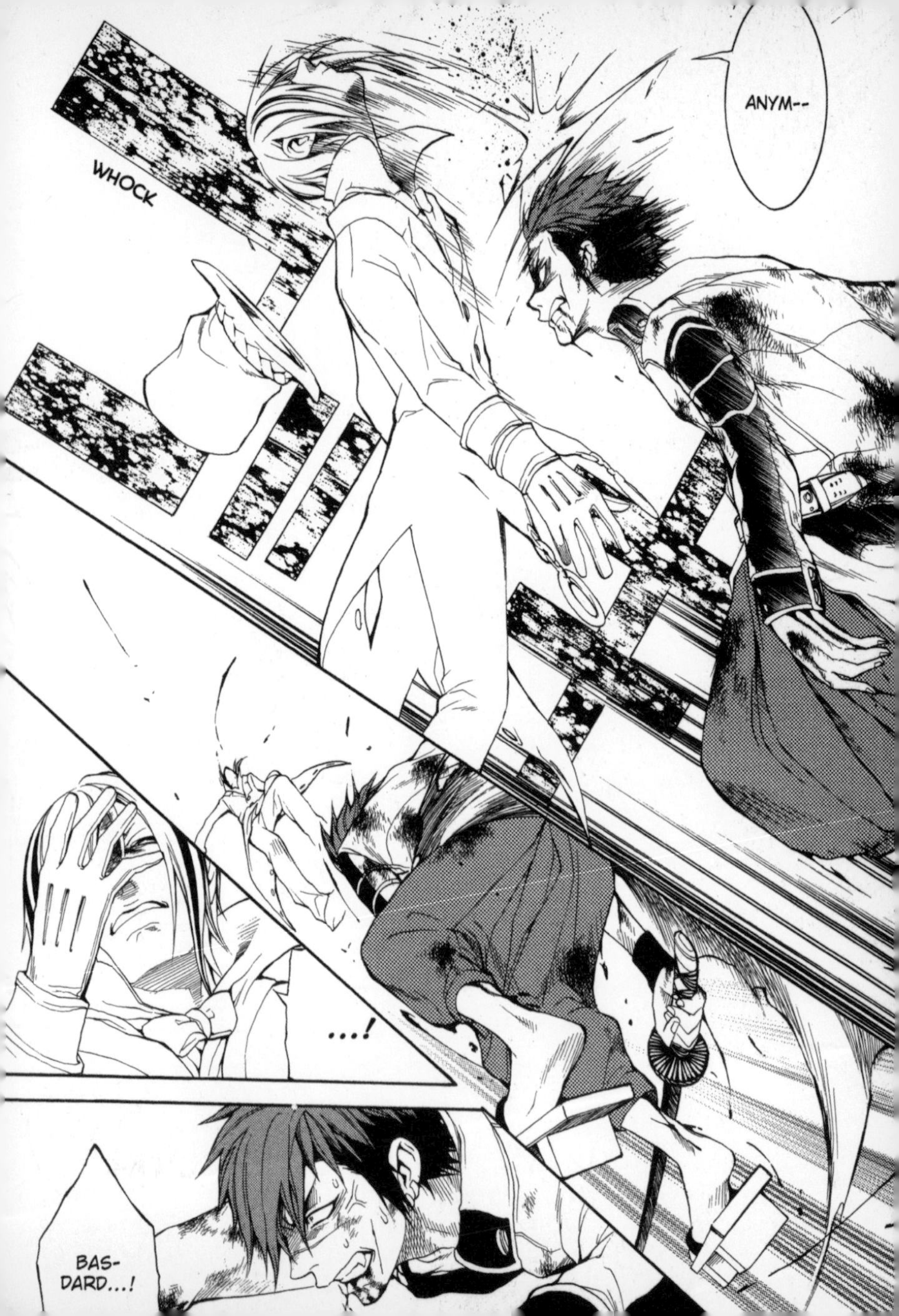
ANYM--
WHOCK
...!
BAS-
DARD...!

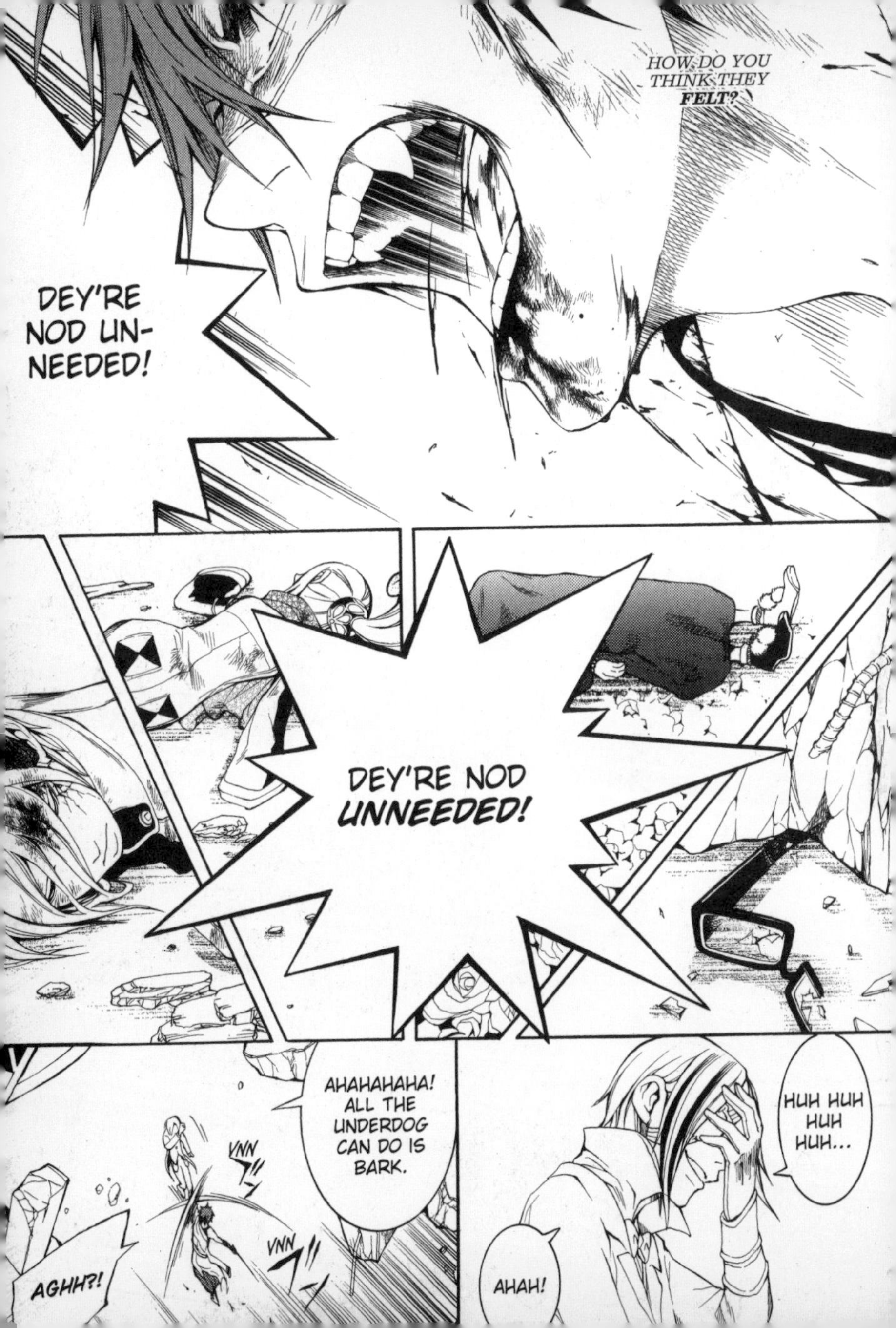
HOW DO YOU THINK THEY FELT?
DEY'RE NOD UN-NEEDED!
DEY'RE NOD UNNEEDED!
HUH HUH HUH HUH...
AHAH!
AHAHAHAHA! ALL THE UNDERDOG CAN DO IS BARK.
VNN
VNN
AGHH?!

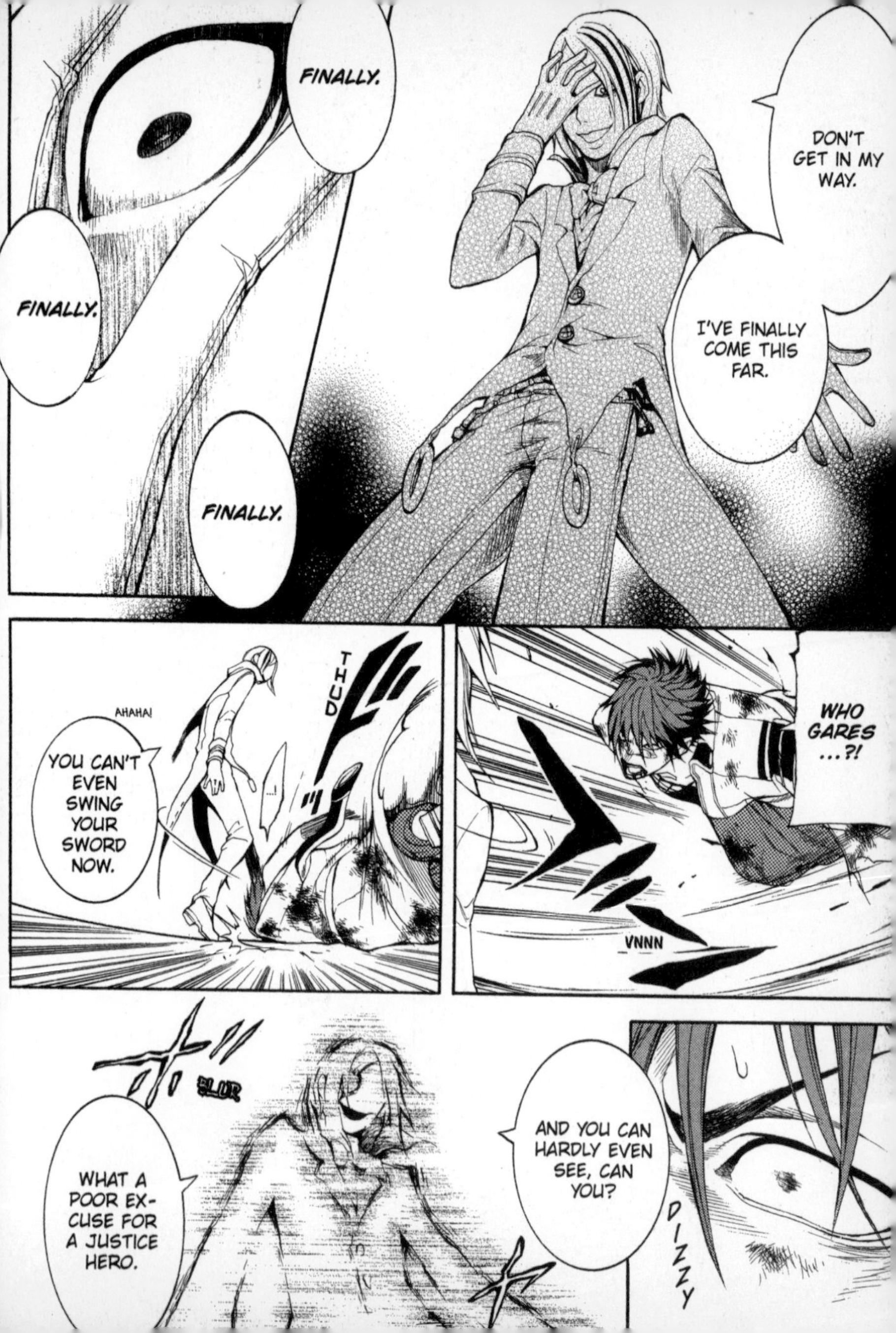
DON'T GET IN MY WAY.
I'VE FINALLY COME THIS FAR.
FINALLY.
FINALLY.
FINALLY.
WHO GARES ...?!
VNNN
THUD
AHAHA!
YOU CAN'T EVEN SWING YOUR SWORD NOW.
...!
AND YOU CAN HARDLY EVEN SEE, CAN YOU?
DIZZY
BLUR
WHAT A POOR EX-CUSE FOR A JUSTICE HERO.

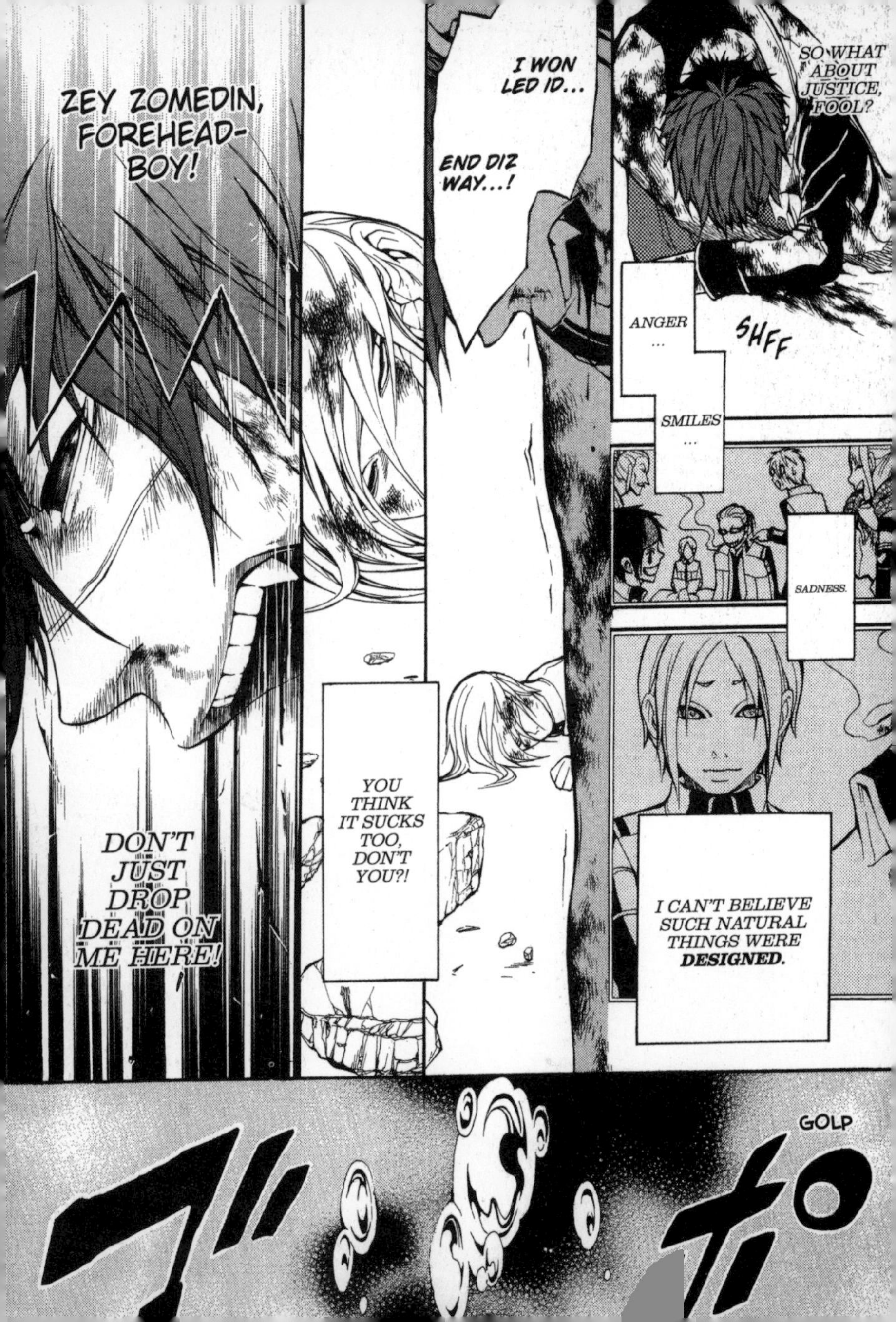
SO WHAT ABOUT JUSTICE, FOOL?
SHFF
ANGER ...
SMILES ...
SADNESS.
I CAN'T BELIEVE SUCH NATURAL THINGS WERE **DESIGNED**.
I WON LED ID...
END DIZ WAY...!
YOU THINK IT SUCKS TOO, DON'T YOU?!
ZEY ZOMEDIN, FOREHEAD-BOY!
DON'T JUST DROP DEAD ON ME HERE!
GOLP
ゴポ

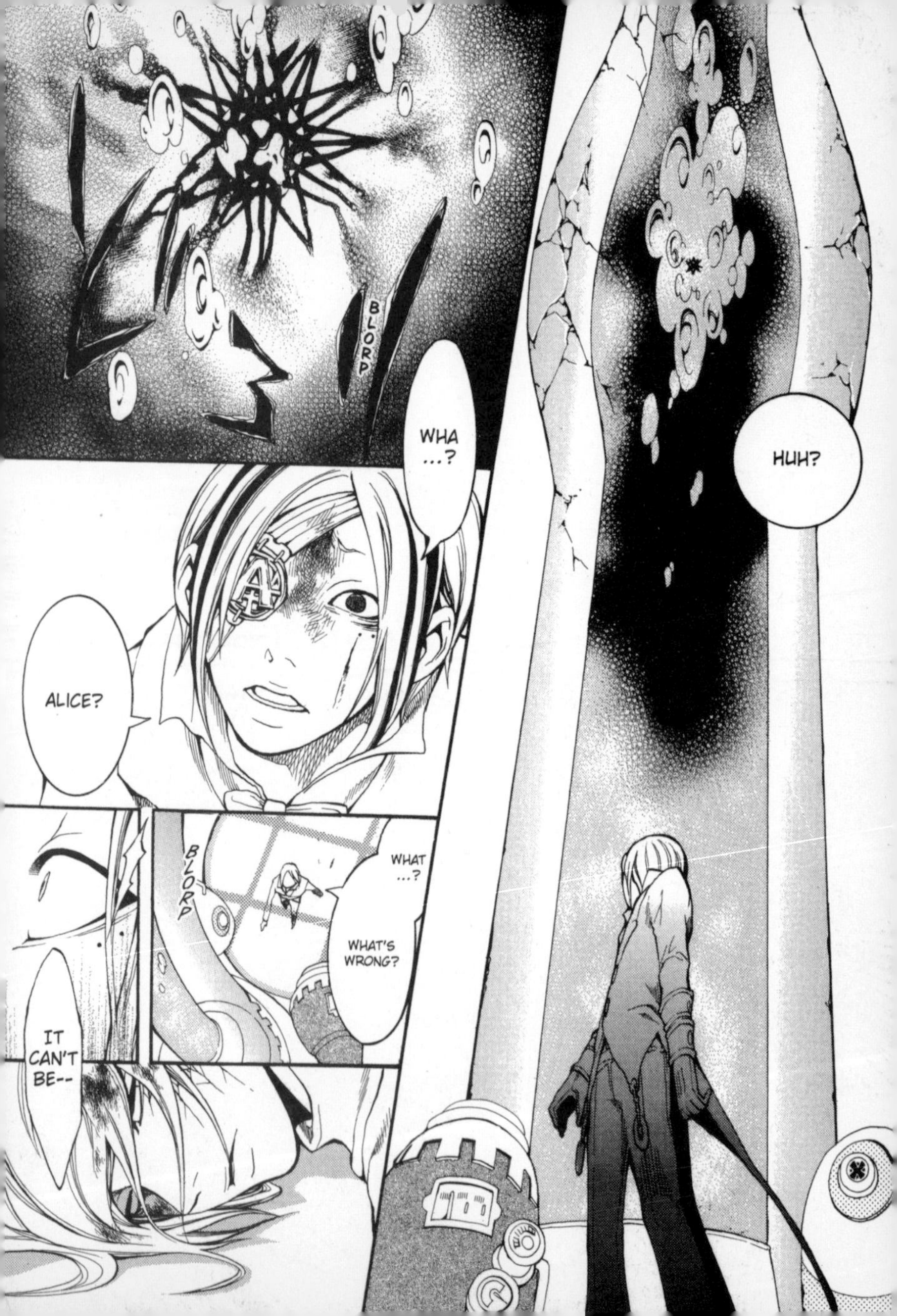
HUH?
BLORP
WHA ...?
ALICE?
BLORP
WHAT ...?
WHAT'S WRONG?
IT CAN'T BE--

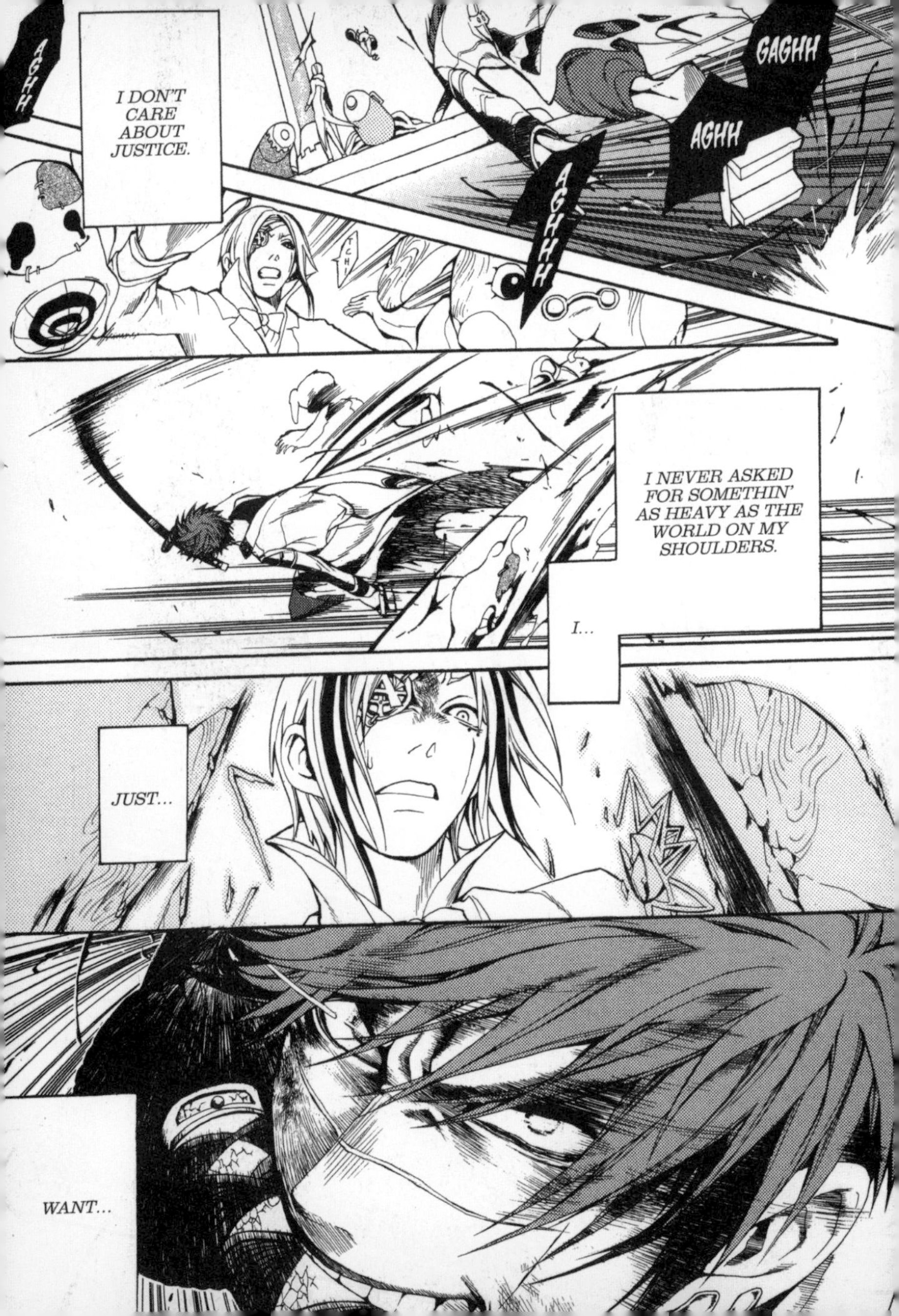
GAGHH
AGHH
AGHHH
I DON'T CARE ABOUT JUSTICE.
AGHH
TCH!
I NEVER ASKED FOR SOMETHIN' AS HEAVY AS THE WORLD ON MY SHOULDERS.
I...
JUST...
WANT...

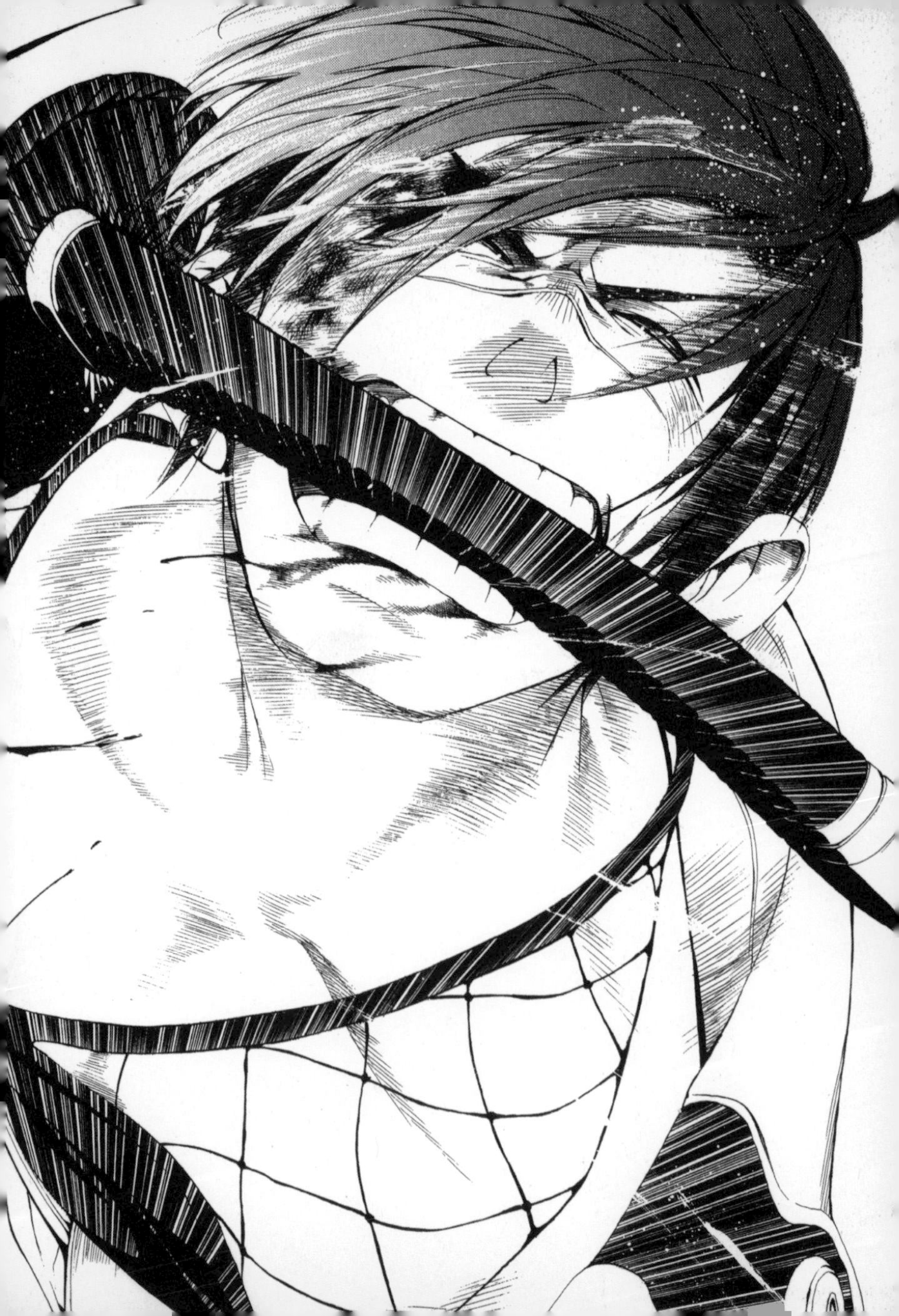

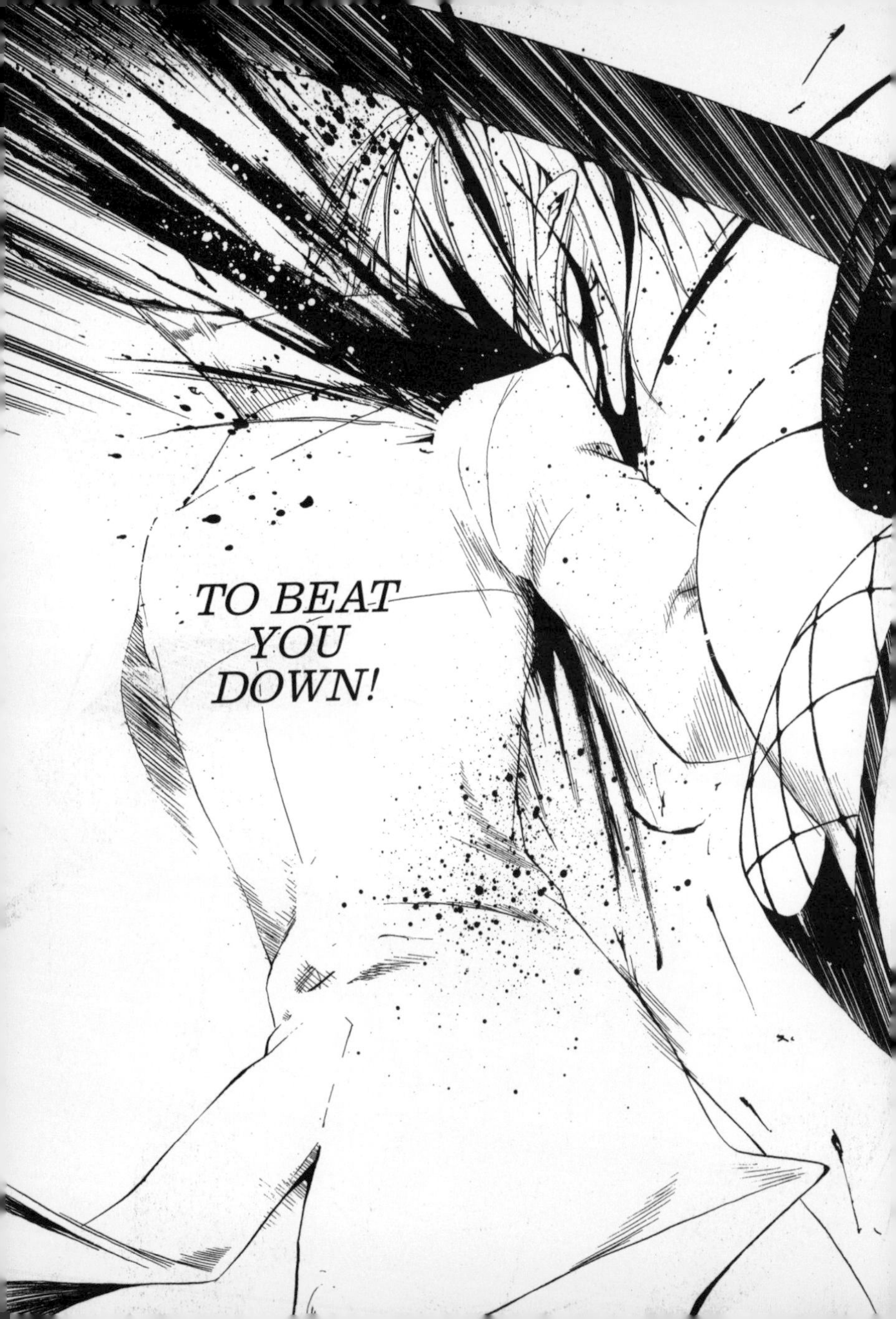
TO BEAT YOU DOWN!

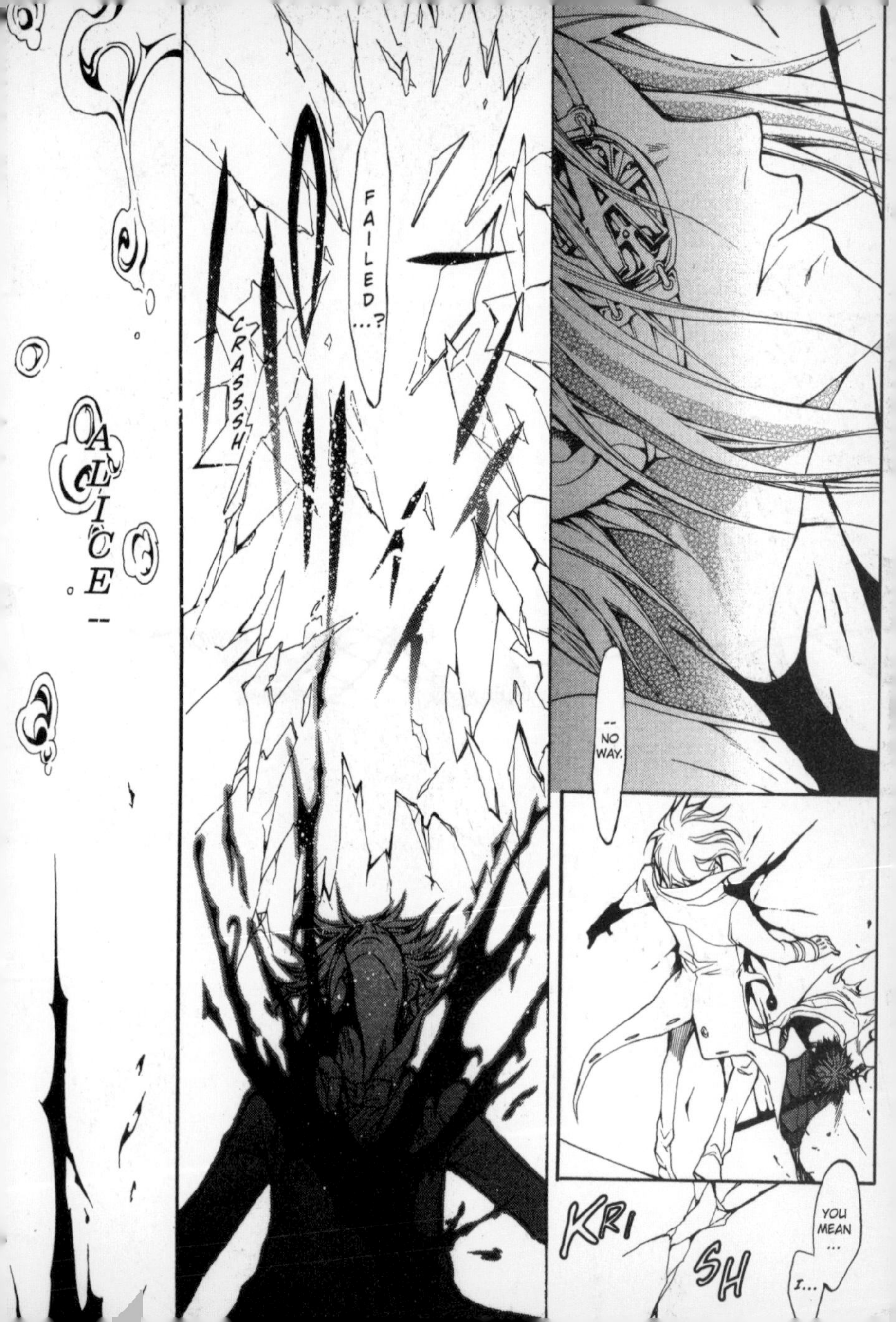
-- NO WAY.
KRISH
YOU MEAN ... I...
FAILED ...?
CRASSSH
ALICE --

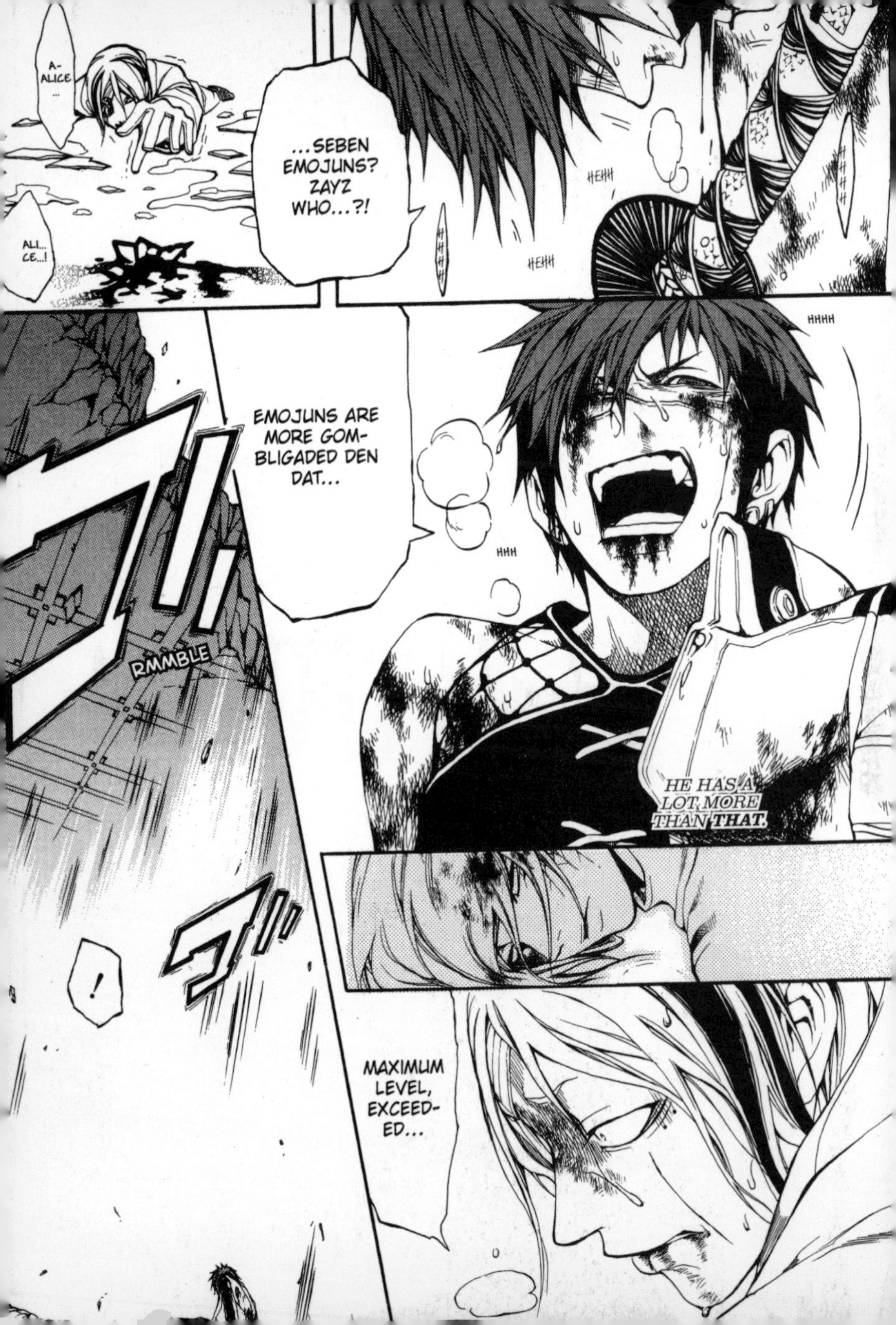
HEHH
...SEBEN EMOJUNS? ZAYZ WHO...?!
HEHH
A- ALICE ...
ALI... CE...!
HHHH
EMOJUNS ARE MORE GOM- BLIGADED DEN DAT...
HHH
HE HAS A LOT MORE THAN THAT.
MAXIMUM LEVEL, EXCEED- ED...
RMMBLE
!

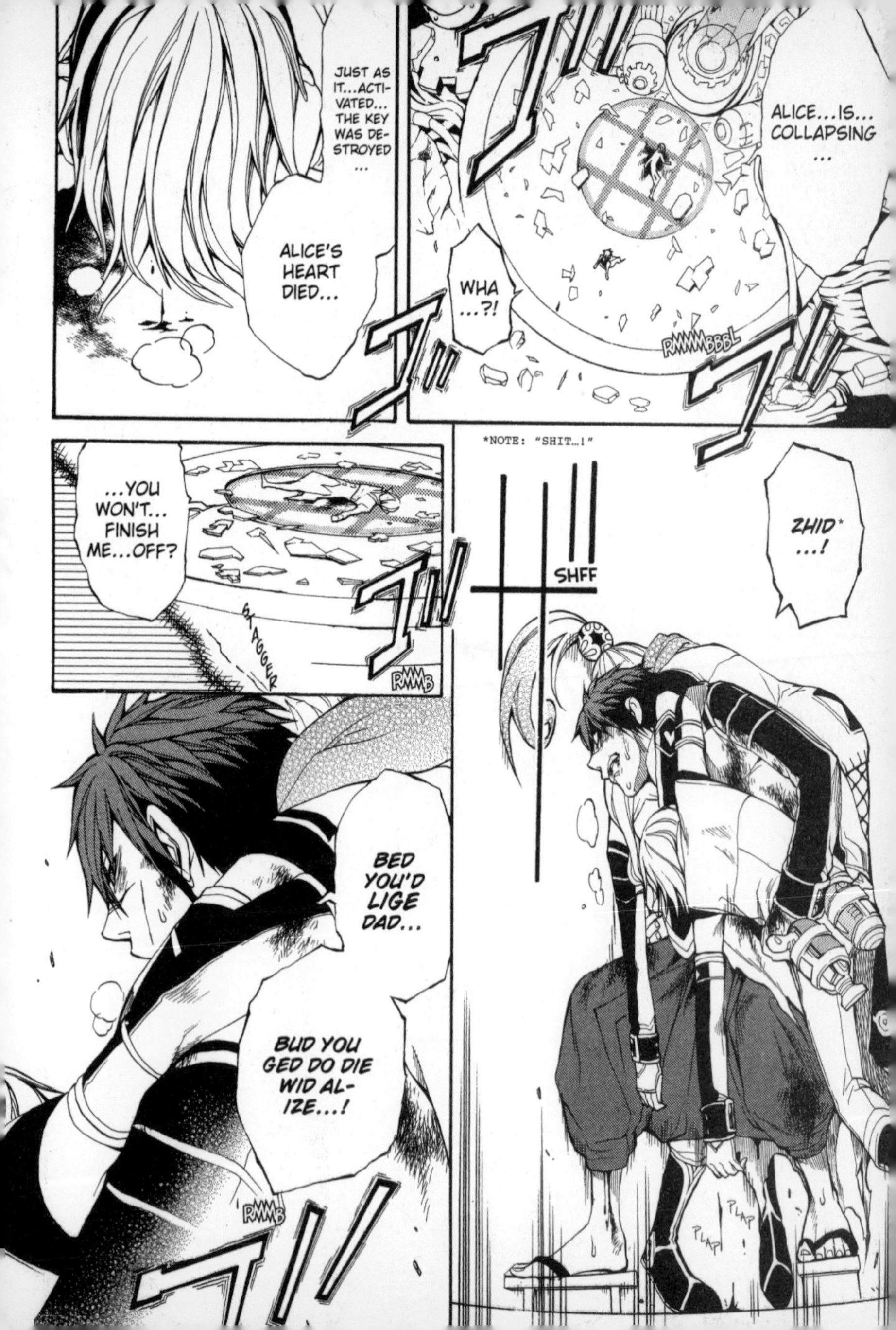
ALICE...IS... COLLAPSING ...
WHA ...?!
RMMMBBBL
JUST AS IT...ACTIVATED... THE KEY WAS DESTROYED ...
ALICE'S HEART DIED...
*NOTE: "SHIT...!"
ZHID* ...!
SHFF
PLAP
PLAP
...YOU WON'T... FINISH ME...OFF?
STAGGER
RMMB
BED YOU'D LIGE DAD...
BUD YOU GED DO DIE WID AL-IZE...!
RMMB

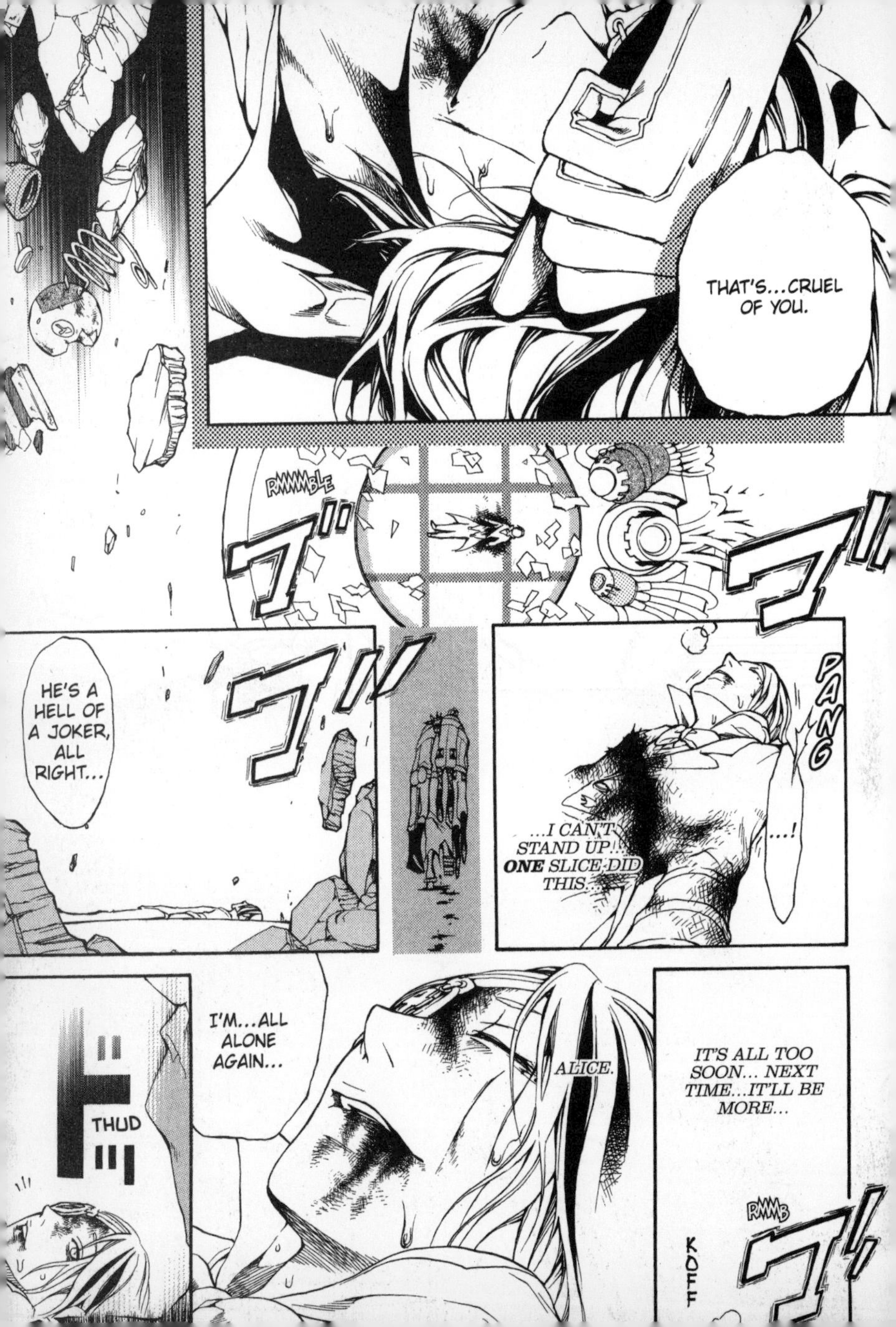
THAT'S...CRUEL OF YOU.
RMMMBLE
PANG
...!
...I CAN'T STAND UP... ONE SLICE DID THIS...
HE'S A HELL OF A JOKER, ALL RIGHT...
IT'S ALL TOO SOON... NEXT TIME...IT'LL BE MORE...
RMMB
KOFF
ALICE.
I'M...ALL ALONE AGAIN...
THUD

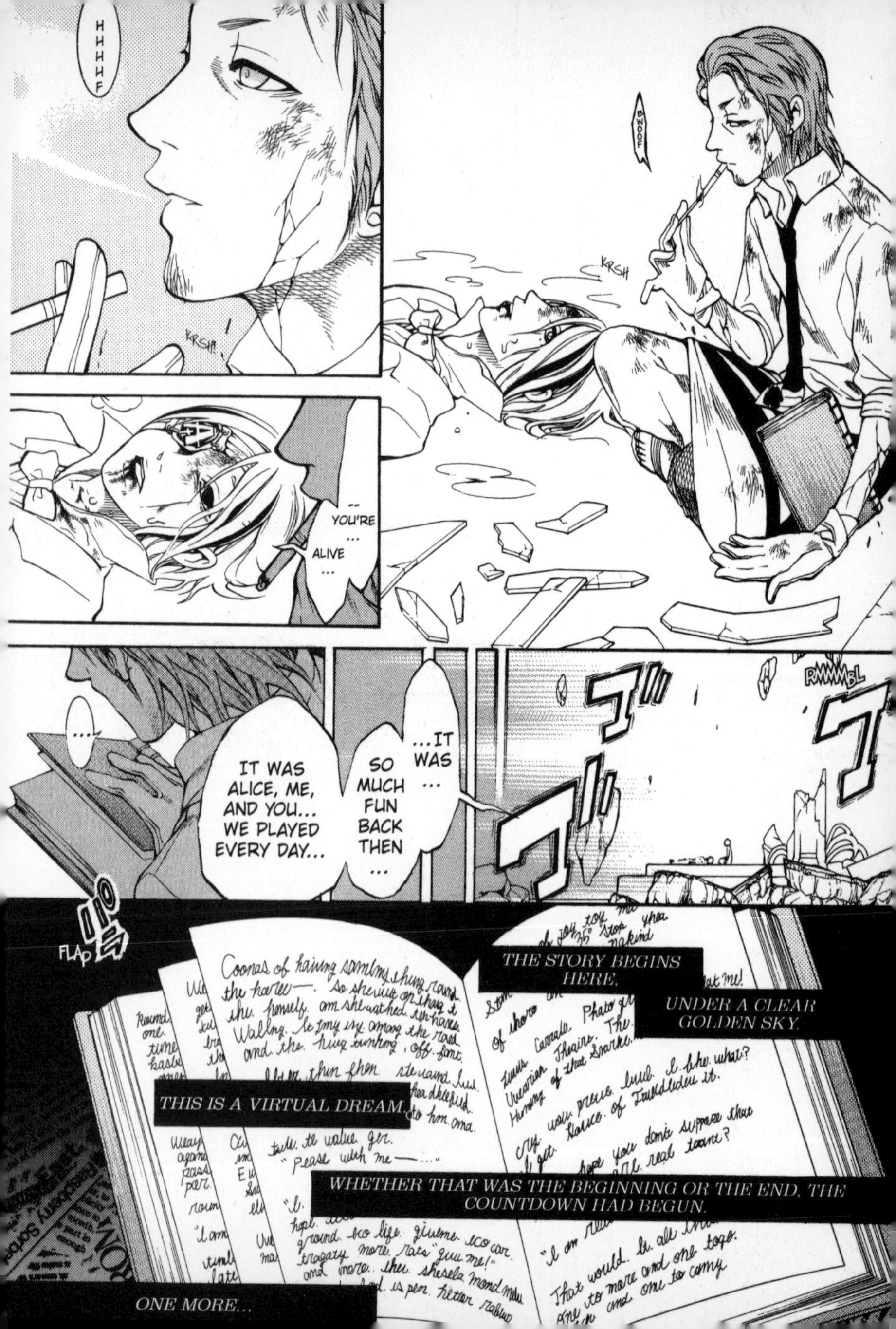
BWOOF
KRSH
HHHHF
KRSH!
--YOU'RE ... ALIVE ...
RMMMBL
...IT WAS ...
SO MUCH FUN BACK THEN ...
IT WAS ALICE, ME, AND YOU... WE PLAYED EVERY DAY...
...
FLAP
THE STORY BEGINS HERE.
UNDER A CLEAR GOLDEN SKY.
THIS IS A VIRTUAL DREAM.
WHETHER THAT WAS THE BEGINNING OR THE END, THE COUNTDOWN HAD BEGUN.
ONE MORE...

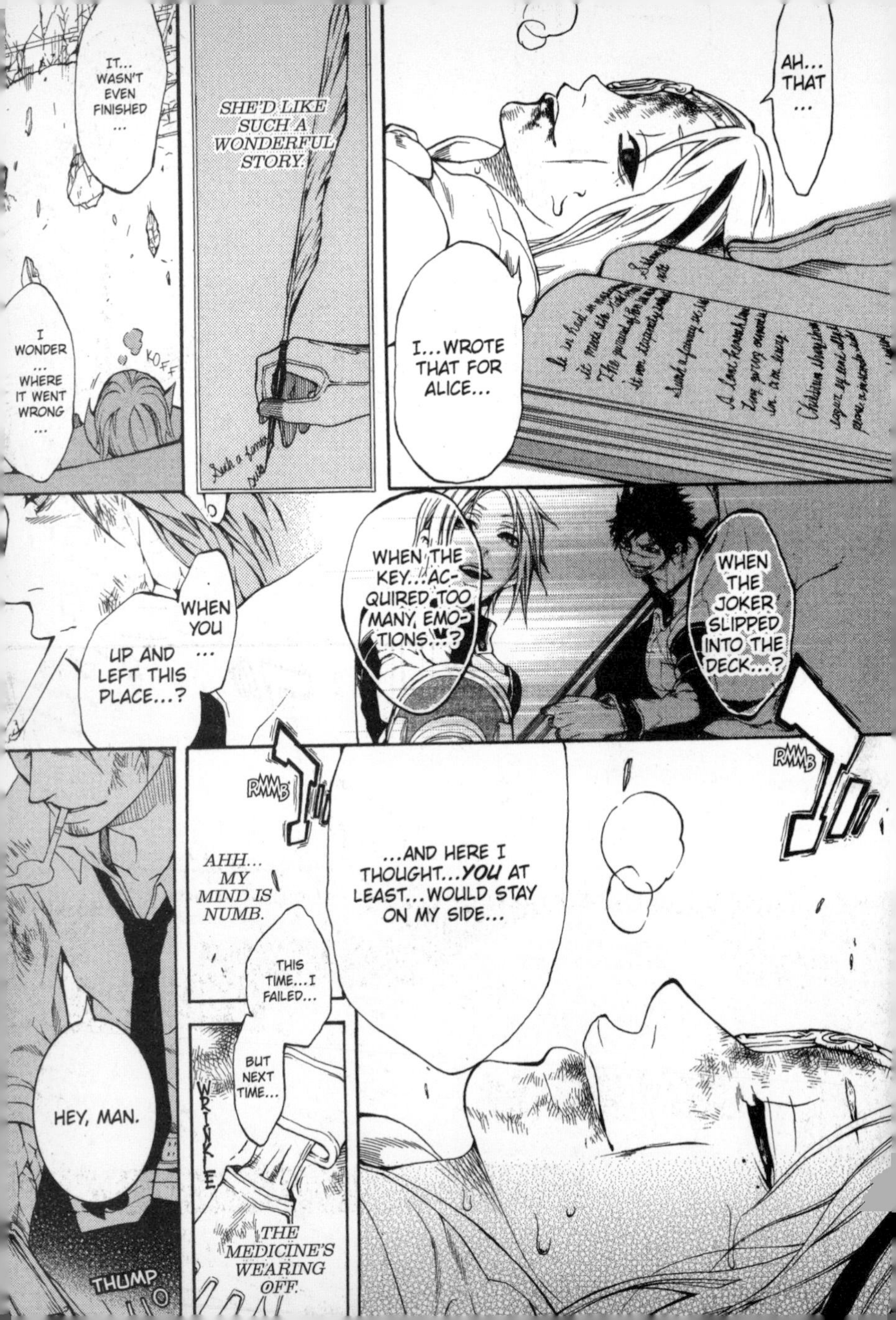
AH... THAT ...
I...WROTE THAT FOR ALICE...
SHE'D LIKE SUCH A WONDERFUL STORY.
IT... WASN'T EVEN FINISHED ...
I WONDER ... WHERE IT WENT WRONG ...
KOFF
WHEN THE JOKER SLIPPED INTO THE DECK...?
WHEN THE KEY...ACQUIRED TOO MANY EMOTIONS...?
WHEN YOU ...
UP AND LEFT THIS PLACE...?
RMMB
RMMB
...AND HERE I THOUGHT...YOU AT LEAST...WOULD STAY ON MY SIDE...
AHH... MY MIND IS NUMB.
THIS TIME...I FAILED...
BUT NEXT TIME...
WRINKLE
THE MEDICINE'S WEARING OFF.
HEY, MAN.
THUMP

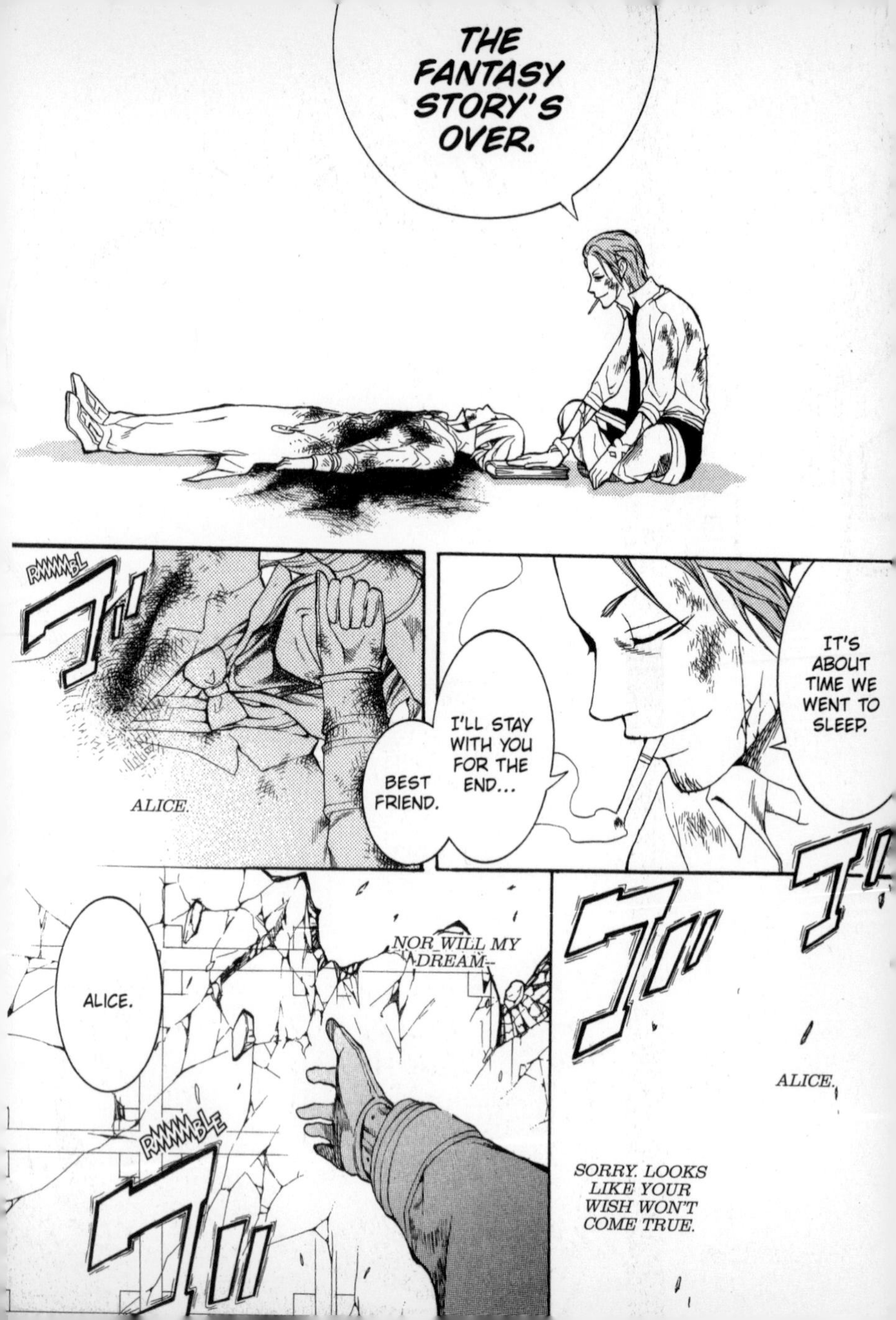
THE FANTASY STORY'S OVER.
IT'S ABOUT TIME WE WENT TO SLEEP.
I'LL STAY WITH YOU FOR THE END...
BEST FRIEND.
RMMMBL
ALICE.
ALICE.
SORRY. LOOKS LIKE YOUR WISH WON'T COME TRUE.
NOR WILL MY DREAM--
ALICE.
RMMMBLE

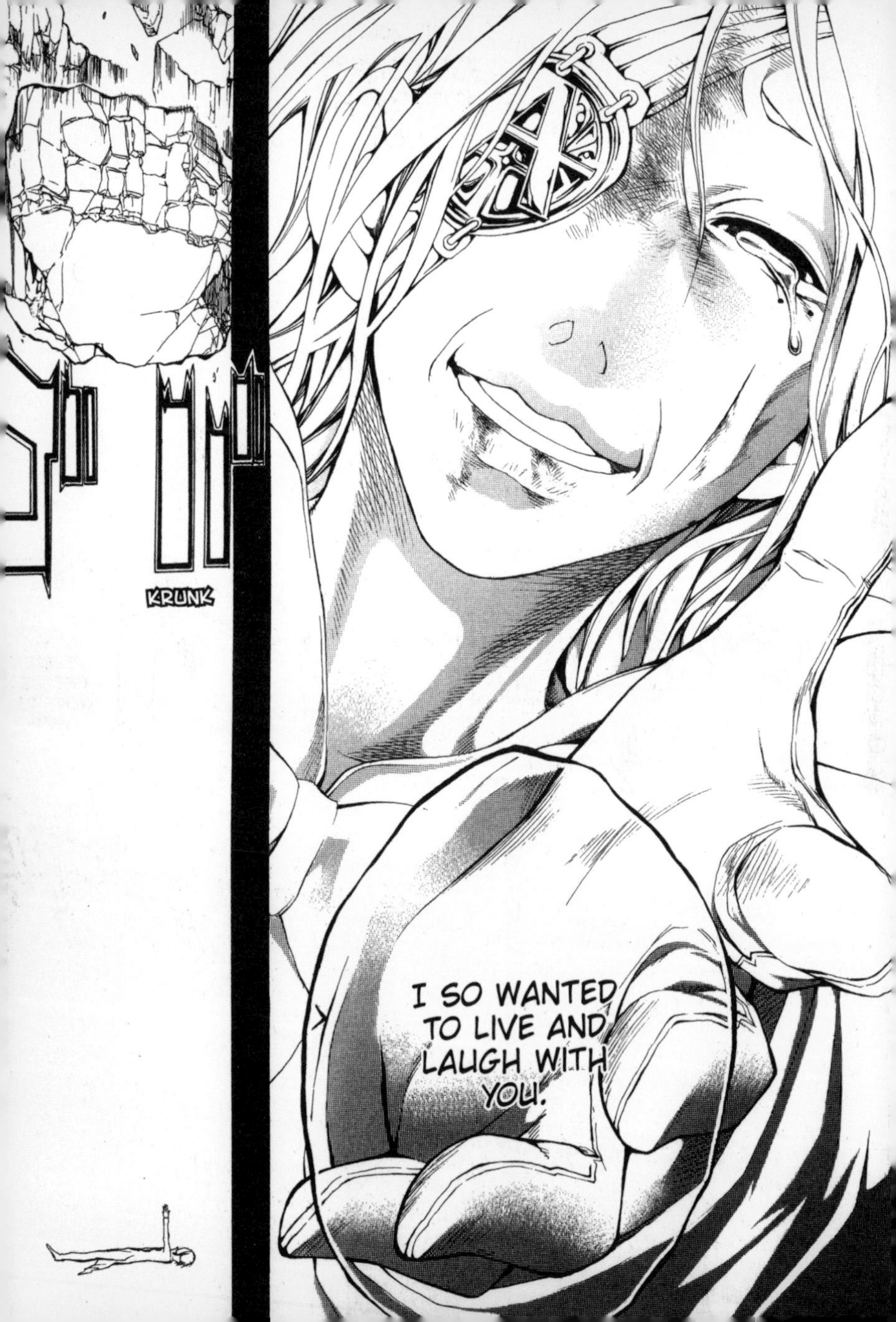
I SO WANTED TO LIVE AND LAUGH WITH YOU.
KRUNK

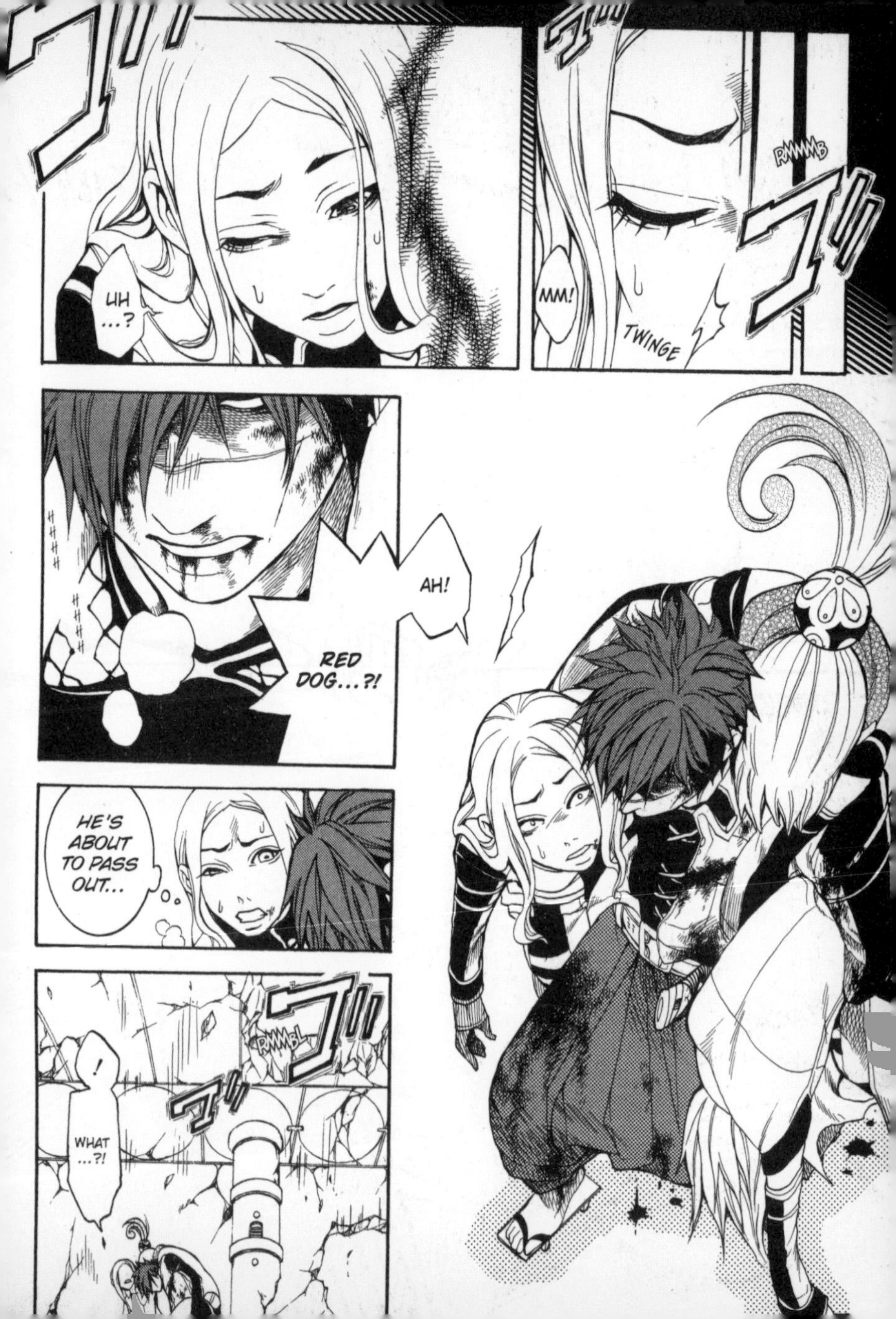
RMMMB
MM!
TWINGE
UH ...?
AH!
RED DOG...?!
HE'S ABOUT TO PASS OUT...
!
RMMBL
WHAT ...?!

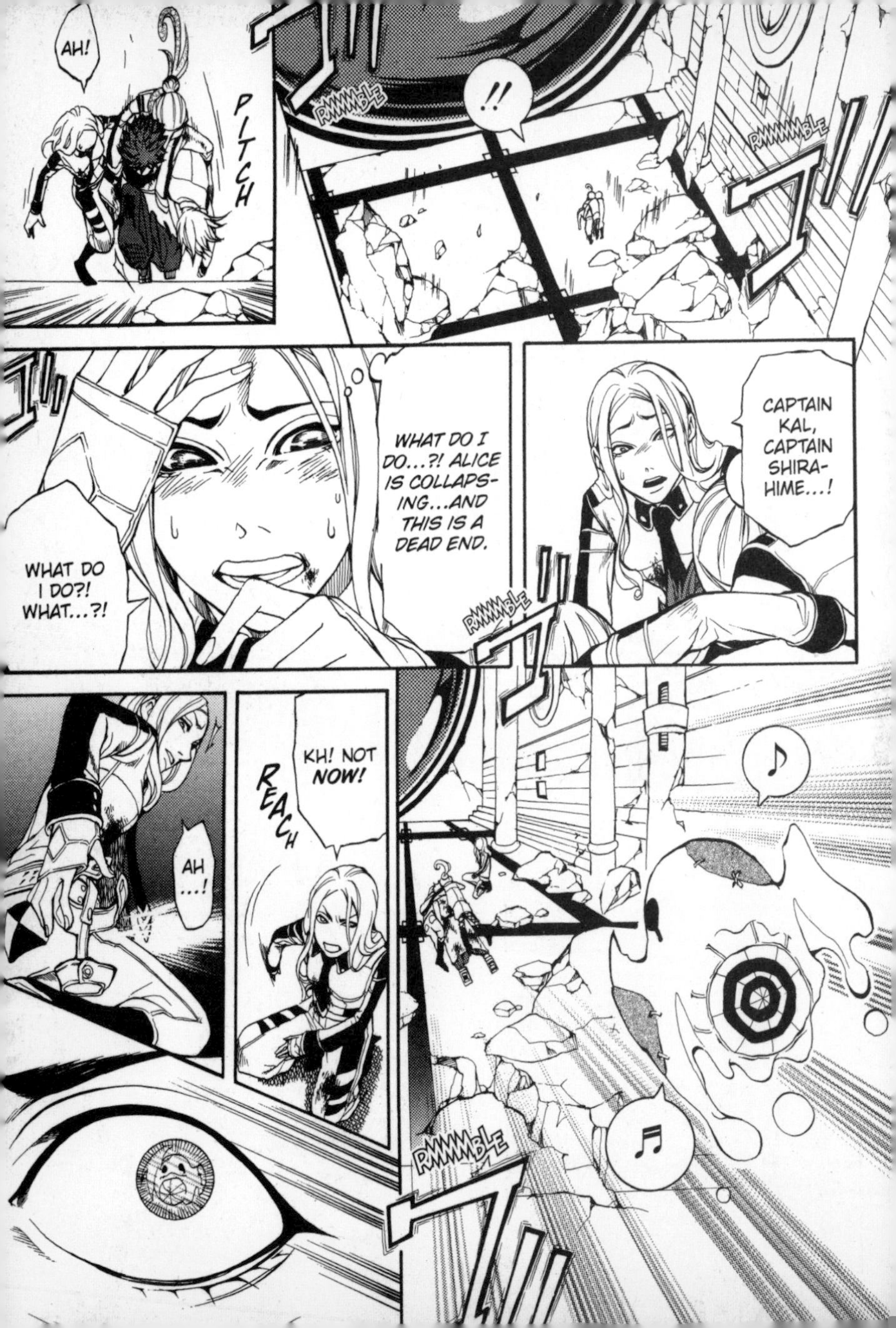
!!
RMMMMBLE
RMMMBLE
AH!
PITCH
CAPTAIN KAL, CAPTAIN SHIRA-HIME...!
RMMMBLE
WHAT DO I DO...?! ALICE IS COLLAPS-ING...AND THIS IS A DEAD END.
WHAT DO I DO?! WHAT...?!
♪
♫
RMMMBLE
KH! NOT **NOW**!
REACH
AH ...!

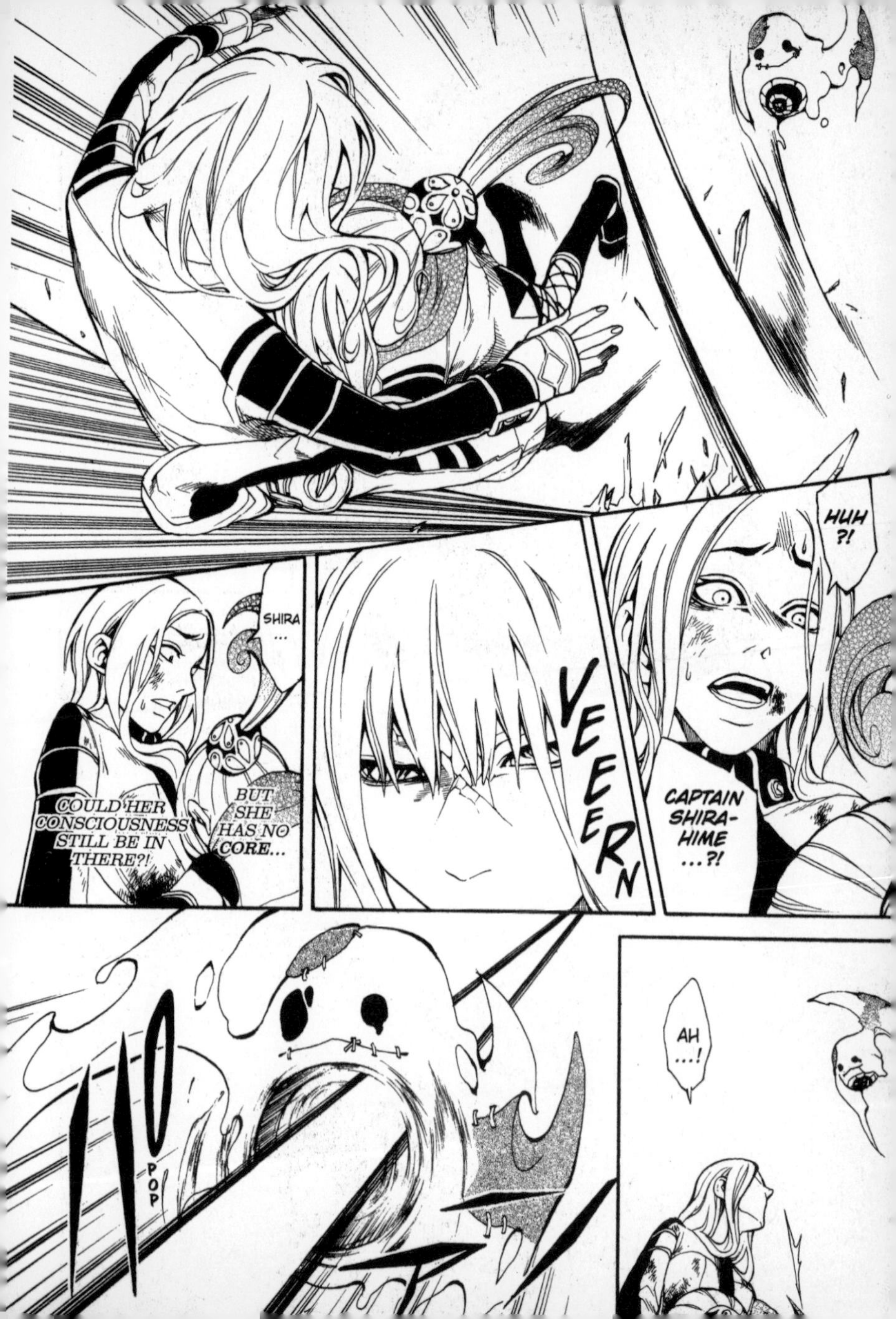
HUH?!
CAPTAIN SHIRAHIME...?!
VEERN
SHIRA...
BUT SHE HAS NO CORE...
COULD HER CONSCIOUSNESS STILL BE IN THERE?!
AH...!
POP

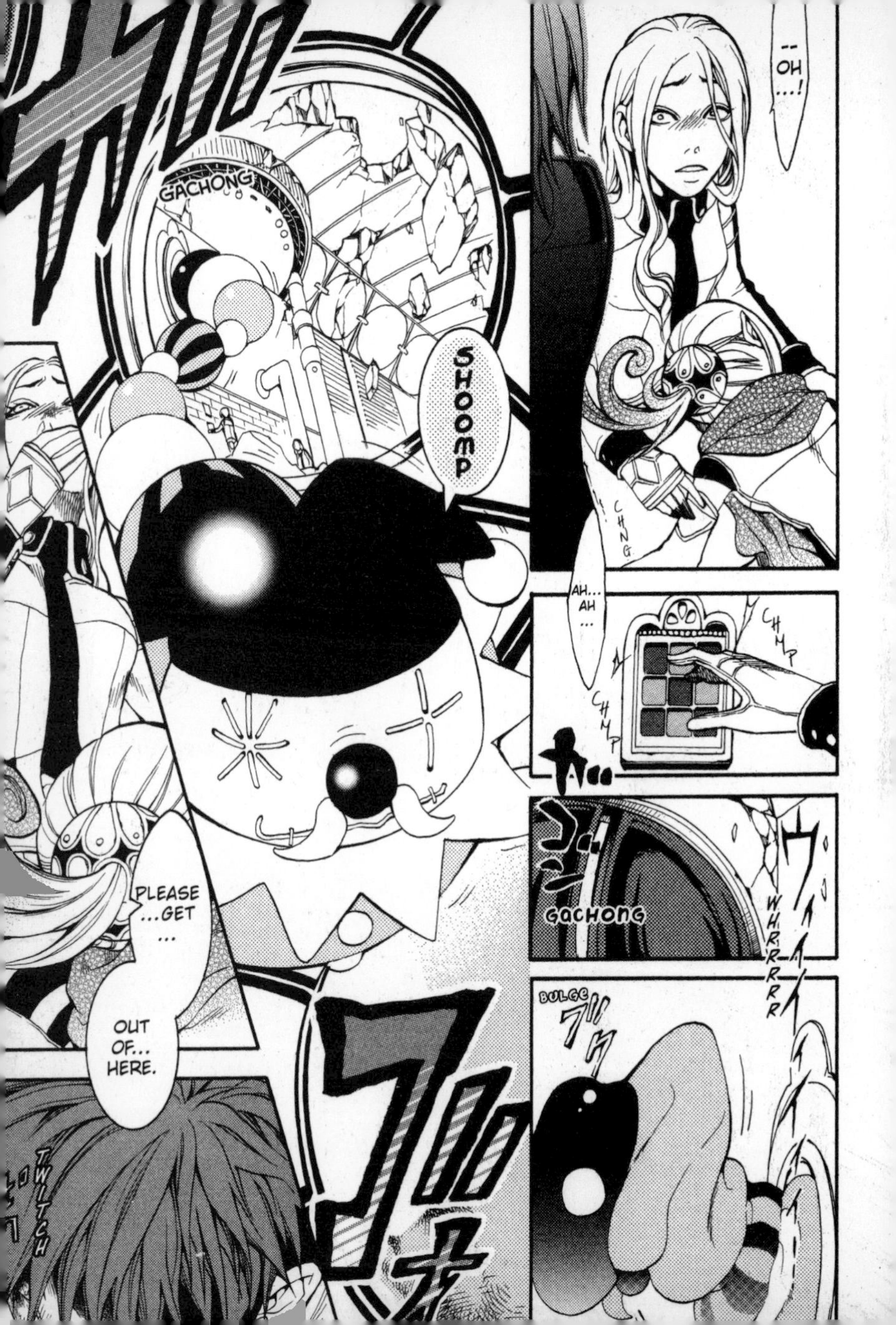
--OH...!
CHNG
AH... AH ...
CHMP
CHMP
GACHONG
WHRRRRR
BULGE
GACHONG
SHOOMP
PLEASE ...GET ...
OUT OF... HERE.
TWITCH

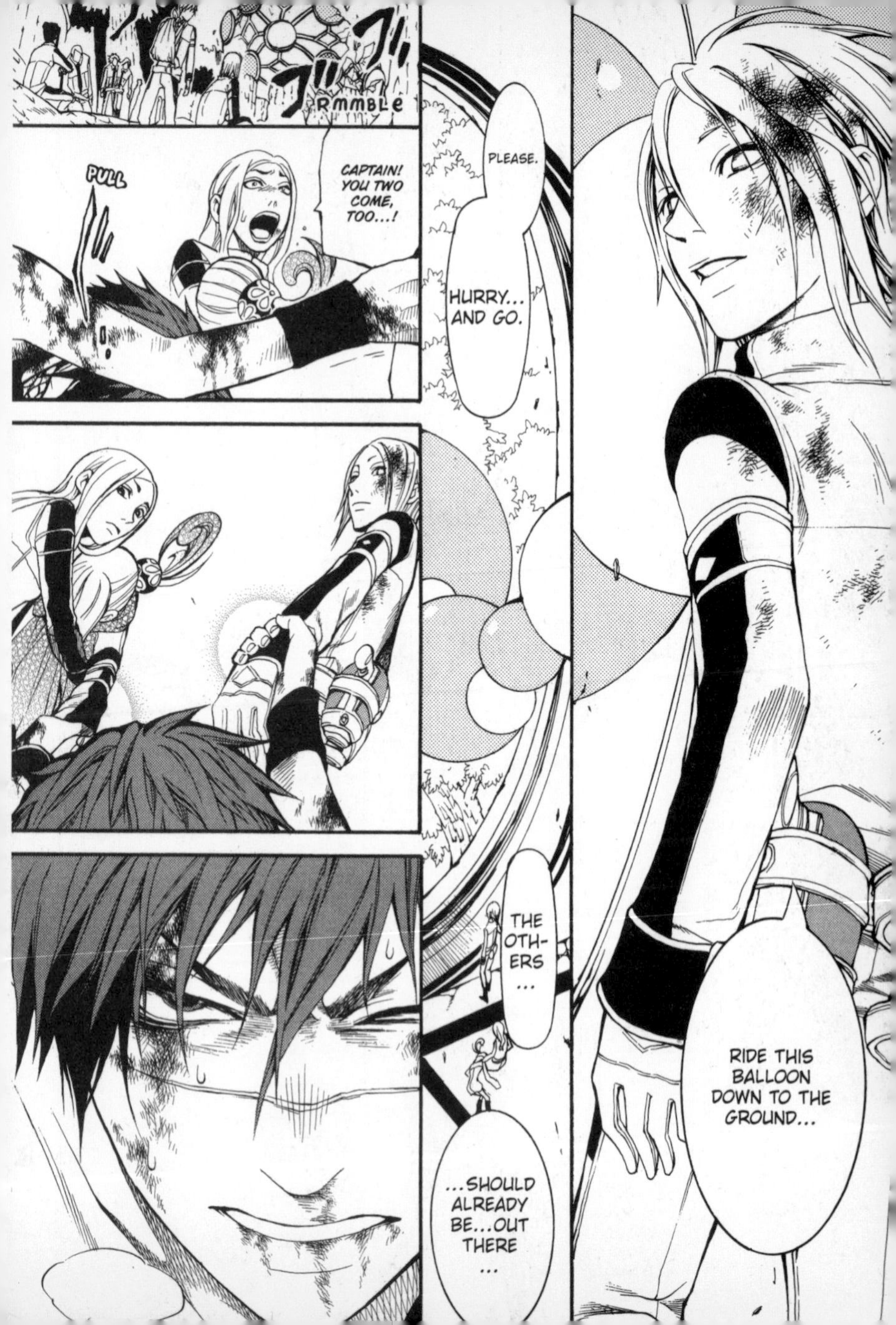
RIDE THIS BALLOON DOWN TO THE GROUND...
THE OTHERS...
...SHOULD ALREADY BE...OUT THERE...
PLEASE.
HURRY... AND GO.
RMMBLE
CAPTAIN! YOU TWO COME, TOO...!
PULL

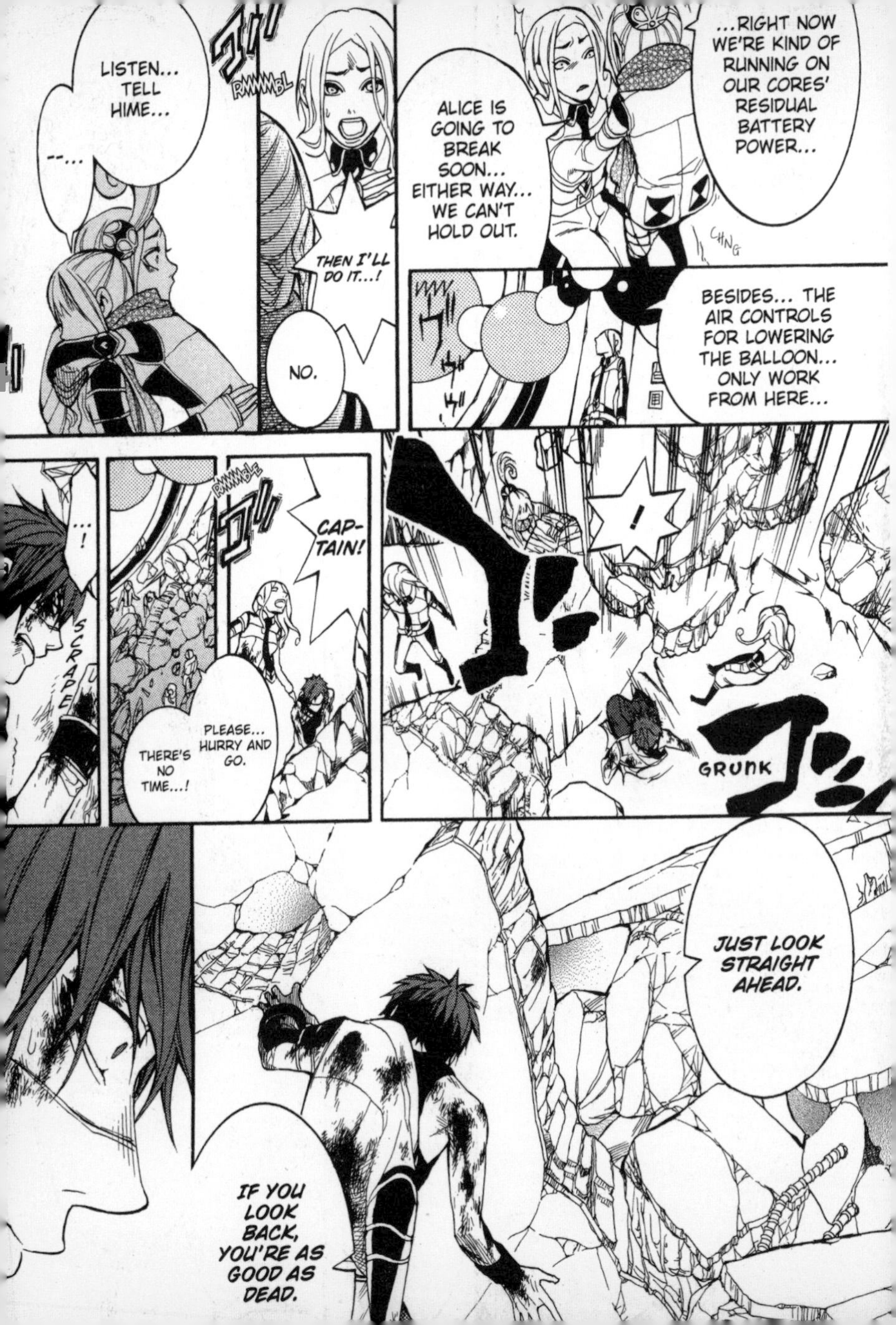
...RIGHT NOW WE'RE KIND OF RUNNING ON OUR CORES' RESIDUAL BATTERY POWER...
ALICE IS GOING TO BREAK SOON... EITHER WAY... WE CAN'T HOLD OUT.
CHING
BESIDES... THE AIR CONTROLS FOR LOWERING THE BALLOON... ONLY WORK FROM HERE...
RMMMBL
THEN I'LL DO IT...!
NO.
LISTEN... TELL HIME...
--...
!
GRUNK
CAP-TAIN!
RMMMBLE
PLEASE... HURRY AND GO.
THERE'S NO TIME...!
...!
SCRAPE
JUST LOOK STRAIGHT AHEAD.
IF YOU LOOK BACK, YOU'RE AS GOOD AS DEAD.

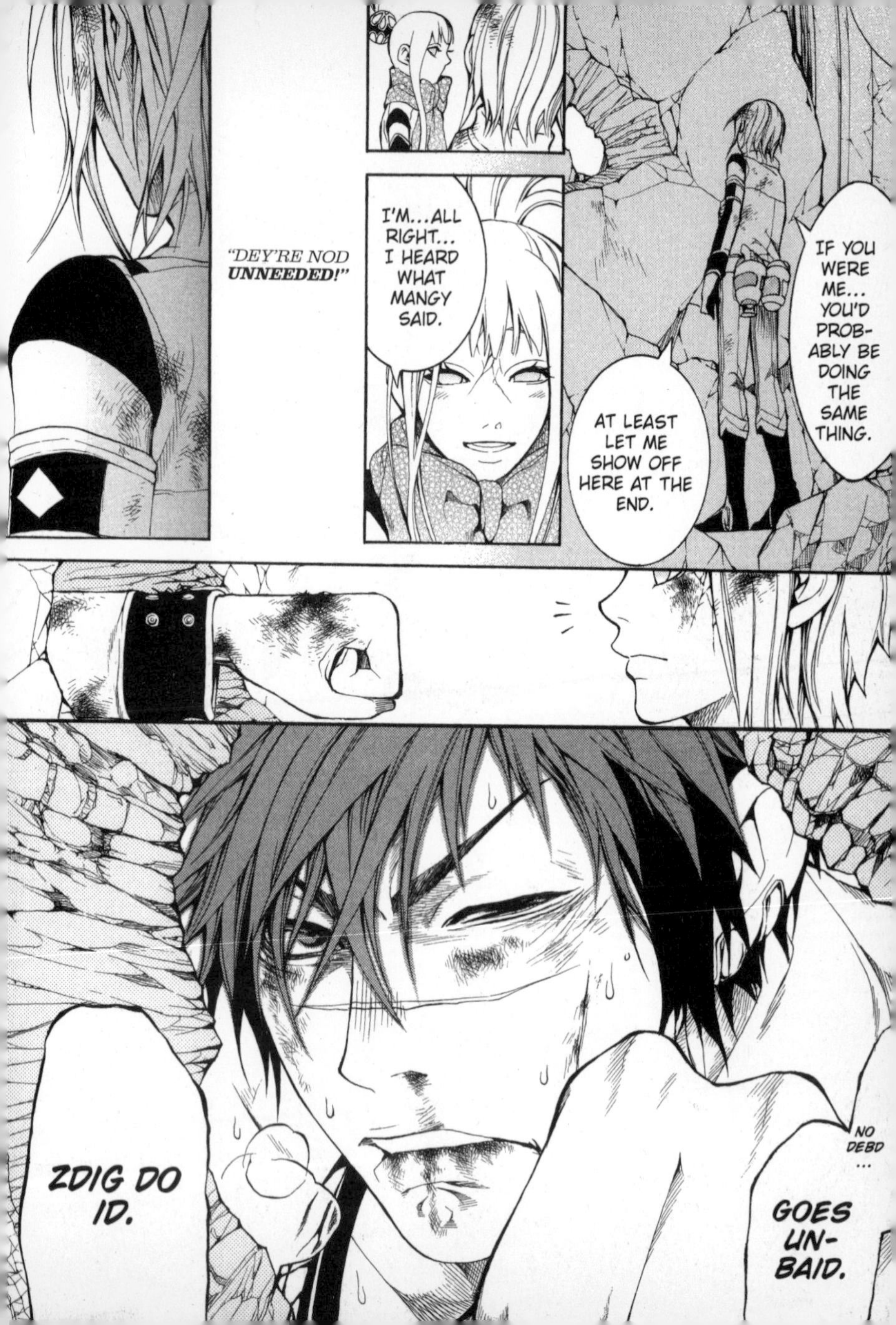
IF YOU WERE ME... YOU'D PROB-ABLY BE DOING THE SAME THING.
I'M...ALL RIGHT... I HEARD WHAT MANGY SAID.
AT LEAST LET ME SHOW OFF HERE AT THE END.
"DEY'RE NOD **UNNEEDED!**"
NO DEBD ...
GOES UN-BAID.
ZDIG DO ID.

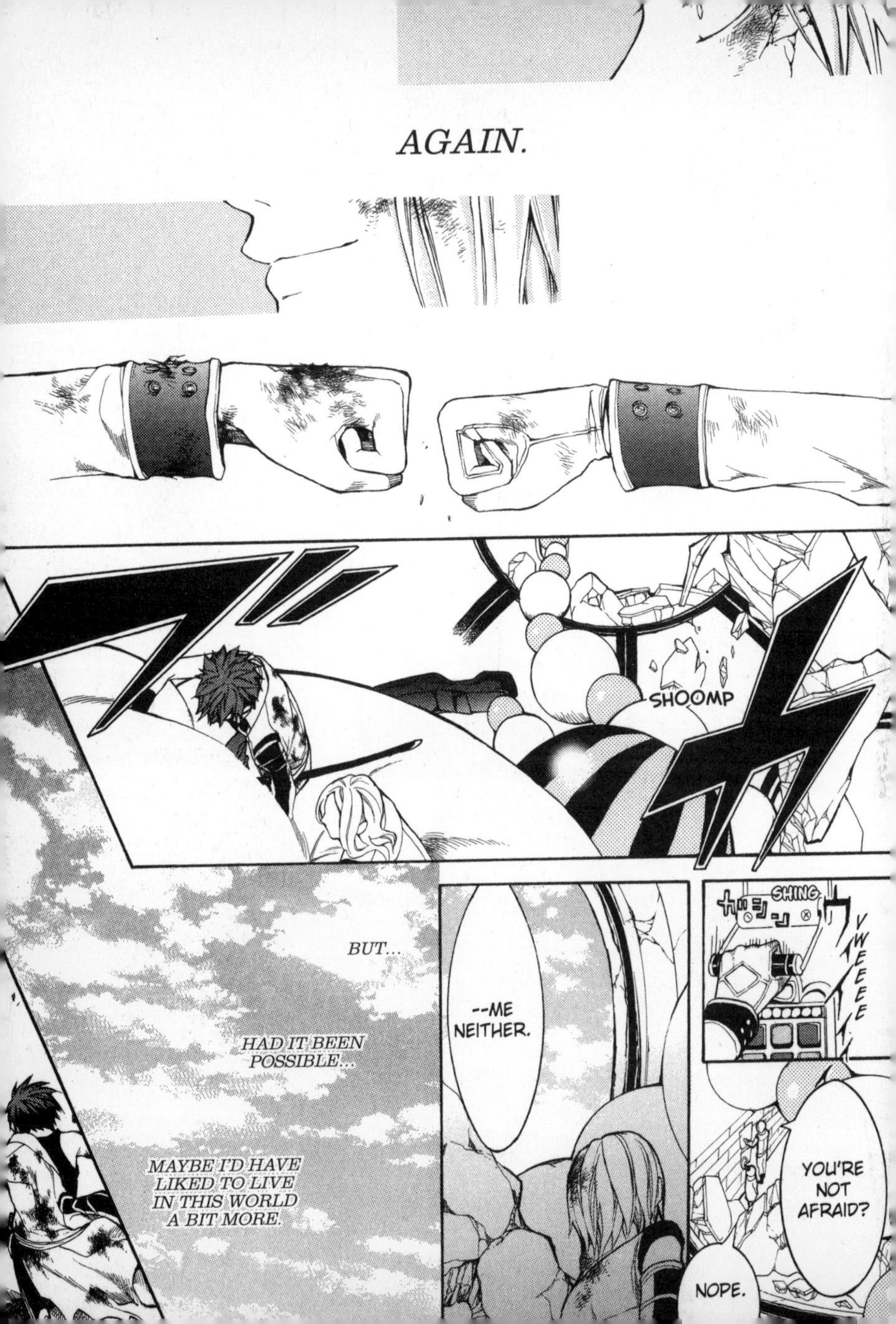
AGAIN.
SHOOMP
SHING
VWEEEE
YOU'RE NOT AFRAID?
NOPE.
--ME NEITHER.
BUT...
HAD IT BEEN POSSIBLE...
MAYBE I'D HAVE LIKED TO LIVE IN THIS WORLD A BIT MORE.

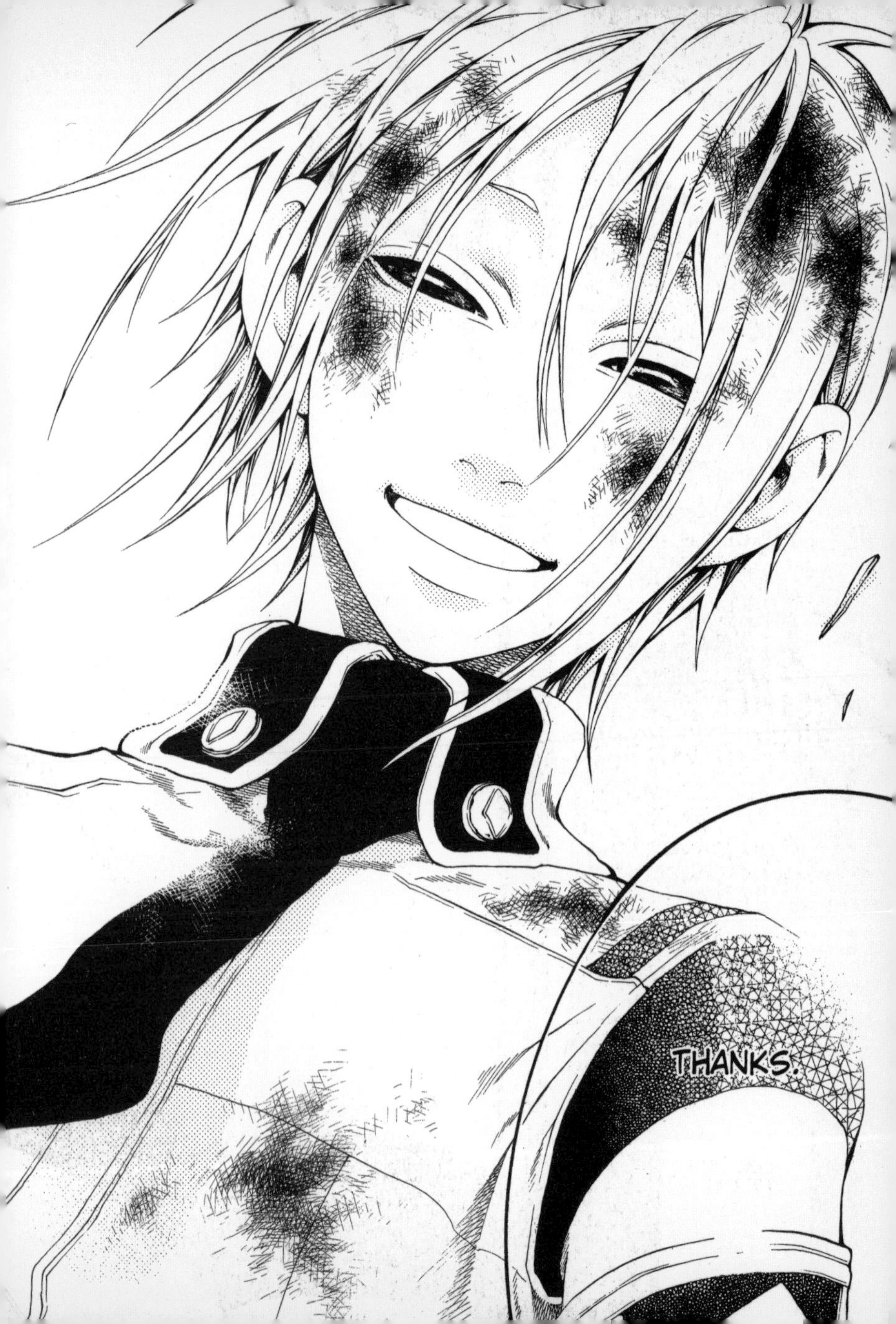
THANKS.

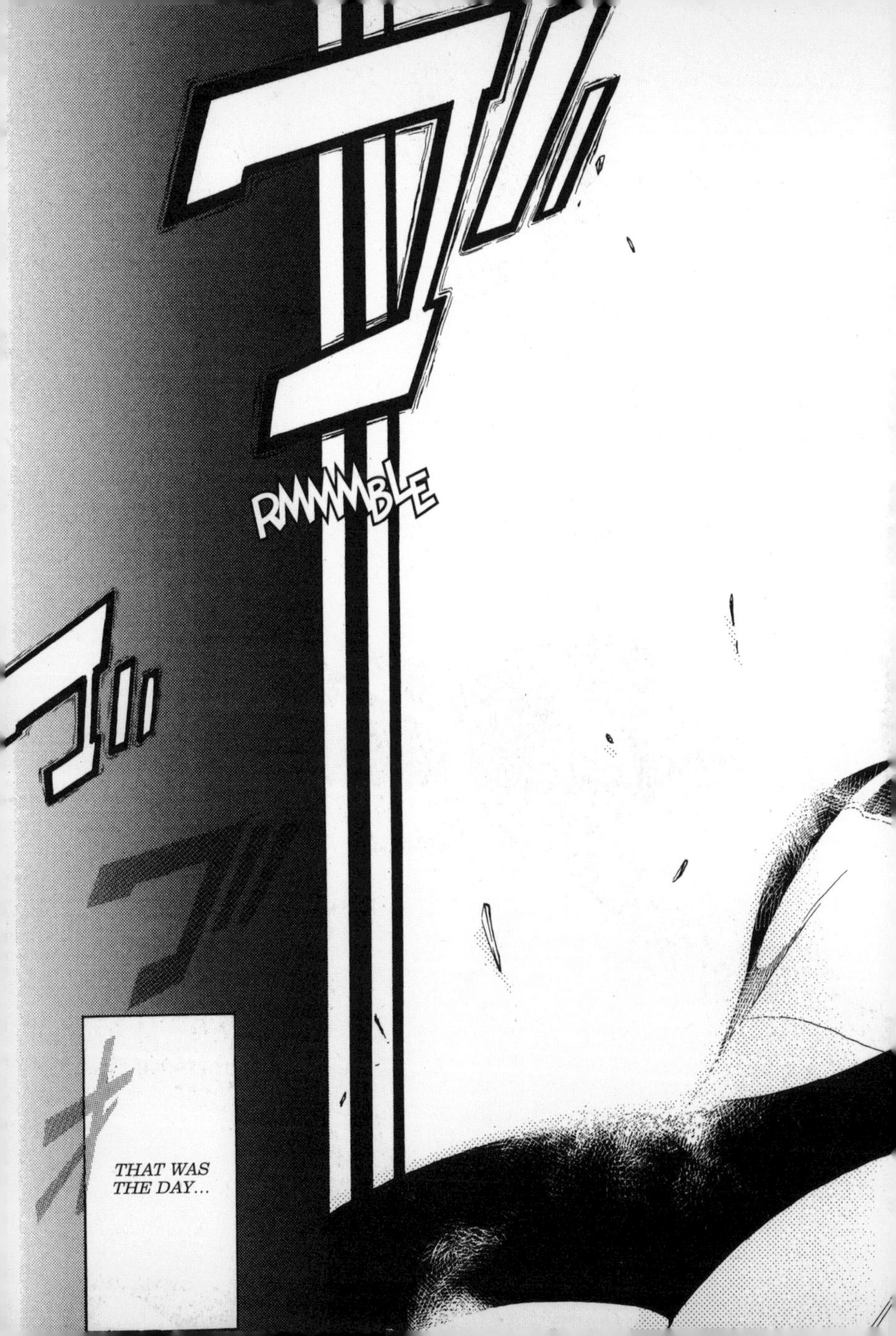
RMMMBLE
THAT WAS THE DAY...

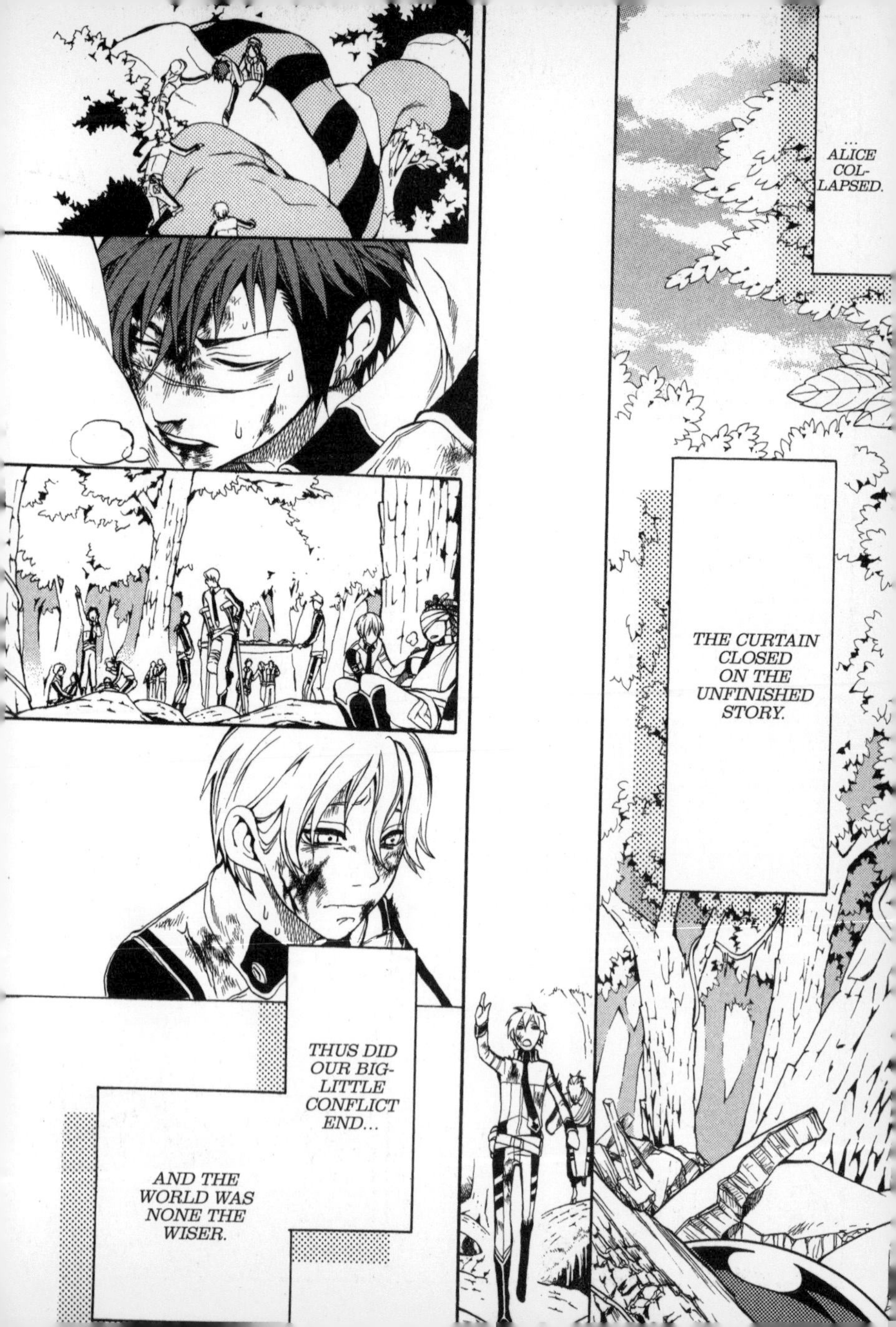
...ALICE COL-LAPSED.
THE CURTAIN CLOSED ON THE UNFINISHED STORY.
THUS DID OUR BIG-LITTLE CONFLICT END...
AND THE WORLD WAS NONE THE WISER.

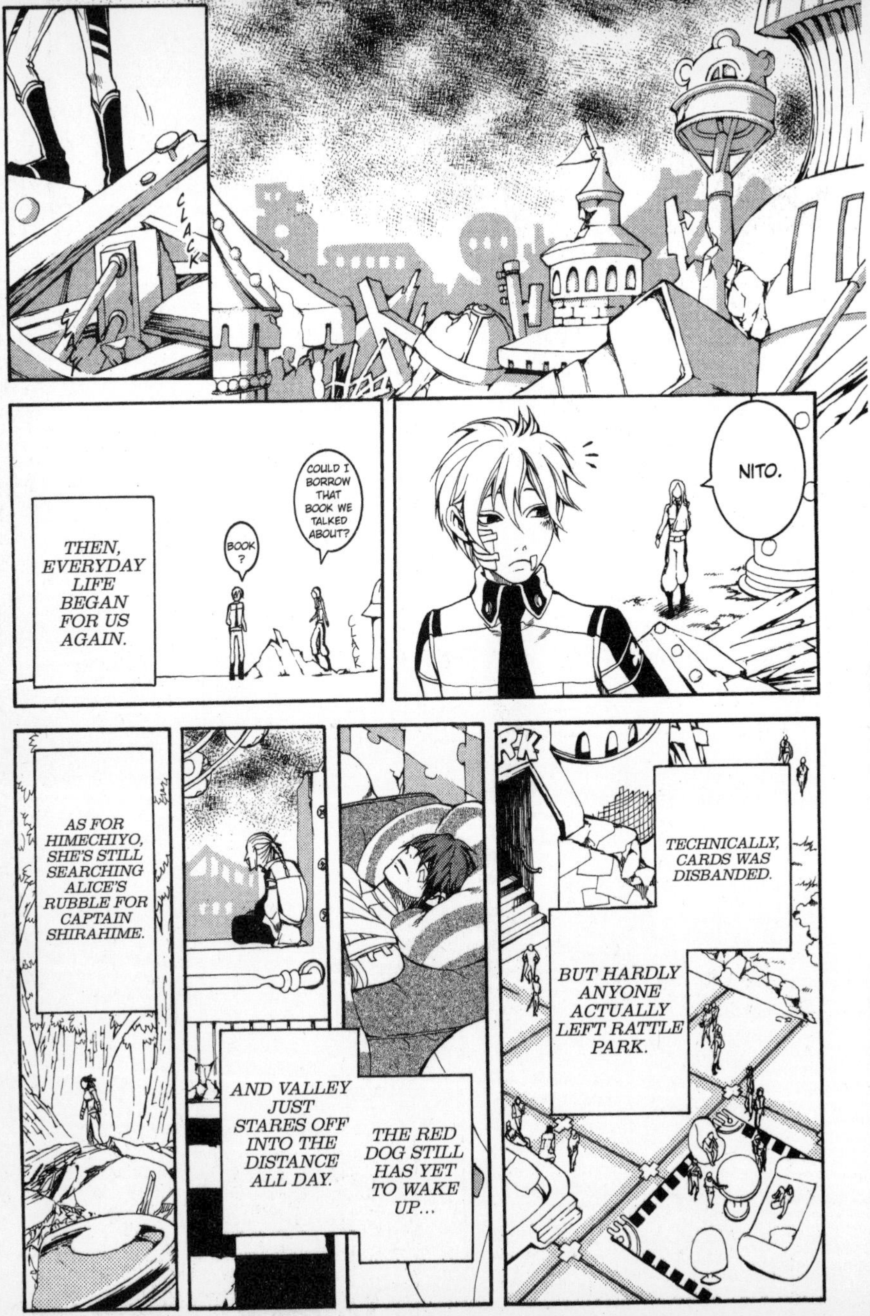
CLACK
NITO.
COULD I BORROW THAT BOOK WE TALKED ABOUT?
THEN, EVERYDAY LIFE BEGAN FOR US AGAIN.
BOOK?
CLACK
TECHNICALLY, CARDS WAS DISBANDED.
BUT HARDLY ANYONE ACTUALLY LEFT RATTLE PARK.
THE RED DOG STILL HAS YET TO WAKE UP...
AND VALLEY JUST STARES OFF INTO THE DISTANCE ALL DAY.
AS FOR HIMECHIYO, SHE'S STILL SEARCHING ALICE'S RUBBLE FOR CAPTAIN SHIRAHIME.

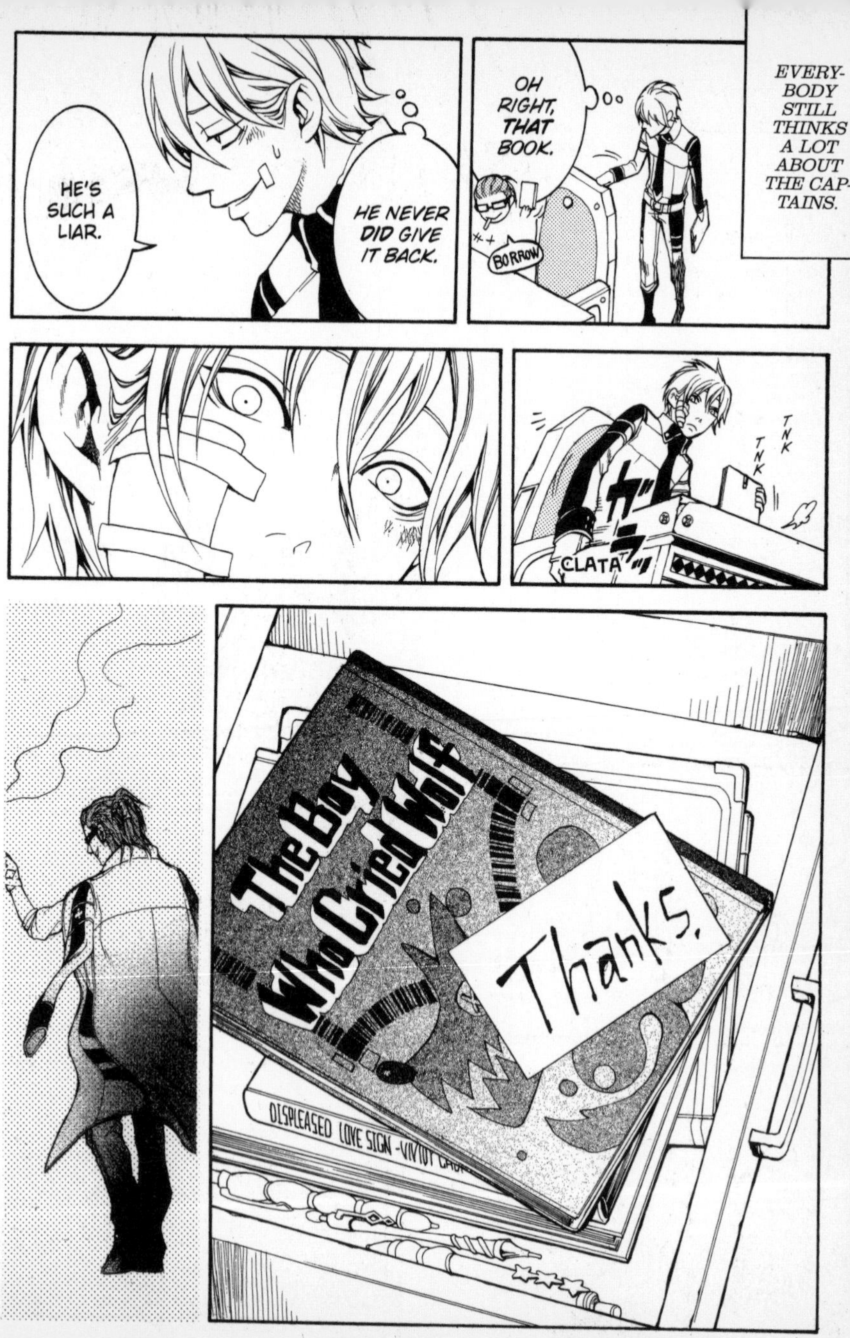
EVERY-BODY STILL THINKS A LOT ABOUT THE CAP-TAINS.
OH RIGHT, THAT BOOK.
BORROW
HE NEVER DID GIVE IT BACK.
HE'S SUCH A LIAR.
TNK TNK
CLATA
The Boy Who Cried Wolf
Thanks.
DISPLEASED LOVE SIGN -VIVID

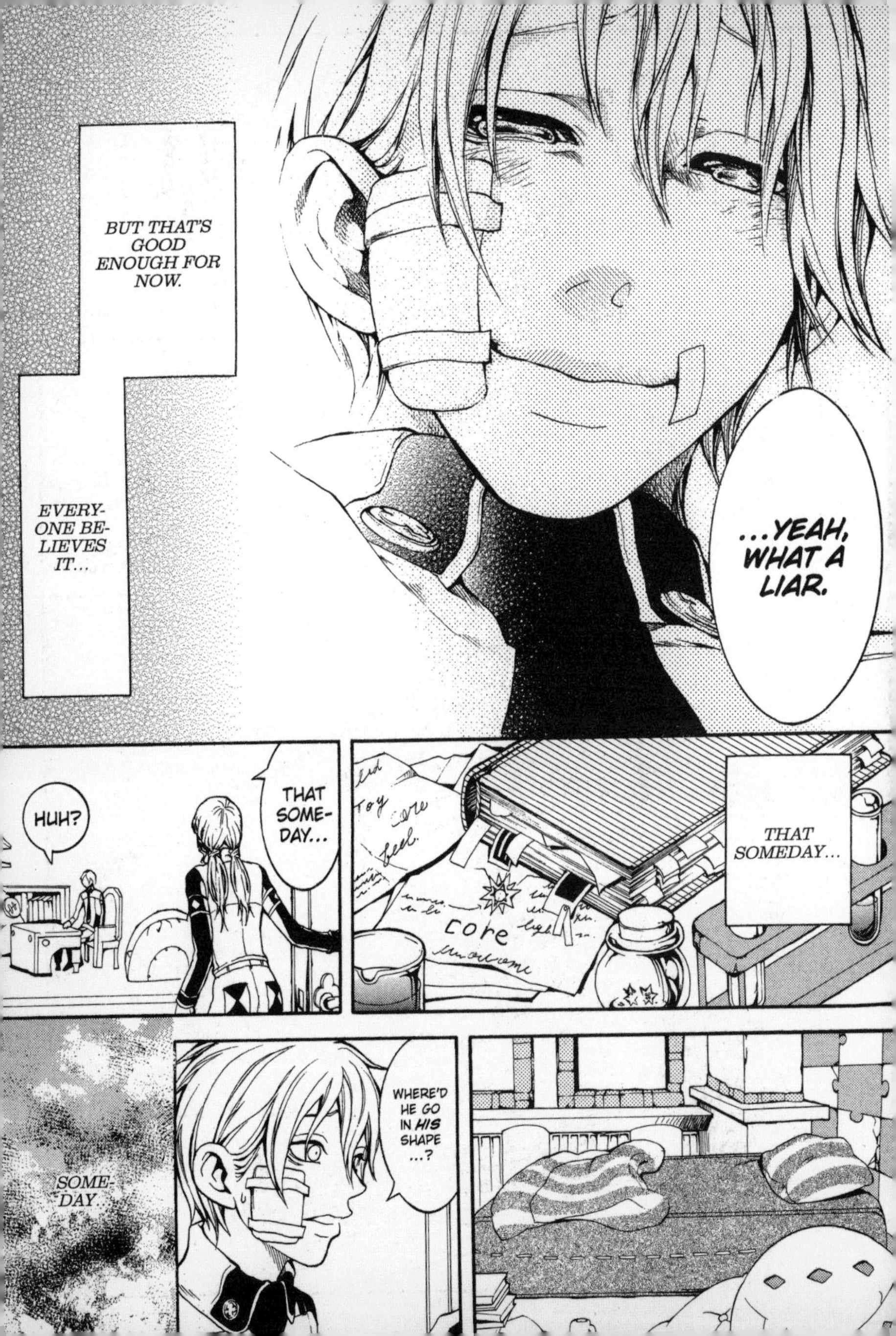

...YEAH, WHAT A LIAR.
BUT THAT'S GOOD ENOUGH FOR NOW.
EVERY-ONE BE-LIEVES IT...
THAT SOMEDAY...
THAT SOME-DAY...
HUH?
WHERE'D HE GO IN *HIS* SHAPE ...?
SOME-DAY.

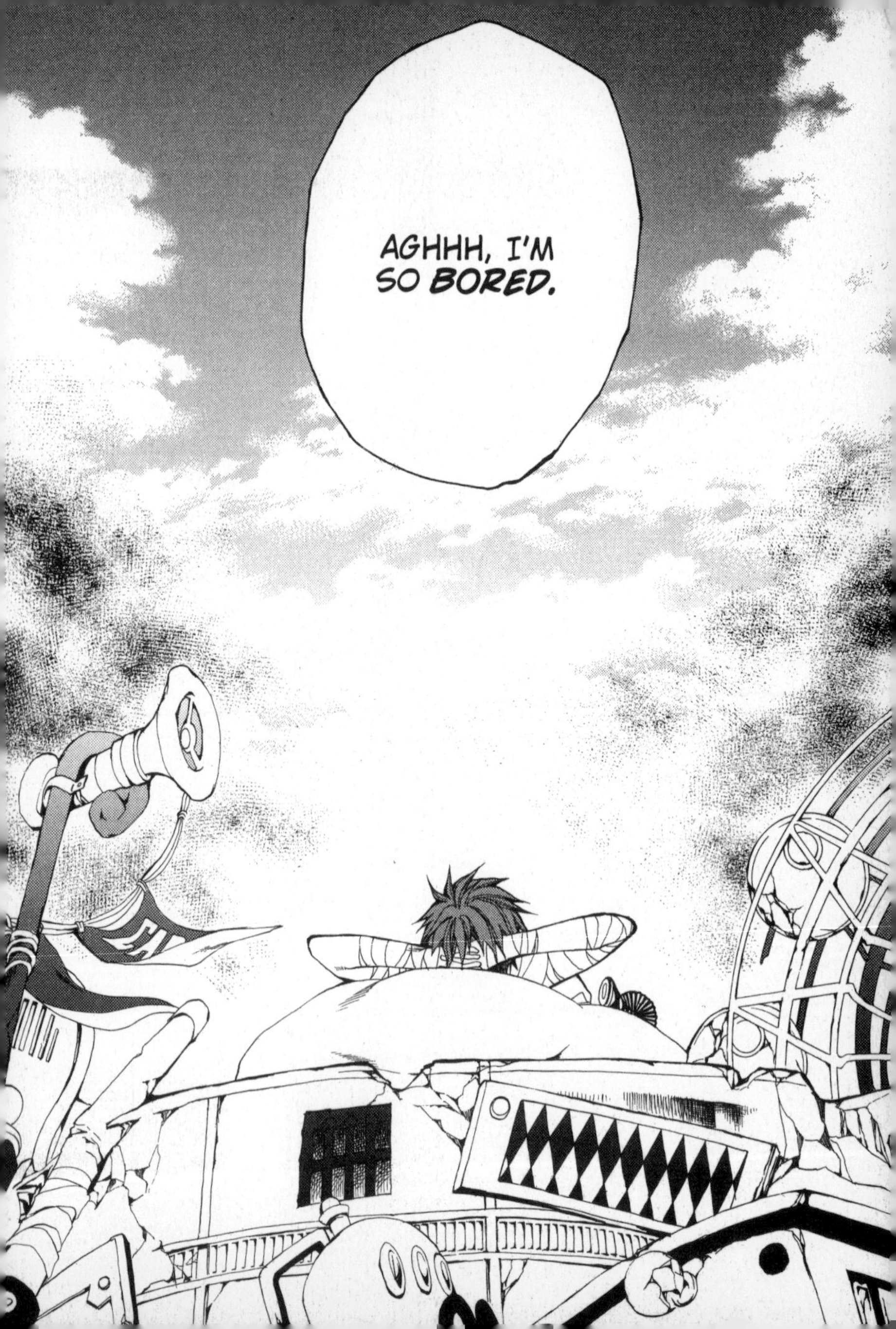
AGHHH, I'M SO BORED.

WE'LL GET TO
SMILE TOGETHER
BENEATH A
PEACEFUL SKY.

REPLICA THE END

Read&Tweet

Because manga should be enjoyed socially.

Follow us!
@DigitalManga

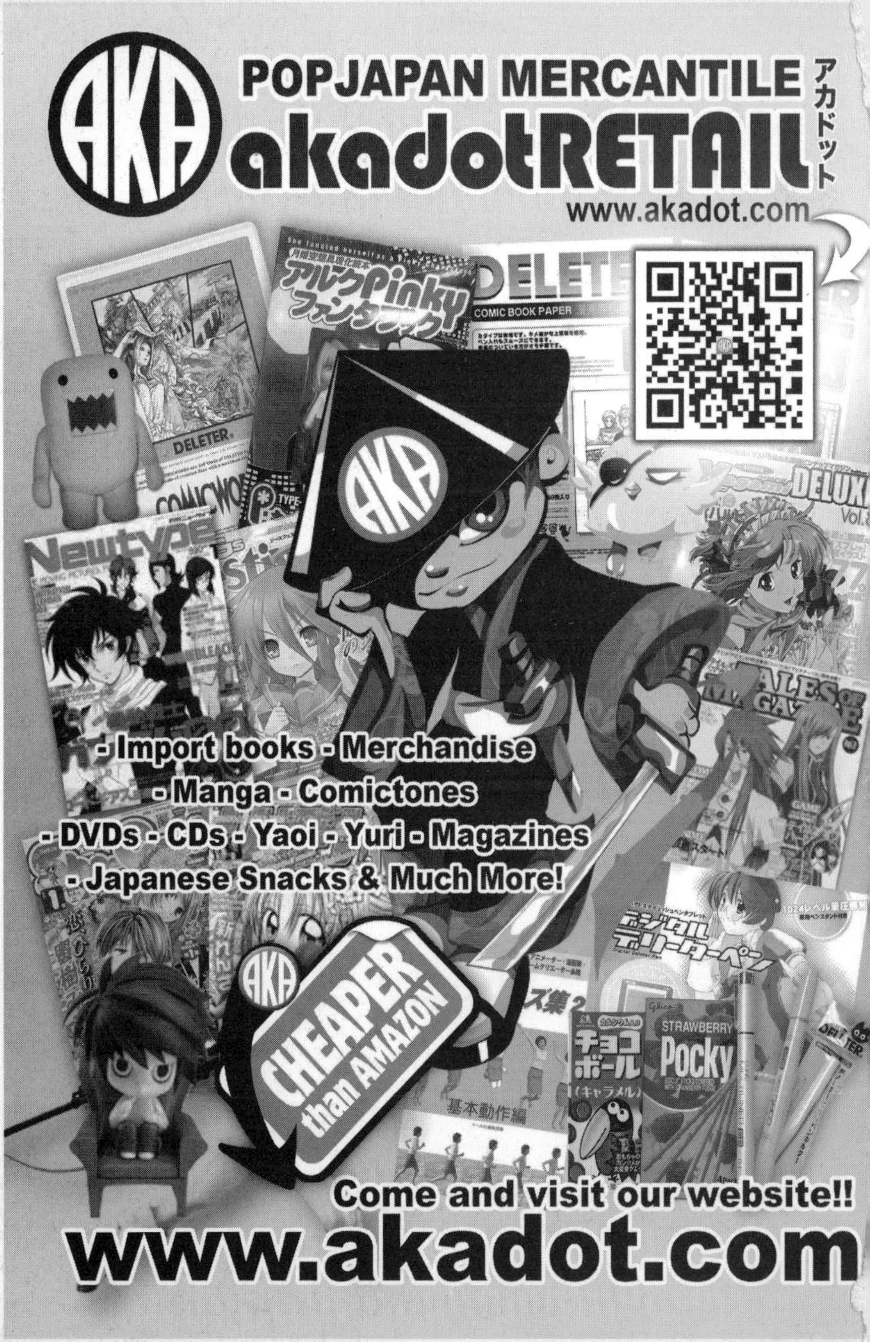

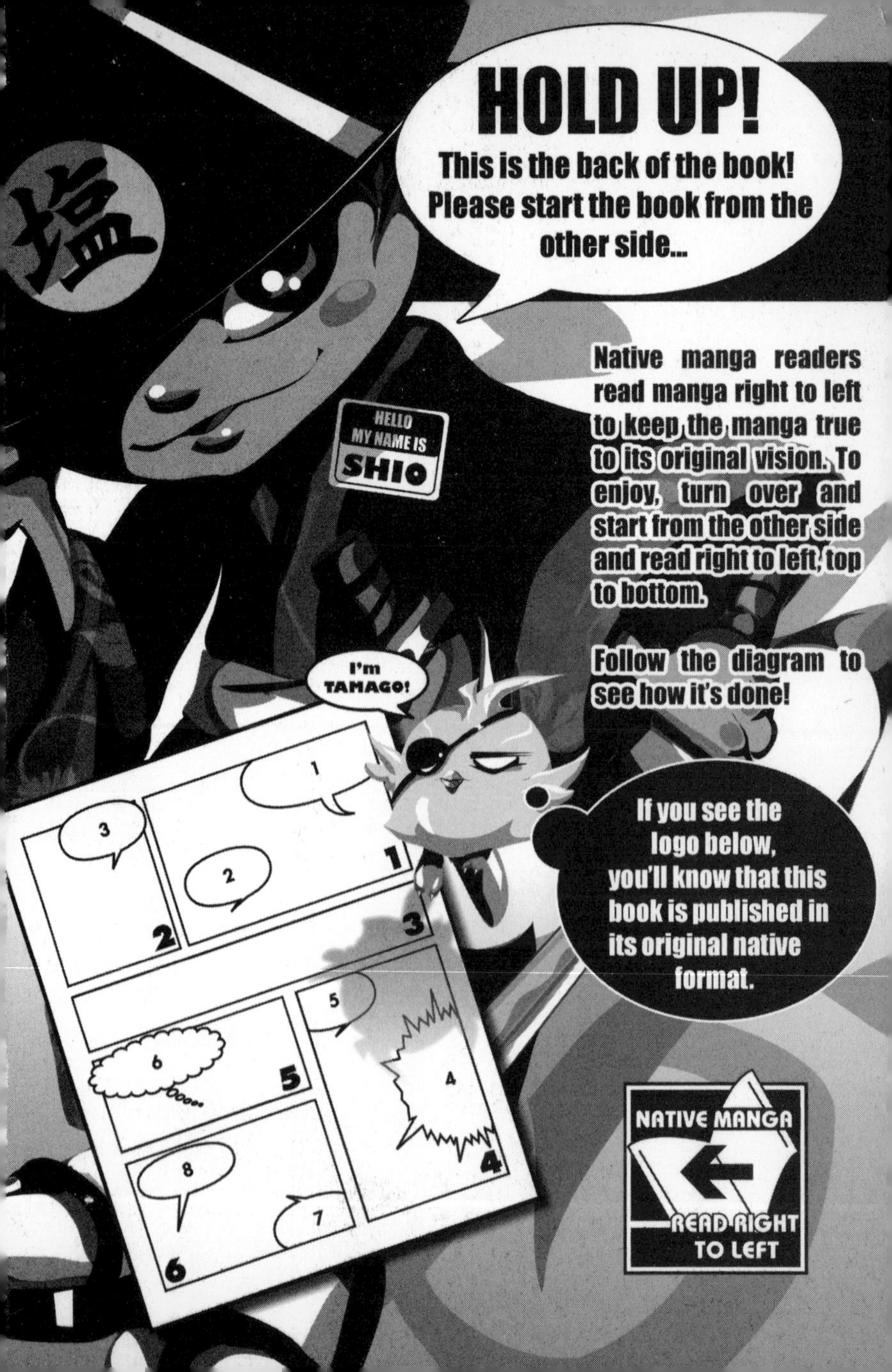
HOLD UP!
This is the back of the book! Please start the book from the other side...
HELLO MY NAME IS SHIO
Native manga readers read manga right to left to keep the manga true to its original vision. To enjoy, turn over and start from the other side and read right to left, top to bottom.
Follow the diagram to see how it's done!
I'm TAMAGO!
If you see the logo below, you'll know that this book is published in its original native format.
NATIVE MANGA
READ RIGHT TO LEFT